The Future of Coaching

Siegfried Greif

The Future of Coaching

Building Bridges Between Science and Practice

Springer

Siegfried Greif
Institute of Psychology
Osnabrück University
Osnabrück, Niedersachsen, Germany

ISBN 978-3-031-96191-5 ISBN 978-3-031-96192-2 (eBook)
https://doi.org/10.1007/978-3-031-96192-2

This Springer imprint is published by the registered company Springer Nature Switzerland AG
The registered company address is: Gewerbestrasse 11, 6330 Cham, Switzerland

Contents

About the Author

Siegfried Greif, Dr. phil., retired professor, University of Osnabrück (Germany, Chair of Work and Organizational Psychology). His current work and research focus are on expanding and improving the effectiveness of coaching methods.

He has published 20 books, including a monograph on "Coaching und ergebnisorientierte Selbstreflexion" (2008, Hogrefe) and "Was ist Coaching?" (2021), and is a coeditor of the "International Handbook of Evidence-Based Coaching" (2022, Springer). He is the author of many articles in specialist journals and various book chapters. He conducts scientifically based and certified coaching training for practitioners in a project of the Chair of the Division of Social, Organizational and Economic Psychology, Prof. Dr. Rudolf Kerschreiter at the Free University of Berlin, Germany, together with the association "Arbeit, Bildung und Forschung e.V."

Siegfried Greif is a member of the German Psychological Society and founder of the Innovation Award of the Division of Work, Organizational and Business Psychology, as well as a member of the German Federal Association of Coaching (DBVC, Senior Coach) and the International Society of Coaching Psychology (ISCP). He was a Research Fellow of the British Psychological Society (1984), held the Wilhelm Wundt Chair at the University of Leipzig (1991/92), and has been a member of the Scientific Advisory Board of the Research Council of the Institute of Coaching (IoC) at Harvard Medical School, USA, since 2016.

Homepage University of Osnabrueck:
https://www.home.uni-osnabrueck.de/sgreif/english/index.html

Coaching training "Result-oriented Coaching", which is based on science:
https://www.abfev.de/leistungen/coaching-ausbildung/

Homepage Research Gate (publications and downloads):
https://www.researchgate.net/profile/Siegfried-Greif

Chapter 1
Bridges Between Science and Practice

1.1 Coaching Based on Science

Coaching can be fascinating for both clients and coaches. For clients, it provides opportunities for great individual changes as well as changes in environmental conditions. For coaches, it is an opportunity to participate in that process and facilitate permanent changes in their clients' real-life conditions. This is at least true for coaches who engage in scientific practices with the aim of solving practical problems (Greif, 1993; Herrmann, 1979). Coaching based on science refers to coaches regularly seeking information about scientific findings and taking them into account in their practice. Of course, no one, including me, can stay abreast of every scientific finding. However, I am constantly finding exciting new developments that are useful for coaching.

The future of coaching depends on more science-based coaches who can provide practitioners with comprehensible and brief summaries of scientific findings and intervention methods, thereby helping bridge the gap between science and practice. We need more practitioners who are interested in understanding, reflecting, and adapting this knowledge to their coaching. Science here is understood as the ongoing attempt to describe, analyze, and explain what happens in and around us and to obtain insight into how it can be successfully changed. Without science, our analyses remain superficial and naïve. Undoubtedly, coaching today is shaped mainly by practitioners who rely on concepts and methods based on their practical experiences, which are only very loosely connected—if at all—to scientific theories and research-supported findings. However, there are already some established bridges, as well as some that are under construction, which may be useful for practitioners. We need various bridges because the worlds on both sides are diverse and constantly changing. The diversity of the practical world is one of the reasons why working as a coach is an extraordinarily challenging job. The people we meet live in this complex world and the issues they bring to coaching are as varied and interesting as life

S. Greif, *The Future of Coaching*, https://doi.org/10.1007/978-3-031-96192-2_1

can be. Coaching can change their lives and ours. Helping clients clarify their themes and achieve their goals can be very satisfying.

The scientific literature on coaching has identified many impressive concepts and methods for which new research would be promising. Often, scientific research on intervention methods exists in practice fields outside of coaching. In the science fields, there is a steadily growing body of application-oriented research—with and without direct reference to coaching—that has the potential to be useful in analyzing and explaining the effects of coaching or in improving coaching methods. It is therefore worthwhile to build not just one but many bridges between practice and science.

The picture of the bridge in Fig. 1.1 was designed for this book by Michael Griem, a Berlin artist with a gallery in Ahlbeck (Usedom Island, Germany). The swinging bridge speaks to the future and conveys the imperative for its construction to be completed.

The worlds of practice and science require their own expertise. Anyone who works as a scientist and also has a coaching practice is aware of the differences in requirements between the two worlds. In coaching practice, one must conduct every session in a way that the client finds stimulating and that supports them in achieving their desired results. In science, on the other hand, it is more important to use theories, hypotheses, and findings precisely. Publications and research studies are expected to lead to new findings, which are always under the critical eyes of other scientists. In the coaching practice literature, authors usually refer to scientific

Fig. 1.1 Building bridges between science and practice

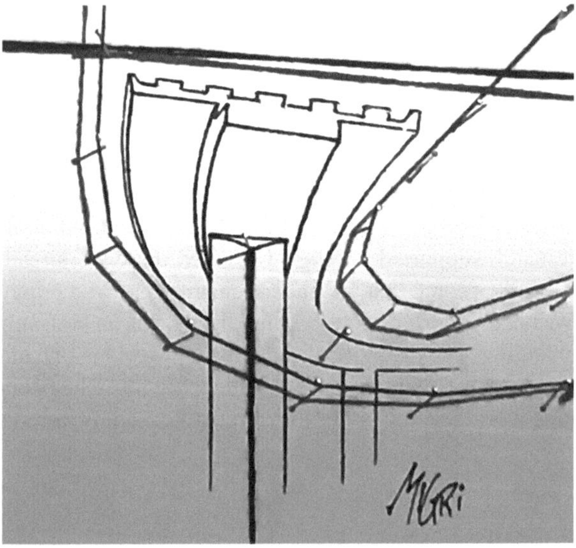

theories in very general ways. A deepening of scientific references requires precise analysis and openness to criticism. In this book, therefore, common practical (and scientific) concepts, theories, and methods are examined and discussed as closely as possible through a scientific lens. My purpose is that of a scientist who aims to provide useful suggestions for the further development of both coaching practices and coaching research. The use of scientifically based coaching methods is a quality criterion required by almost all coaching associations.

1.1.1 To Which Topics or Themes Do We Need Bridges?

Few surveys have been conducted on the subjects that clients want to address through coaching. Bono et al. (2009), in a small study, identified the following list of topics often addressed in coaching:

- Interpersonal skills
- Stress management
- Strategic thinking
- Time management
- Conflict management
- Staffing
- Management style
- Leadership
- Communication
- Adaptability/versatility
- Motivation
- Delegation
- Planning
- Sales or financial performance
- Mentoring

Middendorf (2018, 2020) has periodically conducted detailed surveys in Germany on important coaching topics. The most common topics brought up by clients in coaching are as follows:

- New tasks
- Self-reflection
- Leadership skills
- Personality/potential development
- Relationship issues
- Professional problem situations
- Change management
- Team development
- Stress management, burnout, work-life balance
- Career and job
- Self-management

The largest international survey of the coaching industry to date was performed by the International Coaching Federation (ICF, 2020). It included 22,457 survey respondents from 161 countries and territories. One survey question addressed the main future areas and opportunities in coaching over the subsequent 12 months.

The resulting list and respondent percentages are as follows:

- Relationships 43%
- Life vision and enhancement 42%
- No speciality 42%
- Health and wellness 40%
- Career 37%
- Other 37%
- Leadership 36%
- Executive 34%
- Business and other organizations 33%
- Small business 33%

According to an ICF survey (ICF, 2023b), "Leadership was the main area of coaching most frequently mentioned in the 2022 survey (34%), followed by executive coaching (17%) and business/organizations (13%). The proportion identifying business coaching as their main specialty has been steadily rising, up from 62% in 2015 to 65% in 2019 and 67% in 2022."

Coaching areas and coaching themes are constantly expanding. Clients bring challenging old and new questions and life situations into coaching conversations. When clients achieve important goals or clarify significant themes through coaching support, it also results in feelings of success for their coaches. As a coach, I am almost always learning something new from my clients' real-life questions and solutions. I therefore understand very well why many like to work as coaches.

Coaching is also an attractive profession from an economic perspective. Many become coaches with hopes of high earnings. Unfortunately, since the title of "coach" is not protected by law, some self-proclaimed "coaches" with no adequate training engage in coaching practices. In addition, the general demand for coaching is high and growing. According to an international survey of the ICF, the estimated total revenue from coaching in 2019 was $2.849 billion US dollars (45.5% in North America and 32.2% in Western Europe). This was an increase of 21% over the 2015 estimate. That is very strong growth.

However, the individual revenue from coaching is lower than that of consultants and other high professional services. Globally, the individual average annual income from coaching (USD) is only $47,100 (North America $62,500 and Western Europe $51,100), according to the ICF study. This can be attributed to, among other things, the fact that coaching appointments can rarely be seamlessly scheduled on coaches' workdays without interruptions. This results in a comparatively low number of weekly coaching hours of 13.9. A total of 94% of the coach practitioners in the ICF survey therefore offer services in addition to coaching, which increase their income (especially 60% consulting, 60% training, and 54% facilitation services). Only 26% have more than 14 clients. A comparable proportion of coach practitioners (27%) have four or fewer clients. This means that coaching must very often be considered merely a part-time activity. However, undoubtedly, especially for socially minded people, coaching is one of the most satisfying part-time activities, and according to my personal experience, it can be performed well into old age.

According to anecdotal accounts, large companies invest more than 1 million USD annually in coaching their executives and professionals. Initially, executives and managers or executives from large companies were the main target group for coaching. The focus was on improving their leadership behavior and dealing with conflicts in teams or their individual careers. In the meantime, coaching has been introduced at small companies and craft businesses (Busch et al., 2022). In addition, the market for coaching paid for by individuals seeking to address important personal issues is expanding. This book aims to illustrate the diverse range of topics and target groups, with numerous practical case studies, different types and concepts of coaching, and especially the many established and new practical coaching methods.

According to the scientific problem-solving approach of science (Greif, 1993; Herrmann, 1979), coaching based on science should serve not only as a hallmark of quality for the reputations of coaching associations, coaching training courses, and coaches but also as a strategy for constantly reviewing the effectiveness of coaching. This can be accomplished by studying new scientific findings and intervention methods and learning from errors and best practices and thereby improving the overall coaching process. Chapter 7 of this book summarizes existing methods and results for reviewing coaching effectiveness. There is still much room for improvement.

1.1.2 Selection of Topics in the Book

Two criteria were used to select the content in this book:

1. Practical significance
2. Scientific foundation

It is my conviction that both criteria work well together. Science should not only theorize but also address and clarify practically significant issues. Like reflective scientists, reflective practitioners (Schön, 1983) should analyze, question, and improve their own practices repeatedly. Foundational scientific knowledge should be examined in terms of whether it can be clarified or improved. In this way, solid bridges can be built between practice and science. Following the problem-solving conception of science (Greif, 1993), scientific theories in applied science disciplines serve as "tools of thought" for solving practical problems.

1.2 From Traditional Coaching to Posttraditional Coaching

We live in a world that is always changing. Economic crises, climate change, the digital revolution, the COVID-19 pandemic, and wars have generated complex changes that have directly or indirectly affected large populations. The sociologist Giddens (1991) analyzed the challenges of complex global changes for societies and organizations and their influences on individual day-to-day social life. Traditions and habits that in the past provided security are no longer tenable. Modern, post-traditional society has replaced former sureties with the principle of radical doubt, questioning everything and considering knowledge as only hypothetical (Giddens, 1991, p. 2).

1.2.1 Traditions as Principles and Rules

According to several dictionary definitions including that of the Britannica Dictionary, a "tradition" can be defined as "a way of thinking, behaving, or doing something that has been used by the people in a particular group, family, society, *for a long time*".[1]

> The origin of the word "traditional" is the Latin "tradere," which means "to pass on." Traditions are passed on by informal or formal communication. One characteristic of traditions is that they are conveyed as commonly shared imperatives, often with little questioning. They can endure over long periods, and they can also be short-lived. Hobsbawm noted that traditions can be deliberately created, referring to the "invention of tradition". (Hobsbawm & Ranger, 1992)

1.2.2 Fast Emergence of Traditions in Business Coaching

Lane et al. (2010, p. 379), in their analysis of the future of coaching as a profession, expressed doubt as to whether coaching could be strictly considered a profession. They referred to Bennet (2006, p. 242), pointing out critical gaps in the criteria that must be met for consideration as a profession, such as generally accepted, identifiable and distinct skills for coaches, required training and/or education, general recognition as a profession, and defined theory on which coaches base their practice. In their view, coaching could be described as an emerging profession. They further noted that in the future, professionalization, and not general recognition as a profession, should be prioritized. In her historical and sociological analysis of the professionalization of coaching, Fietze (2017, p. 3) concludes that for coaching, "the clarification of responsibilities of and autonomy in order to ensure the quality of professional work continue to remain crucial challenges even today."

---

[1] Britannica Dictionary, https://www.britannica.com/dictionary/tradition (retrieved Jan. 4th, 2023).

Coaching services in the business field, as established since the 1980s/1990s, are comparatively young for a profession. New professions require principles and rules of conduct for professional behavior. Their function can be understood as providing distinction from other professions, means of quality assurance, and certainty about what one may do and what one should not do as a professional. Such principles or rules can also be seen as "traditions" since they are not often questioned.

It is remarkable how quickly and self-confident basic coaching principles and rules were propagated by coaches at early congresses and in the first coaching associations. They were communicated and negotiated as a common understanding. Many such principles and rules are still being propagated today and are also rarely questioned. I remember the first European Coaching Psychology Conference 2008 in London and especially a coaching congress in 2003 in Wiesbaden, Germany, organized by different German language associations and coaching groups. My impression was that we witnessed informal power struggles over the definition, principles, and rules for coaching and a quick emergence of coaching traditions. Prominent speakers very self-confidently laid down basic principles of coaching behavior. Nonconforming coaching behavior was marginalized and dismissed as "not coaching." It would be interesting to explore these early power struggles in our profession using historical research methods.

1.2.3 Examples of Basic Principles of Coaching

1.2.3.1 Coaching Is Not Counseling

An outstanding example of a basic principle of coaching is the distinction between coaching and counseling. Speakers in early conferences with almost complete agreement emphasized the behavioral differences between business coaching and management consulting. A common assumption about coaching is that coaches are not supposed to give advice. Another is that coaching is not counseling but helping people help themselves. The idea of helping clients help themselves is the traditional basic principle of the coaching profession.

A Google search (November 2022) on "differences between coaching and consulting" yielded nearly 27.9 million hits. It is often emphasized that no advice is to be given in coaching. The International Coaching Federation (ICF, 2021) demands that the coach "maintain the distinctions between coaching, consulting, psychotherapy and other support professions." What is the underlying goal or purpose of strictly differentiating coaching from counseling? This distinction is deemed so important that the ICF has even elevated it to an ethical standard. Is it unethical to provide advice during coaching? Why exactly? Is it harmful to all clients or the profession? How is "counseling" defined for coaches and for modern counselors? What kind of advice is implied? Could counseling be a means of helping people help themselves? Do coaches believe that they are the primary partners for helping people help themselves?

Section 2.4 returns to these important questions and seeks to provide posttraditional answers without neglecting the specificities of coaching and the importance of facilitating clients in developing their own solutions. In a metaphorical sense, they are the "owners" of the goals and the paths to the goals.

1.2.3.2 Coaching Is Not Teaching

Another fundamental distinction is that between coaching and teaching. In his definition of coaching, Sir John Whitmore (1992), for example, stated the following: "Coaching is helping clients learn rather than teaching them." This means that as a coach, I should avoid providing my clients with specific knowledge or information. Analogous to counseling, the assumption is that teaching cannot help clients learn by themselves. Does that mean that it is not allowed to share expert knowledge with our clients, e.g., on how to effectively help themselves or how to overcome difficulties in achieving their goals? For many years, there have been humanistic teaching methods that activate reflective, self-directed, or self-organized learning, which differ from traditional teaching methods (cf. Greif & Kurtz, 1998). A current example is the psychoeducational enlightening of clients in the field of healthcare. This approach has been shown to promote self-help and client self-management. The opinion of experts in these coaching fields is that especially neuroscientific coaching and health coaching do not work without psychoeducational interventions. Section 2.5 explains the principles of psychoeducation. In the chapter on methods (Sect. 6.5), the example of the challenge of changing one's behavioral habits is used to show how, through psychoeducational clarification, intensive "Aha! experiences" can be evoked and how psychoeducation and accompaniment of the implementation typical feelings of shame and self-devaluation after failure experiences can be overcome. The results show that clients experience pride in developing new self-management abilities.

1.2.3.3 Are Coaches Against Online Coaching and AI Tools?

Not long ago, many coaches vehemently rejected online coaching or e-coaching and digital coaching tools or artificial intelligence (AI) tools in coaching. Melanie Maier (2020) wrote a dissertation under the supervision of Harald Geißler and performed intensive interviews with coaches on their reasons for choosing or rejecting digital media. I was the second supervisor of that dissertation and remember the results and the vehemence of the coaches' rejection of online coaching that were observed by the interviewer. Just as the study was completed, the COVID-19 pandemic changed our world. The pandemic was a shock to many "anti-online coaches." Openness, at least to online coaching, became a matter of professional survival for them. We could all experience the worldwide radical changes that this pandemic had not only at the societal level but also at the professional and personal levels. In *Sect. 6.9* of this book, current and future developments in online and e-coaching as well as the use of AI coaching tools are addressed. In Sect. 10.2, future developments in the coaching market, digitalization, and AI are discussed. Scientific studies can help clarify the risks and opportunities of digitalization and AI for our clients, for our interactions with clients, and for the coaching profession. In any case, digitalization and AI are challenging our traditional coaching principles and roles.

1.2.3.4 Detailed Examples of Coaching Principles

Some principles have been propagated by leading coaching, which aims to regulate coaching behavior in detail. For example, speakers at coaching conferences and meetings often oppose the use of *closed questions* in coaching (to avoid influencing or committing clients to a few alternatives given by the coach). However, as empirical evidence from an observational study shows (see *Sect. 6.3* on *Question Techniques*), coaches seem to use closed questions even slightly more often than open questions. This study did not find that closed questions result in lower stimulation of clients. Communication culture is important in this regard. In Japan, the use of open-ended questions can even be problematic in coaching, as Peter Dreyer (2010) demonstrated at a coaching conference. They may even raise fears of "losing face" (see *Sect. 6.3*).

Another rule, formulated in the early phases of coaching, referred to the *maximum number of coaching sessions*. At the 2003 Wiesbaden congress in Germany, without contradiction, one speaker claimed that the ideal number of coaching sessions was eight to ten to prevent clients' psychological dependence. I remember this very well because shortly before that, I had conducted from 15 to 50 coaching sessions each with the CEO, project manager, and core team in one of the largest European industrial services companies to support a fundamental customer-oriented restructuring and, in another case, had even coached a company owner over several years when required by him in critical situations. Should I truly have stopped doing that because I had made these very confident individuals dependent on me? Coaches in a recent online seminar noted that they no longer consider this rule appropriate. One participant said that long-term coaching shows that clients have great trust in the coach.

1.2.3.5 The Future of Posttraditional Coaching

Strictly examined, the described traditional principles and rules of coaching are prohibitions that tell coaches what they should *not* do. It would be basically paradoxical if we were to attempt to help our clients use and expand their possibilities by applying unquestioned restrictions to our own professional behavior. Posttraditional coaching should focus more on principles and rules that extend the possibilities and potentials of coaches. This book therefore aims to determine, for example, how coaches can ask questions that activate clients' intensive self-reflections, how brief psychoeducational enlightenment can generate new insights that improve clients' self-regulation, or how reflective suggestions can be introduced and formulated in such a way that clients are empowered as owners of their goals and decisions.

Many early defined principles and rules of coaching are still maintained today without much dispute. Some such principles have been included in the standards of coaching associations and are communicated in coach training. However, the coaching profession has been confronted with complex and radical changes since the initial definition of these principles and rules. Therefore, for the future of coaching, we need to ask which traditional principles and rules must be critically examined and changed or reformulated so that they can be adapted to the challenges of the ongoing social and technological changes in society, organizations, and private life. Posttraditional coaching does not abandon principles and rules that can be implemented in a meaningful way but rather seeks to reflect on the original objectives and to revise them in light of scientific and practical experience so that they can be applied more effectively today and in the future. As mentioned above, the model here is the "reflective practitioner" (Schön, 1983) and scientific analysis of coaching's explicit and implicit definitions, assumptions, and predictions. For this purpose, we need open discourses with critical reflections on both practical observations and scientific examinations of the practical actions of coaches and clients and their effects. According to the ideal basic principles of science, these discourses should be conducted rationally and without personal attacks, on an equal level, without considering the social rank of the participants. We need much more reflection and discourse between scientists and practitioners. A vision for the future of coaching is that through many discourses, many bridges between science and practice can be built. The general purpose is to further the capabilities of the coaching profession to address today's and tomorrow's complex changes.

Undoubtedly, coaching today is shaped mainly by practitioners who rely on concepts and methods based on their practical experiences; those concepts and methods are only very loosely connected—if at all—to scientific theories and research-supported findings. As noted above, in the coaching field, some bridges between science and practice have been established. These bridges are needed because the worlds on both sides are diverse and constantly changing. The diversity of the practical world is one of the reasons why working as a coach is an extraordinarily stimulating job. The issues clients bring to coaching are as varied and interesting as life in today's world can be. Coaching may change their lives and ours. Helping them clarify their themes and achieve their goals can be very satisfying.

1.3 Overview of the Contents of the Book

This book is a translation of the original German publication (Greif, 2021). It has been thoroughly revised and expanded and includes ten chapters. The chapters that follow this one are structured as follows:

Chapter 2: What Is Coaching? (Why is a scientific definition important for practitioners? Differentiating coaching and consulting, explaining one's own coaching concept at the first meeting).

Chapter 3: Comparing Coaching with Other Methods (similarities and differences: sports coaching—psychotherapy—supervision—mentoring—goal setting and promotional interviews by superiors—consulting by friends).

Chapter 4: Different Types of Coaching (individual coaching—group and team coaching—business coaching—life and career coaching—leadership coaching—intercultural coaching—stress management and health coaching—self-coaching—e-coaching and virtual coaching).

Chapter 5: Directions and Concepts (the GROW model—evidence-based coaching concepts—solution-focused coaching—systemic coaching concepts—hypnosystemic coaching—cognitive-behavioral coaching concepts—narrative coaching—neuroscientific approaches—how to detect pseudoscientific concepts and charlatans).

Chapter 6: Posttraditional Coaching Methods Through a Scientific Lens (definition of methods—classification of coaching methods—questioning methods—meaning, vision, values and strengths—changing behavior, social interactions and conflicts—stress management, burnout prevention and health—team coaching—coaching through organizational change—future perspectives).

Chapter 7: Reviewing the Effectiveness of Coaching (evaluation model—methods and criteria).

Chapter 8: Processes in Coaching (what are the processes?—methods for analysis).

Chapter 9: Result-Oriented Coaching (assumptions and integrative overall model of general success factors—process guidance, appreciation, and emotional support—result-oriented reflections—affect and emotion regulation—goal clarification and conscious wanting—resource activation—implementation support—sustainable change of habits).

Chapter 10: Future Perspectives (developments in the coaching market—consequences of digitalization—impact of AI for job changes and the life of our clients, their reflection, and special forms of life and career coaching—AI bots as coaches or AI-augmented coaching methods—the future of posttraditional coaching and practical coaching based on science).

Box 1.1 Coachee or Client?

The people who ask for coaching are often called "coachees." In this book, "client" is preferred. This term is common for the clients of lawyers or psychotherapists. It is preferred because it does not have the slightly belittling connotation of a "coachee." An alternative, but not yet common, term would be "coaching partner."

Chapter 2
What Is Coaching?

2.1 Controversy Over Coaching Definitions

The controversy about coaching definitions has great relevance in discussions among coaches and in conversations with clients when they ask what is meant by coaching. A clear definition would help in describing coaching specifics and in differentiating coaching from other person-centered interventions.

The first "coaches" were experienced coachmen (coaches) in the nineteenth century who guided the horses of traveling carriages "with great sensitivity" and accompanied passengers "safely and swiftly to their destination" (Steinke & Steinke, 2019, p. 25, free translation). As Steinke and Steinke (2019, p. 26 ff.) found in their specialized historical research, private tutors, tutors, or repetitors have been called "coaches" in Great Britain since the nineteenth century. However, there are many questions about what coaching is today.

All coaches are familiar with the question, "What is coaching?", which arises in social conversations and with potential clients. In answering this question, coaches seek an appropriate and well-formulated explanation. In doing so, they often emphasize coaching as "helping people help themselves," asserting that coaching is a "solution-oriented" process and that they activate the strengths and potentials (or resources) of their clients:

> "Coaching is partnering with clients in a thought-provoking and creative process that inspires them to maximize their personal and professional potential".

S. Greif, *The Future of Coaching*, https://doi.org/10.1007/978-3-031-96192-2_2

2.2 Scientific Criteria for Definitions

Strictly speaking, the ICF definition reproduced above is not a definition that enables coaching to be distinguished from other consulting or training interventions. Rather, it is a statement crafted with the intention of appealing to potential clients and customers. From a scientific perspective, it can be classified as an interest-based, "persuasive definition" (Gabriel, 2004). However, such definitions are by no means forbidden. It is quite legitimate to use catchy, promotional phrases to highlight what is exceptional about coaching. Coaches should, however, be prepared for the fact that not everyone will be taken in by such catchy phrases but may ask precise questions about the meaning of the terms used. For example, what exactly is meant by "partnering," what is meant when consultants are not seen as partners, and what is the difference between coaches and mentors? There are other person-centered interventions that strive to stimulate partnering, thoughts, and creative ideas as well as to develop human potential, e.g., person-centered learning methods. Coaches therefore need answers when critical clients want to know how coaching can be clearly and unambiguously distinguished from other methods.

The classical criteria for scientific definitions, which have been formulated in definition theory (Gabriel, 2004; Menne, 1973) for so-called real definitions, can be helpful for this purpose. This means definitions that contain statements about the essential characteristics of an entity or an object. The entity "to be defined" (here, "coaching") is called the "definiendum." Its meaning is delimited or specified by statements about its characteristics, the so-called definiens. The classical criteria for the formulation of the definiendum are described in the following passages (Menne, 1973; Offermanns, 2004, p. 30 ff., Sarkar & Pfeiffer, 2006).

2.2.1 Adequacy

The definition of coaching must not be too broad, e.g., "Coaching is individual counseling," but also not too narrow, e.g., "Coaching is a conversation between a coach accredited by coaching association X and a client that lasts 45–60 minutes."

2.2.2 Clarity

The meaning of the expressions and terms used in the definition must be known or explained. Common clarity for different people is also called intersubjective verifiability. For example, coaching is often defined by the adjective "systemic." As Kriz (2018) noted, "systemic" has very different meanings depending on the underlying systems theory or individual understanding. Without explanation or reference to the system theory meant in each case, it remains unclear what is meant (see also Kriz, 2022).

2.2.3 *Simplicity*

The definition must be as simple as possible and should not contain redundant statements.

As will be presented below, there are coaching definitions that are very long because they list many characteristics. If those characteristics are not repeated, the criterion of simplicity is not violated.

2.2.4 *Logically Stringent and Without Circular Reasoning*

Definitions must not contain illogical formulations, e.g., "Coaching of employees by their superiors is not allowed, except for team leaders who coach their team members." Logical circles occur when the definiendum is also contained in the definiens. It is not easy to detect circularity. For example, definitions that state in the definiens that coaching is performed by coaches would be risky. Such definitions result irresolvably in logical circles because it is hardly possible to define what a "coach" does without a separate definition of "coaching."

2.2.5 *Meaningfulness and Essence*

The statements in the definition must say a lot about the defined object or "subject matter." It must reflect the "meaning" or "essential" features or be substantial.

This criterion is central but undoubtedly difficult to apply. Its application often depends on the theory favored. For example, a follower of cognitive-behavioral psychological theories will describe the essence of coaching in terms and statements from that theoretical perspective in terms of cognitions and behavior. A communication scientist, on the other hand, might attempt to reconstruct the essence of coaching on the basis of communication processes.

2.2.6 *Further Classical Criteria*

Gabriel (2004) lists other commonly used criteria (set forth below).

Naming of the Associated Generic Term or Superordinate Term
Is there a superordinate term or category (Latin: genus proximum) to which the definiendum belongs? An example of this is a description of coaching as a "person-centered consulting process (…)" (Rauen, 2001, p. 64, free translation). Accordingly, coaching would be subordinated as a subgroup of consulting processes.

Naming the Distinguishing Characteristics (Differentiae Specificae)
How does the subject matter/object to be defined differ from others? This is the question that was addressed at the beginning of this section and is meant by most when they ask about the distinctive features of coaching. The following section focuses on this criterion with examples from common definitions.

A complaint that is often expressed is that there is no common definition of coaching among coaches or between associations. From a scientific point of view, it is imperative that the coaching profession obtain clarification about the criteria on which a scientifically defensible definition and professional explanation for clients should be based. In her dissertation, Martina Offermanns (2004) made inroads into this process by reviewing the existent coaching definitions using the abovementioned criteria (see below). However, she did not find a single definition of coaching that met these criteria.

Beautifully formulated and creative statements such as those in the ICF definition can be used to attract clients. However, scientific standards demand that definitions should be "noncreative" (Gabriel, 2004). If creative (or "newly invented") terms and statements are used in a definition, it is necessary to define each new term in an intersubjectively unambiguous way. For example, the ICF definition would need to clearly define what is meant by "partnering with clients." What exactly is special about this? Could it not be said that the individually adapted instruction of a teacher in how to use a new computer program is also "partnering"? What is meant by "thought-provoking" in the ICF definition? Any briefing on a new program stimulates thought, but the thoughts that are stimulated in coaching are usually very different. How could a definition describe these differences? This question will be addressed further on in this chapter.

There would be little progress in clarifying coaching definitions if the competition for appropriate definitions were merely to formulate a sentence that is particularly beautifully and engagingly or creatively worded. "Coach" is not a legally protected professional title such as "medical doctor" or "psychotherapist." Anyone can call themselves a "coach" and offer "coaching," regardless of the person's understanding of those terms. This makes it all the more important for the profession to define and explain precisely and clearly what is meant by "coaching" and how coaching can be distinguished from other person-centered interventions.

However, there will probably never be complete agreement between all associations and coaches on the definition of coaching. The scientific views and underlying coaching theories and concepts are too varied for such agreement, and they are reflected in the respective definitions and the range of highlighted features and statements. However, if standard criteria for definitions are observed, the differences in the definitions can contribute to transparency with regard to how different coach providers or associations differ in their understanding of coaching.

2.3 The Problem of Insufficient Distinguishing Characteristics in Common Coaching Definitions

2.3.1 *Programmatic Definitions*

Sir John Whitmore is one of the most internationally known coaching pioneers. His programmatic definition is often quoted (see the coaching definition in the glossary of the EMCC, 2018):

> "Coaching is unlocking people's potential to maximize their own performance. It is helping them to learn rather than teaching them." (Whitmore, 1992, p. 10)

This definition continues to be a source of inspiration. It stands for potential-oriented coaching concepts. With his formulation, Whitmore integrates the idea of actively promoting the potential of the individual, an approach rooted in humanistic psychology. He explicitly distinguishes coaching methods from teaching methods. However, he neglects the fact that this idea by no means has been propagated only in coaching. Activating interventions for potential development have existed for a long time as learning methods in psychology and education (Greif & Kurtz, 1998; Schunk & Greene, 2018). Methods of self-regulated or self-organized learning in schools and universities therefore also serve to "unlock people's potential to maximize their own performance." Whitmore's compelling formulation is therefore not suitable for distinguishing coaching from teaching.

2.3.2 *Coaching as Person-Oriented Counseling*

Wolfgang Loos, one of the pioneers of coaching in Germany, initially formulated it in very general terms:

> "Coaching is person-oriented individual counseling of people in the world of work". (Looss, 1991, p. 13, free translation)

Loos thus classified coaching in general as "individual counseling." Initially, he saw the world of work as the area of application. Later, however, he characterized coaching more broadly as "counseling without an explicit request" and as a "reflective partnership." Today, he restricts his earlier specifications, but as before, he asserts that the coaching term is merely a "label" that is "contentless," which is why, in his view, coaching needs to be explained and concretized as a "communicative practice." This, according to this approach, can be done only through the "cocreation of practice and science" (Ebermann, 2018, p. 16 ff.).

A simple way to define coaching is to identify it as individual counseling. One example is the definition by Wahren (1997, p. 9, free translation):

> "Coaching is the individual counseling of individuals or groups in work-related, technical and/or psychological-sociodynamic questions or problems by the coach."

The first part of this definition classifies coaching as the "counseling" of individuals or groups. The reference to "technical and/or psychological-sociodynamic questions" is apparently intended to distinguish the content of coaching from other types of counseling. However, if we consider it more closely, it is not possible to make a clear distinction because similar questions can occur in all forms of personal counseling sessions, e.g., in employee interviews, in mentoring, in conversations with friends or in career counseling. The reference "by the coach" in the definition is not unproblematic because it creates a logical circle. It would be better to delete this part of the definition.

In the early days of coaching, the practice was limited to the world of work as a field of application, as was initially the case with Loos. Soon thereafter, however, coaching was offered, e.g., for self-paying clients, as "life coaching" with all the themes brought in by the clients from their everyday lives. Today, the application of coaching in companies is often referred to as "business coaching." The German Coaching Federation ("Deutscher Bundesverband Coaching," DBVC) has still limited its definition of coaching to this field (DBVC, 2012, free translation):

> "Coaching is the professional counseling, guidance and support of persons with management/control functions and of experts in companies/organizations. The objective of coaching is the further development of individual or collective learning and performance processes with regard to primarily occupational concerns."

Kilburg (1996) emphasized the organization's interests in coaching and offered the following definition:

> "Executive coaching is defined as a helping relationship formed between a client who has managerial authority and responsibility in an organization and a consultant who uses a wide variety of behavioral techniques and methods to help the client achieve a mutually identified set of goals to improve his or her professional performance and personal satisfaction and, consequently, to improve the effectiveness of the client's organization within a formally defined coaching agreement."

2.3.3 Coaching as a Solution-Oriented Process

Internationally, a definition by Stober and Grant (2006, p. 3 f.) from their classical "Evidence Based Coaching Handbook" is often referred to. The authors include other target groups in addition to executives and do not focus on performance or effectiveness improvement in business contexts:

> "Coaching is a solution-focused systematic process (...) typically directed at fostering the ongoing self-directed learning and personal growth of the coachee."

The term "solution-focused" here is related to the approach of "solution-focused counseling" as used by de Shazer to refer to brief therapy (de Shazer & Dolan, 2008). This coaching concept is discussed in more detail below (see *Sect. 5.3*). In complementary explanations, Stober and Grant use an expanded view and emphasize that clients are autonomous adult learners. They can learn and reflect on their actions in a self-directed way on the basis of their experiences and knowledge. Those authors refer to the concept of reflective practice by Schön (1983) mentioned above in *Chap. 1*. Some of their defined terms follow Whitmore, but other terms are more oriented toward basic psychological theories. However, their definition does not allow for a differentiation of the specifics of coaching in comparison with other methods but rather serves as a conceptual classification of coaching as self-regulated and reflective learning (cf. on these approaches Greif & Kurtz, 1998, Schunk & Greene, 2018).

2.3.4 Coaching as a Socratic Dialog

After reviewing various definitions, Passmore et al. (2013) prefer the following explanation. It describes what they believe coaching is, how it is performed, and for whom.

> "A Socratic-based future focused dialog between a facilitator (coach) and a participant (coachee/client), where the facilitator uses open questions, summaries and reflections which are aimed at stimulating the self-awareness and personal responsibility of the participant". (Passmore & Fillery-Travis, 2011, cited from Passmore et al., 2013, p. 3)

In this definition, the dialog between coach and client is specified much more precisely than in many other definitions. This clearly distinguishes coaching from professional consulting or teaching and learning in educational organizations or instruction with instructional methods because they cannot be performed only with open questions. However, not every conversation in which one person asks another open-ended questions should be classified as "coaching." In TV, talk show moderators typically use open-ended questions, and no one would consider them to be coaches. The authors themselves note that in their definition, the outcome of coaching is only vaguely formulated. However, they describe process features not found in other definitions. Additionally, they point to "Socratic questions." Socrates' method of questioning has also been called the "midwifery method" because it assumes that respondents already have the answers within themselves. Through persistent questioning and inquiry, respondents can bring forth the answers themselves. In posing questions, coaches merely serve as facilitators.

According to this understanding, Socrates could be called a "coach." However, if we consider the focus and results of Socratic questioning, we still consider Socrates to be a philosopher as he was concerned with general philosophical clarifications and the search for generally valid explanations and knowledge, not with the typical themes and questions raised by clients in the coaching process as described in Chap. 1. A complete coaching definition requires specification of the content and goals or outcomes of coaching.

2.4 Coaching Is Not Counseling

2.4.1 Help for Self-Help

Among coaches, it is controversial whether coaching should be classified as a special form of counseling. "Coaching is not counseling" is a statement often repeated by coaches. Anyone who describes coaching as a special form of "counseling" may be met with vehement opposition. A Google search on "differences between coaching and consulting" (October 2021) yielded nearly 30 million hits. It is often emphasized that coaching is not about giving advice. The International Coach Federation (ICF) seeks to promote and standardize professional coaching standards by defining core coaching competencies. As part of their ethical standards, coaches are required to be competent in maintaining and communicating the distinctions between coaching, counseling, psychotherapy, and other support professions: "Maintain the distinctions between coaching, consulting, psychotherapy and other support professions" (ICF, 2021). In German-speaking countries, coaches often make claims like the following:

"Coaching is not counseling; it is helping people help themselves."

However, helping people help themselves is by no means a principle that applies exclusively to coaching. It is a classic concept for the sustainable activation of personal initiative. It has long been propagated, for example, as a consulting concept in the field of development aid for third world countries but also as a basis for other interventions. It is therefore not a special feature sufficient for delimiting counseling activities.

2.4.2 What Is Understood by "Counseling"?

Concepts of counseling are constantly and dynamically evolving. It is questionable when coaches and coaching associations through in their definitions limit counselors and counseling associations to certain traditional methods. Basically, it is not legitimate to define the principles of other professions without discussion and agreement. There are counseling concepts that designate "counseling" as "helping people to help themselves." Häcker and Stapf (2009) offer the following definition (free translation, simplified and summarized):

> *Counseling* is a problem-solving process methodically designed by the counselor to support the self-efforts of those seeking advice and to improve their skills in coping with the tasks or problems they are facing.

A practical case example can serve as an illustration. During my work as a management consultant in the Felix Schoeller Group, a global leader in photographic and specialist papers, I was asked to help reduce recurring long standstills of a large and complex paper machine that led to strenuous additional work for the employees, high production costs, and delivery problems that even threatened the existence of this special business field. The causes were not clear. Maintenance engineers, mechanics, and crews were increasingly arguing vehemently among themselves. To find the causes and solutions, I explained to the shift foremen a simple brainstorming method modified for use with the shift workers (with visualization of the causes and proposed solutions written on cards that were pinned to a board). A reserve shift foreman conducted the process independently with employees on all shifts without my further assistance. The mechanics and engineers were also able to contribute their own proposed solutions. In this way, more than 40 possible solutions were created in a very constructive and peaceful atmosphere. Points were obtained from the different shifts and ranked according to the perceived likelihood of finding a solution and tested one at a time. A solution from the employees that ranked fourth led to success. The employees were naturally very proud that they had succeeded in solving the problem by their fourth solution. This example shows how consulting can be designed to help people help themselves.

Accordingly, even "expert advice" can be performed in a person-oriented manner and as "help for self-help." Through this approach, the expert may pass on knowledge in a way that is different from conventional "instruction methods," in which individuals are told exactly what they must do and how. A professional consultation, e.g., for the use of a computer program, which is designed as "help for self-help," would be recognizable by the fact that the expert "instruction" is provided on the basis of individual prerequisites and preexisting knowledge and thereby activates learners to understand the program and promotes independent self-active trials and step-by-step learning from the beginning.

Constructivist concepts of counseling, such as the systemic concept of "integrated counseling" by Handler (2007), also distinguish themselves from traditional methods of professional counseling. Therefore, it does not make sense to claim that coaching can be generally distinguished from counseling when certain forms of counseling must also be seen as help for self-help.

2.4.3 *Coaching as Counseling Without Advice?*

A systemic concept by Raddatz (2018), which is very well-known in Germany, proposes coaching as "counseling without advice." She assumes that "the client determines which goal is to be achieved, and the coach mainly asks the right questions and leaves the finding of the answer to the client" (loc. Cit., p. 25, free translation). She assumes that counseling with an "expert attitude" creates a top-bottom relationship. "The counseler (…) knows the solution (top) and the client (…) does not know it and therefore has to ask for support (bottom)." The price for this is dependence and a lack of independence on the part of the client (loc. Cit., p. 89). For counseling staff, this creates "enormous pressure to be successful," which, in their opinion, can even lead to burnout (loc. Cit., p. 91, free translation):

> In systemic coaching, we see ourselves as purely supporting the client in solving problems on his or her own responsibility—problems that arise in private life, at work, in the company or between these three areas. The problems we work on in systemic coaching are hardly related to an increase in performance, but to the development of new behavioral patterns. Since the client formulates the goal himself and works out the solution himself, he achieves maximum implementation success. (Raddatz, 2018, p. 87, free translation)

Not only for Raddatz but also presumably for most coaches and coaching associations, it is a general guiding principle that the goals of coaching are fundamentally determined by the client and that coaches should stay informed about and decide on the methods used. (The role of the companies or clients funding the coaching will be discussed further below.) However, if they are to be taken seriously, such far-reaching statements about the negative consequences of an expert attitude and the generalized positive consequences of clients working out solutions only on their own, which Raddatz cites to justify her concept, are unsupported assertions that need to be verified by practical observations or, better yet, by scientific studies.

On the basis of my own observations, I question whether counselors and coaches are in fact placed under such "enormous pressure to be successful" that they are threatened by burnout, as Raddatz asserts, just because they give advice to their clients. According to current research findings, burnout is based on excessive demands due to persistent stress over long periods of time (Burisch, 2010; Greif & Bertino, 2022). Transferred to the question of advice, this would mean that coaches must give advice permanently and in so doing overburden themselves. If a coach suffers from burnout, I would look for other, less absurd causes (see *Sect. 8.3* below for research on the negative side effects of coaching for coaches).

Furthermore, one might ask whether, as Raddatz additionally assumes, clients generally feel inferior to coaches when coaches make one or more suggestions and whether they become dependent when coaches make several suggestions. It is difficult to imagine that self-confident clients would subordinate themselves to a counselor or coach after receiving a few pieces of advice, no matter how good. Executives will likely protest immediately if they do not like a proposed solution. They are confident in their ability to enter the solution development process with their own critical considerations. Some explicitly ask the coach to act as a sparring partner because coaching allows them to safely test different views and possible solutions in discourse. Coaches who show relevant expertise, social skills, and methodological competencies in such exchanges in my experience are accepted as coaches "at eye level." Coaches can be stressed by the fear of being devalued in such dialogs because of too little competence from the perspective of their clients. If a practitioner does not trust himself or herself to engage on that level, he or she should not take on those kinds of clients. The very abbreviated case study in Box 2.1 illustrates how quickly a coach is required to be able to give insightful opinions and provide advice derived from those opinions. The following example is from my own coaching practice.

Box 2.1 Case Study: Preliminary Coaching Discussion with a CEO

A young project manager had suggested me to the CEO of one of the largest European industrial service providers as a coach for the CEO, for himself, and for the core team in a difficult and risky customer-oriented reorganization of all companies and work areas. The CEO was a lawyer who had been involved in restructuring at the corporate level but had little experience as a manager. He opened the conversation at our first meeting straightforwardly with the following question: "What do you think of dual leadership in companies?"

The implications of this question were immediately clear to me. In his company, he was not the CEO alone. There was another, very experienced, older CEO with whom he had to somehow get along. With his question, he wanted to test my competence and support in conflicts with the senior CEO. If I did not express a competent opinion on the issue at that moment, e.g., by returning the question like a nondirective conversational psychotherapist with a counterquestion (e.g., "What is on your mind with this question?"), the coaching would have ended before it started. Therefore, I began to briefly enumerate possible conflict risks that came to mind when I imagined two CEOs running a company together. I did not forget to briefly point out that the conflicts depended on the relationship between the two and that if the relationship was harmonious, there could also be a good division of labor where each could contribute his strengths to the company.

I then added that this would require learning more about the constellation of the company and his experiences. After hearing, and apparently accepting, my comments, he answered this question and my follow-up questions in detail. Basically, this was the beginning of our subsequent, very intensive and productive, coaching process, which included many exchanges of opinions as a basis for the joint development of solutions "at eye level."

The conflict with the senior CEO in the organizational change process later came to a temporary climax until, in the end, the concept for realignment was approved after its presentation to the representatives of the company's shareholders. The planned changes were implemented very successfully.

2.4.4 *"Reflexive Suggestions"*

It is always psychologically risky for a coach to express a "one-sided opinion" from which recommendations or suggestions for the development of proposed solutions arise (e.g., the conflicts between the two CEOs in the case example). A coach must always be aware that clients are the "owners" not only of goals but also of solutions and decisions. This means, on a behavioral level, that a coach should only make "suggestions for reflection" and "suggestions that can be rejected at any time" and pay close attention to how clients react to them. Coaches should be ready to drop their own suggestions if they are not accepted by the "owner" and if he or she prefers tenable alternative solutions. In our first meeting, I usually explain that it is important that the client work out solutions independently and that my suggestions are intended only to stimulate thought and reflection. Such suggestions are therefore not simple advice but "reflexive" or "circular" suggestions (see *Chap. 6 Coaching methods,* below, for more on suggestions that stimulate new insights and AHA! experiences as highlights of coaching from the client's perspective). Reflexive suggestions are meant to encourage dialog to broaden perspectives and self-reflection on solution ideas as well as promote reflective decision-making by the clients.

> *Coach:* "When I sometimes make a suggestion, it is important that you see it only as a suggestion for reflection and consideration of alternatives. Please always consider very carefully whether the suggestion suits you and whether you want to implement it. It is not me who must bear the consequences, but you. Perhaps, my proposed solution will inspire you to develop a better alternative solution of your own. You are the owner of your goals and solutions and all decisions that are created in the coaching process!"
>
> My observation is that many clients appear more self-confident after hearing the above explanation, sit up straighter, and show a self-confident facial expression. If further suggestions are introduced by the coach later in the coaching conversation, this explanation should be repeated. The expectation is that clients will learn through such reflexive suggestions to reflect carefully on the solutions proposed by their coach and others before adopting them.

However, in my experience, a particularly attentive and more cautious approach is recommended when clients behave insecurely and helplessly and rarely or only hesitantly contribute their own suggestions. The solutions such clients have tried or considered in the past have often not always been based on their own ideas but rather on solutions that other people have strongly advised them to try. Much time and calm, empathic listening are needed in such cases. Standard coaching questions include "What have you tried thus far?"; "What has your experience been?"; "What advice do other people give you, and how do you rate that advice?"; and "What are possible advantages and what disadvantages might follow?" Even with negative experiences, it is psychologically uplifting to the client if the coach express respect for the difficulty of the situation and for the client's courage in attempting to find solutions and in doing so gaining experience. Posing such questions and expressing support can lay the groundwork for the client to explore and affirm his or her resources and strengths, which can then serve in developing solutions (for resource activation, see below *Sect. 6.4.4 Analyzing and Reflecting on Client Strengths, Sects. 6.6.4* and *9.3.2* on *Resource Activation*). Helping self-insecure clients strengthen their self-esteem allows them to be more able to make their own suggestions or respond confidently to "reflective suggestions" from the coach with their own alternatives or improvements.

2.4.5 The Client as the Owner of Goals, Solutions, and Decisions

The discussion concerning coaching and consulting can be summarized in a reformulation of the traditional principle.

The Client as the Owner of Goals, Solutions, and Decisions
The client is the *owner of the goals, solutions,* and *decisions* that are obtained in all phases of the coaching process. It is the important task of the coach to repeatedly and convincingly communicate this to the client and to verbally and nonverbally encourage and prompt him or her to consciously make relevant decisions for himself or herself in a self-determined manner and to regard the suggestions of the coach merely as suggestions for reflection.

Importantly, the client should always be fully aware that he or she is making all relevant decisions. The coach should express this in an encouraging way. Psychologically classified, this is a matter of actively promoting the client's self-determination in coaching and in the implementation of the solutions that have been developed. According to Deci and Ryan's (2008) *Self-determination Theory*, an explicit emphasis on self-determination has been empirically shown to increase autonomous motivation and behavior change. As mentioned above, the observation that, after hearing that they are the owners of goals and decisions, many clients sit up straighter and express self-confidence is a nonverbal support of assumptions of self-determination theory.

The reformulated principle of self-help and not prohibiting all forms of advice frees coaches from a problematic prohibition of all forms of advice. It shows how coaches can behave in a way that systematically psychologically promotes clients' self-determination. For clients, this can have a twofold liberating effect:

1. They retain the freedom to ask their coach for practical advice without having to fear that the request will be rejected by the coach, with the understanding that the coach does not give advice because it violates the principle of helping people help themselves.

2. They are repeatedly made aware of their freedom and autonomy in the coaching process and thus consciously make decisions for themselves.

A positive side effect of this process is that we can expect clients to transfer such reflections and motivational self-determination to reflective interactions with others who make suggestions to them or who advise them. The reformulated principle can be traced back to well-confirmed assumptions of the theory and research of Deci and Ryan (2008). It assumes that autonomy, competence, and relatedness are basic human needs, which are related to the vitality or energy that is empowering people to act more self-regulated and persistently at important activities.

2.4.6 *A Multifaceted Coaching Definition*

Christopher Rauen (2001) published a review of various older coaching definitions. He summarized the commonalities in the following short definition:

"Coaching is an interactive, person-centered counseling and support process that can include professional and personal content and is time-limited." (Rauen, 2001, p. 64, free translation)

With this formulation, Rauen classifies coaching as a consulting process. He merely specifies that it is "person-centered" and "time-limited." These characteristics are also shared by other intervention methods, such as guided training or mentoring. It is only through his following explanations and additional characteristics that delimitations become possible.

Explanations and additional characteristics (Rauen, 2001, p. 64, free translation):

- "No advice blows," but "individuals process counseling in the sense of preventive help for self-help and self-responsibility."
- The basis is a "counseling relationship" with "sustainable mutual acceptance" and several voluntary and confidential sessions.
- For a specific person or precisely defined group.
- Counseling with psychological and business knowledge as well as practical experience in thematized problem areas.
- The coach provides information about an elaborate "coaching concept" that describes the methods and techniques used with the intentions pursued as well as the conception of man.
- "The goal is always the (re)establishment and/or improvement of the self-regulation abilities of the client."

In contrast to professional counseling, no "advice blows" (i.e., advice, experienced as "blows") are given. The alternative term "process counseling" is explained as "help for self-help and self-responsibility." As explained above, however, specialist consulting can also be designed as help for self-help.

Rauen's limitation to processes seems to be very narrow. Coaching is also open to a description of momentary feelings and many other themes. A process or course does not always have to be analyzed. Additionally, the characteristic "sustainable mutual acceptance" is not suitable for delimitation but forms a conducive basis for all kinds of counseling and probably many other services. "Voluntariness" is a difficult demarcation criterion (see below in *Sect. 2.5* on *Offermann's Definition According to Scientific Criteria*). "Several confidential sessions" could serve as a concrete demarcation criterion from most very short professional consultations. This will be returned to below.

Rauen considers it necessary for coaches to base themselves on an "elaborated coaching concept" to describe the methods and techniques used with the intentions pursued with them. Rauen (2001, p. 192, free translation) bases this on Schreyögg (1995). In principle, it would be advisable for coaches to formulate their coaching concept and make it available to their clients in written form. However, it is questionable whether it makes sense to list all the methods and techniques that can potentially be used by the coach. The list would be very long and would have to contain comprehensible descriptions. New methods would have to be added in an updated form. It would rather make sense and point to specialized literature that describes the basics and methods in more detail. However, most methods have not been developed specifically for coaching. Additionally, it would be problematic to define coaching as applying a defined list of methods and techniques. Who determines whether they belong to coaching?

Rauen also demands that coaches formulate their underlying "idea of man". However, if this emphasizes special experiences, development potential, self-reflection abilities, social competencies and skills, or other things, it can be whitewashing and not very credible.

The last specification that Rauen (2001, p. 64) lists is that the goal "is always the (re)establishing and/or improving the client's self-regulation abilities." According to psychological findings, self-regulation abilities are an important general basis for successful learning and can be promoted by learning methods that teach self-regulation strategies for learning at school and at work (Landmann et al., 2009). Therefore, this specification is not an appropriate "differenzia spezifica" of coaching. Self-regulation abilities are very beneficial for the implementation of the planned behavior changes developed in coaching. However, coaching is by no means "always" about behavior changes. Examples include the development of new perspectives or creative problem-solving solutions.

2.5 What Are Distinguishing Characteristics of Coaching?

2.5.1 Offermanns' Definition Based on Scientific Criteria

The core characteristics listed in the above definitions are seldom precisely defined. To my knowledge, Martina Offermanns (2004, p. 35 ff., free translation) was the first to discuss different common definitions of coaching on the basis of the standard criteria described above and to present a critical summary of typical coaching definitions. To meet the criteria, she developed the following definition:

> "Coaching is voluntary, time-limited, methodology guided, individual counseling that assists the person(s) being counseled in achieving professional goals. Excluded is the treatment of mental disorders."

With her definition, Offermanns classifies coaching as a form of individual counseling. Its limitation to "professional goals" would not be made today, as stated above. By using the adjectives "voluntary, time-limited, methodology guided," Offermanns seeks to distinguish coaching as professional counseling from everyday conversations and goal-setting interviews in companies. Everyday conversations can also be engaged in voluntarily and for a limited period of time; however, they are seldom "methodology-guided." In the case of goal-setting interviews with team members, managers often receive special training in methodology and are expected to perform such interviews in a methodologically guided manner (sometimes using a form). Some companies tie performance to voluntary participation. Would that then be coaching according to this definition?

Voluntariness is a difficult criterion to define scientifically (Wilks, 2018): Is it still "voluntary" when a client is strenuously advised by his or her superiors to undergo coaching or does so under social pressure (from friends or colleagues)? A precise definition is seldom is given. To what extent is it possible to decide completely "freely" (e.g., free of subconscious influences, inner emotional pressures, or firm behavioral habits) is an old question and, owing to neuroscientific research, one that continues to be controversial (Greif, 2008, p. 73 ff, Wilks, 2018).

On the other hand, Offermanns' suggestion to distinguish coaching from psychotherapy is clear. "Mental disorders" can be clarified by reference to the definitions in the commonly used international classification system of mental disorders (ICD-10 or IDC-11) (see Gureje, 2018). This formulation used by Offermanns also appears later in other definitions.

2.5.2 Coaching to Promote Result-Oriented Reflections

Like psychotherapy, coaching is characterized by intensive and systematic self-reflections on one's own behavior, strengths and weaknesses, or self-image. Other terms used to characterize coaching are self-awareness or reflective consciousness. Psychological analyses go back to the work of William James (1892).

Self-reflections can be triggered by various stimuli (Greif, 2008, p. 86 ff.): looking in the mirror, difficulties with working tasks, filling out questionnaires with questions about self-description, feedback from superiors, exams, memories of a success or failure, conversations with friends, conflicts, participation in an assessment center, and others. Spontaneous reflections are rarely very structured or systematically sequenced but probably consist mostly of short associative thoughts. Personally important themes, especially experiences of failure, can lead to long-term circular thinking and rumination. In his neuropsychological theory, Julius Kuhl distinguishes between "action-oriented" and "state-oriented" persons. In his questionnaire, "state-oriented" persons indicate that they "don't know what to do with themselves on days when they fail at very many things" (Kuhl & Kazén, 2003, free translation). They tend to brood about their situation and problems"

> One of my clients told me that after failing an exam in his master's program at a London University, he became depressed and ruminated about his failure at almost every opportunity during the day and after waking up at night. (In parallel with coaching, he was receiving psychotherapeutic treatment. In Section *9.1, Result-oriented Reflections,* I describe the coaching method employed in this successful case example).

The promotion of reflections in coaching should not lead to increased aimless rumination but rather to advance further results. These can be changes in behavior or plans for change, as well as new insights. Such reflections can be called "result-oriented reflections" (see the definition below).

To interrupt circular thoughts, it is necessary to proceed psychologically in a very systematic way, analyzing the eliciting and accompanying affects and feelings of the client and supporting his or her emotion regulation (see Sect. 9.1 *Result-Oriented Reflections*). This process seems to be more successful if the client perceives these reflections as "intensive." Coaches (and psychotherapists) aim to promote "intensive and systematic result-oriented reflections" in psychologically appropriate ways that are adapted to the client to stimulate the regulation of negative emotions and thoughts, giving rise to new insights and/or activating successful behavior changes (Greif, 2008, p. 58). This psychologically sensitive procedure and competence of coaches, adapted to individual differences, is not required in standard education and training or professional counseling interventions.

Through intensive and systematic "result-oriented reflections," opportunities for self-change can be found (Greif, 2002). That coaching promotes such reflections can be empirically proven by observational studies (see *Chaps. 7 Effectiveness of Coaching* and *8 Processes and Procedures in Coaching*). The intensive and systematic promotion of result-oriented problem-solving and self-reflection is a particular characteristic of coaching that can be used to define coaching. However, this process is similar to that of psychotherapy. In its demarcation from psychotherapy, however, coaching excludes the treatment of mental disorders. The application of psychotherapy requires qualification and a license to practice as a psychological or medical psychotherapist. The complete definition is as follows:

Definition of Coaching (Greif, 2008, p. 59, Free Translation)
"Coaching is an intensive and systematic promotion of result-oriented problem- and self-reflection as well as counseling of individuals or groups to improve the achievement of self-congruent goals or to conscious self-change and self-development. The counseling and psychotherapy of mental disorders are excluded."

The technical terms used in the definition are each based on scientific psychological theories (Greif, 2008). The central terms are briefly summarized below.

In the term "problem reflection," the term "problem" is used. The general theoretical background is problem-solving research, particularly Dörner's (2003) research into the difficulties and possibilities for humans in solving complex problems and his definition of the term "problem."

Definition of "Problem" (Greif, 2008, p. 123, Free Translation cf. Dörner, 1979, p. 10 ff)
"A person, group, or organization has a problem when it is in an undesired initial state and wants to achieve a desirable goal or end state but does not currently have opportunities or means to achieve the goal."

Some avoid the term "problem" to avoid possible negative connotations and blocks to creative thinking. There is a common desire to view "problems" as opportunities and a preference to talk about "opportunities" instead. In my experience, however, it is difficult to maintain this in coaching practice. Many clients spontaneously name what they perceive as a "problem," which they want to solve. (Even if they otherwise use the formula "problems are opportunities" in their business.). Their negative evaluations are associated with perhaps long-standing experiences and intense feelings. They can hardly "unfeel" them immediately.

Furthermore, it is artificial and linguistically slightly absurd to rename some "problems" "opportunities." For example, if a computer keeps breaking down, should this even be called an opportunity to fix the computer? Especially if clients see a given but ethically questionable goal as problematic, this should generally not be renamed an "opportunity" at all. Psychologically, it generally seems more beneficial to allow clients to speak freely and openly about their negative experiences and feelings during coaching.

It is important, however, not to get stuck in long, negative stories together but to repeatedly provide understanding summaries of the descriptions and to look for opportunities to solve such problems and show the client respect for having been able to endure such a difficult situation and ask how they managed to do so. In this way, the coach addresses the client's resources. They usually react very positively to this surprising, appreciative broadening of their perspective. In *Chapter 6* on *Coaching Methods*, "resource activation," which is also very important in psychotherapy, will be discussed in detail.

The term "self-reflection" refers to research and theories on self-awareness, self-concept, and self-representation following the neuropsychological motivation and personality theory of Kuhl (2001) (cf. Greif, 2008, p. 21 ff.).

Definition of "Individual Self-Concept" (Greif, 2008, p. 24, Free Translation)
"A person's individual self-concept comprises the totality of all conscious, subjectively important imaginations that a person has of himself or herself as a real or ideal person, including all characteristic goals, needs, characteristics, and developmental potentials that are subjectively valued as important, as well as norms and rules to which he or she is oriented or strives to be aligned."

Following Kuhl's (2001) neuropsychological theory, it is assumed that "self-access" is a prerequisite for people to consciously think through and explicate their self-representations or self-concepts. Quirin and Kuhl (2018) refer to the well-known aphorism "Know thyself" written above the Oracle of Delphi in ancient Greece. Self-knowledge can be seen as a virtue. To achieve this goal, great effort is needed.

Recent research shows that self-access regulates feelings and behaviors that are congruent with needs, values, and goals (Quirin et al., 2011). Quirin and Kuhl (2018) noted that people differ in their self-access and the extent to which they can identify their self-congruent needs, values, and goals. Applied to coaching, an obvious (as yet untested) assumption would be that coaching improves the client's self-access by posing reflective questions and other methods to allow the client to reflect on his or her needs, values, and goals. After all, various studies have shown that result-oriented self-reflection increases during coaching (Greif & Berg, 2011; Greif & Rauen, 2022).

On this basis, it is possible to define what is meant by "individual result-oriented self-reflection."

Definition of Result-Oriented Self-Reflection (Greif, 2008, p. 40, Free Translation)
Individual self-reflection is a conscious process in which a person thinks through and explicates his or her ideas or actions that relate to the individual's real and ideal self-concept. Self-reflection is result-oriented if the person focuses on new insights or develops inferences for future action and changes.

The concept of self-reflection partly overlaps with the concept of *mentalization*, a complex method of reflection recently transferred from psychodynamic psychotherapy to coaching. Mentalization is a comprehensive psychological concept linked to a particular method of reflection. It includes facets that have been integrated from other concepts and theories, such as mindfulness, self-reflection and empathy. According to Taubner and Kotte (2022), mentalizing involves exploring the client's thoughts and feelings, particularly their goals, wishes, and motives, as well as their relationships with important people in their environment and their expectations and interpretations of others' behavior. According to a basic assumption of the method, these reflections are already formed in early childhood attachment experiences and transferred to relationships with other attachment figures in adulthood. Through an empathic, joint exploration of thoughts and feelings toward attachment figures, problematic impairments can be recognized and changed. Through these reflections, the client's curiosity and ability to mentalize are encouraged. As a result, they gain new insights into themselves and others and explore new behaviors (see *Sect. 9.3.3 Success factors at the Metalevel*).

The sociologist Giddens noted that, today, with the radical changes of our post-traditional societies, the sureties of tradition and habit have been replaced with the principle of radical doubt, questioning everything and considering knowledge only as hypothetical (Giddens, 1991, p. 2). The more diverse the options between which individuals must choose anew every day, the more important it is to institutionalize self-reflexivity as a "reflexive project of the self," which consists of developing a coherent, continuously revised self-identity despite uncertainties (Giddens, 1991, p. 5). Stelter (2013, p. 412), referring to Giddens, emphasizes the importance of coaching in opening a "reflective space" with "time for self-reflection" in the search for meaning and new possibilities for action.

In addition, the digital revolution and artificial intelligence systems are leading to further complex and uncertain changes through fundamental technological transformations (see *Sect. 10.2*). In addition to result-oriented self-reflections on the significance of such changes for individual development, reflection on problems should include the selection and design of technologies. Coaching can provide an important space for both types of reflection. In the integrative *theory of result-oriented coaching* presented in *Chap. 9*, a result orientation and self-reflection are classified as general meta-level coaching success factors.

2.5.3 Similarities to and Differences from Psychotherapy

Observational studies have shown that coaches and psychotherapists exhibit behavior that can be classified as promoting their clients' ability to engage in result-oriented reflections (Borsum, 2008; Schmidt & Thamm, 2008). Problem and self-reflections can be distinguished by trained observers on the basis of behavioral descriptions in an observation manual (Greif et al., 2010). In a pilot study, result-oriented problem and self-reflections and reflections on relationship problems were also found in psychotherapy (even somewhat more frequently); however, there are notably more reflections on feelings in psychotherapy than in coaching (Borsum, 2008).

2.5.4 Coaching as Counseling for Self-Help

In the coaching definition, coaching can also include "the counseling of individuals or groups." The term "counseling" is understood here, however, in contrast to directive professional counseling according to the counseling concept which is reproduced above as "help for self-help" or resource activation with self-regulated implementation.

2.5.5 Psychoeducation in Coaching

Enlightening clients about how to perform interventions and conveying relevant knowledge about psychological and other consequences are referred to as "psychoeducational interventions." Vogel (2020) emphasizes that, in addition to providing information, such interventions are intended to provide emotional relief and competence development and, as "help for self-help," to promote self-management or self-regulation. When used in coaching, psychoeducational interventions expand the range of coaches' tasks and roles.

Originally, psychoeducation was used in medical psychotherapy (Donley, 1911) to help clients better understand the causes of their disorders and how to comply with therapy. According to available studies, such intervention increases adherence to therapy and reduces relapse in the medium term (Zhao et al., 2015). Psychoeducation should also prevent misunderstandings or feelings of shame and self-devaluation. By contrast, in coaching, the use of psychoeducation is rarely explicitly denoted. In health coaching, psychoeducational interventions are often essential (see Sect. *6.6 Coaching Methods*, *Health Coaching*). McCay and Kemp (2019) recommend such interventions, especially in neuroscientific coaching. Similar to the perspective of this book, they consider imparting enlightening knowledge specifically useful in changing habits because clients tend to engage in self-devaluation when they fail to change their "bad habits." *Section 6.5* on *Changing Habits* describes how psychoeducational enlightenment can be used in coaching conversations when seeking to make changes in habits.

2.5.6 Self-Congruent Goals, Self-Change, and Self-Development

The coaching definition further emphasizes that coaching supports improvement in reaching "self-congruent goals or conscious self-change and self-development."

The "self-congruency" of the client's goals means that such goals should be in line with the client's self-concept. The client is the "owner" of his or her goals. As owner, the client should decide which goals to pursue (in a socially responsible way). This is true even if the coaching is paid for by the employer and if the goals are dictated by the employer. The client must consider and decide if and how he or she can incorporate those goals. The coaching process can involve dialog about what the consequences will be if the client cannot accept the employer's goals as his or her own and how he or she can clarify any discrepancies with his or her superiors.

Coaching is not always about concrete, precisely definable goals. Sometimes, it is about discovering opportunities for professional or personal development. For example, executives may want to improve their leadership skills, whereas others may want to "become more relaxed" and cope with their many daily demands and stresses with greater internal tranquility and composure. According to the coaching definition, such concerns are multifaceted conscious "self-changes." The conscious planning and implementation of self-changes usually extend over a longer period of time and often include a variety of behavioral changes and goals.

In the above definition, "self-development" stands for all concerns and themes that are not related to limited concrete goals but rather to questions about real and ideal self-concepts as well as "self-discrepancies." These include the client's unmet expectations of himself or herself (Wechsler & Schütz, 2022). This process involves questions such as, "Who am I?", "Who do I want to be?", and "Who do I have to be?" Questions about one's own values and identity or broader questions of meaning are also part of that process.

Boyatzis and Akrivou (2006) draw on various theories to develop a comprehensive model of the ideal self-concept. According to them, three components come together in the ideal self-concept, which are themselves formed by several components:

(1) Imagery of a desired future (the person's dreams, aspirations, and fantasies).
(2) Emotionally fueled by hope (degree of the person's optimism and self-efficacy).
(3) Core identity (unconscious set of enduring individual characteristics, unconscious motives, and traits, as well as roles adopted consistently in social settings).

According to the model, the ideal self influences the person's vision and visualization of desired behavior. Boyatzis and Akrivou (2006, p. 626 ff.) assume that the planning of intended behavioral changes is influenced by the ideal self and the reflection on the person's vision. *Section 6.4* on *Coaching Method*s (esp. *Narrative Coaching and Vision Development*) addresses how reflections on the ideal self-concept can be promoted in coaching.

2.6 When and How Is Coaching Explained in the First Meeting?

Since coaching is something new for many clients, it is a good professional practice to explain one's own understanding of coaching in the first meeting. Some coaches start this right at the beginning of the first session. I think it is psychologically more appropriate to do this rather at the end or in the course of the first coaching session, when the clients have seen how a dialog in coaching with me proceeds. If clients ask questions about it before that time, I will, of course, provide information beforehand. However, clients do not come to the coaching session primarily with the question of how the coach defines coaching but with a personal concern or goal. Therefore, right at the beginning, they should be given the opportunity to describe what they expect from coaching. A more suitable time for explaining the coaching concept is at the end of the session, after the client's concern has been clarified in the coaching conversation with follow-up questions from the coach, or the goal has been roughly outlined and perhaps initial experiences of the previous solution attempts have already been touched upon. In the initial conversation, the client experiences how the coach asks questions and responds to the client's answers. Thereafter the coach may build on this experience and explain his or her understanding on the basis of examples from the coaching conversation. It is advisable that coaches maintain their coaching definition as background knowledge and limit descriptions of how coaching differs from other modalities; clients will usually ask if they need further information. Answering such questions and providing the definitions and explanations set forth above can be useful. In general, however, it is only important to provide a brief, clear description of one's own understanding of coaching:

An example from a transcript of a first coaching conversation with a young team leader can serve as a concretization of this approach. In his first leadership position, the client was very uneasy about his behavior. As a preliminary goal, he said that he wanted to gain "more self-confidence and acceptance by the team." In the last phase of the first session, I explained my understanding of coaching as follows (free translation):

Coach: "Let's talk briefly in general terms about what coaching is about and how we work together in the process. In essence, it is simply about us taking time together to analyze themes or problems, as you have mentioned them, in more detail, to clarify your goals, to develop solutions, to talk about how it will be possible for you to achieve your goals. You bring your experiences in, and we take much more time and address issues more thoroughly than in everyday conversations. Coaches contribute on the basis of their experience and methodological knowledge."

(The coach pauses and offers a prompting look to encourage comments or questions from the client.)

Client: "Is it always just conversations in coaching then?"

Coach: "We can also write important points about the themes on small cards and arrange them on the table. This sometimes helps us keep an overview and can enable new perspectives and solutions. Depending on the theme, there are other methods I can propose to you."

Coach: "Basically, the coaching continues much as we have just started. You bring in your themes and goals, through your questions and mine. Together we try to get as accurate a picture as possible about the situation, about the goals or changes that suit you and that you want to accomplish, and what solutions can lead to your goals and what plans you want to implement. What you mentioned earlier is already quite tricky, and it's worth taking the time to do a detailed analysis and develop the solution." (The coach briefly summarizes the issue and asks if he understood it correctly.)

Client: "Yes exactly, and important to me is (… added)."

Coach: "My role is to support you with this. What is important is that you set the goals and decide what you are going to do. You are the owner of the goals and all decisions what you will make, supported by our coaching."

(The coach pauses and offers a prompting look.)

Client: "Yes, that's important that I decide that."

Coach: "That, very briefly, is my approach to coaching. If you'd like, I'll be happy to explain it in more detail. You are always very welcome to ask questions about coaching and coaching methods later in the coaching process."

If the employer is covering the costs and has formulated targets, the coach should briefly address the fact that these targets are important and should be considered:

Coach: "It is one of the basic rules of coaching that your employer knows that in this process, it is *you* who determines what you personally want to achieve and whether you want to be supported by coaching to achieve it."

As the example shows, some references to the coaching definition are provided, but the focus is on the concrete concerns of the client, supplemented by suggestions about further methods and basic rules. Instead of abstract technical terms such as "problem and self-reflection," it is clearly stated that "we take time together to analyze themes or problems as you have raised them in more detail, to clarify your goals, to develop solutions." Importantly, the client makes the decision about which themes to work on and which goals to achieve and how.

2.6.1 Confidentiality and Other Rules

Coach: "A very important rule in coaching is strict confidentiality. So, everything that is discussed between us here remains confidential. If your boss wants to be informed about the progress of the coaching, we will discuss together how you or we together will inform him. I will not talk about you without you being present."

Client: "Yes, that would be very important to me. I definitely don't want my employer or coworkers to know what I told you today…".

In some companies, all those interested in coaching receive written information on confidentiality and other ethical and practical coaching rules. Some coaches give their clients a separate printout at the end of the session listing the contractual requirements and services of the coach and client.

2.6.2 Coaching Contract and Conclusion of the Conversation

The question subsequently arises as to whether the client would like to continue the coaching process:

Coach: "Can you imagine engaging in the coaching process with me on that basis? Do you want to try it together?"

Client (often similar): "Yes, that's a good match, and I'd like to work with you."

Coach: "Great, I can also imagine working together very well, and I'm looking forward to it."

Both written agreements with signatures and such oral agreements can create a legally binding contract. Important components of oral or written contracts in coaching are described by Fielder and Starr (2008).

At the end of the coaching session, I often ask clients for their takeaway and feedback".

Coach: "What is your overall takeaway from our first conversation? How would you evaluate our start?"

Clients' responses are recorded, as are answers to the final question about expectations and wishes for the next conversation:

Coach: "What are your expectations and wishes for our next conversation?"

2.7 Questions for Repetition and Remembering

(1) Briefly state and describe standard scientific criteria for definitions.
(2) To what extent can coaching also be regarded as "counseling" from your point of view? Please briefly justify your opinion.
(3) What are the characteristics that distinguish coaching from other personal intervention methods?
(4) How can you explain your understanding of coaching to clients in a short and clear way?

Chapter 3
Comparison of Coaching with Other Methods

3.1 Many Similarities

Where does coaching differ from other methods? This question is often asked. Because coaching has much in common with other person-centered intervention methods, this makes it difficult to answer this question. The differences are usually gradual only for many characteristics. However, when the entire profile of all the characteristics of coaching is considered, this can be used to identify coaching very clearly, as explained below. In our coaching training, we often started the first session with the question of which concrete similarity coaching has with goal-setting interviews of managers with their employees and with psychotherapies and only afterward, which differences might exist. Two groups described the similarities between the two intervention methods on cards, and two presented the differences. It is remarkable how quickly very concrete characteristics can be collected and how clearly coaching can be distinguished from goal-setting interviews or psychotherapies at the end. However, the similarities show that there are also many overlaps and that delimitations are consequently difficult.

In the following, the similarities and differences of coaching with five intervention methods are described, which are often compared with those of coaching. There is also the opinion that one does not need coaching because one can better turn to friends for advice instead. There is also a section on this question.

1. Sports coaching
2. Psychotherapy
3. Supervision
4. Mentoring
5. Goal setting and personal development interviews
6. Counseling by friends

S. Greif, *The Future of Coaching*, https://doi.org/10.1007/978-3-031-96192-2_3

3.2 Sports Coaching

In sports, coaching was already established in the nineteenth century. The first sports coaches acted as private instructors. They passed on their practical experience from their sporting successes to others. Steinke and Steinke (2019, p. 73 ff.) have performed research in this field. Sports coaching subsequently became established primarily in Anglo-American countries, especially in preparing athletes for competitions in sports that were cultivated at upper-class schools and universities, such as rowing and American football. Early on, the emphasis was not only on physical fitness, as opposed to training but also on strategy and teamwork, as well as character building. According to Steinke and Steinke (2019, p. 79 ff.), the amateurism of the first coaches only gradually became professional from the 1950s, although, as they noted, the American psychologist Coleman R. Griffith (1926) had already begun to provide a scientific foundation in the 1920s through insights from motivation, learning, and personality psychology and initial considerations for researching and evaluating effectiveness. As they note, Griffith's book is still a stimulating foundation today.

Sports coaching is not only based on psychological findings but also on sports science, which itself draws on many disciplines, such as psychology and pedagogy but also biomechanics and the science of human movement, physiology and sports medicine, sociology, and management sciences (Steinke & Steinke, 2019). According to Cassidy et al. (2016), sports coaching today includes not only the training of individual athletes or the athletic management of teams but also the individual support of athletes and the question of how coaches should communicate their feedback to athletes.

Typically, in competitive situations, athletes are present together with their coaches. As in soccer, they are often even evaluated together in parallel. In business coaching, on the other hand, coaches remain in the background. It is rather rare that executives are renowned with the name and reputation of their coach. However, the fact that top athletes can achieve peak performance with the support of coaching is an advertising argument that is often transferred to business coaching to emphasize the usefulness of coaching.

Steinke and Steinke (2019) classify the orientation of today's sports coaching as a solution-oriented approach and emphasize an improvement in the psychological prerequisites and competencies for athletic performance, especially during competitions. Like business coaches do, sports coaches differ in the practical and scientific knowledge bases and methods they use. The following compilation of commonalities and differences between coaching in sports and in business coaching in Table 3.1, as well as in private themes and goals, is therefore not generally valid but describes hypothetical comparative characteristics that, strictly speaking, need to be verified by representative studies. Accompanying and observing the implementation in competition, so-called shadowing is a matter of course in sports but rather rare in coaching. However, there are exceptions. In *Sect. 6.5*, we describe how shadowing in a special variant is routinely used in result-oriented coaching in other coaching fields.

Table 3.1 Sports coaching and business coaching or coaching of other people

Similarities	*Examples*
Goal reflection	What do I want to achieve (in sports)?
Self- and problem reflection of one's own behavior and the contextual situation	What are my strengths and potentials? What problems and obstacles do I face? Where do I rank in comparison to other athletes?
Supporting the implementation of behavior modification	Supporting motivation and willpower during implementation
Solution orientation	Orientation to chances, own strengths and opportunities
Encouraging motivation	Stop brooding about failures and difficulties and be motivated by hopes of future success
Competence development	Concrete plans for developing one's own competencies to achieve goals
Differences	*Examples*
Joint planning of exercises and evaluation of performance improvements	Individual interval training in rowing with the rowing training machine with protocols of the achievements, pulse and blood pressure values
Focusing on achieving best performance	Comparison with the achievements in the respective league, at least as a background: Where are the best achievements in Olympiads today?
Routine use of shadowing in the implementation situation. (this has been rare in other coaching fields, except for the systematic use of shadowing methods in result-oriented coaching, see *Sect. 9.3.3 Sustainable Implementation Support as a Meta-level Success Factor*)	The sports coach observes the athlete in the competition and gives feedback, and together they draw conclusions from the observations
Use of knowledge from sports medicine, physiology, and physio-technology	Use of the best permitted drugs and measurements and analysis techniques for performance evaluation and promotion
Tough competition and selection of athletes and coaches based on the achieved performance successes	For example, boxers want to be trained by the coach with the best successful boxers in the world

If we look closely, we can find interesting ideas for the future professionalization of coaching not only in terms of similarities but also in terms of differences between coaching in sports and in business coaching or other coaching fields (Steinke & Steinke, 2019). In sports coaching, for example, the specialization of experience, expertise, and methodological knowledge for various sports disciplines is much more advanced than is the case in business coaching or in other types of coaching today. This could become a model for the future professionalization of coaching.

In the following presentation, "coaching" is used for the sake of simplicity as a generic term for all fields of application outside of sports, especially business coaching or coaching for themes related to private life.

3.3 Psychotherapy

Psychotherapy, with its various directions and methods, strongly influenced the development of coaching in its pioneering days in the 1960s and 1970s. Leni Wildflower (2013), herself a coaching pioneer, analyzed these roots of today's coaching methods. This period of new beginnings was inspired by anti-authoritarian student movements in Western countries and the humanistic-oriented self-help movement in the USA. Humanistic concepts in psychology, especially in psychotherapy, were incorporated into coaching. Wildflower (2013) described as precursors Carl Rogers with his humanistic nondirective psychotherapy, the Gestalt therapist Fritz Perls, the systemic family therapist Virginia Satir, and "psychodynamic" methods (also called "psychoanalytic" methods), transactional analysis, and cognitive-behavior therapy. (In *Chap. 5* on *Directions and Concepts*, some particularly current concepts are explained.)

Based on her observations in the coaching field, Wildflower (2013) states that these roots are hidden or unknown to most coaches. Whether coaches are unaware that they are using methods from conversational psychotherapy, psychoanalysis, or behavioral therapy could perhaps be discovered through an empirical survey. In my opinion, it is not only ignorance but also a deliberate concealment of psychotherapeutic roots that coaches often engage in vis-à-vis their clients and principals. Proximity to clinical psychology is seen as problematic by clients because it would be damaging to their image if they could be implicitly seen as "mentally sic" or "disturbed" by proximity to psychotherapy:

> The methods of behavior modification used in behavior therapy are by no means unique to people with mental disorders. They are based on general principles of learning psychology and are broadly applicable to every-day behavior analysis and the modification of human behavior (Hautzinger, 2022). One example is interventions that can be used to change behavior through 'stimulus interventions.' For example, when a client has all too many erroneous dropouts of a new computer program, it acts as a stimulus for him or her to trigger stress and feelings of panic as a 'learned' behavior pattern and frantic attempts to 'save' the processed file. In this situation, coaching can look for new stimuli to remind the client that, in this situation, it is better to calm down, restart the program and accept inevitable loss of data.
>
> Additionally, Sigmund Freud's classical psychoanalysis was by no means developed only for analysis of mentally disturbed persons. In his basic method of interpreting dreams, he first analyzed himself (Freud, 1939). Möller et al. (2022) describe how coaching an executive uncovers and helps work through unnoticed defense mechanisms that influence his behavior or distort his interpretations and how this results in important additional reflections.

The rootedness of coaching in psychotherapeutic methods makes demarcation difficult. However, there is a clear and simple criterion already highlighted in the coaching definition above: coaches who have no psychotherapeutic training and license to practice are not allowed to treat mental disorders. A distinguishing characteristic is that the costs of psychotherapy can be covered by health insurance companies upon application. In addition, as mentioned above, there are further differences between psychotherapy and coaching. Rarely are the goals of companies or other organizations in which they work or organizational structures organizational changes, economic crises in industries or in the world economy. In business coaching, clients often bring these themes into the first session and analyze them systemically (Greif, 2008, p. 297 ff.; see *Sect. 6.7* on *Procedure for Multilevel Coaching*). The fact that these themes are hardly ever addressed in psychotherapy may also be related to the fact that clients do not expect psychotherapists to be competent partners for reflection in this field.

Owing to many similarities with coaching, the transfer of psychotherapeutic methods has not only been fruitful in the past but has also remained so to the present. A current popular example is the *method of narrative coaching* described in *Sect. 6.4.1*, which was transferred from narrative psychotherapy.

In Table 3.2, individual characteristics are listed and described by common methods as examples. Many more features could undoubtedly be found among the similarities.

Even if coaches behave cautiously—in the interest of their clients—and do not always reveal references to psychotherapeutic methods, they should not leave these roots and references unnoticed. They should be able to use diverse, innovative suggestions from the classical and current directions of psychotherapy in a modified form.

Table 3.2 Psychotherapy and coaching

Similarities	*Examples*
Detailed analysis of behavior, thoughts, and feelings as well as triggers and consequences	Methods for behavior exploration
Self- and problem reflection on one's own behavior and the contextual situation	Self-concept: What do I want and what can I (realistically) achieve? What problems and obstacles need to be overcome?
Activation of the client's resources	Reflection on own potentials and planning to use them
Creation of new behavior	Behavior exercises
Solution orientation	Analysis of options for change
Methods of interviewing, question techniques and numerous other methods of analysis and intervention	Open questions, reflective (or circular) questions, visualization methods, relaxation, and meditation exercises
Differences	*Examples*
Specialization in mental disorders	ICD-10 catalog of mental disorders
Cost coverage for psychotherapy by health insurance companies	Covered by health insurances, in the case of coaching by employers or self-payers
Usually, larger number and time span of sessions	In Germany, up to approx. 60 therapy sessions over a period of 14 months. In coaching, the average is 12.3 sessions (Middendorf, 2018)
Focus on the individual level and rarely on stimulating changes the organizational context as in business coaching	Modification of the individual behavior of the clients during psychotherapy

"Psychotherapists" are allowed to call themselves "psychologists" or "physicians" if they can provide evidence of relevant university degrees and subsequent qualifications with a state-approved license to practice psychotherapy. There are only a few normally explicitly defined exceptions. For example, in Germany, nonmedical practitioners can practice psychotherapy under the Law on Nonmedical Practitioners (the so-called Heilpraktikergesetz) after a special qualification. In contrast, anyone can call themselves a "coach" without any regulation and without any prerequisite or state-approved qualification.

3.4 Supervision

When comparing coaching methods with supervision methods, it is important to consider the historical background, theoretical roots, and fields of application. Historically, today's method called "supervision" emerged at the end of the nineteenth century in the USA from a training program for helpers in voluntary work, when it was noted that voluntary commitment quickly weakened if the helpers felt exploited or if their work was not successful (Kotte & Zimmerman, 2022; Loebbert, 2016; Schreyögg, 2004). Supervisors were therefore supportive in the early days of helping professionals and were often physicians who took on a kind of mentoring role.

The methods used early in supervision involved systematic reflections on case work. To characterize problematic help relationships, the psychoanalytic concepts of transference (the person seeking help transfers his or her desire for affection to the person helping) and countertransference (the person helping transfers his or her need to help and his or her own experiences with solutions to the person seeking help) were used (Schreyögg, 2022). Transference can interfere with "self-help" and client independence. Clinicians with psychoanalytic education brought these concepts into supervision.

After these beginnings, during the professionalization of supervision, a psychodynamic orientation and clients in the helping professions emerged as the first main target group. In the meantime, however, the profession has opened other theories and directions, especially systemic approaches (see Sect. 5.5 *Systemic Coaching Concepts*) and other target groups. Loebbert (2016, p. 2) accordingly no longer sees any fundamental differences between supervision and coaching today, apart from the practical and theoretical roots described. He classifies supervision as "a specific form of coaching" or "coaching for helping professions" (e.g., medicine, nursing, social work) with a focus on the specifics of the activities in these fields of work. Table 3.3 lists some of the many similarities and the few (by no means invariably) differences to be found between supervision and coaching. One variant, which is not considered in the following, however, is the supervision of supervisors or coaches in their activities and casework to ensure the quality of their work (Kotte & Zimmerman, 2022).

Since supervision and coaching have strongly converged today, numerous similarities could therefore be mentioned.

Table 3.3 Supervision and coaching

Similarities	*Examples*
Exploration of behavior as well as thoughts and feelings together with their triggers and consequences	Method of behavior exploration
Self- and problem reflection of the own behavior and the context situation	Self-concept what do I want and what can I (realistically) achieve? What problems and obstacles are there?
Activation of the client's resources	Reflection on one's own potentials and planning to use them
Creation of new behavior	Behavior exercises
Solution orientation	Orientation to opportunities, own strengths, and possibilities
Use of methods of interviewing, questioning techniques and numerous other methods of analysis and intervention	Open questions, reflective (or circular) questions, visualization methods, relaxation, and meditation exercises
Differences (not found throughout)	*Examples*
Specialization on clients in the helping professions and the special requirements (there are supervisors who offer coaching in other fields of activity)	Supervision of nurses in a psychiatric hospital
Greater consideration of psychodynamic theories and methods	Team supervision based on the model of Balint groups
Reflection and overcoming of the helper syndrome among supervisors	Reflection on transference and countertransference between supervisor and client

3.5 Mentoring

Like coaching, mentoring is a person-centered intervention aimed at promoting mentees' potential. The *European Mentoring and Coaching Council* (EMCC) defines very broadly that "mentoring is a learning relationship, involving the sharing of skills, knowledge, and expertise between a mentor and mentee through developmental conversations, experience sharing, and role modeling. The relationship may cover a wide variety of contexts and is an inclusive two-way partnership for mutual learning that values differences."[1]

Mentoring has many characteristics in common with coaching. However, the role constellation and qualifications are generally different. In mentoring, a very experienced, usually older person supports a younger mentee in his or her development. Typical areas of support are professional development, gender equality, or cultural integration. The aim is generally to pass on experience to promote development and avoid making mistakes but also to provide psychosocial support (Kerschreiter et al., 2018, p. 252 ff.).

[1] https://www.emccglobal.org/leadership-development/leadership-development-mentoring/ (retrieved 14.4.2022).

Table 3.4 Mentoring and coaching

Similarities	*Examples*
Open questions as the main method	"What do you want to achieve in your career?"
Self- and problem -reflection of experiences	Self-concept "what do I want and what can I (realistically) achieve in my career?" "what are the obstacles to this in our company?"
Activation of the client's resources	Reflection on one' s own potentials and planning to use them
Planning the next professional steps	What is the next step and what should I consider?
Differences	*Examples*
Role constellation of mentor and mentee	For example, the mentor is an experienced, older manager and the mentee is a young team leader
Voluntary cooperation of the mentors	Promotion of the mentoring program with a flyer or note in the online information system of the firm
No or merely short training for mentors	The mentors receive a short instruction manual and a brief introduction to their mentoring task
Describing and sharing experiences	A mentor describes his or her experiences and successes in detail as a kind of model and responds to the mentee's questions
Rarely systematic clarification of goals and concrete definition of objectives	Rough ideas about desired behavior modifications
Often direct advices what to do by the mentor (in coaching, clients should be activated more intensively to search for their own solutions)	A mentor tells the mentee what to do after listening briefly

Mentoring is probably beneficial if mentors have coaching skills and implement them in discussions (Strikker, 2016). However, they usually receive only a very brief introduction to these methods, if at all, if the activity is voluntary or is only carried out as informal mentoring. The number of meetings depends on the willingness of the mentors and mentees to invest time in this purpose. In formal mentoring programs in companies or other organizations, there are sometimes short seminars to qualify the mentors.

Table 3.4 summarizes the similarities and differences between mentoring and coaching.

The results of mentoring depend very much on whether the mentors engage with the mentees with their goals, questions, and differences. It is problematic if they implicitly assume that their own personal career paths and solutions to problems can simply be "adopted" by the mentees. Mentoring has positive effects on satisfaction with the situation, a feeling of belonging to the company, learning, and perceived career success according to meta-analyses (Kerschreiter et al., 2018, p. 252 ff.). However, the effects are rather weak for objectively measurable career outcomes. Accordingly, mentoring is not a cost-effective substitute for coaching. Ebner and Kauffeld (2019) expect that outcomes that can be achieved through career coaching are more effective (e.g., goal clarification, strengthened self-efficacy expectations, and more self-regulation). Coaching would also be preferable for concrete, precisely defined performance goals. In my opinion, the benefits of mentoring lie in the promotion of a feeling of belonging and informal networking with experienced members of the organization.

3.6 Goal Setting and Personal Development Interviews

Goal setting and development interviews are among the management tools that are very widespread today. They are similar to one-on-one coaching in that they are conducted in individual counseling sessions by leaders or superiors with their employees. In organizations in which these instruments are used, leaders usually conduct them at least once or twice a year with all their staff. The subject of goal-setting meetings is usually an improvement in work results (Kerschreiter et al., 2018, p. 231 ff.). In contrast, development interviews focus on employees and their development of their potential (e.g., in terms of changing their behavior) and, in addition, on participation in further training measures. Goal setting and development interviews can also be combined in a single meeting. At the end of the meeting, the planned actions are recorded and form the basis for reviewing their implementation (primarily by the employees themselves) in the follow-up meeting.

Goal-setting meetings can be based on the psychological goal-setting theory of Locke and Latham (2002), briefly described in *Sect. 5.2*, or a definition of goals according to the SMART criteria (Doran, 1981). They are also explicitly used in goal-oriented coaching concepts. The effectiveness of goal-setting methods has been well demonstrated by numerous studies in various companies and countries (Kerschreiter et al., 2018, p. 231 ff.). As assumed in *goal-setting theory*, performance increases for goals that are specific and difficult, as opposed to nonspecific goals; for example, if the supervisor merely says, "Your performance needs to get better." However, careful training is required for leaders to accurately implement these and other principles (e.g., supportive feedback) when setting goals or to conduct development interviews in a motivating mode.

The similarities and differences listed in Table 3.5 apply only to coaching that serves to define goals or develop potential. As reflected in *Chap. 6*, there are also coaching methods, such as *narrative coaching*, which differ fundamentally since they are *not* focused on concrete goals.

Some authors see great similarities between goal setting and development interviews with coaching and even propagate the idea of qualifying leaders as coaches or expanding the coach role of managers, such as "managerial coaching" (or "manager-as-coach"). To this end, special training measures are offered in which managers learn to coach their direct subordinates (Lawrence, 2017). However, it seems problematic if this merely involves the linguistic relabeling of managers as coaches without changing the hierarchical role constellation between managers and employees. If the manager continues to evaluate the performance of his or her employees and decides on the basis of which tasks they are to complete or whether they are to

Table 3.5 Goal setting/development interviews and coaching

Similarities	*Examples*
Psychological *goal-setting theory* as a basis	Goals should be challenging, but measurable
Application of SMART criteria in goal definition	Goals should be specific, measurable, accepted, realistic, and time-framed
Support of the development of potential	Develop a plan to develop performance improvement
Differences	*Examples*
No or only brief training for managers.	Half-day module in a leadership training seminar
Mostly focus on performance goals that are derived from the goals of the organization	"Acquire 20% more customers in the next 12 months!"
The leaders are supervisors of their employees and evaluate the implementation of the plans and their performance improvement—Therefore the principle of confidentiality of the clients' reflections in coaching is violated	Employees emphasize their positive achievements. Open self-reflection on one's own weaknesses or critique of leadership measures could have a negative impact on the employee's career
Much smaller number of meetings than coaching	The leader rarely manages to have a conversation with each of his or her team or meet several times with all team members
Quick to give advice and instruction	After listening for a short time, the leader tells the employee what to do

be put forward for promotion, he or she cannot expect the employees to talk openly with him or her about their self-reflections or especially about managerial misconduct. Managerial coaching with subordinates in their own line is therefore problematic. Participation in coaching training can nevertheless be beneficial for managers if they want to familiarize themselves more intensively with methods of conducting interviews and conducting confidential coaching sessions outside their hierarchy with employees from other departments. If employees turn to them in confidence, they do not have to turn them away but should regard this only as a kind of preliminary interview and frame it as a short "coaching episode" and advise the employee to look for a coach from a coaching pool of suitable coaches to continue (Greif, 2008, p. 165 f.).

3.7 Advice from Friends as an Alternative to Coaching

"I don't need coaching! If I'm looking for advice, I will ask my friends or colleagues." We often hear these sentences. Of course, open conversations with family and friends about problems are important and extremely valuable. An intensive exchange about what is on our minds and emotions allows our friends to share in it. We establish closeness and trust and seek understanding and support in difficult situations. Coaching cannot and must not replace this. Conversely, can conversations with friends fully replace coaching, as some seem to think? I dealt with this question in a section of my first coaching book (Greif, 2008, p. 65 f.). My initial, obvious assumption was that friends or colleagues usually do not conduct conversations in a methodically structured way and nearly never over several weeks with a fixed schedule. From experience, I assumed that only a few of the friends like to listen for a long time but immediately give their advice on what we should do—because they think they already know us and our current problem well and because they lack the professional patience and accuracy of listening of coaches. The irony of seeking advice from such a friend is that after the conversation and problematic advice, we not only continue to have our unresolved previous problem but also an additional problem with the friend because we did not follow his or her advice. However, there are also friends or dialog partners in the family who take the time to listen to us with understanding. That alone helps us. If they then help us find solutions ourselves to cope with difficult situations, this can be very similar to a coaching session! However, at least if the situations and goals of those seeking advice are complex or require special experience and expertise, it would make sense to seek the support of professional coaches.

Basically, how counseling sessions with friends and professional coaching differ is an empirical question. I was able to win Franziska Kaiser (2018), a psychology student, to conduct a pilot study on this topic in her bachelor's thesis. In ten interviews each after coaching sessions and after counseling with friends, she explored the perceived differences. Despite the small sample, the differences are significant and show very high effect strengths. According to her findings, coaching sessions promote more result-oriented self-reflection and are more focused on goal clarification and concrete outcomes. Open-ended questions are also used in friendly conversations, but in coaching, the method-repertoire is more diverse. In addition, coaches are more reluctant to share their own experiences and seldom give direct advice. We can therefore further assume that the differences in counseling conversations by friends and professional coaching are greater than the similarities. Table 3.6 below captures these hypothesized differences, as well as similarities. Larger follow-up studies are needed to test whether the results can be generalized.

Table 3.6 Advice from friends and coaching

Similarities	*Examples*
Open questions to those seeking advice	"What's wrong?"
Time to talk	Friend takes time
Initiation of reflections	Friend stimulates to reflect on his or her points of view
Stimulate search for solutions	"What can you do, in your situation?"
Differences	*Examples*
Very narrow repertoire of methods of the advisor	Asking fewer questions and describing more of one's own experiences
Not systematic analyses	The resulting descriptions of the situation and outcomes remain vague
Jumping reflections	Seldom result-oriented reflections
Quick insertion of advice	Friends tell the counselee what to do after a short listening. (Coach activates clients to find or adapt possible solutions to his or her preferences.)

Considering these differences, and in addition to the normally lower professional experience and competence of the friend in comparison to a professional coach, one should not seriously claim that it makes no difference to seek advice from friends instead of coaches. Basically, this would be as naïve as if a high-performance athlete would think that he does not need a sports coach because he can receive advice from a friend and that this would lead to the same performance results. Coaches to whom this argument is held up by potential clients or customers may prepare themselves against such—basically profession-damaging—arguments referring to the differences described above.

3.8 Questions for Repetition and Remembering

(1) Briefly name and describe differences and similarities between coaching and psychotherapy.
(2) Briefly name and describe differences and similarities between coaching and mentoring.
(3) What is to be said against supervisors labeling their goal-setting meetings as "coaching"?
(4) What arguments can you use to convince someone that the advice of friends or colleagues cannot generally replace professional coaching?

Chapter 4
Different Types of Coaching

4.1 Individual Face-to-Face Coaching

Individual coaching, or one-to-one coaching, is the most common classic form of coaching. It has been carried out not only in coaching appointments with clients and coaches, such as face-to-face coaching or online coaching (Berninger-Schäfer, 2022) with online video but also as distance or remote coaching by telephone and computer video or through time-delayed communication with media such as email or messenger systems (SMS, WhatsApp, or Signal). There are also coaching sessions in which multiple media are used. For example, one-to-one coaching can be started face-to-face and later continued as distance coaching by phone and video or by email or messenger systems, e.g., WhatsApp or Signal for specific questions. Examples and a brief description of e-coaching methods follow below in several chapters.

In companies and other organizations, there is often a list of reviewed coaches, the so-called coaching pool or coach pool, from which clients can select someone by themselves. According to an online survey of 750 HR professionals in Germany (XING & Jonas, 2018), 69.7% have their own coaching pool in their companies. A total of 58.8% rely on personal recommendations when coaches are selected.

Internal coaches are employed in the same organization as the clients, whereas external coaches are not. The advantages mentioned for *external coaches* are independence from the company (37.5%), neutrality (32.8%), and acceptance and trust (12.4%). For internal coaches, these include knowing the company, structures and processes (73.5%), being part of the company (16.1%), having lower costs (5.2%), and being available (5.2%) (XING & Jonas, 2018).

S. Greif, *The Future of Coaching*, https://doi.org/10.1007/978-3-031-96192-2_4

4.2 Group and Team Coaching[1]

By definition, a social group is three or more people interacting with each other. A couple or dyad, on the other hand, consists of only two people interacting with each other. The specialist literature on couple coaching is scarce. An interesting exceptional case is coaching recovery and burnout of small business owners and their spouses (Busch et al., 2021). Special problems such as the coaching of double tops of companies are treated by Schreyögg (2005), and the challenges of married couples on foreign assignments are treated by Schmelz (2009).

The terms "team" and "workgroup" are often used interchangeably and are indistinguishable, as Dick et al. (2018) note. Both terms refer to individuals who share common goals, for which they are responsible, and who interact to achieve the goals. A "team" in Germany is often additionally attributed positive group characteristics, such as good cooperation and a strong "sense of we" (Kauffeld, 2001). Workgroups or teams are often embedded in organizations and linked to a broader system and task environment (Kozlowski & Ilgen, 2006).

In general, the term "team coaching" is more common than "group coaching". In this presentation, team coaching is defined analogously to the definition of individual coaching above.

Definition of Team Coaching
Team coaching is an intensive and systematic promotion of result-oriented problem- and self-reflections as well as consulting groups to improve the achievement of self-congruent goals or to consciously change and develop the teams (Greif, 2008, p. 59, free translation). Therefore, the result-oriented reflections on the level of the group refer to the real and ideal self-concept of the team or its characteristics.

With this definition, team coaching can be distinguished from team development interventions, which refer only to shared performance criteria or performance improvement tasks and exercises. However, there are concepts for team development that can be classified as team coaching at the same time, since they explicitly promote result-oriented team reflections (see especially West and Anderson (1996) and the adaptation as Team Coaching by Greif (2008), p. 342 ff. and below *Sect. 6.7* on methods of *team coaching*). If teams are encouraged to regularly reflect on the common tasks, processes, and specifics of the team and immediately derive improvements from this, this leads to an increase in innovations in the teams and well-being as well as increased satisfaction, according to numerous studies now available (Dick et al., 2018). Team reflexivity can be measured by a short questionnaire before and after the implementation of this new reflection and improvement routine in the team.

[1] I thank Christine Gockel for valuable comments on this section.

In his much-cited review, Clutterbuck (2007) emphasized that team coaching can be seen as a "reflexive space" (op. cit., p. 131). However, he does not address the importance of promoting "result-oriented" team reflexivity. Clutterbuck does, however, analyze other important aspects, especially the roles of team leadership and coaches, team performance, conflict, feedback, and cultural diversity in teams. In a recent review of team coaching, Slagter and Wilderom (2018) address three foci of effective team coaching: (1) stimulating reflections, (2) promoting self-leadership and responsibility for work, and (3) developing a working relationship. How team coaching can be conducted is elaborated below in *Sect. 6.7* of this book.

4.3 Business or Executive Coaching and Leadership Coaching

The classic field of application of coaching outside sports coaching is the so-called business sector. "Business coaching" covers not only fields of work in companies or business enterprises but also a very broad field of all commercial, business, and "busy" activities. This secondary meaning of active action may also have contributed to the international preference for the English term "business coaching" in countries outside the English-speaking world. Accordingly, very broadly, it can be understood as the application of coaching to clients of all types of organizations and positions and their professional and social fields of activity. In this presentation, many different areas of coaching in these fields have already been addressed above and are described below.

Initially, "executive coaching" was addressed primarily at the top leadership and management levels. In the meantime, all management levels as well as activities without management functions, who are responsible for the administration and execution of a project, activity, or business, are included.

Within business coaching, leaders are the most important target group to date (Kerschreiter et al., 2018). In English, leadership coaching is also known as "leadership and executive coaching." The themes according to our own observations and in a survey by Middendorf (2020) are leadership responsibility, leadership competence development or organizational change, and change management. Other themes are transformational leadership (Felfe & Elprana, 2022), conflicts (Vollmer & Vetter, 2022), time management and stress (Greif & Palmer, 2022), or new tasks when new positions are taken. More often, it is also about the relationships among work, family, and leisure time, as well as the fear of burnout due to permanent stress (Greif & Bertino, 2022). The spectrum is extraordinarily diverse and ranges up to individual situations and goals. Some coaching methods are presented below in *Sect. 6.5*.

Taylor et al. (2019) researched leadership coach effectiveness and proposed an integrative model based on self-determination theory (SDT; Deci & Ryan, 2000) and intentional change theory (ICT; Boyatzis, 2008). They propose that the clarity of three inherent human needs in the leader (autonomy, relatedness, and competence) facilitates self-discovery and purposeful action on the part of the leader.

When these needs are met, motivation and sustainable change are achieved. Specifically, they assert that, through facilitated self-discovery and purposeful action, clarity of the ideal self, prior to actual self-discovery, creates clarity, purpose, and a desire for behavioral change. The approach is similar to the concepts of self-development and self-discrepancy and involves changes stimulated by expectations of oneself (Wechsler & Schütz, 2022), as mentioned above in *Sect. 2.5.6.*

4.4 Intercultural Coaching

Companies increasingly employ people from different countries and cultures. This has led to increased demand and specialization in "intercultural coaching" or "diversity coaching." The most cited author internationally is Philippe Rosinski (Rosinski, 2003; Rosinski & Abbott, 2006). He strives to expand coaching by considering cultural differences (between ethnicities, countries, organizations, groups, or professions) to activate human potential. It draws on general principles of intercultural psychology as well as methods of transactional analysis and neurolinguistic programming (for a critique of neurolinguistic programming (NLP), see *Sect. 5.7*) and ties them together with practical examples.

Stout-Rostron (2022) more systematically addresses the basic findings of intercultural research, such as differences between cultures with individualistic and collectivistic orientations. She also considers current findings on managing intercultural diversity. As she noted, coaches who have grown up in multicultural countries have prerequisites to avoid stereotypes and simplifications in their work.

4.5 Life Coaching

In contrast to business coaching, which is usually commissioned and financed by the employer, focused on personal life goals, "life coaching" has emerged as a counterbalance that is normally privately financed. The focus of life coaching is usually on themes from the private sphere and questions related to general or health-related well-being, one's own biography, personal development goals, or a clarification of the meaning of life.

Promoting overall well-being throughout life refers to the professional world as well as the personal world (Neenan & Dryden, 2002). From a practical perspective, Purdie (2010, pos. 376) understands this to mean simply: "A purposeful conversation that inspires you to create your best life." This means that all themes belong here that clients bring to coaching with the goal of improving their lives. However, since not only private but also professional themes can be addressed, distinguishing it strictly from other areas is almost impossible. Perhaps a narrower definition of the content of life coaching according to the main theme "well-being coaching" would make more sense. As outlined below in *Sects. 4.6* and *6.6*, "health coaching" is also developing in this field. Pragmatically, it would make sense to distinguish between coaching paid for by employers and coaching paid for by clients themselves and to explore what the main contents are. In my experience, the overlap is very large.

4.6 Stress Management and Health Coaching

Stress often occurs on the other side of high performance. Therefore, *stress management* is often a theme in business coaching. However, stressful situations are often experienced in private life. Greif und Palmer (2022) refer to the general definition of stress, which embraces all types of situations. According to this definition, stress is "a permanent state of negative tension that in the long run leads to impairment of mental well-being and health" (p. 863). According to recent scientific stress models, coaching can be applied to improve stressors (especially the reduction of structural stress conditions) and resources such as decision latitude and social support, as well as individual coping skills (changes in behavior) and relaxation. Popular general intervention methods are time management, relaxation, and mindfulness exercises (see *Sect. 6.6* on *stress management*).

Permanent overload by stress can result in emotional exhaustion, which is seen as the core symptom of *burnout* (Maslach, 1982). If long-term emotional exhaustion results in depression or other symptoms of mental illness, it is necessary to consult experienced psychotherapists. Coaches should limit themselves to the prevention of burnout and mild forms of burnout (Greif & Bertino, 2022; see also *Sect. 6.6* in this book).

Health coaching has developed into an expanding field of its own in recent years. Very broadly, it can be defined as "practice of health education and health promotion within a coaching context to enhance the well-being of individuals and to facilitate the achievement of their health-related goals" (Palmer et al., 2003, p. 92). This understanding of health coaching also includes themes related to mental health well-being and overlaps with *life coaching* (see *Sect. 4.5*).

Sforzo et al. (2019) developed a compendium of methods and research on "health and wellness coaching." Coaching has proliferated to support or follow up medical therapies, especially when medication regimens and dietary rules are complicated and require special care. Notably, the Sforzo et al. compendium does not list or describe coaching for stress management and burnout prevention, even though they can reduce well-being and lead to mental and/or physical impairment and illness. However, as they show, the number of 150 research studies published between 1989 and 2017 has grown impressively by 81 in the next 2 years (Todorova, 2022). They reported research that mostly demonstrated the effectiveness of health coaching as an adjunct to medical therapy, particularly for patients with high cholesterol levels and diabetes, heart disease, and hypertension. An increasing number of studies also exist on coaching for obesity, although not all have positive results, and the dropout rate of participants is high. Studies of coaching for well-being (self-efficacy, perspective change, irrational beliefs, stress, anxiety, and depression) have shown inconsistent results.

In a recent publication, Todorova (2022) highlighted the future importance of health coaching in chronic disease treatment and the interrelationships and additional roles that coaching can play in pandemics. She showed that in the case of COVID-19 prevention, the reduction of chronic disease as an additional risk was especially important. Measures of preventive behavior change "through changing attitudes, beliefs, and motivations" (p. 440) must be applied by coaches.

4.7 Career Coaching

Kauffeld et al. (2022, p. 138 f.) describe career coaching as "a specialized coaching method, supports a client in defining their career goals and devising strategies to meet those goals." Stable careers are becoming rare, and clients often have to prepare for sudden significant job changes following the economic crises of their firms or the digital revolution, especially the replacement by or use of artificial intelligence (AI) in their firms. Therefore, the preparation, development of an individual strategy and accompaniment of clients in emotionally demanding job changes, acceptance and regulation of emotions, rational planning of possible career steps, and the search for new jobs are very important in the coming field of coaching.

Career coaching is different from career counseling. Career counselors have expert knowledge of the situation in the job market and the requirements of different professions and often use psychological tests to assess the interests, knowledge, and abilities of job seekers. Clients should also take advantage of this advice. Conversely, career coaching focuses on answering questions such as "What career goals should I pursue?" and "How do I shape my career in such a way that my personal values are fulfilled and I can fully contribute my skills?" (op. cit., p. 146). This is why coaching methods for analyzing and reflecting on the client's personal vision, values, and strengths (see *Sect. 6.4* below) play a major role here.

It often takes a long emotionally straining time for clients to regulate often experienced frustrations and anxieties and to prepare and discover the best possible development opportunities. This requires correspondingly long and trustful accompaniment through coaching sessions for each new situation that arises and motivational encouraging work of the coach. As Kauffeld et al. (2022, p. 146) call for, longitudinal studies are needed in this field to measure the success of career coaching. *Section 10.2* takes a closer look at the complex future challenges of digitalization and AI for clients and coaches. Specialized methods of career coaching, including AI knowledge, are necessary.

4.8 Self-Coaching

"Self-coaching" refers to coaching performed independently by clients without a coach (human person or AI coach), for example, with written instructions or otherwise.

In the early stages of our coaching research, we expected self-coaching to be less effective than coaching with a coach. Therefore, we believe that it would be optimal if, in studies on the effectiveness of coaching, in addition to the usual waiting control group, a subgroup with self-coaching would be a suitable comparison group (of course with clients randomly assigned to the groups). In her dissertation, which I supervised, Martina Offermanns (2004) accordingly divided managers into these three groups. Self-coaching was conducted in groups using a guideline text with autonomously completed questions for goal clarification, solution development, and implementation planning. Three experienced coaches provided individual coaching sessions. We were surprised to find that no numerically significant difference in rated goal achievement or the other outcome scales could be demonstrated between the self-coaching and coaching groups. (As expected, however, both showed substantial differences in comparison to the control group without a coach or self-instruction). A similar result for self-coaching was reported by Sue-Chan and Latham (2004).

I remember when Martina presented her remarkable result in the dispute for her work, she was thoughtfully asked by Jürgen Kriz, who too was examiner of her dissertation, 'Isn't coaching always self-coaching?' When her paper was she published, formulated a remarkable title: 'Does Coaching Need a Coach?' (Free translation.)—However, all participants in the self-coaching group were dissatisfied with the setting and desired coaching by a coach. In addition, this group had a very high risk of dropping out. Only because she asked these participants 'on her knees' not to endanger her dissertation did they continue.

An obvious possibility is for a person to be "psychologically present" to clients as a coach during coaching but to use self-coaching tools in a supportive way. E-coaching and AI tools in coaching would also be suitable for this purpose, which will be discussed below.

4.9 Online Coaching, E-Coaching, and Coaching with Artificially Intelligent Systems

Geissler (2022) uses the term "E-coaching" for all "coachings in which electronic media are used" (free translation). Alternative media include face-to-face communication or the use of felt pens, flip charts, etc., in coaching (p. 115). Other terms for coaching with so-called new media are "virtual coaching," "online coaching," "digital coaching," and "Internet coaching." Other authors name it "remote coaching" or "distance coaching" when the bridging of distances between the client and coach is emphasized. Classic here is "telephone coaching" or newer "online coaching" with systems such as Zoom or Teams. If systems with so-called artificial intelligence (AI) are used, these variants are called "AI coaching."

Geissler (2022) sees telephone coaching as the "undisputed number one" among the media for remote synchronous communication. As he points noted, the restriction to the acoustic communication channel not only has disadvantages but also leads to clients being able to focus more on the coaching themes. Among the media that can be used asynchronously, email and SMS are particularly common. As the greatest advantage, he sees the possibility that much more time and carefulness can be spent on the formulation here. Geissler and Rödel (2023) recommended an introductory overview of common online coaching methods and a description of specific success factors.

A special variant is virtual coaching with avatars. Clients can each choose an avatar for themselves (a virtual person or 3D figure) and another for the coach. Afterward, the avatar can be navigated through different 3D spaces with different tasks and questions, as we know them from face-to-face coaching sessions (Berninger-Schäfer, 2022; Geissler, 2016).

Clutterbuck (2022) described the future potential of learning and adaptive artificially intelligent chatbots in coaching. They can also be used in coaching when asking questions to clients (see Sect. 6.3 *Questioning Methods*). Can social chatbots ask and answer as coaches do? At the end of this book, future perspectives of online and AI coaching are discussed, along with their potential and risks (see Sect. 10.2 *Consequences of Digitalization and Artificial Intelligence*).

4.10 Questions for Repetition and Remembering

(1) List all the different types of coaching you are familiar with.
(2) How can the business coaching field of application be distinguished from that of life coaching?
(3) Please name examples of health coaching functions.
(4) What kind of coaching would you like to acquire? Please give reasons why you have chosen this one.

Chapter 5
Directions and Concepts of Coaching

Wildflower (2013) has historically reconstructed the theoretical and methodological roots of coaching. She finds that most coaches' roots in psychotherapeutic concepts are hidden or unknown to coaching practitioners. Moreover, some coaches deliberately try to conceal these roots so that coaching with executives is not rejected as clinical "couching" (laying on the couch, as is psychoanalysis). However, there is little point in covering these roots because they are far too obvious. From the dawn of coaching at the end of the 1950s through the 1980s, every classical concept of psychotherapy has found a counterpart as a coaching concept. This is true for psychoanalytic or psychodynamic concepts (Sigmund Freund, C.G. Jung, Alfred Adler and others) and behavioral and cognitive-behavioral psychotherapy methods (behavior modification, Ellis' rational-emotive therapy). Humanistic psychotherapy (e.g., Rogers' client-centered psychotherapy), solution-focused brief therapy (de Shazer), bioenergetics, Gestalt therapy, or various systemic approaches (Satir's family therapy, hypnosystemic therapy) are very important. It is impossible to even briefly acknowledge all the concepts here. In the following, only a selection of very influential coaching concepts rooted in psychotherapy are presented, and at the end, various concepts related to evidence-based coaching, which are broader and more rooted in general psychological research, are also presented. At the end, a section on charlatanry and pseudoscientific concepts in coaching and how to recognize them follows.

Wildflower (2013) described the special stimulating importance of different approaches and basic positions of *Humanistic Psychology* for the self-understanding of coaching pioneers. It emerged in the USA in the 1960s against the background of the *Civil Right-Help* and *Self-Help* movements, as well as the *Human Potentia*l movement. In 1962, the Esalen Institute was founded in Big Sur, California (USA), and functioned as a creative discourse center in which humanistically oriented scientists, especially psychologists and anthropologists, as well as natural scientists and writers, competed with each other to develop innovative concepts. Esalen was open to different views of science in terms of extraordinary diversity and ranged from research-based theories and methods to spiritual concepts.

S. Greif, *The Future of Coaching*, https://doi.org/10.1007/978-3-031-96192-2_5

As Wildflower (2013) noted, several pioneers who are still well-known today contributed to the development of today's coaching concepts. Abraham Maslow, with his humanistic motivational theory with self-actualization as the highest level of human development; Carl Rogers, with his *Humanistic Psychology* and *Client-centered Therapy*; Fritz Perls and his *Gestalt Therapy*; Virginia Satir with *Family Therapy*; Timothy Leary with his plea for free access to psychedelic drugs; the anthropologist Gregory Bateson with his systemic communication theory; the physicist Fritjov Capra with a holistic-systemic approach, linking to Taoism and Far Eastern mysticism; Alexander Lowen with his *bioenergetics*; the Viennese neurologist and psychiatrist Viktor Frankl and his existentialistically oriented psychotherapy as a search for the meaning of life; Albert Ellis with his *Cognitive–Behavioral Therapy* and analysis of irrational beliefs; the psychiatrist Eric Berne and his *Transactional Analysis* (TA); the computer scientist and psychologist Richard Bandler and the linguist John Grinder, who together developed the concept of *Neurolinguistic Programming* (NLP); or Sir John Whitmore, who, influenced by humanistic psychologists such as Maslow and Rogers, developed his internationally known *GROW Model* of coaching.

The following overview provides brief introductory presentations of selected coaching approaches. Critical aspects are also addressed. For more in-depth reading, please refer to the original and reference literature (Palmer & Whybrow, 2018; Wildflower, 2013). It starts with the *grow model*, which was one of the first well-known coaching concepts. The next is the complex group of *Cognitive Behavioral Coaching Concepts*, which were inspired by psychological methods of behavior modification. The third is the group of different approaches, which are programmatically inspired by the idea of *evidence-based coaching* methods on the basis of scientific theories and research. Later, further relevant approaches and concepts will be outlined.

5.1 The GROW Model

Sir John Whitmore won many car races as British touring car driver in the 1960s. In his second career, he studied psychology and was particularly impressed by Maslow's and Rogers's humanistic psychology. Against this background, he developed a practical coaching concept that is now known worldwide. His standard work "Coaching for Performance," first published in 1992, is very catchy to read (Whitmore, 1992). *GROW* stands as an acronym for the initial letters of goal setting (short- and long-term goals), reality checking (implementability in the current situation), options (choices and alternative strategies), and will to act (or intention and what needs to be done, when, by whom, or "wrap up" (where am I and what is to be done next). Each individual coaching session, as well as the entire coaching process, should be divided and structured into phases according to this model.

In defining goals in coaching, Whitmore refers to Locke's and Latham's (2002) *goal setting theory*, according to which goals should be specific and challenging. At the same time, he calls for goals to be defined using the SMART criteria (cf. Doran, 1981). For Whitmore, this abbreviation stands for specific, measurable, agreed, realistic, and time-phased (op. cit., p. 62).

Whitmore's GROW model provides a good example of a concept that describes how coaching can be done in a practically illustrative and stimulating way. In addition, there is the catchy acronym, which has certainly contributed to its dissemination. However, terms from scientific theories and methods are merely mentioned (sometimes without references), are eclectically placed side by side, and are often not accurately reproduced. For example, the criteria for defining the goals that are central to the concept are listed briefly side by side on only one page without references to sources and are rephrased and supplemented in the process without any substantiation.

In Anglo-American countries, the GROW model has been very common until recently (Grant, 2011). According to a Europe-wide survey (Passmore et al., 2018), most coaches use solution-focused methods (68%). In contrast, cognitive-behavioral methods and GROW are cited by only 49%. In the UK, these percentages reverse from 70% to 40%. In German-speaking countries, it is also known, but overall, it is less frequently used as a basis.

Grant (2011) criticized the model and variants that are now being promoted because there is no research that confirms the assumed phases. Thus, each attempt to achieve a goal is usually followed by a review and evaluation. A "RE-GROW model" would therefore be more appropriate according to Grant and can be underpinned with psychological theories of self-regulation in the pursuit of goals (see *Sect. 5.3 Evidence-Based Coaching Concepts: Tony Grant's Goal-Oriented Coaching*).

5.2 Cognitive-Behavioral Coaching Concepts

As shown above, psychoanalytic or psychodynamic concepts are particularly important within supervision approaches. However, coaching approaches are more often oriented in Anglo-American countries to cognitive-behavioral methods of psychology, which are based on findings of psychological learning theories and methods of behavior modification derived from them. They claim general validity, not only for behavior modification of clients intended in psychotherapy but also, for example, for school learning or adult vocational learning (Hautzinger, 2022). Examples include behavioral exercises to establish new behavior or problem-solving training to improve autonomous coping in the face of future difficulties. A systematic behavioral analysis often serves as a starting point, in which the situation or stimuli that trigger the behavior (S), the organism variables (O, also person characteristics), reactions (R, including emotions and cognitions), contingencies (K, relationships between R and C), and consequences (C, rewards and punishments) are analyzed according to Kanfer and Philipps' (1970) S-O-R-K-C model, for example, to find the starting points for change.

A cognitive-behavioral concept of psychotherapy frequently referred to in coaching is the ABCD model by Ellis (1993). It is used to analyze and change behavior as well as the cognitions and emotions involved, especially irrational beliefs. It begins with a description of the events that are perceived as activating or adverse (A). This is followed by an analysis of the subjective beliefs (beliefs, B) associated with the events and the emotional consequences (C). After disputation (D) with clients, irrational beliefs are identified and consciously changed. Ellis expects that this will result in positive modifications of the emotional consequences and effects (E).

Cognitive-behavioral coaching approaches are often not based on a single model. They use various methods of behavior modification and make use of current developments and findings from extensive worldwide applications and research in this field. An example of such an integrative approach to coaching is the approach to coaching of Palmer et al. (2008). It draws on a modified Ellis model, problem-solving methods, imaginative methods, and stress and self-management methods.

5.3 Evidence-Based Coaching Concepts

Evidence-based coaching was first propagated by Grant (2003) in his keynote address to the first *evidence-based coaching conference* in Sidney, Australia. In the introductory chapter of their *Evidence-Based Coaching Handbook*, Stober and Grant (2006, p. 5 f.) refer to principles of evidence-based medicine. Applied to coaching, they understand by this a foundation of coaching by broad empirical-scientific and theoretical knowledge and "an intelligent and conscientious use of the best current knowledge integrated with practitioner expertise." The *American Psychological Association* has adopted principles for evidence-based practice in clinical psychology and defines it similarly to "the integration of the best available research with clinical expertise in the context of patient characteristics, culture, and preferences" (APA, 2006, p. 273).

The beginnings of evidence-based medicine and studies with randomized control groups can be found in the 18th century (Boylston, 2014). In psychology, William Stern (1903) published the first comprehensive program for applied psychology on a scientific basis. Hugo Münsterberg (1915) compiled the practically usable scientific findings already available at the time in his textbook on business psychology, which is still stimulating today and draws on application-oriented studies in the first psychological laboratory in the USA at Harvard University founded by him (see Greif, 2007).

In the following, two evidence-based coaching concepts are presented as examples: (1) *positive psychological coaching* and (2) *goal-oriented coaching* according to Antony Grant. Chapter 9 follows my concept *of result-oriented coaching*, which can also be classified here.

The best methods—or the "gold standard," so to speak—(Stober & Grant, 2006, p. 5 f.) highlight studies with quantitative measurements of the effectiveness of the interventions, which were carried out with control groups and assignments of persons by chance ("Randomized Controlled Trials" RCT) and summaries of the results of as many RCT studies as possible in the form of meta-analyses. As will be explained in Chap. 7 on methods and studies on the evidence of coaching effectiveness, these studies can also have some shortcomings. It is often advisable to conduct additional qualitative observations to concretize and validate the quantitative measurements. Coaching practitioners can contribute by carefully documenting the observed coaching processes. Not all theories and research need to be conducted in the coaching field. It is legitimate to integrate empirically well-confirmed assumptions and theories from interdisciplinary basic and applied research from other fields, which can be transferred to coaching. The concepts of evidence-based coaching reproduced below make use of such integrations.

The evidence-based practice in this book is not limited to RCT studies but is understood more broadly. The general definition of "evidence-based" is "conscientious application of the best current scientifically based knowledge combined with practitioner expertise." Concepts, theories, and intervention methods should be rejected if they have not been underpinned by qualitative or quantitative research and precisely described practical observations or at least plans for future studies. Coaching concepts and methods whose effectiveness has been claimed by a self-confident person merely on the basis of his or her "experience"—sometimes labeled "eminence-based" methods—may be stimulating but must be supported by empirical research before we adopt them as trustworthy.

This is similar in other disciplines. Medical eminences that elevate themselves above other people and research evidence with supposedly infallible knowledge are called "gods in white." In coaching, we also find "eminences" who want to convince us that they know more about people and coaching than nearly anyone else does (especially they criticize the scientific "theorists") and that their experiences are worth more than scientific evaluation studies:

> In the history of medicine, market criers who praised salves and other often ineffective remedies were pejoratively referred to as "quacks". However, not everything that "quacks" used in treatment in past centuries was nonsensical and ineffective. They used some means that had effects. However, when they mix up some tinctures and sell them as miracle cures, which they know very well do not work, we rightly call them "charlatans" (see Sect. *5.9 Recognizing Pseudoscience and Charlatans in Coaching*).

Coaching involves not only scientists but, much more often, practitioners who invent new effective intervention methods on the basis of their experience and sensitivity. However, since the application of coaching methods and concepts serves to support humans with important goals and potentials, they must not be used negligently. Practitioners or scientists must face scientific and practical scrutiny of their effects and side effects, as is common in services to persons and in science.

5.3.1 Positive Psychology Coaching

Martin Seligman is regarded as the founder of "positive psychology" (Seligman & Csikszentmihalyi, 2000). He sees coaching as "a practice in search of (…) a scientific, evidence-based backbone and a theoretical backbone" (Seligman, 2007, p. 266). As he suggested, positive psychology practice can provide this with interventions and measurements that work, as well as qualifying coaches. Seligman (2007) propagates positive psychology as a "new discipline." However, it would be more appropriate to call it a "programmatic approach" or "research program" that encompasses all subfields of psychology. Its object is the measurement and scientific study of positive mental processes, especially positive emotions, such as feelings of happiness, as well as strengths and other positive developments that enable "well-being" and a "good life" or "flourishing development." At the same time, it encourages scientific research on how they may arise and be facilitated (Seligman & Csikszentmihalyi, 2000). It takes its cue from humanistic psychology and highlights its contrast to deficit-oriented approaches to psychology as a distinctive feature of its programmatic approach. Like the concept of *solution-focused counseling* (see Sect. 5.4), fixations on negative emotions and experiences are to be avoided in interventions.

Kauffman et al. (2010) identify a primary goal of *positive psychology coaching* as promoting positive emotions. They point to hundreds of studies showing that positive affect leads to concrete outcomes such as higher wages, customer satisfaction, creativity, physical health, or job performance (Lyobomirsky et al., 2005). As typical examples of interventions to activate positive emotions, they mention the method "Three good things." It involves writing down three good things that went well during the day every night before going to bed. Another method is to imagine that everything will go the way one wants it going in the future. MacKie (2014) used a strengths-based coaching approach to improve transformational leadership, using a list of 60 strengths from the *Realize2* online questionnaire (now called the *Strengths Profile*) to reflect on and increase the use of one's strengths. Additional examples of methods can be found in the reader by Green and Palmer (2019). From a future perspective, Green and Palmer (2019) believe that it is necessary to develop integrative theoretical frameworks to provide an overview of techniques and strategies that can be used in coaching, *referred to as* "integrative cognitive–behavioral coaching" (ICBC) (Dias et al., 2017).

The development of methods that promote positive emotions or strengths empirically confirmed is undoubtedly an important extension of the evidence-based method pool, also for coaching. Since positive psychology encompasses all subfields and psychology research that addresses the promotion of positive developments of people with their consequences, extraordinarily diverse individual methods can be adapted to coaching.

Positive psychology does not attempt to formulate a closed general theory but rather sees itself as a research program that is open to theory but is always evidence-based. However, the focus of the program, primarily on positive emotions, processes, and developments at the same time, restricts this openness and can hardly be maintained unchanged according to recent research findings. For example, Oettingen's (2014) (2015) research revealed that stimulating exclusively positive emotions and positive fantasies about the consequences of achieving a goal is not at all conducive to goal attainment. It is more effective in addition to the imagination of positive results and feelings to reflect on the internal and external obstacles (often filled with negative emotions) that need to be overcome before the goal can be achieved and how this can be done. According to her findings, wallowing in positive fantasies leads only to a weak commitment to the goal and activates little energy for goal achievement in the face of difficulties. Those who set overly optimistic goals but then face unexpected obstacles give up prematurely. A simple program of positive psychology would at least have to be differentiated and consider reflection and conscious constructive coping with negative affect and obstacles:

> Strict adherence to the programmatic imperative to focus only on positive emotions is, in my experience at least, not always practically feasible. If clients want to talk in detail during coaching about their negative emotions and experiences with important critical life events such as separations, illnesses, professional failures, or conflicts, or even just about their ongoing stressful situation at work that they are currently experiencing adversely, it would hardly be comprehensible for the clients if their coach did not react with understanding and in detail. According to my own practical experience, however, it is always possible in the coaching conversation to smoothly reduce the circling process of updating and deepening the clients' negative emotions and thoughts while listening to such descriptions at appropriate points and to respectfully enquire how they were able to cope with this difficult situation and how they thereby prevented the situation from becoming even worse. By doing so, I can immediately gain their attention and slowly encourage them to develop more positive evaluations and feelings (see Sect. 6.3.4, the method of supporting positive "change talk" by *motivational interviewing)*, activate self-efficacy beliefs and resources (see below the success factors in Chap. 9 on *result-oriented coaching*). As a coach and listener, I am, in a way, "always on the lookout" for obvious and hidden resources (especially individual potentials of the client and support resources in the social environment), which the clients were not aware of before. According to my practical experience, it would not be appropriate or necessary to avoid or distract clients from describing negative feelings and situations. It is more appropriate to follow a resource-activating approach permanently. (Research testing this hypothesis would be helpful!)

Green and Palmer (2019) described the development of a "second wave" of "Positive Psychology 2.0" (Lomas & Ivtzan, 2016), which also takes into account people's negative experiences in addition to their positive experiences. According to this approach, negative emotions such as anxiety and pessimism are not harmful per se but may be necessary in a dialectical way for the "flourishing development" of people. However, with this approach, the central programmatic position of positive psychology is, in a sense, given up. Even the incriminated theories and interventions by positive psychology, which take negative emotions and characteristics into account by no means aimed at making people become worse with their interventions, always achieve positive improvements. Positive Psychology 2.0 cancels itself out and leads to a general evidence-based psychology that encompasses all interventions that can be scientifically proven to promote positive developments.

In addition to the umbrella program of positive psychology, the following evidence-based coaching concepts rely on specific empirically based models or theories with definitions of terms and assumptions that have been applied to coaching.

5.3.2 Tony Grant Goal-Focused Coaching

The concept of goal-focused coaching by Antony (Tony) Grant and O'Connor (2022) is essentially based on the cognitive psychological model of self-regulation by Carver and Scheier (1998) and applies it to coaching processes. According to this theory, self-regulation processes begin, as in the cycle in Fig. 5.1, with an issue from which a goal can be derived.

To achieve the goal, an action plan is needed, which subsequently must be carried out through actions. The performance and outcomes of the implementations are observed by the acting person. (This is called "self-monitoring" or self-reflection.) The observed implementation is then evaluated by the acting person according to a standard. If, after the execution, the achievement of the goal is evaluated as a "success," the process ends. In some cases, however, it is necessary to repeat successful actions (e.g., to ensure success in the long term). If it is not successful, then whatever did not work may be improved, and the whole cycle starts again from the beginning (with modifications of the issue, goal or action plan).

Grant, following Austin and Vancouver (1996, p. 388), defines "goals" as "internal representations of desired states or outcomes." As research findings indicate, it is important to distinguish between different facets and types of goals. Examples include short-term and long-term goals, positive goals and avoidance goals, self-concordant and discordant goals, performance goals, and learning goals. Grant recommends using these distinctions in coaching for greater effectiveness. He brings these distinctions together in a complex integrative model of goal-focused coaching (Grant, 2006, 2022). The starting point is the perceived coaching need and the goal selection process. The end point is goal achievement. Important characteristics on the client side are the social and organizational context, as well as characteristics such as readiness for change, resilience, and mindfulness, which have a moderating influence on context and effects. In goal selection and planning, the abovementioned characteristics of the goals act as moderators. The self-regulation cycle shown in Fig. 5.1 begins with goal selection and planning.

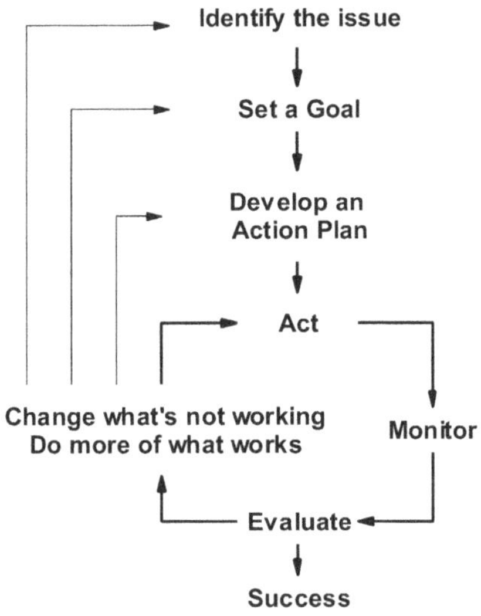

Fig. 5.1 Model of goal-directed self-regulation (simplified after Grant, 2006)

Grant's coaching concept can be regarded as a prototype of a scientifically founded or evidence-based concept. The cyclic model is based on goal theories from general psychology research with precisely defined distinctions and terms adapted for coaching. In addition to general psychological research, Grant refers to studies in the coaching field that have been validated (some of them with RCT):

> In German-speaking psychology, the self-regulation model of Carver and Scheier (1998), which Grant is based on, has received little attention, perhaps because here, the more detailed action regulation theory of Winfried Hacker (2014), with its exploration and differentiation of various levels of regulation (intellectual, perceptual-conceptual, and sensorimotor levels), has gained great attention. A common basic assumption of these models is that mental regulation processes are activated by (conscious) goals and changed or maintained by feedback. (For an introduction in English, see Windlinger, 2021). In Julius Kuhl's complex neuropsychological theory of action, in contrast, affects activated in the situation build the starting point. Depending on whether the affect is positive or negative, different mental regulatory systems are activated, as experimental studies have shown (Kuhl, 2001; for an introduction in English, see Kuhl & Beckman, 1994). Transferred to the promotion of self-regulation skills in coaching, this means that it is important for clients to recognize and learn to counterregulate their initial problematic affective and cognitive reactions to critical situations (Engel & Kuhl, 2022). In this context, self-motivation (even "being able to find something positive in unpleasant things") and self-calming ("self-regulating of negative affect" and developing new alternative actions) are usually important for intention formation (loc. cit., p. 38).

As the two theories of self-regulation show, the research and further development of psychological self-regulation processes is an extraordinarily complex field. It is worthwhile to follow the current findings of basic research and use them in the coaching field for more precise assumptions and research (see *Chap. 9, Result-Oriented Coaching*).

5.3.3 *Acceptance and Commitment Therapy as an Approach in Coaching*

Acceptance and Commitment Therapy, referred to in short as ACT (spoken as a single word, not by the initials), is a new "third wave" of evidence-based approaches in behavioral and cognitive psychotherapy. The number of research studies and fields of psychological difficulties showing that ACT methods improve psychological flexibility are impressive. The Association for Contextual Behavioral Science lists more than 1000 randomized controlled studies on the effectiveness of methods in diverse areas of psychotherapy.[1]

[1] https://contextualscience.org/act_randomized_controlled_trials_1986_to_present (date of last access: Jan 10, 2024).

Effectiveness is measured by a short self-report questionnaire developed by David Chantry called the ACT Advisor.[2] It is based on a psychological flexibility model, referring to six assumed core ACT processes (McCracken & Morley, 2014):

1. Acceptance
2. Commitment and taking action
3. Attention to present
4. Defusion
5. Values identification
6. Self as observer

The resulting psychological flexibility score is based on questions, which allow the user to choose a rating position between two opposite statements for each dimension. The examples for *acceptance* are "I willingly accept my thoughts and feelings, even when I don't like them." The opposite: "I constantly struggle with my thoughts and feelings." *Commitment and taking action:* "I identify the actions I need to do to follow my values and I see them through."/"I don't manage to act on the things I care about." Values Identification: "I am clear about what I choose to value in life."/"I don't know what I want from life." Self as observer: "The person I called knows what I am thinking and feeling."/"The person I called is my thoughts and feelings about myself."

McCracken and Morley (2014) do not mention any studies on the reliability and validity of the ACT Advisor or describe other statistical test quality criteria. It is surprising that it was not possible to find any studies on the reliability and validity of the ACT Advisor. However, many outcome studies have been performed on therapy for chronic pain and other clinical symptoms using other therapy-specific self-report measures, with known reliability. In the therapy of clients with unavoidable pain, which cannot be completely reduced by drugs, learning to accept the pain and learn to live with it seems to be very plausible. However, there are also other applications where it seems to be useful. Barret et al. (2019) reviewed studies on changing values that applied value-based psychometric tools in ACT therapies. Most of these studies are based on adequate statistical criteria. However, in their conclusion, more standard measurement instruments are needed in the field of values. To date, studies in the field of coaching seem to be lacking. Here, the use of reliable and valid self-report measures, which are recommended in coaching outcome research, and behavioral observations or physiological measures, as described in *Chap. 7*, are recommended.

One of the basic assumptions of ACT therapy is that suffering is normal for humans (Hayes, 2005, p. 4 ff.; Hayes et al., 2011). Persons who have learned how to create peace of mind are rare. Approximately 80% suffer from serious psychological problems. Enormous sums of money are spent to reduce their degree of psychological pain. The consumption of antidepressants is so high that rivers and

[2] Available only for members of the Association for Contextual Behavioral Science: http://contextualpsychology.org/act_advisor_psychological_flexibility_measure

fish have become polluted with them. The new approach of ACT is to stop fighting against natural negative thoughts, feelings, and pain and instead focus on (1) mindfulness, (2) acceptance, and (3) value-based living.

Hayes (2005) published a challenging self-help book that describes many intensive exercises and how to calmly and mindfully "just notice and accept" the situation, especially one's own thoughts and negative emotions. The goal is not to overreact but to talk to yourself more realistically and come to terms with yourself and with improved psychological flexibility to move toward valued behavior.

The approach is based on *Relational Frame Theory* (Hayes et al., 2001). This theory analyzes the functional context of human language and cognition (Hayes et al., 2011, p. 30 ff.). It is rooted in a pragmatic philosophy of science and a holistic approach. Human action is analyzed by its proximal history and situational context. The central intervention method is behavior and context analysis and seeking workable behavior through questions. Verbally stated goals can be assessed by the degree to which practices have been achieved. The focus is on changeable contexts and is therefore linked to practical concerns. Successful work toward a goal therefore functions as a useful guide for science. "Successful working" and reaching goals on the basis of values constitute the criterion by which contextualists evaluate events.

Additionally, therapeutic interactions are evaluated as they reach the client's chosen values and goals. The pragmatic issue is always workability (whether they work in practice) and not "objective truth" (op. cit., p. 34). "What is true is what works." The central method of therapy is behavior and context analysis and seeking for workable behavior through questions (p. 38).

Looking for methods that possibly result in pervasive changes in the client's behavior, Hayes refers to experimental analyses of the role of human language conversation between a client and a therapist (op. cit., p. 39–40) and the relation of language framing the behavior of people. In the ACT interventions, they also refer to the classical learning and conditioning theory of B.F. Skinner (1969). Their example is a child who has been scratched while playing with a cat cries and develops a phobia. After the child has learned that the animal is called a "cat," through stimulus generalization, hearing he child sounds the mother saying "Oh, look! A cat!" may elicit crying and running away, even if the child has not been taught to fear the word "cat." Similarly, Hayes et al. (2011, p. 42 ff.) explain the activation of memories and framing of cognitions and emotions, which are very difficult to change. In addition to behavior and context analysis, the methods of ACT apply observing and accepting unwanted individual thoughts and emotions evoked in a situation or by words (the "constant stream of evaluative chatter" of the mind, op. cit., p. 252) through mindful contemplation and loosening inflexible relationships through psychoeducational exercises (mental experiments and trying to change the situation) (see in detail in *Sect. 6.4.5 Mindful Self-Acceptance and Analysis of the Own Values* in this book).

Hayes (2002, p. 6 ff.) recommends using this new approach to look at our negative thoughts, pain, or negative emotions, e.g., not to try to regulate them but to increase acceptance and mindfulness in today's busy world. In his view, our human race has become the dominant race on our planet because we are able solve undesirable external problems, e.g., predation, colds, or floods. However, according to Hayes, it does not work in the same way if we try to reduce our internal psychological pains or unpleasant feelings.

In his keynote at the Annual Conference of the Institute of Coaching in Boston 2023, Hayes (2023) introduced the approach for the field of coaching. Examples of the special exercises of the self-help book of Hayes (2005) are summarized and discussed in *Sect. 6.4.5* on methods for *mindful self-acceptance and analysis of one's own values.*

This approach is provocative because it focuses on the acceptance of self-critical thoughts and negative feelings as a radical counterposition to the basic principles of *positive psychology*. To date, evidence of the effectiveness of ACT methods in many areas of application has been very convincing, with impressive numbers of methodologically careful studies. The methods are generally as effective or better than other therapeutic methods. No relevant negative adverse effects have been reported to date. However, as noted in *Sect. 6.4.5*, after a detailed description of the exercises and their theoretical bases, there remain open questions about the neglect of relevant alternative psychological theories and findings on more effective intervention methods, as well as possible limitations and unconsidered side effects. They will be discussed below.

5.3.4 Perspectives of Evidence-Based Coaching

The advancement of scientifically sound evidence-based coaching is a program that has a future. However, if we take a more critical look at some of the concepts, such as *positive psychological coaching*, it becomes apparent that by focusing exclusively on immediately positive aspects, it appears to be very one-sided. The extension, *positive psychology 2.0*, which now recognizes the importance of negative emotions and perhaps not immediately positive but long-term effective positive interventions, questions the previously propagated core statements. The idea of *positive psychology* to take up all findings and methods that have direct positive effects and promote the happiness of people, without paying closer attention to possibly contradictory or heterogeneous theoretical foundations of individual interventions that are not comparable with each other, must also be classified as "naïve eclecticism" in terms of the philosophy of science:

> An eclectic enumeration of different evidence-based methods without systemizing a theory leads, especially in the case of similar methods, to the question of which criteria should be used to decide which one is to be preferred. For example, one may ask which of the many existing instruments should be used to analyze client strengths. There are various lists of strengths listed in *positive psychology*. (How such strength cards are used in coaching practice is described in *Sect. 6.4*.) Therefore, which instrument should be used to identify strengths? Should the online *strength finder* test (Rath, 2014), originally developed in a Gallup survey, be used or should the *values in action* (VIA) questionnaire be preferred with its list of 22 "character strengths" (Peterson et al., 2010) or the online *Realize2/Strengths Profile* questionnaire mentioned above (Linley & Dovey, 2012) because it captures "perfor-

mance strengths" and, as MacKie (2014, p. 121 f.) suggests, provides "a broader view" by asking about both utilized and previously untapped strengths. In Germany, 24 "strength cards of positive psychology" are distributed as a variant (Härtl-Kasulke & Kasulke, 2018). The well-known Positive Psychologist Boniwell (2015) recommends the interactive method her published 50 "Strength Cards". These are picture cards with headings to designate each strength, such as "Motivation", "Creativity", "Action", "Leadership", "Communication", and "Harmony". Brief descriptions are shown on the backs of the cards. The respondents are asked to select the cards that suit them or that they want to activate in the future. By doing a Google search, one can find more strengths cards. Without decision criteria based on scientific theories and research, the choice between different strength cards is merely based on a pragmatic or subjective preference. From a scientific point of view, this means "arbitrariness."

In their concluding chapter on the future of Positive Psychological Coaching, Green and Palmer (2019, p. 119 ff.) refer to Seligman's (2011) *PERMA model*, in which he lists the activities he has found to enhance well-being (the acronym stands for pleasure, engagement, relationship, meaning, and accomplishment). They refer to their own earlier *RAW model* with resilience, achievement, and well-being as core competencies (Green & Palmer, 2019, p. 11 ff.). They are to be reflected upon and activated repeatedly in coaching. Finally, in an *integrative cognitive-behavioral coaching model* (ICBC), other models are included with their characteristics and intervention methods (see Green & Palmer, 2019, p. 119 ff.). The model is used to systematically classify the different types of interventions and important features of the coaching process. The model focuses on the coaching relationship and the use of guided exploratory and imaginative methods. Since the integrative model contains assumptions about which features and methods are particularly important in coaching, it can be seen as a framework model, a preliminary stage for the development of a coaching theory. What would be necessary for further development, however, would be not only to list the features and interventions and assign them to processes but also to explain important references through precisely formulated assumptions and support them by research.

Grant's evidence-based approach is based on a general basic psychological model of self-regulation of human behavior and research findings on different types of interventions for different types of targets. The sophistication of the practical implications deduced from this theory is remarkable. For me, even after his much too early death in early 2020, he is and remains an international frontman of evidence-based coaching and a role model for an orientation of the coaching profession on fundamental theories of psychology. He was open to insights from *positive psychology* and integrated appropriate findings into his assumption. In my view, Grant's approach is a model of how coaching concepts can be founded on the basis of general psychological theory and research.

Acceptance and commitment therapy as an approach in coaching can be seen as a different and fresh restart of evidence-based coaching rather than independent of the theories of other coaching approaches. Its roots are interventions derived from Skinners' classical behavior theory and theories on the role of human language in behavior modification and integrate knowledge from the popular support of mindfulness. (The radical behaviorist B.F. Skinner would have protested vehemently against this inclusion of such not directly observable focusing of the mind. However, it is a courageous modification.) Its voluminous research evidence and practical successes in the field of psychotherapy show how an evidence-based approach can attract the attention of researchers and practitioners very quickly. It probably will find many followers in the field of coaching. Simple self-report measures of the core criterion of psychological flexibility and other simple outcome measures also stimulate research on the effectiveness of the method and comparisons with other interventions. However, if we look at the instruction for therapists and coaches or especially the self-help instructions of the approach, we find that there are stimulating fresh interventions, which should be tried, but many open questions, psychologically implausible or difficult practical procedures and a neglect of important theoretical and practical alternatives remain. Additionally, among evidence-based approaches, the discourse always remains open.

After the description of the grand approaches above, in the following subchapters, four concepts of coaching, which have found their followers, are introduced. Some are older, such as the concepts of solution-focused coaching and systemic coaching. Others are younger, such as *hypnosystemic coaching* and *narrative coaching*.

5.4 Solution-Focused Counseling

The concept of solution-focused counseling was developed by Steve de Shazer as a method of brief therapy (De Shazer & Dolan, 2007) but is also frequently used in coaching. According to the already mentioned Europe-wide survey (Passmore et al., 2018), in German-speaking countries, relatively most coaches use solution-focused methodology, with 68%. In the UK, this figure is significantly lower at 40%. This coaching concept involves methods that, as a kind of help for self-help, try to completely avoid advice given by coaches or passing on knowledge. It also avoids retrospective problem analysis (or behavioral analysis such as in *cognitive-behavioral approaches*) because this approach might lead to change resistance or problem fixation. Instead, the aim is to focus clients on their own ideas for solutions. The well-known wonder question serves this purpose:

> Imagine that tonight a miracle happens and the problem we are talking about is solved.—Then, what might that small change be when you wake up in the morning, so that you will say: Great, something must have happened—the problem is gone! (short summary from de Shazer & Dolan, 2007).

It is assumed that the clients themselves have the necessary knowledge of solutions and that this can be evoked by the miracle question. De Shazer and Dolan (2007) demonstrated the general effectiveness of their method as a psychotherapeutic brief therapy:

> The approach of the wonder question is similar to the well-known problem-solving technique "working backward", in which the previous solution steps are to be found by going

backward from the target state (Anthony, 1966). Through this technique, difficulties in finding the important "first step" to the solution can be overcome, and psychological fixations caused by a difficult initial situation can be reduced. This can explain why "Aha! experiences", and new insights can be enabled by this method (Greif & Riemenschneider-Greif, 2018; Müller & Greif, 2022).

However, if the miracle question is repeated several times for several problems with the same client, one will hardly achieve any surprise effects. In this case, it seems better to continue with the classic working-backward problem-solving technique. Additionally, De Shazer and Dolan (2007) do not address the fact that their fair story is not accepted by all individuals. In one of my supervisions, the coach who used it reported that the image of a fairy spiriting away problem even seduced her client into believing that he did not have to do anything and that his problem would miraculously solve itself. This could be seen as a special functional fixation inherent in the fairy image ...

People differ in their solution knowledge and creativity in developing solutions. It becomes very tedious in coaching sessions if they cannot quickly think of suitable solutions at once. Another problem is that they want to use solutions that obviously cannot work or want to implement ethically problematic solutions.

To date, investigations that verify the basic assumptions of the method, according to which all clients have all the necessary solution knowledge, are lacking. The assumption suggested by the concept that (reflexive) suggestions by therapists or coaches have problematic side effects could presumably be refuted quite easily by basic psychological research. As Greif and Riemenschneider-Greif (2018) noted, the strict prohibition for the coach to provide any suggestions for solutions contradicts the assumptions and research results of *Gestalt psychology*, which have been confirmed to a good degree, according to which restructuring to solve problems often requires at least small stimulations or impulses. This was discovered by Wolfgang Köhler more than 100 years ago and by Norman Raymund Maier in his experiments in the 1930s. In *Gestalt psychology*, it is called *fixation* when a person fails to change from one way of looking at something or changing his or her perspective. A *functional fixation* is formed by a particular habitual use or context. Few previous experiences with misleading solution attempts can disturb mental solution access. As has been demonstrated by much research (Beeman & Kounios, 2015), such fixations can be very easily reinforced. In this context, while Beeman and Kounios (2015) repeatedly emphasize in their research review that, on the basis of the available evidence, we can assume that we often have much more solution knowledge than we believe. Like the Gestalt psychologists, however, they assume that we need an impetus to rethink to dissolve fixations and gain new insights. Therefore, in coaching, it is purposeful to first activate and explore these knowledge resources of our clients (e.g., through working backward or other problem-solving methods). The question to be clarified empirically is, through which individually optimal methods we can activate this knowledge if the access to this resource is blocked by fixations or if the blockage is not recognized. Often, clients need small impulses or nudges so that they can "restructure" their knowledge or other existing resources and use them differently than before.

Simple fixations can be solved with reflexive questions. The so-called "headstand technique" is also suitable in some cases. For this, one asks the client if and how the problem could be further worsened. For some, the specific negative influences come to mind much more easily. One subsequently asks them to turn these factors around ("put the solutions on their feet") to generate approaches for solution ideas using this method.

In the case of strong emotional fixations, clients are, figuratively speaking, "locked up" in their own world of thought (Beeman & Kounios, 2015). In our experience, such fixations cannot be solved with methods such as the wonder question or simple creativity techniques. Here, for example, the abovementioned disputation methods can be used, as Ellis uses them to dissolve irrational beliefs (Ellis, 1993), combined with impulses to mentally destructure the mental construction (Greif & Riemenschneider-Greif, 2018).

As the explanations show, solution-focused counseling according to de Shazer is not a concept that is suitable for all clients and all problems but rather a method that stimulates clients to find their own solutions if they have the necessary solution knowledge and if appropriate solutions are not blocked by fixations. As the discussion shows, a prohibition of any hints or nudges for finding solutions by the coaches or of reflexive suggestions would not be adequate in all cases.

5.5 Systemic Coaching Concepts

"Systemic coaching" is regarded as a kind of trademark, especially in German-speaking countries, and is therefore often highlighted by coaching training courses on the internet. In the USA or Great Britain, on the other hand, this is rare in advertising coaching training (Greif, 2014b). A recent search by me in the self-representations of coaches on Rauen's internet database for searching coaches in Germany, Austria, and Switzerland revealed that out of a total of 1001 coaches, 44% mention "systemic coaching" in their profile.[3]

In his article with the provocative title "Systemic—what else!", Nowak (2017) criticizes the inflationary use of the label "systemic" in counseling and coaching. On the basis of various concepts, he noted that systemic principles "have always been integral components of most educational-psychological counseling procedures and the addition of 'systemic' is thus in many cases superfluous and misleading" (op. cit., p. 477, free translation). In his response to this position, Kriz (2018), while highly sympathetic to Nowak's appreciation of classical counseling concepts, rebuts that "not all are systemic" and calls for an accurate use of the term "systemic" and that it be stated to which of the different systems theories "systemic coaches" refer in each case. He also explains the emergence and importance of systemic concepts in psychotherapy and coaching and discusses the differences between various systemic theories (Kriz, 2016, 2018, 2022).

Scientists with a radical *constructivist systems theory* orientation reject quantitative research methods, such as those commonly used in psychological and neuroscientific research. The oppositions between these and other views of science appear almost irreconcilable, and the disputes about this and quantitative research methods have also been carried out in the coaching field (Greif, 2011). Very fundamental

[3] https://www.coach-datenbank.de/coach-suche.html, research 7/15/2020.

theoretical disputes exist, particularly with respect to whether organizations or other social systems are "open systems" that share interactive exchanges with their environment (Bertalanffy, 1948; Katz & Kahn, 1966) or must be viewed as "operationally closed systems" without direct environmental interactions (Luhmann, 1995). Nevertheless, other systems theories analyze processes of human cognition and communication "systemically," drawing on classical Gestalt psychological insights or assumptions of *Synergetics* (Haken et al., 1995). In this systems theory, processes are often assumed to self-organize through nonlinear systemic interactions and backactions. To some extent, they are measurable, and they can be modeled mathematically. An example of an integrative systemic coaching concept referring to *synergetics* is the person-centered approach of Jürgen Kriz (2016, 2022). In regard to concrete examples of systemic intervention methods in coaching, reference can also be made to "circular questioning" (see below *Circular Questions* in *Sect. 6.3*) or "reflexive suggestions" (see Sect. 2.4).

As a conclusion from these brief notes on *systemic* coaching, the differences and points of disagreement between different systemic approaches are so severe that it is always necessary to specify exactly which scientific view and system theory is meant in each case and why a certain system theory and research methodology is preferred. Coaches who understand "systemic" rather casually and perhaps only as a synonym for "holistic "and are not familiar with systems theories should inform themselves carefully and ask whether it makes sense to use the extremely heterogeneously used term, which requires explanation. Furthermore, it would be desirable if they carefully apply systemic methods in their coaching practice and observe exactly what happens and which processes are activated.

5.6 Hypnosystemic Coaching

Gunther Schmidt (2022), a medical doctor, director of the Milton Erickson Institute Heidelberg (Germany), has developed a refined approach that integrates the hypnotherapeutic methods of Erickson (cf. Erickson et al., 1976) with an analysis of systemic interaction patterns between the individual and the environment and refers to neuroscientific knowledge. The "hypnosystemic" approach also refers to research results on embodiment and priming. For a short introduction in English, see an interview by Strelzig (2015).

In his coaching, Schmidt basically uses trance inductions of hypnotherapy. However, similar to Erickson, he rejects the use of direct suggestions of traditional hypnotherapy. Instead, after an exploration of the problem of the client, he or she asks him or her to close the eyes and explain the problem and its context or roots, sensitively offering alternative images and thoughts that encourage the client to understand his or her own wishes and situation better and more deeply. It is important that clients realize that they are competent and independent creators of their experience.

The systemic approach is inspired by family therapy (especially Stierlin, 1994) and its approaches to understand and work with interactional patterns between people and their surrounding contexts. Transgenerational loyalty bonds in relationships, interactional feedback loops that influence experience, etc., are reflected. Therefore, at the same time, it is possible to intervene at an intrapsychic level via hypnotherapeutic methods and at an interactional and context-related level by reflective questioning methods adopted from family therapy. The inclusion of the influences of interactions and relationship factors in the view of Schmidt increases the effectiveness of hypnotherapeutic interventions. The ideal is that the client "can react better to any influence from the outside in utilizing it to trigger unconsciously helpful solution patterns and so reacting more independently" (Schmidt, cited from the interview by Strelzig, 2015).

Schmidt has published a lot in German, and the approach is very popular in Germany. As far as I know, there is no specific research on the processes and results of the coaching intervention. It can be classified as a scientifically informed, very refined approach. Like Ericksen, the popularity of Günter Schmidt at least partly comes from his sensitive video demonstrations (sorry: they are also in German) and courses. Coaches and researchers, who are interested in the application of hypnotherapeutic methods in coaching, should consider this approach.

5.7 Narrative Coaching

Coaching is by no means always about precisely definable goals and how they can be achieved. *Narrative coaching*, for example, is primarily about the client's self-concept or identity and the clarification of meaning issues. The original basis is *narrative psychotherapy* by White and Epston (1990). They assume that individual identity is formed by the stories that the individual repeatedly tells about himself or herself from his or her own life in an intimate environment. Psychologically, experiences of important failure events appear to be examples if they are told with strong emotional involvement. These narratives are analyzed and "deconstructed" by questions. In therapy, external influences and attributions should be focused on. Through this "externalization" of the narrative, clients gain some distance from their issues and stories and develop a more detached analysis of their stories and possible influences. The narrative of the problem and context becomes "richer" as a result. Failure experiences are no longer attributed only to one's own failure alone but also to the influences of other people and thus are "reauthorized." By looking at the problem from a higher level, it becomes easier for clients to revise it. Clients can also reconfigure the story as an important life experience and discover a deeper positive meaning in it. Drake (2010, 2017a, b) transferred these therapy principles to coaching:

Externalization resembles the method of *"Self-Distancing"*, which has been studied by Kross and Ayduk (2017, p. 87 f.). In their experiments, they instructed the participants: "Go back to the time and place of the experience you just recalled and see the scene in your mind's eye. Now, take a few steps back. Move away from the situation to a point where you can now watch the event unfold from a distance and see yourself in the event. As you do this, focus on what has now become the distant you. Now watch the experience unfold as if it were happening to the distant you all over again. Replay the event as it unfolds in your imagination as you observe your distant self …". In contrast to an instruction to remember one's own negative feelings in the situation, participants focused less on the negative emotions arousing features of their experience and more on reconstructing it with insight and closure after self-distancing (e.g., "I was able to see the situation more clearly and understand why it happened."). The shift in thought content results in lower rumination and reduced long-term distress than does the distraction method.

In narrative coaching, it is important to separate the implicitly nonlinguistically conveyed story from the action ("emplotment") and to note and highlight what has been omitted or not said. For example, if a client "presses around" with his head down and does not express that he sees an experience as a failure, the coach calmly and appreciatively says the presumably avoided word "failure." He assumes that argumentative discourses between coaches and clients about narratives have a great impact on identity development. Richer narratives and retelling are possible and open spaces for new insights into the "old stories" of the person and a reorientation of identity.

Stelter (2014, 2018, 2022) designs his narrative coaching as very free, to a certain extent philosophical conversation about questions of meaning. Following the Danish existential philosopher Kierkegaard, he emphasized that a person is never finished with himself. The ongoing search for meaning will take place through questions about the meaning of topics and concepts that are important to clients (e.g., "What does 'freedom' mean to me?") and will occur through self-reflection, in which one distances oneself from oneself and returns to oneself. Stelter refers here to the psychiatrist Victor E. Frankl, who placed the "will to search for meaning" at the center of his logotherapy (Frankl, 1970). According to this approach, man is not fixed in his development. By becoming aware that he or she "can always-also-become-another," the person starts asking for the meaning of facts and for the meaning of his or her own being.

To my knowledge, whether clients' narratives about their important experiences become "richer" through the questioning style of narrative coaching and whether this also promotes identity development and answers questions about meaning has not yet been precisely investigated with scientific research methods. This could be done through qualitative analyses of transcripts of narratives comparing the narratives at the beginning and end of the coaching. Additionally, we could use interviews and questionnaires to capture changes in self-concepts and identities and questions about how clients answer questions about their construction of meaning before and after the intervention. However, as long as these and other assumed results of narrative coaching are only casuistically supported with case histories, the interesting concept is open to scientific attack. Stelter could draw on the qualitative methods of phenomenology and social constructivism that he favors in future research (Stelter, 2014). However, as will be illustrated in *Sect. 6.4.1*, studies using combinations of qualitative and quantitative research methods could be envisioned.

The performance of narrative coaching and other ways to test assumptions are also described below in the *Narrative Coaching* subsection of *Sect. 6.4.1*.

A description of the selected *neuroscientific approaches* is provided in the following of this chapter. Some see them as the inspiring future of coaching.

5.8 Neuroscientific Approaches

5.8.1 Neuroscience-Based Founded Work for Coaching?

As Jack et al. (2019, p. 421) noted, "relatively little guidance has been available in the management literature for scholars seeking to integrate neuroscience and organizational science in a balanced, informative, and methodologically rigorous manner" in the field of organizational research. They review the neuroscientific methods of functional magnetic resonance imaging, electroencephalography, lesion studies, transcranial magnetic stimulation, and transcranial direct current stimulation, with an eye toward how these methods might be combined to produce converging evidence. To date, however, there are limitations to the various designs in this field, which also apply to the field of coaching since the necessary standardized conditions for the application of these methods are rarely met.

The German neuroscientist Gerhard Roth and psychologist Alica Ryba, according to their own opinions, published the "first neuroscience-based founded work for coaching" and a comprehensive introduction into relevant basic knowledge about the areas and processes of the human brain and their functions (Roth & Ryba, 2016). A general focus in all chapters is the question of how human behavior and feelings are regulated by the brain and how they can be influenced and changed by interventions. The core question of what is possible and especially what is not possible is scrutinized very closely and critically. In his recent book about the difficulties of changes for humans, Roth (2019, p. 426 ff., free translations) emphasized that "Humans change throughout their lives, but the changes that occur can vary greatly in type and extent." The possible changes are determined by a large range of factors, including the following:

1. The genes involved (they explain mostly unspecific effects of the psyche and personality).
2. Epigenetic control factors (depending on pre- and postnatal environmental influences; more specific effects, which can be partially altered).
3. Prenatal hormonal influences of the body and brain of the expectant mother on the brain of the unborn child (especially severe stress and trauma).
4. Postnatal and early childhood factors (influences of the parents).
5. Factors that occur later in childhood, adolescence, and adulthood.

These factors promote or inhibit each other in complex ways and influence personality development both simultaneously and sequentially. The second and third factors, namely,

> prenatal epigenetic and hormonal influences, are particularly important because they determine the basic component of personality (Roth, 2019, p. 426 ff., free translation).

Roth bases his conclusions on a reception of current findings on the development and functions of brain areas and the limbic system (of animals and humans) and implications for behavior modification by coaching.

In his book with Ryba on the neurobiological foundations of effective change concepts in coaching (Roth & Ryba, 2016, pp. 127 ff., free translations), a distinction is made between four levels of personality and psyche:

1. The vegetative-affective level (limbic-vegetative basic axis of the brain, drives and affect states as largely genetically determined, only slightly controllable; all processes are unconscious).
2. The psychic-limbic level is the site of emotional conditioning of individual learning (linking emotional, predominantly negative or surprising events associated with basic feelings of joy, fear, anxiety, defense, and surprise; shaping of early bonding experiences as prerequisites for the development of our self-image and our ability to empathize).
3. In the upper limbic level, conscious, predominantly socially mediated emotions (limbic parts of the cerebral cortex, impulses, inhibitions for the strong affects of the lower, limbic level and infantile drives; socially mediated through experience and upbringing; and the formation of the conscious self, morals, and ethics).
4. Cognitive-linguistic level (neocortex, areas of action planning, Broca's language area; rational ego, mind, and intelligence).

As Roth and Ryba (2016, p. 132 f.) noted, the cognitive-linguistic level has only a few direct connections with the limbic centers, which explains why "rational advice and insights alone are not able to have a lasting influence on people, while our emotions, especially in the form of stress, fear and pain, can have a strong influence on our thoughts and actions (op. cit., p. 132, free translation)."

After a critical examination of classic personality traits such as extraversion and neuroticism, Roth and Ryba (2016, p. 135 ff., free translations) distinguished six basic psychoneural systems that can be characterized by the interaction of neuromodulatory substances in limbic and cognitive brain centers:

1. Stress processing system (coping with physical and psychological stress).
2. Internal calming system (damping and calming; suppression of harmful impulses to act).
3. Evaluation and motivation system (positive/negative evaluation of experiences with regard to the consequences for one's own well-being).
4. Impulse control system (tolerance of reward deferral; effective impulse control).
5. Attachment and empathy system (emotional coupling between infant and mother; differentiation of one's own emotional world under the influence of the primary attachment person).
6. Reality and risk perception system (realistic assessment of consequences of actions; recognition of advantages and risks of a certain situation; control of attention, learning, and memory).

According to Roth and Ryba, these systems have basic tasks and functions, as briefly mentioned in the list above. They release different brain substances, such as adrenaline and noradrenaline, cortisol, serotonin, and opioids.

In the following chapters of their book, Roth and Ryba describe and discuss critical conclusions from basic neurobiological findings on the development of the human personality, learning, and memory; the unconscious, motivation, and problems of behavioral change; the importance of interpersonal relationships; and various psychotherapeutic approaches, from Sigmund Freud to Milton Eriksson's hypnotherapy as well as behavioral therapy, systemic and humanistic forms of therapy, and coaching methods. In particular, they criticize that, from a neurobiological view, many interventions are not very effective because they cannot capture the genetic mechanisms or processes in the human brain that have already been shaped during pregnancy or processes that are regulated unconsciously. Roth and Ryba (2016, p. 345 ff., free translations) refer to Grawe's (2006) model of effect factors in psychotherapy and the modified success factors inspired by it according to Greif (2008, see also the revised success factors in *Chap. 9*) as positive approaches to change. As starting points for problem-solving in coaching, they differentiate (op. cit. p. 353 f., free translations):

Unspecific starting points

1. Clarification of goals (concrete and precise description of goals and possible solutions to problems).
2. Resource activation (reference to strengths and the possibility of experiencing and behaving in this way).
3. Problem actualization and experience activation (activation of those neuronal networks that are involved in the problem).

Specific starting points

1. Circumventing the problem (avoiding the problem or changing the framework conditions).
2. Elimination of the problem or symptoms.
3. Cognitive-motivational change of perspective (insight into the background or the experience and behavior through result-oriented self-reflection and problem reflection).
4. Emotions and bodily sensations (visualization and re-experiencing of emotions as well as attenuation and self-calming).
5. Procedural rehearsal of better adapted behaviors (for lighter stress in cortical limbic structures, for heavier stress in subcortical limbic structures).
6. Building new skills and important experiences (systematic continued development, catching up on important experiences).
7. Restructuring of the inner map (leaving narrow frames of reference and reorganization).
8. Decision-making and letting go processes (separation from ideas and fantasies that have become dysfunctional).

9. Implementation support and evaluation (promoting the implementation of goals in everyday life, action plans, or timetables, thinking through implementation options, anticipating possible obstacles, planning rewards, monitoring success, and making improvements if necessary).

Roth and Ryba are not the first to apply neuroscientific findings to improve the effectiveness of coaching. The neuropsychological personality systems interaction (PSI) theory described below in this chapter is an example. However, the significance of Roth and Ryba's work lies in their use of comprehensive basic neurobiological knowledge for a differentiated discussion and clarification of the effectiveness of success factors and interventions in coaching. What is missing in their approach, however, is systematic empirical research to confirm their assumption in the coaching field. Preliminary studies are reported in the following subchapter.

5.8.2 Researching Brain Activities in Coaching Conversations

Pusba (2022) published an overview of beginning neuroscientific research in the field of coaching and offered a framework of neuroscience principles in coaching. She calls this approach *brain-focused coaching*. In her view, research in this field must answer two questions (op. cit., p. 78): "(1) what happens in the brain during a coaching conversation, and (2) what kind of changes in the brain (…) drive behavior change to attain the goals."

Innovations in recording real-time brain signals allow the assessment of brain processes during coaching sessions and before and after studies. In her contributions, she refers to the goal-oriented coaching approach of Grant (see *Sect. 5.7*) and starts with a citation of recent general research on brain processes during goal clarification, decision-making and planning, motivation and volition, and changes in behavior habits (see also *Habit Change* in *Sect. 6.5*). She differs in four processes of behavior change: *clarity, awakening, resolution, and empowerment.* Her first studies measuring qEEG and activity of the left and right frontal lobes and during coaching sessions show first evidence that coaching is accompanied by plausible different observable activities of the human brain in these processes (Puspa et al., 2018, 2019).

5.8.3 Neuropsychological PSI Theory and Coaching

Neuroscientific research on coaching methods is a challenging field for the future. Neuropsychological assumptions have been integrated into coaching methods (see, e.g., the research on self-access *in Sect. 2.5* or the methods for changing behavioral habits in *Sects. 6.5 and Chap. 9*). Specific questions concerning the general role of affects and inhibition in human motivation and emotion, thinking, intuition, and behavior have been researched by Julius Kuhl (2001). He has developed a complex neuropsychological theory, named *PSI* theory (personality systems interaction), and fundamental assumptions that have been supported by laboratory experiments.

A recent broader summary of the importance of PSI theory in coaching has been published by Engel and Kuhl (2022, pp. 28 ff.). The theory differs between four macro systems of the brain:

1. *Extension memory* (right prefrontal brain: feeling, coherent context and self-knowledge; "parallel processing integrating a virtually unlimited number of separate experiences," including "the perception of one's own inner states, goals, needs, abilities, and behavioral options for solving" and autobiographical memories and self-representations).
2. *Intention memory* (left prefrontal brain: conscious thinking, maintenance of explicit intentions, planning, sequential-analytical attention).
3. *The object reception system* (left parietal brain: sensation, incongruence-emphasizing attention; it involves two opposing modes that are characterized by inhibition vs. facilitation).
4. *Intuitive behavior control* (right parietal brain: intuitive behavior routines).

> The main function of the object recognition system is to focus on one detail at a time (i.e., an 'object'). This process demands separating the object from its specific context, as in figure-ground contrast. According to PSI theory, object recognition is intensified when novel, unexpected, incongruent, or incorrect information is detected (op. cit., p. 30).

These systems are associated with the activation or inhibition of negative or positive affect. As an example, the observation of a difficulty by the object reception system is associated with negative affect. By activating positive memories in extension memory, negative affect can be reduced. The resulting process is self-relaxation.

Coaching should aim at supporting the client's affect regulation. The implementation of difficult intentions (action control) requires an interaction between intention memory and intuitive behavior control. It would be optimal if the coach stimulates a change from low positive affect to high positive affect. In the difficult task of learning from one's own mistakes (an example of self-growth), the client often needs support in activating resources in his or her extension memory (or "self"). The change here is from high negative affect to low negative affect. A first step in the development of self-competence according to PSI theory is raising awareness through self-reflection, a standard method in coaching. The second step focuses on developing the ability to self-regulate affect. This "inner resourcefulness" is needed for self-regulatory competences and can "be trained and developed in coaching" (op. cit. pp. 32 f.).

Basis assumptions of PSI theory have been incorporated into coaching at an early stage (Greif, 2008). They can be used to clarify core coaching assumptions about the importance of self-representations and difficulties in accessing the self through self-reflection if an arising negative affect is strong. Access to the self is easier if it is mild. This reduction can be induced by asking the client, who is observably highly emotional, to describe his or her emotional state. According to the assumptions of PSI theory, this question should activate conscious reflections in the frontal lobe of the brain and thereby reduce strong accompanying affect. As a coach, you normally can observe how the client after this question suddenly sits up, concentrates, and starts to talk in a more rational and less emotional way about his or her emotions. This intervention can be directly applied in coaching to stop strong affect and is integrated into our theory and methods of *result-oriented coaching* (see *Sect. 2.5.2 and Chap. 9*).

5.8.4 Future Challenges of Neuroscientific Approaches in Coaching

Better understanding, what works and what does not work in coaching, changing affect and emotion, unconscious processes and rational reflections, thinking and decision-making, and the development of self-regulation competences. Coaches are wise to acquire neuroscientific background knowledge and pass it to their clients through psychoeducation and stimulate Aha! experiences and more realistic trials in changing affects, thoughts, and behavior. An example is the application of neuropsychological knowledge in the field of habit change (see *Sect. 6.5.2 and Chap. 9*).

However, even if newer technologies allow the measurement of neurobiological signals of the brain in coaching sessions, they are not independent of artifacts produced by body movements or speaking and need many replications of the same interaction to be reliable. (I discussed my naïve plans to start neurobiological research on habit change together with a neuropsychologist. However, he explained that it would be necessary to design very artificial repetitive habits and coaching behaviors. Therefore, I postponed my plans to future technological developments, which might allow to study more real-life coaching interventions.) In the future, these measurement problems can be solved. Until then, neuroscientific informed coaching has been an existing and promising approach.

5.9 Pseudoscientific Concepts and Charlatans

Coaching is an attractive and expanding service. Anyone is allowed to call him or herself a "coach" without any regulation and refers to his or her own education, knowledge, and experience. One can also offer coaching training without having to undergo quality control. These are favorable conditions for charlatans who claim to be experts and promise services that they cannot deliver. This discredits the seriousness of professional coaching services provided by well-trained coaches. Coaching associations increasingly see this as a major threat to the future of coaching. In this chapter, criteria are described, which can be applied by associations, coaches, and clients, allowing the identification of charlatans in the coaching field. From a scientific point of view, there is a particular threat from associations that offer coaching training on the basis of concepts, which look to laymen at first glance as if they were practical and scientifically founded. Only through close inspection can one determine that this is not the case at all. The following criteria are discussed, which are related to the basic criteria of the philosophy of science (e.g., Chalmers, 2013 or Lakatos, 1981), and practical rationality can be used to recognize that a coaching concept is pseudoscientific. In scientific discourse, such criteria are always open to challenge and must be discussed.

5.9.1 Criteria for the Identification of Pseudoscientific Concepts

Hansson (2013), on the basis of the general philosophy of science, defined the general characteristics of a pseudoscience across directions and fields of application. In contrast to science, pseudoscientific statements can be recognized by the fact that they refer to similar large areas as scientific theories. However, they are unreliable and merely pretend that their statements are reliable (Hansson, 2013, p. 70 f.). The application of Hansson's criteria, whether there are comparable scientific areas and how the reliability of statements is to be assessed, requires scientific expertise.

Macho (2016, p. 186 f., free translations) suggested that pseudoscience in the fields of medicine and psychology can be recognized by the following two general criteria:

1. "Pseudoscience rejects accepted methods and testing standards. It attempts to diminish the value of these methods or to classify inferior methods as equally good."
2. "Pseudoscientific theories are characterized by an ontology that contradicts that of the established sciences. This includes dubious entities (such as life energy or energetic fields and regions of the body) and mysterious mechanisms of action (such as the transmission of the effect of substances through water that has once come into contact with these substances—even if the substance is no longer detectable)."

According to Macho, the rejection of recognized test methods and the weakening of strict evaluation criteria lead to "sand being thrown in the eyes of the public by presenting inadequate test methods as equivalent to recognized methods. As a result, not only are consumers harmed by being expensively sold ineffective therapies, but the advances of medicine and psychology as a whole are endangered" (Macho, 2016, p. 192, free translation). The acceptance of the claims by their supporters is typically uncritical.

Macho's criteria list important negative consequences of using pseudoscientific intervention methods. However, without the advice of scientists who know how to determine whether the evaluation methods are reliable and which "ontology" (fundamental assumption on the existence or reality, basic categories, and the features of these entities) are only usable by scientific experts. Against the background of

Hansson's and Macho's criteria, I have tried to translate the essence and formulate criteria that can also be used by laypersons independently, at least to a large extent. According to these criteria, concepts, and theories as well as intervention methods are considered pseudoscientific if they meet the following criteria.

Criteria for the Identification of Pseudoscientific Concepts

1. Intervention methods that are claimed to have exceptionally strong effects are recommended. However, these claims are only anecdotally supported by referring to individual cases or "experiences."
2. Confirmations of the assumptions and effects of the intervention methods by scientific evaluation studies are lacking, or negative research results are concealed.
3. Scientific evaluation methods are rejected categorically.
4. Scientific theories and intervention methods are cited to justify and validate, but the citations are associative, inaccurate, or distorting.

1. Reports of exceptionally strong effects may impress people who wish they could achieve such extraordinary results themselves. However, even laypersons can check whether these effects are claimed but are supported only by anecdotal descriptions of individual case examples, and they can ask whether they are also supported by scientific evaluation studies. If the protagonists of the methods persistently point to case examples with unbelievably good results and merely to whatever "experiences" that have not been systematically documented in a written and technically comprehensible form, this should make everyone suspicious.
2. The second characteristic of a pseudoscientific concept is the lack of scientific confirmation of the assumptions and evidence of the effectiveness of the methods through as many evaluation studies as possible. This absence is, in my opinion, the most important characteristic of pseudoscience. However, in regard to new theories or methods that have only recently come into existence, one should consider that, in the beginning, assumptions and methods are often based only on initial unsystematic observations of individual cases and single studies. However, the authors of the concept should address this lack of confirmation by research in an open and self-critical manner. Furthermore, authors should start from the beginning to carefully formulate their assumptions about contexts and results and name appropriate scientific research instruments that seem suitable for evaluation (see *Chaps. 7* and *8 Examining Coaching Effectiveness* and *Processes in Coaching*). Especially problematic are pseudoscientific theories and methods that are several decades old and still do not refer to serious confirming scientific effectiveness studies with systematic qualitative or quantitative methods.
3. It is extraordinarily problematic whenever negative research results on efficacy or side effects are withheld. The deliberate concealment of negative effects known through scientific publications can even be labeled fraudulent.

4. Charlatans and pseudoscientists often categorically reject scientific evaluation methods. This is listed as the third characteristic. Because one can explain why existing scientific studies can be completely rejected or why there are no scientific evaluation studies, this is a simple way out. By this argument, it seems to be possible to defend the concept in principle against all past and future possible scientific test results from the outset. In addition, all scientists who have found negative research results are accused that their evaluation studies have been performed with methods that are completely inappropriate or have been distorted by prejudices against the concepts and methods. It seems strangely self-contradictory when, despite this, the claim of scientificity is made. To recognize whether these are only protective claims, one should ask the representatives which scientific evaluation methods they accept and to justify exactly why they are better than the existing methods are.
5. The fourth characteristic describes how pseudosciences give themselves a scientific appearance. Typically, they quote well-known scientists as a source or "proof" for the validity of their theory or the effectiveness of their methods. For example, popular neuroscientists known from the media are often quoted. However, if one then reads the cited literature in the original and compares what has been made of it, one can determine whether the reproduction is inaccurate, glossed over, or even completely wrong to make it fit in the meaning of one's own claim.

Those unfamiliar with the subject and the literature can easily be blinded and impressed by embellished citations. To prove inaccurate or distorting scientific citations, expert knowledge and research in the cited literature are needed. However, often, a short Internet search (e.g., in Google Scholar with the keyword "NLP pseudoscience") can already be helpful.

5.9.2 How to Recognize Charlatans

According to the Duden Online dictionary, charlatans are people who "fake abilities and thereby deceive other persons" (free translation).[4] They shamelessly promise fantastic successes that they cannot deliver and fraudulently conceal or disguise negative effects. The first criterion, therefore, is similar to the first criterion for identifying pseudoscientific methods. However, the second criterion is a deliberate deception of their customers.

Criteria for Identifying Charlatans

1. They recommend their methods and claim that they achieve exceptionally strong results using them, but they cannot deliver these results.
2. They know that their methods do not achieve promising results. However, this and possible harmful side effects are concealed or hidden from their customers.

Whenever extraordinary successes are promised, caution is always called for, as is a critical review of whether they have been demonstrably and without any doubt reliably delivered. Charlatans must especially fear and avoid independent scientific testing. Charlatans can also expand their methods with pseudoscientific arguments. Thus, it becomes more difficult to identify them. If they truly believe in the successes, even if they do not occur, they are, strictly speaking, not "charlatans" but "whitewashers."

Proving that someone is deliberately concealing or covering up knowledge about missing effects or side effects is difficult to verify unequivocally. As in judicial fraud trials, there would have to be testimony from the person or testimony from others who heard him or her admit to it.

5.9.3 Neurolinguistic Programming as a Pseudoscience

Neurolinguistic programming (NLP) is a theory that, with its principles and intervention methods, is very widely used in coaching training and among coaches (Greif, 2014b). It was originally created by its developers Bandler und Grinder (1975) as a short psychotherapy. By naming their theory, they refer to processes in the brain ("neuro"), linguistic communication ("linguistic"), and "programming" of clients' behavior. Essential to NLP (Linder-Pelz, 2010, p. 19), it is a very broadly understood "modeling," understood as the formation of successful new patterns of thought, behavior, and language, as well as perceptions, emotions, beliefs, and assumptions. Bandler and Grinder mention constructivist systems theory, linguistics, learning psychology, cybernetic psychology, and psychotherapy as theoretical foundations. They borrow and modify the concepts and assumptions of these approaches. They adopt psychotherapeutic methods after analyzing the language structures of successful therapists such as Gestalt therapist Fritz Perls and family therapist Virginia Satir. They conceive a so-called meta-model for analyzing the surface and deep structure of human communication and refer to the linguistic syntax theory of Noam Chomsky (2017). Later, they incorporated the hypnotherapeutic methods of Milton Erickson (Erickson et al., 1976).

At first glance, the program seems impressive. However, why is NLP considered a pseudoscience by scientists (Kanning, 2014) and criticized as a pseudoscience on Wikipedia? While Wikipedia is not an untouchable professional source of information, in the case of inaccurate statements, NLP supporters can demand corrections.[5] Notably, long-term published NLP criticism in Wikipedia has not yet been corrected. One does not have to be a pronounced subject matter expert to recognize; according to the four basic criteria taken together, as listed above, NLP can be considered a pseudoscience (Greif, 2022a, b):

---

[5] In 2008, Wikipedia introduced a review system and procedure to correct any incorrect information.

1. Claims of Extraordinary Effects

   In the classic and, until today, recommended introduction to NLP training[6] (Bandler & Grinder, 1979, p. 5 ff.), the author of the preface, John O. Stevens, claims that through NLP principles, "deep and lasting changes" are brought about "quickly and easily" and lists the following examples.

   In "less than an hour":

> "Cure phobias and other feeling responses" or overcoming "learning disabilities" (e.g., spelling and reading problems) in children and adults.
>
> "Within a few treatment sessions":
>
> "Eliminate unwanted habits (smoking, alcohol consumption, overeating, insomnia, etc.), make change of negative interactions of couples, families, and organizations so that they can act more satisfactorily and productively."
>
> and many physical problems, most of which are already recognized as "psychosomatic."

Stevens himself says that "these are strong claims," but "experienced NLP practitioners can back them up with solid, visible results." It is astonishing that not all readers have reacted skeptically to such fantastic claims of effectiveness. These claims in this "NLP-Bible" are communicated without criticism by followers, and the intervention is often even termed "magical." To the best of our knowledge, neither NLP nor other short-term therapies can achieve such great effects. As evidence for the extraordinary effects, very vaguely "experiences" are referred to, and in the book, only anecdotal case descriptions are provided. In the numerous new editions of this NLP standard book, the assertion of the fantastic effects has never been corrected.

2. Lack of Confirmation by Scientific Evaluation Methods

   In their review of a total of 1459 publications on the effectiveness of NLP interventions, Sturt et al. (2012) found only 10 with before-after surveys and five with randomized control groups. The interventions address very different problems, such as anxiety, obesity, morning fatigue, substance abuse, or claustrophobia, during magnetic resonance imaging. The number of therapy sessions ranged from 4 to 20. Only three of the before-after comparisons revealed significant improvements in questionnaire scales, but none of the objective measures (body weight, drug abuse by urinalysis, etc.) improved significantly. Only one of the five randomized control trials showed a significant effect. The authors conclude that NLP cannot be recommended for practical usage.

   Zaharia et al. (2015) performed a meta-analysis on the effectiveness of NLP for the treatment of social and psychological problems. They found a total of 425 studies, 12 of which compared before and after scores (658 subjects in total, from studies with samples ranging from 12 to 115). In six of these studies, effects were tested with randomized control trials. Dormandy and Grimley (2024) recently defended the NLP approach against my critique published earlier (Greif,

[6] In the literature list of the ANLP, the international NLP association, the book is highly recommended as the "NLP-Bible." https://anlp.org/books/frogs-into-princes#reviewform, last access July 31, 2024.

2018, 2022a, b), especially how I discussed the meta-analysis of Zaharia et al. (2015). Therefore, let me add some arguments to the methodological problems of the meta-analysis. I tried to submit a detailed response to all points in the journal, but did not get an accepting response:

Normally, meta-analyses on the effectiveness of psychotherapeutic methods are carried out on a precisely defined rather homogeneous group of psychological problems of the clients or mental disorders. In this meta-analysis, nearly all belong to different groups and vary widely (snake phobia, claustrophobia in the scanner, depressiveness, various anxieties, fatigue, posttraumatic stress disorder, or birch pollen allergy). Additionally, the therapeutic methods and their durations are heterogeneous and include single hours of anchoring sessions up to weekly sessions of NLP therapy over 5 months. The qualifications of the therapists range from students who have participated in training in NLP anchoring techniques to therapists with 10 to 20 years of experience in NLP.

As a measure of the average strength of the effects, the authors calculated Cohen's d-measure across all samples. The mean effect, calculated by Zaharia et al. (2015), is $d = 0.54$, which at first glance is quite strong and significant. According to Cohen (1988), an effect size less than 0.30 is considered small, between 0.31 and 0.50 is considered moderate, and an effect size greater closer than 0.50 is considered large.

However, a look at the results reveals that most of the effects of the individual studies are between −0.18 and 0.35. Accordingly, most effects are small and at most moderately strong, with some even being negative. Only a study of a master's thesis reached a very strong effect of $d = 2.20$. In this study, the NLP anchoring technique reduced the perceived fear of the dentist, as measured by an anxiety questionnaire.[7] (This could also be achieved with common relaxation methods). Such an outstanding high value at first glance should be classified as an outlier. Outliers, which in small studies which increase or decrease the overall mean value, should normally be eliminated. This would be methodologically more correct given its extremely large distance from all other values and relatively simple therapeutic task. The difference from the second strongest effect with $d = 1.25$ is very large here. A standard method for detecting outliers is a formula that, on the basis of differences in interquartile ranges, calculates the so-called "upper fence" (above which the values should be excluded) (cf. Cousineau & Chartier, 2010). This upper fence is 1.14. Therefore, excluding this study with a much higher value of 2.16 is recommended. The resulting reduced mean after exclusion is $d = 0.39$. It is only moderate. Certainly, Dormandy and Grimley (2024), even if they say that this value is "good enough", cannot claim that it is much higher than that which is reached by standard psychotherapeutic methods, as is implied by the claims of Stevens in the foreword of the "NLP-Bible" and those who follow such claims. Of course, not all practitioners and science-oriented NLP followers do that. However, why do they not mention this?

As I explained in my discussion, with the underlying "therapy" (one two-hour anchoring session on the fear of the dental procedures), the exclusion of this study by Pourmansour (1997) can also be justified by the fact that, unlike other therapies, it is possible to achieve strong effects in this field. A meta-analysis of 29 nonpharmacological randomized controlled intervention studies (overall 2.886 patients) for reducing mental distress associated with dental procedures (Burghardta et al., 2018) supports my argument. They reported strong effects, especially for hypnosis (listening to hypnosis tapes). The authors suggested that these strong effects can be explained by the known results of other studies, namely, that the effects of hypnosis depend on the individual suggestibility of the patient.

Dormandy and Grimley (2024) mention that Zaharia et al. (2015) performed statistical tests on so-called publication bias, which I should mention. These tests consider that the mean parameters found in single smaller samples can have a broader range of values than

[7] I wanted to inspect the study, but she did not answer my email.

those found in large samples. There was no significant effect; therefore, Zaharia et al. (2015) included all the studies in their analysis. Such tests are OK, but they do not imply that outliers that increase the mean value to an extreme degree should be ignored.

Dormandy and Grimley (2024, p. 13) state that results supporting a certain NLP technique "could hardly be more devastating" (Greif, 2022a, b, p. 763) and say that the reason is unclear". Apparently, they have overlooked or do not accept my reasons given in the previous sentence (loc. cit.): "If we look at the effects from the randomized samples (only five), we find only one single large effect with $d = 0.65$. Here, two effects are negative, one at $d = 0.00$ and one at $d = 0.07$." If this is the result after 40 years of research, how could such an outcome of randomized NLP evaluation research be judged? "Devastating" or not, even Zaharia et al. (2015, p. 361) conclude: "Although many studies are aimed to determine the efficacy of NLPt, there is a major lack of high-quality data from observational, experimental studies or randomized trials in this field. Until now, there have been insufficient data to recommend this form of therapy strongly for reducing some psychosocial problems."

3. Categorical Rejection of Scientific Evaluation Methods

   To shield themselves from the outset against any scientific investigation of their assumptions and principles, Bandler and Grinder (1979, p. 10) confess that they are "not interested in the 'real' or 'true' nature of things" or scientific data. "We're not offering you something that's true, just things that are useful."

   Bandler and Grinder make strong claims about the validity of their diagnoses and the usefulness of their principles for successful change. They cannot seriously disregard whether the models and assumptions they use are false or inaccurate. It would be very perverted to believe that one could achieve useful positive effects with false principles. Their argumentation is self-contradictory and cannot be maintained in this way. Those who reject scientific evaluation methods should better argue differently.

4. They Refer to Scientific Theories and Intervention Methods to Justify and Validate, But the Citations Are Associative, Inaccurate, or Distortive.

   Dormandy and Grimley (2024) are right to demand that we be cautious and not assume that all NLP followers are science-oriented. The difference between practitioners who are not interested in science and science-oriented NLP followers. In my contributions, I have mentioned science-oriented authors such as Linder-Pelz (2010), who explicitly accepts standard criteria of empirical evaluation research, and Grimley (2016), with his action research approach. In the view of Dormandy and Grimley (2024, p. 3), pseudoscientific authors can be classified as "bullshitters."

   As a scientist, I would avoid calling people "bullshitters." Dormandy and Grimley refer to the provocative essay "On Bullshit" of Harry Frankfurt (2005). He argues that "one of the most salient features of our culture is that there is so much bullshit" (op. cit p. 1). A bullshitter is neither on the side of the true nor on the side of the false. Since his eye is not on the facts at all, he is not a conscious liar. This is different for the liar, who knows that he or she is lying or an honest person, who consciously strives not to lie. Pigliucci (without data)[8] precisely

[8]The editors of the online encyclopedia add no date, since the contributions are revised continuously. My last access was on July 24, 2024.

explicates the relationship between lying and pseudoscience. He cites Moberger (2020, p. 598) that "the bullshitter is assumed to be capable of responding to reasons and argument, but fails to do so" (2020, 598) because he does not care enough. For Pigliucci, "the bottom line is that pseudoscience is bullshit with scientific pretensions." The arguments of Dormandy and Grimley are slightly different. They assume that the groups, which they call "NLP bullshitters," are pseudoscientists who claim scientific status for NLP techniques but do not care about accuracy. They compare this group to salesmen, aiming for profit, who falsely claim that their products have been researched or spuriously downplays research into the dangers of their products. However, the term "bullshitter" in a contribution to the philosophy of science may be amusing but also very discriminating. In my view, it is more constructive to describe examples of inaccurate citations or false claims and hope that in the future, people who care will avoid them in the future. In my view, on the basis of a discourse of the general philosophy of science, we need more than this single criterion to identify pseudoscientists.

Only those NLP representants can be called "pseudoscientists," who claim to be scientific, as Dormandy and Grimley (2024) emphasize. In my view, those who justify and validate NLP in reference to the content of scientific theories and methods can also be accused of behaving in a pseudoscientific manner. They refer to scientific theories and intervention methods by citations, which are inaccurate or distorting. Many such references can be found in the traditional "NLP-bible" of Bandler and Grinder (1979) and newer publications of Bandler and Grinder and their followers. Quotations, technical terms, and assumptions from the underlying scientific theories or intervention methods have to be used accurately and not distortively. To recognize this, expert knowledge is usually required (see Greif, 2018 for literature sources and more information; descriptions of NLP terms and methods according to original formulations by NLP representatives such as Bandler & Grinder, 1979; Linder-Pelz, 2010 and Rückerl & Rückerl, 2008). In the following several distortive citations of prominent NLP authors are summarized.

Modeling

Modeling is a central learning principle of the learning theory of Bandura (1969). NLP originally referred to Bandura but describe it as changing feelings and behavior through observing, listening, asking, activating, and experimenting. This description bears no resemblance to Bandura's six phases of observing and imitating the behavior of a model person (see *Sect. 6.5 Cognitive Modeling*).

T.O.T.E. Strategy

Test-Operate-Test-Exit (T.O.T.E.) is a cybernetic cycle introduced by Miller et al. (1960) that analyzes basic human behavior (the classical example is hammering in a nail). In NLP it is applied very differently as a universal strategy for successfully solving problems that can be guided by the coach step by step.

Chomsky's Generative Linguistic Theory

Chomsky has developed a transformational grammar, which assumes that "deep structures," subconscious syntactical rules or transformations generate the spoken "surface structure" of human language (Chomsky, 2017). Different "surface structures" can result from the same "deep structure" as in the sentences: "John sees Mary" or "Mary is seen by John." Grinder was a linguist, and it is astonishing that he changed Chomsky's term "deep structure," referring it to the unconsciously underlying rules and meanings, without mentioning the different meanings (c.f. Grimley, 2008, p. 196 f.).

Anchoring

Anchoring is very important NLP technique. It is called the "master tool." It aims to create and change emotional states "through unconscious conditioning processes" (Linder-Pelz, 2010, p. 27). Bandler (p. 127 ff.) describes how to apply the exercise. His example is a client who tries to eliminate bad memories starts the anchoring exercise by imagining past very good experiences. He or she then tries to intensify the positive feeling, as if this can be done by raising an imagined "fun lever." The client may strengthen the mental imagination by holding the imagined lever between the index finger and thumb and lifting the hand slightly. After this is accomplished, the next step is applying this skill in triggering negative feelings by mentally raising this fun lever after focusing on the bad memories, supported by the movement of pressing the thumb and index finger together. The idea is that he or she is now able to stop bad feelings by arousing positive feelings.

Bandler and Grinder (1979, p. 110) refer to the well-known experiments of Pavlov, where dogs learned to anticipate food by ringing a bell. The "unconditioned reflex" of the dog seeing food is the salvation. If the bell is rung directly before the exposure of the food, after several expositions, the dog starts to salivate after hearing the bell. This is now a "conditioned reflex" according to Pavlov's classical learning theory. Bandler and Grinder (1979, p. 110) state that their anchoring technique "is (…) straight conditioning. We have simply associated a new set of feelings, namely, competence and strength, with the auditory and visual stimuli." However, it is obvious that the classical conditioning according to Pavlov is completely different. In particular, the conditioning of human reflexes is never as quick as anchoring. An example is conditioning of the eye blink reflex after a short blast of air to the eye. It requires 20 to 30 repeated repetitions of a tone before the closing of the lid is elicited by the tone (Merrill et al., 1999).

Grimley (2016, p. 175) cites Derks (2000), who is very convinced that it is not necessary to evaluate the effectiveness of "anchoring," since it is well confirmed by research on classical conditioning and completely identical to it: "For instance, instead of asking if the use of anchors is supported by scientific research, people wonder if 'NLP' is scientifically sound. However, anchors are just another name for classical conditioning, something based on the Pavlovian paradigm" (Derks, 2000). This contrasts with Grimley's statements in his book on the theory and practice of NLP Coaching (Grimley, 2013, p. 89 f.) Here, he precisely describes Pavlov's classical conditioning study and states that "anchoring is not designed to cause a response in a somewhat linear and mechanical way, like Pavlov's dogs, but rather is designed to keep the boat of feeling and consciousness in a particular positive and useful area on top of the vast sea of unconsciousness."

It would be possible to develop a different hypothetical theoretical model of anchoring and start research, which determines whether the anchoring works as expected for all subjects. It is open to doubt.

A list of more justifications of NLP by can be found in Greif (2022a, b). Also recent examples of distorting citations of scientific theories or research by NLP authors can be found. For example, in Germany, the well-known NLP protagonist Schmidt-Tanger (2006) quotes a model of the neuroscientist von Hüther (2004) about levels in the human brain. It describes how incoming signal patterns become inner images and the role of emotions in this process. However, there are hardly any appropriate references to Hüther's levels for the processes described in her article. Nevertheless, she concludes already in the title: "and NLP is right after all" (free translation). She claims that her method of generating emotional arousal in clients through provocations is neuroscientifically proven by Hüther. I could observe one of Schmidt-Tanger's coaching demonstrations (Schmidt-Tanger, 2014).

> In an interview (Gros, 2010), she explains her approach. "It is essential that the therapist or coach has the courage of provocation by saying things that should not actually be said" (free translation, p. 75). As she describes, she dares, bluntly saying, what intuitively comes to her mind. She describes what stimulates her provocative behavior in an example: "When they come to therapy, many clients organize a church service around their problem. They have told this 22 times, and flowers are brought to the altar every morning. Once a year they light a candle for the problem [...] Yes, and if this worship of the problem is to come to an end, then you can switch to Provo [...] then you can take a look at this cosmic joke that you're indulging in, where the clients themselves sometimes think: 'My God, I'm truly getting on my nerves. I actually need a new problem because I'm truly tired of it." (p. 61, free translation)

It would be interesting to determine by independent studies what different clients think, feel and do if they are confronted by Schmidt-Tanger, e.g., by saying "Don't you get on your own nerves when you emphasize your problems over and over again and organize such a church service around your problem? "Hüther (2020) favors a concept of teaching without pressure and free creative development is completely different. It is absurd to believe that Schmidt-Tanger's method of provocative behavior of coaches is compatible with his emotionally warm approach and would be accepted as an adequate behavior for teachers.

Kanning (2014, p. 126 f., free translation) summarized his NLP criticism: "The 'theory' is characterized by a mess of poorly defined constructs that have been selectively chosen and only loosely connected. Any author of NLP literature can come up with completely arbitrary new concepts without disturbing the overall picture. Moreover, even central terms are used differently or with multiple meanings in different publications. Scientific findings are either incorporated into the canon of methods in a purely associative manner, trivialized, alienated, or persistently ignored if not liked. Thus far, it has not been possible to create a coherent or even contradiction-free model from the multitude of concepts."

In summary, the quotes show that all four criteria for a pseudoscience, the four criteria of a pseudoscience for the "NLP bible" written by Bandler and Grinder (1979), cannot be found for all but also in the contributions of important younger NLP representatives:

1. Intervention methods that are claimed to have exceptionally strong effects are recommended. However, these claims are only anecdotally supported by referring to individual cases or "experiences."
2. Confirmations of the assumptions and effects of the intervention methods by scientific evaluation studies are lacking, or negative research results are concealed.
3. Scientific evaluation methods are rejected categorically.
4. Scientific theories and intervention methods are cited to justify and validate, but the citations are associative, inaccurate, or distorting.

Taken together, the classification of the cited publications is very clear. From the beginning, claims of the effectiveness of NLP were completely exaggerated and implausible. They were supported only by reference to "experiences" or anecdotal case descriptions. Clear confirmation of the claimed exceptionally strong effectiveness of the intervention methods with careful scientific studies is still lacking after approximately 50 years. Scientific verification has been rejected by Bandler and Grinder or some of their followers for strange reasons. Bandler and Grinder and several followers refer to scientific theories and intervention methods to justify and validate their positions, but the citations are associative, inaccurate, or distorting. The philosopher of science Lakatos sees pseudosciences as "degenerate research programs" if they are based on "ad hoc assumptions" and do not allow for new or interesting predictions or applications (quoted from Macho 2016, p. 184). Since the methods of NLP have been borrowed from other scientifically reviewed psychotherapies and their effectiveness is lower than that of the original methods according to the available results, NLP can be classified as a "degenerative program." Therefore, the recent contribution of Dormandy and Grimley (2024) has to be rejected as a trial to whitewash NLP positions, which are still prominent in inaccurate arguments.

However, there are NLP advocates, such as Linder-Pelz (2010), who consider common research methods to be necessary for a scientific review of NLP. She is one of the very few NLP representatives I know who takes up the criticism of the lack of scientific foundation and effectiveness testing of NLP. She also criticizes the NLP community's rejection of scientific research. As a future perspective, she calls for an evidence-based, scientific NLP approach in the coaching field. However, to overcome the classification as pseudoscience, it would be necessary to explicitly reappraise problematic positions and attempts at justification through biased quotes from well-known scientists in a self-critical manner and without regard for the founders Bandler and Grinder or well-known younger NLP-eminences. To a certain extent, NLP would have to restructure and reinvent itself from the bottom up on the basis of realistically assessed positive practical experience. Scientifically committed followers could try to examine the processes and effectiveness of promising intervention methods through careful, qualitative or quantitative research.

5.9.4 Recognize Pseudoscience and Charlatans in Coaching!

NLP is by no means the only concept that can be considered a pseudoscience. Basically, it is easy to develop a new concept, loosely quote well-known scientists, perform a few coaching sessions, and advertise that, according to previous experience, fantastic successes have been achieved. If you search for coaching offers on the internet, you will quickly find authors of new concepts with sounding names or coaching interventions, which promise the solution of currently not completely solved problems such as burnout or new stimulating concepts such as agile leadership coaching. Caution is advised when grandiose effects are promised but can be supported only by individual anecdotal experiences or single customer references. Double caution is needed when no scientific research and reviews on the effectiveness of the interventions are mentioned with precise literature references but when they merely refer to well-known scientists as witnesses but without their real recommendation. It is worth investigating whether the positions of scientists and their research are accurately reported. We make it too easy for self-proclaimed experts if we allow ourselves to be blinded.

Charlatans can be recognized by the fact that, as in the first criterion for pseudoscience, they make claims and promises about fantastic results that they cannot deliver. They refer thereby again only generally to their experiences or miraculous success stories. Some charlatans thereby lack quotations from the scientific literature. Quite a few even explicitly distance themselves from "conventional science" in terms of their analyses and methods. This also applies to some of the esoteric methods that are also widespread in coaching. Some coaches even refer to shamans and occult powers. In a Google search (October 2022), I found more than five million internet entries on "Shamanic Coach."

Modern charlatans use the Internet and produce YouTube films and self-published books. One should become especially suspicious if, as seen recently, coach consultants promise that by buying their marketing support, training, or tools, coaches can earn several hundred thousand dollars annually, even over a million. Largest caution is required if, in the publications to the magniloquently formulated success, no single literature reference is indicated as a basis and source, let alone scientific proof. Some authors get along completely without a literature list. Do they draw their recipes for success entirely from their own knowledge? Some cite no one but themselves. This could perhaps only mean that they are so convinced of themselves and their own words that they proclaim them to us with the utmost certainty. Maybe that they believe in their propaganda and do not deliberately want to deceive us. However, we do not have to adopt their grandiloquent self-belief and better not trust their fantastic promises.

Coaching based on science, supported by well-received scientific theories, research, and an open (self-)critical discourse about the coaching concepts based on them and the results they achieve, is the best rational and practical approach when selecting and further developing our coaching intervention methods. Scientific research also serves in coaching for orientation (information, reflection, and discourse) and legitimation through scientific foundation and thus for the professionalization of coaching (Fietze, 2017). Coaching associations alone are not able to identify and critically examine all pseudoscientific concepts and charlatans. On the basis of the listed characteristics, companies seeking coaches for their employees, coaches concerned about their reputation as reputable coaches, and clients as end customers can at least ask critical questions when suspicions arise. This would put pseudoscientific concepts under pressure to change and make business more difficult for charlatans.

5.10 Questions for Repetition and Remembering

1. List all the coaching concepts that you know.
2. Which coaching concept do you think is particularly suitable? Please specify the reasons for your selection.
3. Which coaching concept do you criticize? Please name your reasons.
4. What characteristics can you use to recognize pseudoscientific concepts and charlatans in coaching?

Chapter 6
Coaching Methods: Reappraisal Under Posttraditional Scientific Magnifying Glass

6.1 What Is Understood by "Coaching Methods"?

The use of the term "coaching method" or "coaching intervention method" can cause protests because the term might suggest that coaches apply rigidly prescribed techniques and rules of behavior with their clients.

- I remember an interview with an experienced coaching practitioner. When I asked her about what methods she preferred, she indignantly replied, "I don't use 'methods'!" However, she had just told me how she had explained to a manager a systematic selection process for choosing team members and recommended it for use. When I pointed out a supposed contradiction, she explained that she had by no means resorted to a predefined method because she had individually adapted the procedure with the inexperienced manager in such a way that it seemed practicable, especially for this client. My "Aha! experience" was that in the future, I should perhaps better speak of "flexible methodical procedures" instead of "methods."

Presumably, almost all coaches emphasize, when talking about their "methods," that they have to adapt sensitively and flexibly to the specific characteristics and preferences of the individual client and to his or her goals, to the particular social and organizational context, and to the specific themes. In the guidelines for coaches, which we use for the training of future coaches, we always note that it is always necessary to reflect such adaptations or changes.

The term "method" is used every day or in common definitions in the literature. For example, the philosopher Rapp (1973, p. 913, free translation) understands it to mean "a consistent method of procedure (…) applied to achieve a particular end." He distinguishes "methods" only from "actions that come about unintentionally and are carried out arbitrarily or uncontrollably." The spectrum ranges from spontaneous but reflected processes of thought and action to precisely defined procedures. The following definition takes this up.

S. Greif, *The Future of Coaching*, https://doi.org/10.1007/978-3-031-96192-2_6

Definition of Coaching Method

A "coaching method" is an intervention started by coaches or by an AI system to activate clients' actions and interactions that can be assigned to a group of interventions with characteristic distinguishing features and that, according to available practical experience and/or scientific evidence, serve to support clients in their chosen themes or goals.

In coaching, performance is usually not rigid and schematic but is flexibly adapted to the specific goals, characteristics, and preferences of the client as well as to their social and organizational context.

Coaching methods are often also called "coaching tools," I am aware that, strictly speaking, coaching methods cannot be called "tools" according to the meaning of the word. The reason why the term "tool" is preferred may be that it has a strong connotation in that the method can be used very well in practice. The practitioner in me too likes this term. I therefore like to use it, synonymously with a flexible understanding of the "coaching method." However, the term "coaching tool" is usually used for procedures that are specified in detail. The term "coaching method," on the other hand, can also be used to refer to higher-level or general procedures (e.g., stress management methods).

Some authors prefer the term "coaching techniques" (see the section of coaching techniques in the journal *The Coaching Psychologist*). Interestingly, in the history of Applied Psychology, the term "technique" became very popular and inspired the founders to name the field "Psychotechnique" (e.g., Münsterberg, 1915).

A "coaching method" can be centered on a single interaction (e.g., a specific open question) or on several consecutive activities (e.g., use and joint interpretation of picture cards for a "strength analysis") or a combination of methods (e.g., stress management coaching: analysis of the stress situation and resources, clarification of goals, planning, implementation and accompaniment of the client in coping with the stress situation, and performing relaxation exercises).

For a more detailed description of individual coaching methods, we use short guidelines in our coaching training.[1] As is explicitly emphasized with respect to the guidelines in our training, the descriptions of the performance are not instructions that have to be rigidly adhered to but merely an attempt to describe possible procedures with their expected results. Variations in performance, as well as the underlying assumptions and research findings, present critical problems, and questions have always to be addressed. The coaches reflect and decide with the clients if and how the described methods are used. The model is the "minimal guidelines" we have used to promote self-active and self-organized learning (Greif et al., 1993; Greif & Kurtz, 1998).

---

[1] An example can be retrieved from my Research Gate publications: https://www.researchgate.net/publication/378899547_Rigorous_Implementation_of_Behavior_Changes

Today, there are attempts to replace coaches completely or partially with virtual coaches (e.g., avatars, cf. Berninger-Schäfer, 2022), coaching bots, or artificially intelligent systems (AI) and AI tools (Clutterbuck, 2022). If they follow a rigid routine (e.g., a program to query and automatically evaluate one's strengths without interpreting and reflecting the evaluation together with the client), I would explicitly not qualify this as a flexibly adaptable coaching method or coaching tool but only as a subordinate instrument in coaching or, according to Geissler (2022), as a problem-solving aid in coaching. In the future, however, flexible virtual AI systems that can be used as alternatives to real coach persons are likely to exist. Without entering here into the questions of how they may perform in comparison with humans as coaches in the future, such flexible and adaptive systems are incorporated in the definition. Section 10.2 of this book provides a comprehensive description of the consequences, risks, and opportunities of using AI as a coach or AI tool in coaching.

The following presentation begins with a brief overview of different groups of common types of coaching methods.

6.2 Different Coaching Method Groups

The participants in coaching training and professional coaches are highly interested in learning about and trying new coaching methods. Books on coaching methods and tools are bestsellers (Megginson & Clutterbuck, 2005, 2009; Rauen, 2007, 2012, 2013; Gorell & Jones, 2012). Most of these methods and tools are based more on practical experience and creative ideas than on scientific evidence. Exceptions can be found in the section "Techniques" of the journal "The Coaching Psychologist" with its short descriptions and my guideline collection of scientifically based coaching tools (Greif, 2025, in prep.). A treasure trove of suggestions for evidence-based methods is Green and Palmer's (2019) account of positive psychology methods. The latest collection by Passmore et al. (2021) includes over 250 coaching tools.

In the coaching literature, different methods are offered depending on their theme or goal and for different types of purposes. However, a research-supported grouping of different types of methods is lacking. The development of a classification system to group and distinguish coaching methods would be a difficult task. After all, coaching can essentially refer to all the conceivable themes and objectives of human life. Therefore, the classification would have to be very comprehensive and open for extensions. In the following presentation, the coaching methods are pragmatically divided into preliminary groups. The individual current methods are subsequently selected for all groups and briefly described.

Pragmatic Grouping of Different Coaching Methods

1. Questioning methods
   (a) Classic questioning techniques
   (b) Mirroring
   (c) Circular questions

   (d) Motivational Interview
   (e) Questions of social chatbots

2. Meaning, vision, values, and strengths
   (a) Narrative Coaching
   (b) Vision development
   (c) Values analysis and reflection
   (d) Strengthening strengths
3. Behavior change, social interactions, and conflicts
   (a) Cognitive modeling
   (b) Habit change
   (c) Enlightenment of the clients
   (d) Communication behavior
   (e) Empty chair exercise
   (f) Conflict analysis and management
   (g) Leadership behavior
4. Stress management, burnout prevention, and health coaching
   (a) Analysis of the stress situation and resources
   (b) Stressor reduction
   (c) Resource activation
   (d) Relaxation and meditation
   (e) Health coaching
5. Team coaching
6. Coaching during organizational changes
   (a) Better communication
   (b) Managing complex and uncertain changes

For more detailed descriptions of how each method is performed, see the guidelines of Greif (2025, in prep.).

6.3 Questioning Methods

Asking questions is not the most common activity of coaches in coaching conversations, but listening is, with a duration of 55% of the time and a frequency of 29% of the activities, as Deplazes (2015) found in her analysis of video recordings of 23 coaching processes of 13 coaches. In an early study on the classification of transcripts of coaching conversations, Geissler (2009) reported that questions accounted for between 26% and 61% of coaches' activities (mostly above 30% and with a significantly higher frequency than other activities, such as explaining, reflecting, and planning). In Deplazes (2015), asking questions 16% in frequency (10% in duration) followed "reflection" (on clients' environment, experiences or perceptions, and coaching process) with 20%.

Questioning is considered an almost always applicable intervention. Through questions, an infinite variety of problems can be explored, reflected upon, analyzed, or clarified together. From a practical perspective, Wehrle (2012) compiles 100 different types of questions and 400 possible follow-up questions. "They are meant to pick up the client where he is right now and take him to where he would like to go, his personal goals" (op. cit., p. 7, free translation).

Graf et al. (2020) distinguish three basic types of questions from a linguistic perspective in problem-related interactions in coaching: elucidation questions ("Do you have an example of this?"), cause investigation questions ("Where does this come from?"), or problem-solving questions ("What should we do next?").

Questions about an example and the subsequent follow-up questions can be used to clarify a problem and deepen understanding. As Spranz-Fogasy et al. (2019, p. 131) state, psychotherapists can point out ambiguities, contradictions, or unusual things by asking follow-up questions. From the clients' perspective, inquiring also shows them the therapists' genuine interest in them and strengthens the bond and working relationship. Through questions, answers, and summaries, new knowledge is cocreated.

As Graf and Spranz-Fogasy (2018) summarize, research on questions in coaching is very unsatisfactory. In particular, they call for studies of the sequences of questions and answers in coaching. Deplazes (2015) conducted the first comprehensive study. Her analyses revealed that coaches ask more closed questions (8.8%) than open questions (6.4%), although many coaches are very fundamentally opposed to the use of closed questions. As expected, however, clients' responses to open-ended questions are longer than those to closed-ended questions. At the same time, the length varies enormously within each group. Notably, contrary to the widespread opinion among coaches, they do not find any differences in the content of the answers, according to which closed questions would be "more stimulating and goal-serving" than closed ones (op. cit., p. 199, free translation). Further studies on the frequencies of and reactions to different types of questions in coaching are necessary to gain firm insights. Research outside the coaching field is also interesting, such as on question formulations for interview and survey methods (Brandon, 2014; Moshagen et al., 2014) or on the use of questions in teaching (Acar & Kiliıc, 2011).

In the following, the formulation of open questions is described as a classic questioning technique used by coaches. This mirroring is subsequently explained in accordance with nondirective psychotherapy. A method characteristic of systemic concepts is circular questioning. Finally, a complex questioning method, *motivational interviewing*, which has become increasingly important in both individual and team coaching for motivating changes, is presented. At the end of this section on questioning techniques, the use of artificially intelligent systems as social chatbots in coaching to support clients is discussed.

6.3.1 Classic Questioning Techniques

Coaches guide the coaching conversation primarily by asking questions of their clients. However, their process guidance is normally intended to support the clarification of the themes or goal achievement of their clients. The clients are the "owners" of the themes and goals and the decisions on how to work with the methods chosen for this purpose. A common maxim is as follows:

Who asks, leads, but in coaching, should not control the answers!

Questions used by coaches to "wrap" hidden advice are particularly problematic (Wildt & Wildt, 2009). In guiding the coaching process through questions, it is important to give clients maximum discretion. This begins with the opening question "What themes would you like to address today?" and ends with the closing question "What is your conclusion for today's session?" These and other "open-ended questions" leave open what clients answer. Through them, clients can be activated to report, tell, and explain or explore a problem or themselves or come up with ideas for solutions. They are often formulated as "W-questions."

- **What** (e.g., "What would you like to discuss with me today?", "What exactly happened in the situation?", "What happened next", "What did you feel in the situation?", "What exactly is your goal?")
- **Who** (e.g., "Who was there in the conversation?", "Who criticized you?")
- **When** (e.g., "When exactly was this?", "When in the situation did you sense something was going wrong?")
- **Where** (e.g., "Where did it happen?", "Where were your thoughts in that situation?").
- **Why** (e.g., "Why do you think your partner behaved this way?").

For behavior and situation analyses or goal clarifications, "what-questions" can usually be used very well. "Why-questions," which remind of inquisitorial questions of parents or teachers ("Why did you do that?!"), should be avoided in coaching. With regard to exploring the subjective explanations of the client, they can usually be rephrased into "how-questions" and softened by suggestions about the situational context ("How do you explain that you behaved like that in the situation?").

For clients to be able to give their answers without time pressure, the coach must be able to endure silence and should not immediately repeat the question or phrase it differently but, as a rule, wait at least a few seconds for the clients to say something.

Questions can also be used to ascertain whether what has been heard has been understood correctly ("Did I understand you correctly that…."). This requires attentive listening and, if possible, literally summarizing and repeating the client's wording. It helps to take notes. However, it takes practice to maintain eye contact with clients while they write. (In coaching training, I demonstrate how to do this with an exercise and ask the exercise clients if my note-taking bothered them. Most don't even notice.) After all, permanent eye contact is by no means optimal; it can be perceived as intrusive.

6.3.1.1 Different Types of Questions

There are various overviews by practitioners on question types. Above, reference was already made to Wehrle (2012), with a total of 500 question types. For some of them, however, one can question whether they can be clearly distinguished or whether they are only variations of similar questions. In a recent publication, Proksch (2016) distinguished "hypothetical questions" ("What would happen if…?") and "circular questions" (see below), "scaling questions" ("On a scale from 0 to 10, how satisfied are you with the achievement of your goals?"), "solution-oriented questions" ("What would have to happen for you to be completely satisfied?"), or "paradoxical questions" ("What could make the situation worse?" also called "headstand questions" because to improve the situation you have to turn the factors that lead to the worsening of the situation around and put them from the head to the feet), "closed polarizing questions" (with alternatives previously named by the clients themselves), and "suggestive questions" and "alternative questions" (answered alternatives, such as "Yes" and "No" or "Solution A or B").

Suggestive questions should generally be avoided (Wildt & Wildt, 2009). However, there are exceptions, e.g., if a decision for an important solution already worked out with the clients is to be enforced. In this case, however, it would be appropriate to draw the clients' attention to the fact that and why one is deliberately asking suggestive questions.

The mentioned practice authors describe plausible concrete advantages and disadvantages of the different types of questions. They are formulated with great certainty as rules, as if they were unquestionably valid. Given that research in this field, which is very significant for coaching, is still in its infancy, we should be cautious with respect to general assumptions about the general effects of certain types of questions with all people. It seems much more plausible to hypothesize that responses to similar questions vary widely across individuals and depend on the preceding interactions and relationships with the questioner. As Deplazes (2015) documents in her analysis of video recordings of coaching conversations, there is a great deal of variation in clients' responses.

At least we should be careful with generalizations that go beyond our cultural context. In a conference contribution, Peter Dreyer (2010) provided a coaching demonstration with a Japanese woman to convey very clearly how different the style of coaching is. Both showed much greater mutual appreciation. In Japan, in his experience, open-ended questions can actually be problematic in coaching according to traditional Japanese rules. They are considered questions where clients do not know which answer is a "correct" answer. This is unsettling and can raise fears of "losing face." In a subsequent skyping with a coach in Japan, we were able to experience this very directly. Peter Dreyer urged us to leave the polite questioning to him while Skyping with the Japanese coach. One German participant could not help herself and asked open questions and follow-up questions in a friendly but persistent manner, as we are accustomed to in our culture. After that, the conversation became noticeably uncomfortable for the colleague from Japan and had to be ended politely and quickly by Peter Dreyer. In other cultures, even the "rhetorical questions" and "leading questions" that are discredited here can apparently be quite appropriate. In Japan, for example, problems and self-reflections in coaching can be stimulated in an appreciative way by well-meaning quotes from famous people, aphorisms, or suggestive questions about commonly shared principles and rules (Dreyer, 2013).

In the coaching field, there is an interesting study by Maurer (2009) from a practical point of view, in which she compared the effects and acceptance of different questioning mirroring techniques in executive coaching. Compared with a control group and a nondirective group, she found the strongest changes in the clients' problem view and satisfaction when the coaches used open-ended questions according to a given list of classical questions. The following questions are examples of this list (op. cit., p. 137):

1. Clarification of the situation (e.g., "What specifically is at stake?" "What are the facts?" "What are your feelings about person X?" "How do you deal with it?")
2. Causes and background of the problem (e.g., "What do you see as the causes of your current situation?")
3. Goals (e.g., "What are the goals?" "What do you want to achieve?")
4. Resources (e.g., "What resources are available to you to achieve your goal?")
5. Action options (e.g., "What other options do you see to address the situation?" "What do you think are the possible consequences of these actions?").

6.3.2 Mirroring

A psychological questioning method adopted from psychotherapy into coaching is "mirroring." This requires careful reflective listening to what the client says and observation of nonverbal emotional responses. The coach describes and empathically accepts the client's descriptions of their experiences and, in particular, their (possibly only slightly shown) sensations and feelings in their own words without evaluating them. Carl Rogers (1942, 1951) by no means understands nondirective counseling and psychotherapy to be merely a "technique." In his view, it is the basis of his humanistic theory and the main way to enable self-development and growth of the personality. By empathically mirroring the contents of experience and feelings, one shows clients that one understands and accepts them. This acceptance is expected to open them up to self-accepting self-exploration and deeper self-reflection. Rogers sees this as a prerequisite for independent psychological growth and self-development.

Stober (2006) transferred this method and the concept of nondirective therapy to coaching, but in doing so (loc. Cit., p. 24) highlights differences in the general objectives between psychotherapy and coaching. Thus, in her view, therapy serves to promote psychological recovery, whereas coaching serves to promote decisions between alternative courses of action for one's own development.

Many coaches emphasize nondirectivity without, however, using Rogers' method and his concept of Rogers accurately and exclusively. They simply refer to "nondirective" in a general meaning as not wanting to dominate or direct the client. For them, "mirroring" is usually just one questioning method among other types of questions.

Maurer (2009) compared leadership coaching using the mirroring method with classical questioning methods. The coaches were given the six levels of reflection according to Finke (2004) as orientation:

1. Reaccentuating repetition (reproducing the meaning of words in one's own words).
2. Picking up on the prevailing feeling (mirroring also the feelings perceived by the coach that were not explicitly mentioned)
3. Clarification of the situational context (suggestions mentioned about the situation are taken up)
4. Picking up on self-reflective feelings (example: "Therefore, it was your supervisor's reproachful look that made you so angry")
5. Picking up on feelings and needs (example: "It was to this anger that you attributed all your frequent feeling of humiliation")
6. Clarifying the life-historical context (suggestions of connections between present feelings and earlier biographical events)

In her study, Maurer (2009) compared the coaching results of three groups of 14 managers each. First, the reflection method (with the levels described) was used; second, classic questioning techniques were used; and third, a control group without coaching was used. The values of various scales for well-being, activation, and self-efficacy were compared. The results revealed statistically significant differences compared with those of the control group. The mean differences between the two coaching groups were only small. There was a tendency for mirroring to promote changes more at the emotional level and questioning to promote changes more at the cognitive level (Maurer, 2009, p. 206). However, the differences are not statistically significant and could be due to random effects. In addition, the variation within the groups is large. Accordingly, the methods have very different effects individually or are used differently by coaches.

It remains an open question whether mirroring emotions in coaching is a generally appropriate method for all themes and goals as well as for all target groups or whether it should be used more specifically for the exploration of emotional experiences and for the promotion of self-awareness and verbalization of feelings. Comparative case studies with analyses of the interactions (ideally videos) of the behavior of the clients and scales, which try to capture the processes and outcomes, would be desirable (see below the research methods in *Chap. 8: Processes in Coaching* and *Chap. 7: Effectiveness of Coaching*).

6.3.3 Circular Questions

"Circular questions" (sometimes called "reflective questions") are a characteristic method of systemic interventions. The special nature is illustrated by the cartoon in Fig. 6.1. A client describes a situation in which he harshly criticizes an employee of the team he leads in front of the other team members. The client explained that he

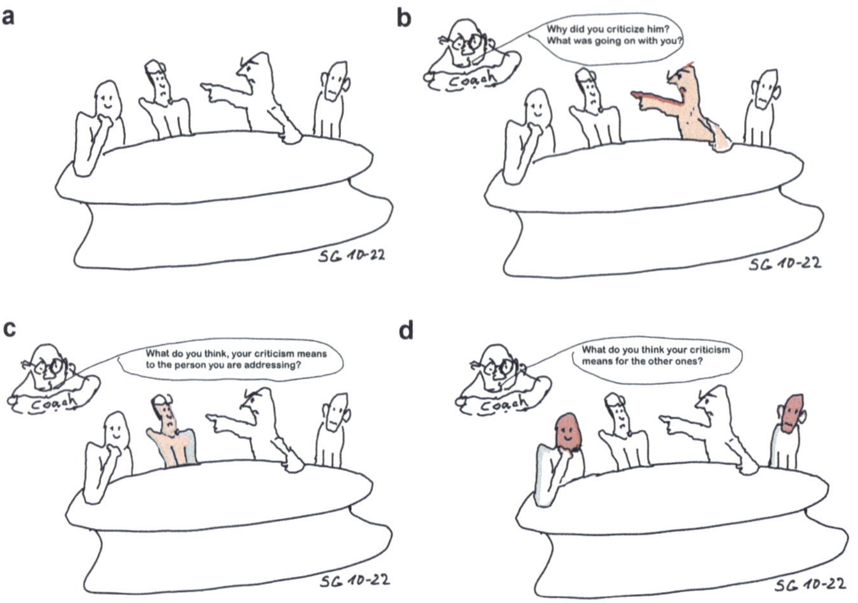

Fig. 6.1 (**a**) A conflict situation, (**b**) Direct self-reflective question of the coach, (**c**) Circular question (individual level), (**d**) Circular question (group level)

was annoyed by his "constant destructive criticism of all proposed solutions." Owing to his harsh criticism, he wanted to stop this behavior of the employee. The coach's first question stimulating self-reflection is "Why did you criticize him? What was going on with you?" The following "circular" question here might be, "What do you think your criticism means to the person being criticized?" In this way, he stimulates the client to imagine his or her counterpart's thoughts, feelings, and behavior and what he or she might be possibly eliciting by criticizing the other person. The following questions also require reflections on the hypothetical thinking and feelings of other people and how this can influence interactions. As Fig. 6.1d shows, they may also stimulate reflections at the group level.

Circular questioning is considered a distinctive "systemic" questioning method for promoting reflection on mutual expectations and interactions among people. It goes beyond the assumption of linear mutual influences between people in their interactions and considers circular interactions that relate to themselves or "self-referential" interactions (Simon & Rech-Simon, 1999). Bateson (1981), one of the founders of systemic psychotherapy, referred to the importance of metacommunication or "communication about communication," which provides a foundation here.

In a modified version, circular questions can also be performed in groups. In a sense, this would be a "gossiping in the presence" of the person being gossiped about, guided by the coach (Schlippe & Schweitzer, 2019, p. 95 ff.). The person being talked about can thereby gain direct insights into the expectations referring to him or her, better understand their reactions, and take these into account in his or her behavior. If coaching is about testing different behavioral options and their effects, the "empty chair exercise" (see *Sect. 6.5: Social Interactions and Conflicts*) could also be used as an alternative in the situation described.

In general, circular questions in psychotherapy and counseling are assumed to promote reflection on the circular interconnectedness of people's actions in social contexts and enable fundamental systemic changes (Bamberger, 1999; Simon & Rech-Simon, 1999). However, only practical case studies can be found in the literature as evidence for this assumption. However, interaction process analyses would be quite possible, as shown by two pilot studies supervised by myself and Arist von Schlippe as diploma theses (Bähre, 2001; Offermanns, 1998). In Martina Offermann's study, seven systemic interviews were performed with project managers in current conflict situations, whereas Marianne Bähre's study included six managers. The transcripts were analyzed and evaluated by trained observers. In the majority, the perceptions and evaluations of the managers' feelings changed after the circular questions. A more differentiated description of the conflict and self-reflection has increased. However, practical suggestions for solutions to these conflicts have not always been developed.

As outlined above (see Sect. 5.4, *Solution-focused Counseling*), providing suggestions and suggestions for rethinking so that clients develop new insights is likely beneficial (Greif & Riemenschneider-Greif, 2018; Müller & Greif, 2022). In the case of strong fixations concerning the mindset of the clients, a self-reflective confrontation of the clients seems to be necessary to be able to dissolve being locked into blockades of their thinking. To determine whether and under which conditions circular questions or other self-reflexive questioning methods promote new ("systemic") insights, further observational studies are needed.

Call: More Bachelor's and Master's Theses on Questioning Methods!
We need many more observational studies to fill the large research gaps concerning methods for coaching. As mentioned above, promising research studies have been started at the University of Kassel, Germany (Deplazes, 2015), and by a team of linguists and psychologists from Austria, Germany, and Switzerland, "Questioning Sequences in Coaching" (QueSCo, head is Eva Maria Graf, University of Klagenfurt[2]) (see Graf and Spranz-Fogasy (2018)).

Many students would like to perform an observational study in the coaching field. However, employees and managers are hesitant because coaches and clients are not ready for observations or because the students do not have the necessary minimal coaching qualifications to lead coaching exercises themselves and would hardly find volunteers for this. Martina Offermanns (1998) and Marianne Bähre

[2]The homepage of the research team is https://questions-in-coaching.aau.at/en/ (last access October 10th 2022.

(2001), as students, were eager to perform a study of coaching methods in their theses. I knew from experience that managers and other employees are quite willing and very open to interviews with young people. My suggestion to her was therefore to act as an interviewer but to use questioning techniques such as those used in coaching. Martina and Marianne were highly motivated to learn and apply the very demanding method of circular questioning in conflicts. For the analyses and evaluations of the transcribed answers in the interviews, they trained observers and checked their consistency with the statistical parameters. As the transcriptions of the interviews and the evaluations of the trained observers and especially the somewhat very positive reactions of the interviewees show, the interview phases with the circular questions are quite comparable to professional coaching situations and reflections with clients. It would be beneficial if Martina's and Marianne's interview studies could encourage further observational studies with these or other questioning methods. We can expect interesting research results not only for question types but also for the resulting interaction processes.

6.3.4 Motivational Interviewing

Who has not heard this: "I would like to change something (e.g., complete my tasks faster and more quickly, not always spend my time on work, familiarizing myself with a new field of interest). However, when it becomes concrete, my priorities change, and I doubt whether I truly want that or maybe something else? Or suddenly, I realize that some inner resistance or ambivalence is slowing me down." How such ambivalences and inner resistance can be overcome is the initial question for the application of *motivational interviewing* (MI). It consists of a complex system of questions and principles designed to activate clients in coaching to evoke deep reflections on their desires for change and to overcome the ambivalence and inner resistance involved. The questioning system was originally introduced by Miller and Rollnick (1991) for counseling and psychotherapy and motivating behavior change in substance abuse, which is undoubtedly a difficult target. MI has since been used in various other fields, such as leadership behavior, change management, and coaching (Klonek & Kauffeld, 2012; Passmore, 2011b; Passmore et al., 2017; Güntner et al., 2022).

According to MI principles, coaches should behave empathically, listen very carefully to their clients, and use open-ended questions to explore the ambivalences and perceived advantages and disadvantages of changing or maintaining behavioral options. Clients' reasoning arguments used to explain why they maintain problematic behaviors are thereby referred to as "sustain talk" (arguments in favor of continuing to maintain undesirable behavior). (Example: "I do want to change, but right now it seems better to put it off until a better opportunity.") Importantly, coaches do not argue with their clients about the pros and cons of these reasons, even if their arguments seem inconsistent. This could increase resistance to the coach and

Box 6.1 Transcript of a Coaching Dialog (Klonek and Kauffeld, 2012, p. 68, Free Translation)

The client talks about her goal of linking her future career with a desire to have children.

Coach: "What's behind that? Why is that very important to you to push through?" (*evocative question*).

Client: "Because I definitely want to have children (*change talk—wish*) and I want to start that in the relatively near future" (*change talk—commitment*).

Coach: "That's actually the big striving then" (*complex reflection*).

Client: "Yes ..., that this is also feasible for me (*change talk—wish*)—and in my time frame." (*change talk - wish*).

Coach: "You then take care with this directly in your application" (*complex reflection*).

Client: "Yes, exactly" (*change talk—activation*).

Coach: "That's good ..." (*appreciation*) (pause) "You would then say, 'Well then I'll go to the competitors otherwise!'" (*complex reflection*).

Coach: "And then when you found the ideal job. You pushed through it—what would happen next?" (*open question—imagining the future*).

Client: "Then, I would choose the workplace too" (*change talk—self-commitment*).

changes. According to the MI question system, it is more appropriate to skip such questions and ask the client about the benefits of the changes and to repeat the benefits of the changes formulated by the clients and to stimulate further change-related expressions, referred to as "change talk." This is followed by planning and implementing the desired behavioral changes. To illustrate these distinctions, Box 6.1 reproduces an excerpt from a transcript of a coaching conversation from a case study by Klonek and Kauffeld (2012) with classifications of question type.

Klonek and Kauffeld (2012) distinguish two phases in MI: (1) stimulating motivation to change and (2) taking action to implement the change. The question types and comments of the coaches refer to four intervention principles:

1. *Empathy* (open questions, appreciation, open listening, summarizing).
2. *Developing discrepancies* (evocative questions, developing themes, looking back, looking forward, goals and values, etc.).
3. *Dealing with resistance* (simple or increased reflection, changing focus, reinterpreting, agreeing with a turn, emphasizing freedom of choice, etc.).
4. *Strengthening the confidence in change* (evocative questions, scaling confidence, strengths and resources, information and advice, reinterpretation, etc.) should be strengthened.

For more specific techniques using MI in coaching, reference can be made to presentations by Jonathan Passmore (Passmore, 2011a, 2011c, 2012a, 2012b, 2013a, 2013b; Passmore & Whybrow, 2008).

MI has references to various scientific theories. Miller and Rollnick (1991) modeled their emphasis on empathy as a basic principle of the nondirective talk psychotherapy of Carl Rogers but simultaneously called for directive or evocative questioning to handle ambivalences. By doing so, they try to help clients identify and overcome their ambivalences. Here, they refer to the cognitive dissonance theory of Festinger (1978), according to which people try to reduce perceived dissonance between attitudes and behavior. By allowing their clients to cite many positive consequences of desired behavioral changes, the clients are, in a sense, convincing themselves. Klonek et al. (2015) mention Deci and Ryan's (2008) *self-determination theory* and use it to justify why it is important for motivation that the freedom to decide for oneself should not be restricted in coaching but should be explicitly emphasized. Further references not mentioned by Miller and Rollnick can be found in the research on the stimulation of behavior changes by focusing on perceived discrepancies between behavior and an ideal self-concept, the so-called "self-discrepancies," already mentioned above in *Sect. 2.4*.

There are numerous studies on the effectiveness of MI in various fields of application. Lundahl and Burke (2009) performed a meta-analysis of studies on the effectiveness of MI compared with randomized control groups in different clinical groups (addiction to alcohol, marijuana, or other drugs). Compared with the control group, they reported significant improvements of approximately 10–20% after MI. At the same time, the effects of the MI in groups are smaller than those in individual applications. Regarding the classic MI application field of substance abuse, Smedslund et al. (2011) performed a meta-analysis of the 59 efficacy studies available at that time with randomized comparisons and control groups. Like Lundahl and Burke did, they reported moderately strong effects of the method compared with control groups without intervention or after simple feedback but no significant differences from other therapeutic treatment methods.

Because MI works neither better nor less effectively than other treatments in clinical applications and because the method is also suitable for other behavioral changes, stronger effects can probably be expected here. Therefore, the focus of efficacy studies has recently increased. O'Halloran et al. (2014) published a review of the state of research and a meta-analysis of studies using randomized groups to determine whether MI can be used to increase physical activity, improve cardiorespiratory fitness, and induce more exercise in individuals with chronic health problems. However, contrary to expectations, the confirmed effects were rather small or moderate. However, this could be partly attributed to insufficient accuracy in the application of the complex method. In studies with controlled application of the method, the effects are greater.

In the coaching field, to date, only the first pilot studies have been conducted. The case study by Klonek and Kauffeld (2012) is especially interesting. In their interaction analyses with trained observers, they categorize coach behavior according to the differentiations of the MI method (see Box 6.1). However, the rigorous implementation of complex principles has proven to be a very demanding task. The achievement of the expected overcoming of ambivalences is methodologically difficult to prove and probably by no means possible with all clients. In the case study of Klonek and Kauffeld, however, maximum frequencies of change talk are reached in coaching, with 91% and 100% self-commitments, respectively. Such implementation rates for the method need to be confirmed by further studies. To achieve sustainable changes, it might be necessary to accompany a very accurate application and rigorous implementation of the method over a longer period (see *Sect. 9.3.3: Sustained Accompaniment of the Implementation as a Metalevel Success Factor*).

Güntner et al. (2022) recommend the use of MI not only for motivating difficult changes in individual coaching but also in team coaching to promote "change talks" in teams. In addition, coaches could teach this method to managers who want to use it in conversations with individual employees or their teams when dealing with difficult goals and organizational change. For this purpose, coaches could introduce their clients to the basics and application of MI (psychoeducational with introductory literature) and then accompany them in the implementation.

In a case example, I explained the MI to a client, the owner of a small company. Using this method, he succeeded in motivating his managing director, who was always skeptical about changes, and frequent arguments did not help at all. Through "change talk," he successfully convinced him that changes are necessary. I explained the principles to him in detail and gave him this text excerpt from the German edition of this book together with the text by Güntner et al. (2022). He found the texts very understandable and the principles comprehensible.

6.3.5 Can Social Chatbots Pose Questions and Answer Like Coaches?

For the scientists involved in the research and development of the so-called artificial intelligence (AI) systems, the "Turing Test" initiated by Turing was only a minor challenge. The goal was to develop a computer program with which humans could communicate linguistically (in writing or orally) but without being able to recognize that they were not talking to a human. Weizenbaum (1966) constructed "Eliza" the first such system, which has passed the test. It simulates the questioning and mirroring as practiced by nondirective therapy in the style of Carl Rogers (see *Sect. 6.3.2: Mirroring)*. It is quite impressive how the program can react to written sentences or descriptions of one's own feelings. Some people said that it was comparable to the reactions of therapists. However, the questions and answers were variable but, in principle, rather schematic and did not provide a deep understanding.

A review of experiments with AI systems and "chatbots" has been published by Shum et al. (2018). Well-known AI assistants include Apple's Siri, Microsoft's Cortana, Google Assistant, Facebook M, and Amazon's Alexa. They are already very versatile speech-based information systems that are suitable for searching and booking restaurants, etc., or serve as assistive reminders. Chatbots also produce research, reports, and comments in social media and newspapers that are hardly recognizable as chatbot productions.

More interesting than standard AI assistants are the newer "social chatbots." They have the potential to provide models for more sophisticated conversations, such as coaching. One example is "XiaoIce" from Microsoft (https://www.msXiaoIce.com/). It presents itself as a virtual companion not only reacting to verbal commands or prompts but also as a socially and emotionally intelligent conversational partner and companion. This chatbot aims to establish an emotional relationship between the user and the chatbot. As a result, it is intended to be used not only for individual tasks but also as a preferred virtual companion over a longer period. This can be seen from the fact that users communicate with these chatbots very often and for an astonishingly long time (up to 24 hours …!) and say "thank you" to the chatbot as if it were a human being for its help. To make this possible, developers have programmed these chatbots by asking questions with an adaptive AI system so that they respond to contextual information, ask queries, and talk to them "emotionally intelligently," evaluating this information "like a friend" and adapting to the users' knowledge and preferences, even with humor or creative solutions. They can evaluate and interpret not only linguistic information but also contextual information or images.

Examples:

- The user wakes up at 3 a.m. and asks the chatbot what time it is. The chatbot registers the unusual time and initially asks, "Can't you sleep?" and answers after that.
- The chatbot recognizes a deterioration in the user's mood in the way he or she speaks and asks what is wrong. It reminds the users of positive experiences and thus demonstrably cheers them up.

Social chatbots are not fully developed at present. If they are created to be user friendly to support coaching processes as special additional tools, they could, in principle, also be quite useful (e.g., as always friendly but persistent reminders, as individualized memory aids or "patient friendly" feedback givers when learning complicated procedures or when recognizing and analyzing changes and creating reports).

Some coaching experts expect that future AI systems will be able to completely replace coaches, at least in simple standard coaching sessions (Clutterbuck, 2022; Rauen, 2018b). However, because such adaptive, self-optimizing AI systems are becoming increasingly complex and nontransparent in their growing simulation of quasi human behavior, I believe that *a cautious, reflective use of AI systems* would be the recommended principle of their usage. At least in the case of constant use of such systems or for very important and difficult goals, it would be advantageous to seek additional advice and support from experienced coaches who are familiar with the advantages and disadvantages of using such systems. *Section 10.2: Consequences of Digitization and Artificial Intelligence* discusses the opportunities and risks of the expected revolutionary changes for the coaching profession in detail.

6.4 Meaning, Vision, Values, and Strengths

Coaching is by no means only about achieving concrete goals. Coaching also supports clients in reflecting on their values, general questions of meaning or significant experiences in the past, as well as their own strengths and future visions and plans for their own lives in the professional or private sphere. They are presented below as examples of coaching methods that are not directly focused on goals.

6.4.1 Narrative Coaching

Narrative coaching is suitable for clients who want to clarify questions about the meaning of their lives, their self-image, or their identity ("Who am I?"). The starting points are often important personal stories that clients tell about their lives and that do not let them go, such as school and career failures or successes but also drastic changes (new job, relocation, or critical life events, such as illnesses, separations, unemployment). White and Epston (1990) assume that an individual's identity is represented and formed by the stories ("narratives") that the individual tells about himself or herself and his or her life. Particularly important are the so-called dominant stories, which are told repeatedly with strong emotional involvement. White and Epston founded "Narrative Psychotherapy," in which these narratives are analyzed (or "deconstructed") through questions in the conversation with the clients. Therefore, it is possible to detach from the problem, as it has been perceived until now. Subsequently, they are encouraged to develop "richer" narratives about the described experiences with the problem situations, especially those with more positive implications.

Importantly, the problems described in the narratives are not only perceived as internal problems of the person ("My problem is …") but also analyzed together from a higher perspective (metalevel), such as an external influence on another person. This "externalization" or "objectification" of the narrative enables a distanced analysis of possible influences. As a result, clients can more easily disengage from their feelings and thoughts and develop alternative perspectives. For example, by "reauthorizing" a client's distanced account of a failure experience, he or she may realize that the cause of the failure was not him or herself but rather a situation that was difficult to cope with. The story and one's own achievement in mastering the situation can now be interpreted more positively or associated with a deeper meaning. A story of failure can be reinterpreted as an important experience that has helped clients move forward in their personal development. With the support of the therapist or coach, clients can then be guided to tell their stories differently in the future. With this "retelling," according to the assumptions of White and Epston (1990), new meaning can be found in one's life, and a positive perspective on life can be promoted.

6.4.1.1 Narrative Coaching According to David Drake

The narrative method has been transferred to coaching in different variants. The first variant and further development was created by Drake (2010). Drake's approach is that the conflict dynamics described in the stories are the central pivot and source for the solution of the problem: "Nothing moves forward in a story except through conflict, and, in fact, the conflict is the axis on which the story turns and the cauldron for the solution" (Drake, 2010).

Drake (2010) emphasized four basic principles:

1. *Identity development is situated:* Clients' stories are always related to concrete situations. In coaching, this reference must be analyzed and, to a certain extent, witnessed and respected.
2. *Development is limited:* Clients may be able to "retell" their experiences and give them new meanings, but additional new experiences are required for wide-ranging identity development.
3. *Discourses are powerful:* The discourse between coaches and clients about narratives is very important for identity development. New positive constructive reflections can enrich their self-image. For this purpose, further stories can also be used as "evidence."
4. *Retelling is possible:* Clients can tell their stories differently and open spaces for new insights into the "old stories" with their enriched reflections. This enables a reorientation of meaning and identity.

Drake published detailed suggestions for the use of his method (Drake, 2017a). He describes numerous case examples and questions of the coach that can be used to stimulate reflections and retelling of one's own stories. By his own account, he has trained (especially with online webinars) over 20,000 coaches and clients in his method.[3]

Figure 6.2 shows the model on which Drake bases his coaching approach. When clients tell him their important stories or experiences from their lives, his analysis starts with a clarification of the situational embedding of the story ("Situate—What is?"). Then, he explores ("Search—What if") what meaning or general purpose the story has for the client. What are the important aspirations of the clients? What if things had gone differently? What experiences have been made thus far?

The coaching conversation then turns to the possibilities of looking differently at the story, shifting ("Shift—What matters?") and focusing in the future on what matters—the fulcrum of the story. Is it possible to change behavior? What can one "experiment" with, what can one try? Finally, evaluate what changes to firmly stick to in the future ("Sustain—What works?"). What is going or working as expected? What is progressing? How does the environment react? How can one express and present the changes?

[3] See https://www.themomentinstitute.com/narrative-coaching (last access November 26th 2022).

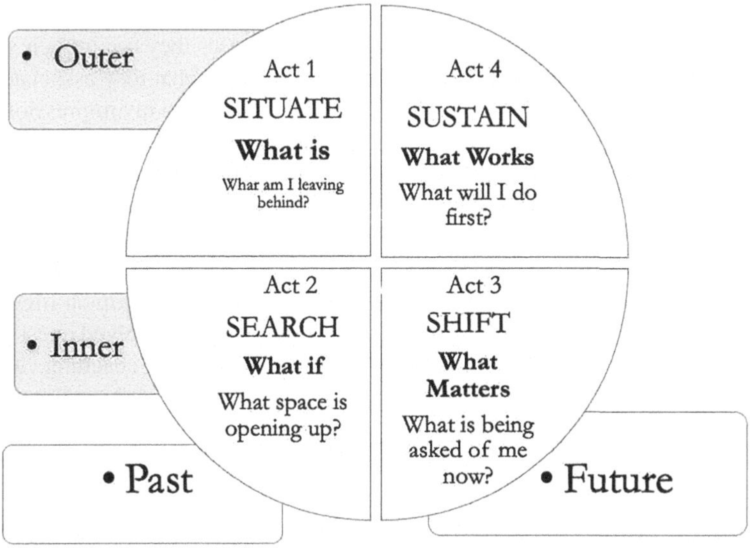

Fig. 6.2 Drake's narrative coaching model (simplified op. cit. p. 230)

As this sequence shows, performing narrative coaching according to this model is a complex coaching task that takes place over several sessions. For simplicity, it is outlined as a sequence of steps. As Drake noted, however, the sequence is by no means linear but goes back and forth.

Drake describes the process in detail using a coaching example (Drake, 2017a, p. 259 ff.). Very briefly, his client "Wayne" has been through several professional "downward spirals," as he says, and basically, they always had something to do with "unfairness." In the first session ("situate"), his professional dreams were the starting point, as were his situations, feelings, and thoughts. The key phrases were "being stuck," "being lost," "being an exile," and "feeling torn between home (his house) and the world." With these formulations, Drake was able to return to the subjective starting point in later sessions. He wanted to live in both worlds without being torn between them. Going deeper into the themes in the second session ("search"), Drake asked his client to develop a story for each of the alternatives. What if I could tell a different story? Wayne then began looking for a better job and contacted another company. In the third session ("switch"), Wayne reported that after the session, he physically felt his energy returned, with a sense of lightness and freedom. In this session, he began to imagine a new place for himself in his relationships with others. A profile of the characteristics of jobs that could bring out his best was developed. The final session ("sustain") discusses how Wayne could consolidate what he had achieved. Drake recommended a professional career counseling expert for him. Wayne said at the conclusion of the coaching session, Wayne felt a great sense of relief that all those burdens had fallen off him that had been weighing him down. However, he saw that this was only the first step on a long road.—Drake later learned during a subsequent coaching session that Wayne had found a new, more satisfying job. The "old stories" keep coming up sometimes, however. Drake feels, however, that the client is better able to deal with them from a stronger starting position.

As the example shows, narrative coaching does not focus on specific goals. Drake reflects with his clients on the individual terms and phrases they use in their stories that are biographically important to them and asks exactly what they associate with them to trace the meaning of the story from their perspective. In my impressions and observations, reflecting on biographically important life events in coaching is an important alternative to goal-oriented coaching. Reflecting on and clarifying questions of meaning is an essential social mission and challenge for all members of society, especially in a time of fundamental social changes and digital transformations in all areas of life.

Drake's method supports clients who repeatedly ruminate on critical life events that they "can't overcome" or clients who want to reflect on unresolved questions of meaning. As the case example described above shows, narrative coaching can help clients clarify these stories in such a way that they become less burdened by them or even gain positive motivational energy.

Even though this method seems very convincing and promising, from a scientific point of view, we cannot be comfortable with Drake (2017a), who merely publishes anecdotal descriptions of case studies on the effectiveness of his method. At the very least, we would expect him to articulate precise assumptions about the expected results and to propose research methods by which they can be tested. In a book chapter (Drake, 2017b, p. 302 f.), he briefly mentions the low amount of research on narrative methods in all fields and calls for more research himself. Drake mentions scientific theories and findings (from Sigmund Freud to neuroscientific research) as his background. However, he mentions them rather loosely and does not go into detail how they can explain the observed effects, e.g., in the case of Wayne. As the only study in the coaching field, he refers to a study on team coaching of young athletes for career development using narrative methods ($N = 31$) with a randomized control group ($N = 46$) (Stelter et al., 2011). However, the effectiveness of the method is only measured here with a brief questionnaire on general social recovery, which bears little relation to the specific individual changes described by Drake. The effects on the team assessed here by the team members after the coaching are significant and moderately strong directly after the coaching; however, they are later small.

6.4.1.2 Philosophically Oriented Narrative Coaching

A variant of more philosophically informed narrative coaching has been presented by Stelter (2013) and in a publication together with Drake (Drake & Stelter, 2014). Stelter (2014) refers in particular to the existential philosopher Kierkegaard and emphasizes that people should try to find themselves, constantly driven by self-reflection, by distancing themselves from themselves and returning to themselves. This process can be seen as a constant search and (re)construction of meaning.

According to Stelter (2018), this search for meaning in coaching can take place in a very freely structured conversation by asking questions about the meaning of words that are important to individual clients (e.g., "What does 'freedom' mean to me?"). Stelter draws on the psychiatrist Victor E. Frankl, who places finding and fulfilling meaning and the will to meaning as the basic human striving and central focus of his logotherapy (Frankl, 1970). Since the human being is not fixed in his development but can always change, he seeks answers to questions about the meaning of his own being. However, these answers are always seen as provisional.

In his scientific approach, Stelter is based on social constructivism and prefers qualitative methods of phenomenology. However, he does not completely reject questionnaire methods in research, as the team coaching study mentioned above shows. Stelter (2022) expects his narrative coaching to have very profound effects.

According to Stelter (2022, p. 555), today, there is a generally socially enforced "individual self-discipline." This discipline, in turn, can lead to depression, self-doubt, burnout, and stress. On the other hand, according to Stelter (2022, p.562), meaning making is "the central perspective" of the coaching dialog and a powerful "source of life fulfillment and self-discovery." By making meaning in narrative coaching, self-discipline can be overcome, thus reducing depression, self-doubt, burnout, and stress.

Stelter's postulations are very far-reaching; however, they are not supported by empirical research and can hardly be reconciled with findings on the development of and interventions for depression, burnout, and stress. Depression is by no means caused primarily by crisis. Even if it in some cases may be partly associated with crises of meaning, it would not be advisable to use coaching for therapy. The diagnosis and treatment of depression require specially trained, qualified medical or psychological psychotherapists (Hautzinger, 2006). The conditions and factors that induce stress are well researched and can be addressed in stress management coaching (Greif & Palmer, 2022). The most common pressures or stressors are strong pressure to perform, work interruptions, and too fast a work pace. How could they be managed through meaning-making? As explained below, it is usually more effective to try to reduce the stressors or activate resources for stress management. (see *Sect. 6.6: Stress Management Coaching and Burnout Prevention*). In coaching, the analysis and development of interventions, which might improve stressful situations and resources as a priority and additionally strengthen coping skills and use relaxation techniques before, during, and after stressful situations, are recommended (Greif & Palmer, 2022). According to the current findings, burnout results from permanent excessive demands due to stress. Therefore, when burnout prevention with coaching, a similar combination of interventions is also recommended (Greif & Bertino, 2022). If burnout leads to depressive episodes, therapy by accredited psychotherapists is necessary. Coaches should therefore only apply coaching as a preventive measure at the beginning of burnout development or in the case of mild forms.

6.4.1.3 Result-Oriented Narrative Coaching

After my own experience and observations with the promotion of self-reflection on important life stories and questions of the meaning of the clients, I can confirm that through the joint analysis of the terms and sentences of important stories of their meaning with a distanced meta-reflection, intensive reflection and rethinking with new insights can be triggered. However, generally, the insights emerge surprisingly quickly in the process. Therefore, in my opinion, Drake's phase model reproduced above does not fit the spontaneous reflections expressed by clients and their lightning-like "Aha! experiences." This process usually takes place within one session.

Once clients have gained new insight into the meaning and significance of their story and self-concept, I suggest that they "retell" this story to me in coaching. Then, they are asked to tell it to a friend. In the next coaching session, we then reflect together on how the person has responded first and what this has done to them. As noted at the outset (see *Sect. 2.5.2*: *Coaching to Promote Result-Oriented Problem and Self-Reflections)*, when promoting self-reflections in coaching, it is important to promote "result-oriented" reflections. "Results" here are predominantly new insights and no fruitless circling rumination but clear new discoveries. The task of "retelling" the story in the coaching session and repeating this with a friend enables changes experienced as outcomes in communicating their new self-perception and role identity in the clients' communications with their significant social contacts, as described in the symbolic–interactionist communication model by Scholl, Lackner, and Grieger (2022).

The question I finally ask in narrative coaching, what the new narrative has done to the client, can in a way be seen as an open qualitative interview question about the possible effects of the method. Clients indicate that the new reframing and "retelling" has moved them emotionally and that they have gained very important and memorable new insights about themselves and that their self-perceptions have changed.

6.4.1.4 Research Impulses

The narrative method is powerful according to my practical observations, in a similar way as Drake expresses it. However, it can no longer rely solely on case example experiences for too long. This also applies to result-oriented narrative coaching. At some points, systematic effectiveness studies are urgently needed, or at least a discussion and planning of suitable research methods and effectiveness studies.

Narrative coaching can promote positive increases in the awareness of individual strengths, making meaning and developing self-concepts. However, I would realistically expect changes in behavior to follow immediately only if clients communicate their retelling to their social environment and if, as a result, their social role changes recognizably for them and for their social environment.

Following Festinger's (1978) classic *theory of cognitive dissonance*, people strive for inner harmony and reduce dissonance between their cognitions (especially principles), feelings, and actions in a subjective way. However, as this theory describes, there are multiple ways in which we can still justify and maintain behavior that contradicts one's principles. Against this background, the high demand of a fundamental construction of meaning is not a process that could be completed in one to three coaching sessions with congruent action or even lead directly to the reduction of stress, burnout, or depression. However, it would already be important if we could prove that narrative coaching provides new insights and impulses that help clients to repeatedly balance their inner harmony, to better clarify their questions of meaning from their point of view, and to expand their self-concept through result-oriented self-reflections of their experienced stories in their lives.

As an impulse for research on the facilitation of self-concept development and meaning-making through narrative coaching, qualitative analyses are suggested first as research methods. Interesting insights could be gained from the transcriptions of narratives from coaching conversations and subsequent open-ended interview questions. As a simple initial approach, clients and their caregivers could be asked directly about perceived changes in their biographical narratives, or structure-laying techniques could be used to reconstruct clients' subjective theories (Greif, 2023, in prep.). To assess changes in positive and negative affect, the well-established *PANAS* (Breyer & Bluemke, 2016) is suitable. A simple instrument focused on the assessment of meaning would be the *Meaning in Life Questionnaire* (Steger et al., 2006). It contains five short questions each about two factors: (1) search for meaning and (2) clarity about the meaning of one's life (optimal would be to ask before and after coaching). Examples include "I understand the meaning of my life" and "My life has no clear meaning or purpose" (7-point response scales from "absolutely true" to "absolutely false").

6.4.2 Development of a Vision

In the present context, the term "vision" refers to imagined conceptions of a desirable future. In the organizational context, the term refers to shared ideas about the future development of the organization. The formulation of a vision of the future often starts with rather sketchy ideas and keywords about long-term objectives and desired future capabilities. Only later do these become precise goals and defining elements, as well as plans for how they are to be achieved. In individual coaching, the focus is usually on what the clients want for themselves personally as an ideal future. The elaborated vision can then be used as a basis for reflection and clarification of the client's goals, in the case of job-related visions, after a comparison of the client's own vision with the vision of the organization. It is important to clarify the personal vision in the case of important decisions in life (career choice, job loss, separation, transition to retirement).

Passarelli's (2015) account of vision development in coaching draws on Boyatzis and Akrivou's (2006) model described in Sect. 2.5.6, according to which the ideal self-concept is the basis for clarifying a person's individual vision of his or her desired personal future. These visions of the future are based not only on their dreams, aspirations, and fantasies about the future as well as their values and outlook on life but also on their assessments of what seems achievable and feasible, as well as the important characteristics and skills that the person ascribes to themselves as strengths as a special feature, ideal self-concept, or "identity."

Megginson and Clutterbuck (2008, p. 45 f.) compiled the following list of questions that can be used in coaching when developing an individual vision:

Visualization questions:

- "Where do you want to be (in what place)?
- Describe what you see - the surroundings, the people. What do they look like?
- What are you preoccupied with?
- Describe how you feel when you are well.
- Describe how the people around you are doing.
- Describe what you hear."

Evaluation questions

- "How is this different from the current state?
- How far is it from how you see yourself?
- What is the distance from how you feel?
- How do you feel about this distance?"

Questions for the implementation of the vision

- "What can you do to make the vision a reality?
- What is your first step?"

It is important to encourage clients to imagine their future as vividly as possible. The last two questions can lead to goal clarification and planning for change.

Passarelli (2015, p. 2 f.) calls the ability to create and communicate a compelling vision for the organization to employees the cornerstone of transformational leadership. A coach supports clients in refining their vision for themselves. "Who do I want to be?" "What values do I want to promote?" Passarelli concludes (p. 10): "In summary, vision-based coaching holds that a clear and comprehensive personal vision mobilizes developmental resources through activation of a positive psychophysiological state that optimizes affective, cognitive, and neurobiological functioning for development. These resources fuel ongoing developmental efforts that endure the test of time, benefiting both the leaders being coached and their organizations."

In the practitioner literature on vision work in coaching, little attention is given to the fact that, according to research by Oettingen (2014), merely wallowing in future fantasies can, however, lead to the rapid abandonment of the pursuit of the goals derived from them if unexpected internal or external obstacles arise. In coaching, it is therefore necessary, as Passarelli also mentions, to prepare clients for possible obstacles and how to overcome them (for methods, see Greif, 2025, in prep.).

6.4.3 Value Analysis and Reflection

The analysis and reflection of the client's values can serve as a background for a deeper reflection on the development of the vision and clarification of the goals and criteria that have been derived accordingly. A variant is the clarification of the clients' own values in comparison to the perceived values of the company, especially if the clients have conflicts with the values practiced in their company or if they have ethical concerns.

6.4.3.1 Value Lists

A simple method in coaching is to ask clients what values are important to them in their lives. The values mentioned by the clients are recorded and explained with keywords. The list then provides background knowledge for the further course of the coaching.

A somewhat more systematic method, but basically the same, is the "hierarchy of values" by Middendorf (2004, the following citations are free translations). The purpose is to "reflect on behavioral patterns and decision-making processes." Especially in the case of questions about professional development or other future developments, the method is intended to serve to better understand "oneself and one's own motives" and to make "more conscious decisions" through this self-knowledge. The method is slightly simplified in four steps:

1. The clients are given an explanation of what is meant by "values" ("values are behind the things that are important to us." op. cit., p. 175) and examples from different areas of life ("nice colleagues, secure job, exciting work …" etc.).
2. The clients are asked to enter ten values in loose succession in a list and then compare them in pairs according to their importance ("What is more important to me? Value 1 or value 2?"). This creates a ranking or hierarchy depending on importance. This ranking should be reflected on together, including which values were not mentioned.
3. The clients compare their values with the central values of fathers and mothers.
4. The clients are requested to compare the values with the company's hierarchy of values.

During these comparisons, differences and similarities or contradictions are reflected.

If it is only a question of asking the values that come to the client's mind at the moment of coaching and forming a ranking order, it is easier to write them down on small colored cards or online, for example, on the whiteboard on which the values mentioned by the client are noted with keywords. On the table or online on the whiteboard, they can be quickly put in order.

Figure 6.3 shows an example of a comparison of one of my client's values with what he perceived to be the prevailing values in the company. In the example, almost all of them conflict with their values. He therefore wanted to quit as soon as he finds a company that suits him better. He was therefore looking for a company that is more in line with his values. As a coach, I can additionally recommend a strength evaluation (see below) and encourage him to continue actively searching for current job offers on the net and to consult a headhunter. In this often lengthy search process with ups and downs, coaching is a suitable psychological accompaniment of career coaching.

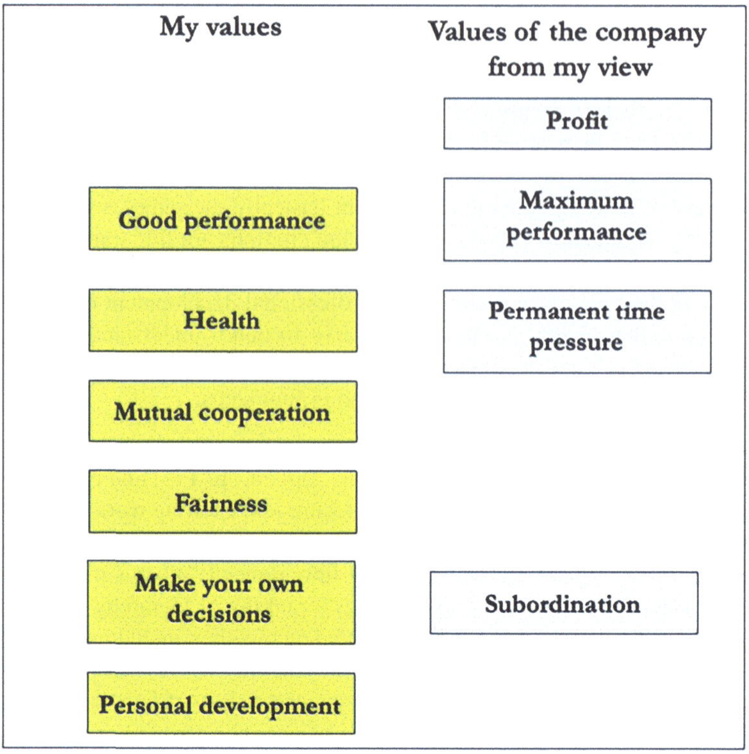

Fig. 6.3 Example of the client's values and the perceived company values

6.4.3.2 Schwartz's Theory of Values and Its Use in Coaching

Notably, the results of the large field of intercultural values research were not considered in the coaching field, although numerous studies have been conducted for decades to determine which values are important for people and what significance they have for motivating and justifying decisions. Boehnke und Hanke (2022) are an exception. In their contribution to values and their importance in coaching, they refer to Schwartz (1994) for definitions of values and human behavior. In summary, values can be understood as "abstract guiding principles, that have an influence on behavior and experience" (op. cit., p. 960). They can be ordered according to their relative importance and are normally "situation-transcending" (not only referring to an individual situation).

Schwartz's value theory is particularly well supported by research. According to P. Schmidt et al. (2007), more than 200 studies have been conducted worldwide. In his introductory overview, Schwartz (2007) distinguishes ten universal values. They apply to all cultures of our world but have different meanings in each culture. The Schwartz Value Survey (SVS) is an established standard questionnaire used to assess ten values (Lindeman, 2005). The importance of the values is assessed on a 5-point scales.

The following descriptions are based on formulations by Schwartz (2007, p. 1 ff.) with additions by Schmidt et al. (2007):

1. *Self-Direction:* Autonomous and independent thought and action; choosing, creating, exploring (creativity, freedom, independent, curious, choosing one's own goals).
2. *Stimulation:* Excitement, novelty, and challenge in life (daring, life full of variety or excitement).
3. *Hedonism* (pleasure principle): Pleasure and sensuous gratification for oneself. (enjoying life).
4. *Achievement:* Personal success through demonstrating competence according to social standards (successful, capable, ambitious).
5. *Influence and power:* Social status and prestige, control or dominance over people and resources (social power, authority, wealth, public image).
6. *Security:* Safety, harmony, and stability of society, of relationships, and of self (family security, national security, social order, not owing anyone anything).
7. *Conformity:* Restraint of actions, inclinations, and impulses likely to upset or harm others and violate social expectations or norms (politeness, obedience, self-discipline, deferential to parents and elders).
8. *Tradition:* Respect, commitment, and acceptance of the customs and ideas that traditional culture or religion provide the self (piety, accepting one's position in life, humility, respect for tradition, moderation).
9. *Benevolence*: Preserving and enhancing the welfare of those with whom one is in frequent personal contact (the "in-group," helpful, honest, forgiving, faithful, responsible).
10. *Universalism:* Understanding, appreciation, tolerance, and protection for the welfare of all people and for nature, considering universal consequences (tolerance, wisdom, social justice, equality, a world at peace, a world full of beauty, unity with nature, environmental protection).

It is possible to apply the "Schwartz Value Survey" (SVS) in coaching. It is an established standard questionnaire used to assess ten values (Lindeman, 2005). The importance of the values is assessed on a 5-point scale according to their importance. As an alternative, in the coaching conversation, the above list of values could be presented to the clients. To ensure that spontaneous nominations of their own values are not influenced, it is advisable to use questionnaires or lists only after an oral interview and the naming of personal values. The questionnaire can then be used with the question of whether there are any values among them that they would like to include and rank additionally in their individual list. This supplementary request can prevent clients from not remembering important values at the moment. For example, religious values are often not mentioned spontaneously. Gaining influence and power is an important personal value that is sometimes not mentioned openly because it seems socially undesirable. In particular, in the case of managers, questions to reflect on this should not be avoided. Interestingly, using the questionnaire allows comparisons of the clients' ratings with the results of numerous international studies. As already summarized by Schwartz (2007), studies show that there are typical differences between various subgroups according to age, gender, and education.

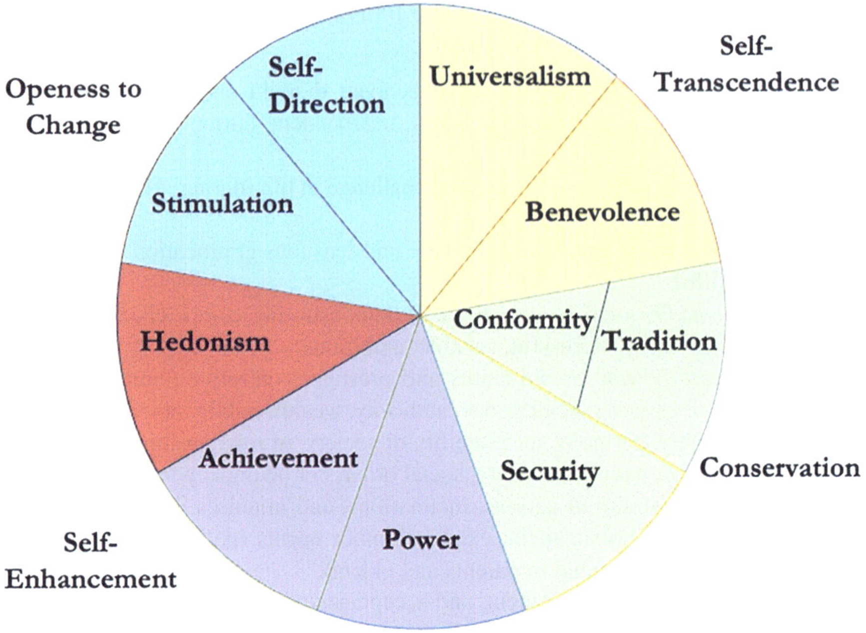

Fig. 6.4 Schwartz value model (2007, p. 3, simplified)

A core assumption of Schwartz's value theory refers to the correlations between the ten values. They can be arranged in a circular model according to the level of their correlations. Those adjacent to each other, according to studies, are perceived to be more similar and closely related, and those opposite are antipodes and are weakly or negatively correlated. Figure 6.4 shows this structure and the more closely related groups. Steinmetz et al. (2012) checked to what extent this assumed circular structure can be confirmed in existing studies. To do so, they subjected 318 correlation matrices from 88 studies and the European Social Survey (total N = 251,239) to meta-analyses with eight cross-cultural clusters. The circular model was not confirmed in all the culturally diverse country clusters. However, three of the country clusters formed in this process—one of them with studies from Northern European countries—yielded values with good fit to the data and good concordance with the theoretically expected circular structure. However, here, as a marginal deviation, self-determination should be localized between hedonism and stimulation.

6.4.4 *Analysis and Reflection of the Strengths of the Clients*

According to my observations, the analysis and reflection of clients' strengths play an increasing role in coaching practices. A Google search on "strength coaching" (3/11/2022) returned approximately 289 million entries. Providers advertise tools and coaching to help discover and promote (hidden or underutilized) "competencies," "talents," "potentials," or even "character strengths" as a basis for success in work and life. "Strengthening strengths" is a slogan that is mentioned quite often.

The methods are usually based on numerous strengths, which are arranged on lists or picture cards and explained briefly in each case. When selecting a method, it is advisable to check whether the strengths listed are based on scientific theories and research. *Section 5.3.1* mentioned tools that draw on *positive psychology*. Strengths analyses lend themselves to decisions about college and career choices, especially as a start in career coaching (Ebner & Kauffeld, 2019). Furthermore, from the perspective of coaches who are oriented toward positive psychology (see *Sect. 5.3.1:* Positive Psychological Coaching), "strength coaching" is a method that can be used almost universally for many objectives and changes. A very important field is coaching after job changes or layoffs resulting from AI systems take over existing human work (see *Sect. 10.2*).

6.4.4.1 Popular Strength Lists

It is reasonable to use questionnaires in coaching that refer to comprehensive lists of important strengths. For the individual questions, the strengths are described briefly in each case and are rated with scales according to their importance to the respondents. In the following, three well-known questionnaires are presented and briefly discussed.

StrengthFinder

The online test StrengthFinder (Rath, 2014) is very well known (renamed CliftonStrengths[4]). It contains a collection of 34 talents, which were generated according to Gallup studies. The studies asked about "talents" that "can be applied to a variety of occupations and functions" (op. cit. p. 26, free translation).

Rath (2014) uses a simple formula as the basis for his definition of a "strength" (op. cit. p. 31):

$$Talent \times Effort = Strength$$

By "talent," he means "a natural way of thinking, feeling, or behaving." By "effort," he refers to "time spent practicing, developing their skills, and building their knowledge base." "Strength" is the "ability to continuously perform at a near-perfect level." However, the assumption in the definition of strengths that one can continuously produce near-perfect performance regardless of the conditions in the context is extremely questionable. The formula assumes that talent with zero effort produces no strength. A great strength, on the other hand, can lead to success with

[4] https://www.gallup.com/cliftonstrengths/en/253850/cliftonstrengths-for-individuals.aspx?utm_source=google&utm_medium=cpc&utm_campaign=germany_cs_ecom_de&utm_term=cliftonstrengths&gclid=CjwKCAjwzY2bBhB6EiwAPpUpZrbKTZrI9BtqP_FbvU2oZoNTaRGFHYzge4Ll8CX2PrPUJUobNNNVOhoCgAIQAvD_BwE (last retrieved 3/11/2022).

little effort, just as a low talent with a great deal of effort can also lead to positive results. These relationships are understandable but very simplistic and therefore open to criticism by scientific evidence. If StrengthFinder is popular despite these inherently easy-to-see criticisms, this may be because it includes well-chosen and vividly formulated strengths that many can identify with. Its characteristics are described in four groups: executing, influencing, relationship building, and strategic thinking, as shown in the following overview (Rath, 2014, p. 202, free translations):

Executing	**Influencing**
"Individuals with strengths in executing have the ability to capture and bring an idea to realization."	"Individuals with strengths in this area take responsibility, speak up, and make sure their voice and/or that of their group is heard."
Examples: Arranger—Carefulness—Discipline - Achievement orientation - Responsibility—Persuasion	*Examples:* Authority—Best performance - Communication Skills—Sociability - Awareness—Action
Relationship Building	**Strategic Thinking**
"Individuals with strengths have a unique ability to create solid relationships. They establish groups and organizations that are far greater than the sum of their individual members."	"People with strengths in this area continually sharpen our sights for the future. They continuously gather and analyze information so that targeted decisions can be made."
Examples: Adaptability - Bonding skills - Empathy—Striving for harmony - Positive Attitudes—Connectedness	*Examples:* Analytical Thinking - Collector of Ideas - Intellect—Strategy—Imagination—Intellectual Curiosity—Future Orientation

6.4.4.2 Realize2/Strengths Profile

The *Realize2* questionnaire, now called the *Strengths Profile,* is an instrument whose statistical test quality criteria have been verified (Linley & Dovey, 2012). It focuses on "performance strength." As MacKie (2014, p. 121 f.) says, it allows "a broader view" because it includes questions about both utilized and currently unutilized strengths.

Linley und Dovey (2012) published manual and statistical parameters. The parameters were collected over several years, and their descriptions were revised repeatedly. After the statistical analyses, 60 strengths remained in the end version. They were grouped into five "strength families" according to their similarities:

1. *Strengths of being* (14 attributes, authenticity, centered, courage, curiosity, gratitude, humility, legacy, mission, moral compass, personal responsibility, pride, self-awareness, service, and unconditionality)
2. *Strengths of communication* (8 attributes: counterpoint, explainer, feedback, humor, listener, narrator, scribe, and spotlight)
3. *Strengths of motivation* (13 attributes: action, adventure, bounceback, catalyst, change agent, competitive, drive, efficacy, growth, improver, persistence, resilience, and work ethic)
4. *Strengths of relationships* (11 attributes: compassion, connector, emotional awareness, empathic connection, enabler, equality, esteem builder, personalization, persuasion, rapport builder, and relationship deepener)

5. *Strengths of thinking* (14 attributes: adherence, creativity, detail, incubator, innovation, judgment, optimism, order planful, prevention, reconfiguration, resolver, strategic awareness, and time optimizer)

There are brief descriptions of all the individual strengths, as follows (p. 120):

"*Adventure:* adventurous people like to take risks and move outside their comfort zone."
"*Authenticity:* people who are strong in their authenticity are always true to themselves, even when pressured by others."
"*Bounceback*: people who are strong in bounceback use setbacks as steppingstones to keep going and achieve even more."

The respondents provided their answers by using 7-point rating scales. For each attribute, respondents are asked to rate three independent dimensions of *energy* ("how energizing they found something"), *performance* ("how good they were at doing something"), and *use* ("how often they were able to do something").

The reliabilities of the strength scales determined in a study are satisfactory to high (with a single somewhat weaker value). They mostly correlate only slightly with each other and are therefore suitable for recording the various strengths independently of each other. Plausible correlations are found with other questionnaire scales. The Realize2/Strengths Profile is therefore suitable for use in coaching.

Linley et al. (2009, p 39 f.) understand "strengths" as the existing abilities of a person to act, think, or feel in an authentic way that enables optimal functioning or developments and achievements. Accordingly, they can also be classified as "individual resources" and make people aware of and use their strengths as "resource activation" (see below resource activation in *Sects. 6.6 and 9.3*). They assume that recognizing one's strengths is the "smallest thing" we can do to make the greatest differences. They use case studies to describe how leadership coaching with Realize2 can reflect on strengths and "make weaknesses irrelevant."

Quinlan et al. (2012) published a review of eight studies on well-being improvement in which participants clarified their strengths with various questionnaires and made choices about which ones they wanted to improve in the near future (using the Realize2). However, the statistical effect strengths were only small to moderate. One might expect that using the tool in coaching and reflecting more intensively during the process would produce stronger effects. As explained in stress management coaching (see *Sect. 6.6*), the effectiveness can be increased considerably if not only the individual but also social resources are made use of (e.g., support by other persons) or existing knowledge and resources provided by favorable working conditions (e.g., expansion of the decision latitude at work).

6.4.4.3 Values in the Action Inventory of Strengths

Another well-known instrument is the *Values in Action Inventory of Strengths* (VIA-IS) questionnaire. It is based on Seligman *(see positive psychology coaching* above). It contains a list of 22 "character strengths" (Peterson et al., 2010). However, the assessments of several strengths are highly correlated with each other, as shown by exploratory analyses of the correlations between strengths in a very large international sample of 447,573 participants (Ng et al., 2017). According to this study, the respondents rate these values similarly despite the different names. Only five statistically independent subgroups of strengths are separable: justice, temperance, coercion, transcendence, and humanity. In addition, many of the strengths correlate with a general factor that the researchers call disposition to positivity, seeing everything positively. Therefore, Realize2 would be preferable as an instrument to capture many different strengths that can be distinguished by the clients.

Every coach can think up and list strengths as he or she sees fit, either at his or her personal desk or together with others. Such lists of strengths, created by coaches themselves, are therefore increasing at an inflationary rate. However, how these lists of strengths are understood by clients, whether they are distinguished as their authors believe, and whether their use by clients yields the intended results can be determined only by careful research. Ng et al. (2017) show the importance of statistical analyses of strength lists to ensure that the values can be distinguished by respondents.

6.4.4.4 Strengths Cards

It is certainly more stimulating when the strengths are not presented as a list or in a questionnaire but instead are presented on picture cards with beautiful and original images. The number of published card sets is also increasing. In the following, only a few well-known card sets are described and commented upon.

Boniwell Strength Cards

The well-known positive psychologist Ilona Boniwell (2015) recommends 50 "strength cards" published by her and applied as an interactive method. The picture cards show headings to designate the respective strengths, such as "Motivation," "Creativity," "Action," "Leadership," "Communication," and "Harmony," as well as short descriptions on the backs of the cards. The respondents are asked to select five strengths that fit them or that they want to use in the future. (The cards can be used in individual coaching for individual strengths or with teams to clarify team strengths.)

The cards have a postcard format. On the front, next to the name of the strength, it is a photo or drawing that stimulates imagination and relates to the subject. For some, the references are immediately clear, as with a photo of two young men arm wrestling to the headline "Competition." Others require some imagination; for example, the strength "Critique" features a pencil standing on its end with a light bulb mounted on it.

To explain what is to be done with the cards, there are four fields on the back of each strength card. For the strength "Critique," the following explanations are given:

Does that sound like you?	**Description**
1. "You are always able to look at the situation in an unusual way. 2. It is very easy for you to criticize at least some aspects of a person's position, even if you quite like it overall. 3. You have heard this a few times: "Why do you always have to question everything? Can't you just accept the argument?"	"If this sounds like you, your strength may be the strength of **Critique**. This means you love to bring an alternative perspective to any situation. You seem to see things differently from others, and can present a range of options, possibilities and alternatives for any scenario. As a result, you will often bring up arguments that other people have missed."
Activate	**Stretch**
1. "When reading an article in a magazine or newspaper, try to find some points with which you disagree. 2. Can you think of someone you admire, who is excellent in constructive critique?"	1. "What do you think of the following: "The strength of criticism lies in the weakness of the thing criticized." 2. How can you make sure that your critique actually benefits the recipient rather than simply activating their defensiveness?"

The 50 strengths are as follows according to Boniwell (alphabetical):

Action	Hardwork	Recognition
Adaptability	Harmony	Resilience
Adventure	Humility	Responsibility
Authenticity	Humor	Self-awareness
Beauty and Excellence	Improvement	Self-control
Communication	Kindness	Self-discipline
Competition	Leadership	Social-connection
Courage	Learning	Social intelligence
Creativity	Listening	Solution
Critique	Love	Spirituality
Curiosity	Motivation	Strategy
Detail	Open mindedness	Teamwork
Empathy	Optimism	Time optimization
Equality	Personalization	Vitality
Explaining	Persuasion	Wisdom
Forgiveness	Planning	Woo
Gratitude	Prudence	

Boniwell (2015) cites the general strengths definition by Linley et al. mentioned above on the importance of clarifying strengths. However, in my literature searches, I could not find publications with research on her card set. She does not explain exactly why and how she selected the strengths and why she defined each one this way and not differently. At first glance, the list is stimulating and comprehensive but in need of completion compared with Realize2. For example, patience, charity, self-reflection, persistence, piety, and constitutionally robust physical or mental health are missing (Boniwell's definition of resilience does not include this), as are a wide variety of very specialized knowledge or job-related skills and competencies. A current example of additional strength in career coaching would be relevant knowledge and experience with the digital systems and computer programs or AI used in the future desired field of work.

6.4.4.5 Exercises of Positive Psychology with the Cards

The strengths cards can be applied for visual imagination in structured positive psychology exercises (also in groups). In the first phase, the cards are used to discover and deepen one's own strengths (remembering contextual situations, favorite strengths, success of strengths, imagining, and deepening experiences). The second phase reflects how to transfer and use strengths to make life easier (prioritize, which ones do I want to use more in the future, tasks to activate these strengths, step-by-step plans, sharing experiences).

Strengths cards can be embedded in Seligman's (2011) *PERMA model* of *positive psychology* to improve quality of life:

Positive emotions
Engagement
Relationship
Meaning
Achievement

There are further exercises with cards related to this model, and at the end, there are supplementary exercises for physical activity and relaxation and for healthy nutrition.

6.4.4.6 Future Research Challenges

Like questionnaire instruments, the described strength cards refer to findings and interventions of *positive psychology*, according to which they have positive effects on well-being and performance if clients reflect on their strengths, use them systematically, and expand them. The use of picture cards is intended to provide a visual, in a sense "analog" anchoring in addition to written explanations. These assumptions are plausible at first glance but need to be researched and confirmed. The abovementioned intervention studies on questionnaire methods show only small to weak effects, and these effects only improve subjective well-being. *Positive psychology* has been revealed as an integrative program that always bases the effectiveness of its methods on scientifically confirmed evidence. As long as convincing evidence is lacking, we must not sell our clients exaggerated expectations of benefits.

Clients like using strength cards. According to my practical observations in face-to-face coaching, they look at the pictures with curiosity and pleasure. This investment of time and an observable stimulation of positive self-descriptions are indications that the method activates positive result-oriented self-reflections. Such effects could certainly be scientifically verified by means of transcripts and surveys. Nevertheless, I would not expect that this alone would directly result in performance improvements or desired behavioral changes without additional support (see *Sect. 6.5.2: Behavioral Change* and especially the difficulties of *Habit Change*). With the clarification of one's values, the reflection of one's strengths is a positive self-occupation that contributes to inner harmony. Together with the activation of individual resources (in addition to the use of the client's social resources and possibilities in the environment), a motivating start can be made that supports behavior changes. These possible effects could and should also be explored by scientific research.

Psychological career counselors analyze very specific job-related interests, skills, and competencies or talents. Instruments have been developed and applied in decades of research in psychological diagnostics (Kersting & Klehe, 2018). Developers of analysis instruments for strengths and career coaches might leave the application of these methods to career counselors (Kauffeld et al., 2022), but they should know these methods, which have been reviewed by many studies, and consider recommending the application by professional experts in addition to their career coaching.

6.4.4.7 Values, Attitudes, and Behavior

In their contribution to the importance of value theories in coaching, Hanke and Boehnke (2022) take Schwartz's theory as a starting point but also refer to other theories and research. An important theme here is the relationship between values and attitudes as well as values and behavior.

Some business consultants or coaches believe that it is enough for their clients to have their values clarified because they assume that behavioral changes will follow directly as a consequence. Unfortunately, however, the correlations between values and attitudes and between attitudes and behavior are rather weak. For example, we all know people to whom the (universalistic) values of protecting the environment are important but who by no means behave consistently in an environmentally responsible manner in their everyday lives. Therefore, as everyday observations and research findings show (Cooke & Sheeran, 2004; Glasman & Albarracín, 2006), the relationships among values, attitudes, and behavior are generally rather weak. This is also because values are by no means constant but vary in their importance (today one way, tomorrow a bit different, etc.) and because values are often formulated in a general and not very specific sense (this allows for different interpretations). If the values are formulated in a stable and specific sense ("it is important to reduce my personal C02 footprint in this year"), closer correlations can be expected with a corresponding behavior (e.g., by buying an electric car, avoiding flights, a solar system on the roof, etc.). However, whether an individual consistently implements value-compliant behavior also depends on a supportive social context. If life partners or colleagues do not join but are against it, consistent implementation is difficult. Coaches should be aware of such difficulties and help their clients assess and manage them in a realistic way.

6.4.5 *Mindful Self-Acceptance and Analysis of the Own Values*

In his psychoeducative self-help book "Get Out of Your Mind and Into Your Life," Stephen C. Hayes (2005) explains and describes a number of challenging reflections and exercises of the new *acceptance and commitment therapy (*ACT), which can also be used in coaching (in *Sect. 5.3.3: Evidence-Based Coaching* approaches, you find an introduction to ACT). The book provides an introduction to the theoretical foundations and central assumptions of ACT and the individual exercises. It can therefore probably be regarded as one of the most systematic and broadest psychoeducational introductions to psychotherapeutic exercises, which can also be used in coaching.

In most exercises, Hayes asks the reader to think about typical thoughts and painful feelings. He asks to make notes, accept painful thoughts, and carry out evaluations or experiments with alternative thoughts and possibilities. The book begins with exercises on human suffering and the role of language here and the trouble resulting from negative thoughts. The next chapters focus on mindfulness and willingness. The last part analyzes human values and how we can commit to and live our values. The following description summarizes some of the exercises.

6.4.5.1 Deepen Mindfulness in Your Life

Hayes (2005, p. 105 ff.) explains the relevance of mindfulness and describes a series of standard exercises through which mindfulness practices should be implemented in daily life. They are asking to pay attention to many different types of experiences. Three principles should be observed during these exercises:

1. *Necessary time:* As a first step, Hayes recommends practicing some form of mindfulness exercise every day and setting a realistic time limit to the practice (as a start between 15 and 30 min at a time).
2. *Relaxation and distraction:* The focus of the exercise is not relaxation, as some people expect. You may be relaxed but also tense. "The point is to be aware of whatever is going on for you without avoidance or fusion."
3. *Feeling too bad to practice?* Hayes noted that a bad feeling should never hinder you from starting exercising. It is normal and an important experience. "Mindfulness is about getting in touch with your own experience moment to moment in a defused and accepting way." Hayes asks to "be gentle and nonjudgmental (even with your judgments!)."

Hayes explains each exercise and gives written instructions that shall be repeated before starting the exercise (in the beginning, e.g., by a record on an audio cassette tape). The following descriptions are short summaries of keywords. The first instruction will be described in more detail to provide an impression. The following are similarly detailed but are only briefly summarized here.

Be Where You Are.

Sit on a chair or lay down on the floor or bed—find a comfortable position—close your eyes—take a few breaths.

Bring your awareness to the tips of your fingers—rub the fingertips—notice the feeling—rest your fingers—feel what they are touching.

Think now of your whole body—where are you sitting or lying—feel the back side of your body—touch the chair or bed—be mindful of the way your body is positioned.

Think about the room you are in—your position in the room—where is the door—what about the ceiling—feel your body in the context of this space—open your eyes and take a look around the room.

Silent Walking

Walking meditations—walk 10 min (or longer) silently—"listen" to the content of your mind—attention drawn to particular objects, thoughts, or feelings.

Cubby Holing

Observe the psychological content as it comes up—to which of the following categories do they belong: emotion, thought, bodily sensation, or evaluation?

Eating Raisins

Discover how it feels to explore the attributes of raisins slowly and mindfully in the mouth.

Drinking and Eating Mindfully

Start with preparing and drinking a cup of tea slowly and mindfully—take time and mindfully attend to an eating experience.

Listening to Classical Music

Focus your attention on specific aspects of complex sets of stimuli repeatedly, e.g., classical music.

Be Mindful of Your Feet While You Read This

Focus your attention on your feet while reading.

Just Sitting

Simply sitting quietly in a position that you maintain—watch what comes up for you in an accepting way.

Hayes encourages the reader to experiment with these exercises and see what works individually. He refers to the meditation called Zazen of Zen Buddhism, which is often called "just sitting" (Hayes, 2005, p. 115 f.) and explains that there is no mystical but that "just" does not mean that nothing much happens. You cannot stop breathing or thinking or residing in some peaceful place. Meditation exercises teach how to watch thoughts and feelings, even painful feelings, "how they come in and go out." This is the essence of the principle of mindful acceptance of the ACT approach.

6.4.5.2 Live Your Values in Your Life

The last practical part of the self-help book of Hayes (2005, 153 ff.) is about reflecting on our own values and how we can live them. The chapters begin with an introduction to the meaning of values and how they can influence our life. For life, he uses the illustrative metaphor of a bus that we drive with many different passengers. The passengers whom we have picked up are our "memories, bodily sensations, conditioned emotions, programmed thoughts, historically produced urges." Some of them we like, some of them we do not like. Some of them refuse to leave our bus. We like some of them and would love to have them around. Others we do not like. Some are so unpleasant (severe anxieties, difficult urges, or painful feelings of sadness) that we would like to make them leave the bus. However, they stubbornly refuse.

Imagine that you have been driving a bus called "your life," with the sign on the front of your bus saying "Values." Like any bus, as you move along, you have picked up passengers. In this case, your passengers are your memories, bodily sensations, conditioned emotions, programmed thoughts, historically produced urges, and so on. You have picked up some passengers you like: these are like sweet little old ladies who you hope will sit up in the front, near you. You have picked up some you do not like: these are like tough, frightening gang members whom you would just as soon have taken another bus. Instead of fruitless attempts to get rid of or avoid these passengers by placing them further back on the bus, Hayes recommends learning to accept them as a given with the mindfulness exercises described above.

"Values are chosen life directions" (Hayes, 2005, p. 154 f.). In the metaphoric bus, we have a compass and must choose a direction to follow, e.g., "I think I'll go east." "Since the road is not perfectly due east, we choose the best possible road, and the compass is our instrument to check whether we are driving in the planned direction. At the end of the road, we again have to decide between a couple of alternative routes. "In this same way, values are intentional qualities that join together a string of moments into a meaningful path. They are what moments are about, but they are never possessed as objects because they are qualities of unfolding actions, not of particular things. Said another way, values are verbs and adverbs, not nouns or adjectives; they are something you do or a quality of something you do, not something you have. If they are something you do (or a quality of something you do), they never end. You are never finished. For example, say one of your values is to be a loving person. This doesn't mean that as soon as you love someone for a few months you are doing, as you can be doing with building a house or doing with earning a college degree. There is more loving to do—always. Love is a direction, not an object." Similarly, values are not goals or outcomes (p. 158 ff.). However, values, especially "ultimate values are perfect for the individual valuing them" (p. 158 ff.), and can make our "life rich and meaningful, even in the face of great adversity" (p. 165 ff.).

Hayes (2005, p. 167 ff.) recommends the following exercises to explore and reflect on our own values. They are very complex. The following list is only a short summary that provides an impression of their content and structure.

Imagine What a Friend Will Say at Our Own Federal

- Close your eyes and take a few deep breaths and observe the thoughts and emotions coming up in an accepting way.
- Visualize the picture.
- What will the friend say in an eulogy about "what you stood for in your life; about what you cared about; about the path you took."
- Write down, what are you afraid, what might be said.
- If you could see inside the head of the speaker: Write down, what he or she might think privately, with no playacting.
- Imagine that all the important people in your life are present. Imagine that someone in an eulogy reflects together with all of these people about what they might see "if your life had been true to your innermost values." What would you most want to have manifested in your life? Be bold and write the eulogy and your values down word for word.

Here Lies … Inscriptions on my Headstone

- What inscriptions would you like to see on your headstone? Write short inscriptions for the following 10 valued domains.
  - Marriage/couple/intimate relationship
  - Parenting family relationships (other than intimate relationships and parenting)
  - Friendship/social relations
  - Career/employment
  - Education/training
  - Personal growth and development
  - Recreation/leisure
  - Spirituality
  - Citizenship
  - Health/physical well-being
- Create a ranking list of the domains of life where you might begin to take action.
- "How well have you been currently living this value on a scale of 1 to 10?" ("not at all" to "extremely well-manifested in my behavior").
- With 1 meaning it is not at all manifested in my behavior to 10 meaning it is extremely well-manifested in my behavior.
- Rate the importance of the value domains (1 to 10).
- Create your "life deviation score" by subtracting the ratings of the actual behavior and the importance ratings and summing the values. Highlights the ratings with the largest gabs.

Taking Bold Steps (pp. 178 ff.)

- "Goals are the guideposts by which you can mark your life's journey (…and) practical means to make your values manifest." Reflect and develop goals that will move you in a valued direction. By which specific can you achieve these goals, which internal barriers need to be overcome?

- Check the goals. Are they:
  - Practical
  - Obtainable
  - Work with the current situation
  - Lead in the direction of the stated value
  - Short- or long-term
  - Choose goals with achievable, obtainable outcomes
- Write down the necessary actions for short- and long-term goals (p. 182 ff.)
  - Define specific actions, you can truly do
  - What barriers will come up, and how can you overcome them?
- Make a firm commitment and do not give it up (p. 188 ff.)
  - Breakdown old behavior patterns!
  - Don't break or quit the commitment!
  - Staying mindful of your values using a worksheet, which reminds you!
  - Behave flexibly as long as you make progress in living your values!

As summarized in the last point of the list above, the new commitment often breaks old behavior patterns. This can be difficult. Hayes offers another worksheet focusing on how to do that. Additionally, there are inner and outer barriers, which must be overcome, and reflecting and advance planning are needed. The essential focus of the client is remaining mindful of his or her values and observing what is happening.

In the concluding chapter, Hayes (2005, p. 195 ff.) explains the new commitment as a "choice to live a vital life." In view of Hayes, typical behavioral patterns follow an *acceptance cycle*, shown in Fig. 6.5, or an *avoidance cycle*. He comes back to his metaphor of driving a bus ("My Values") with some passengers you like and others you do not like. The acceptance cycle involves four ideal phases, created by reflections that can be repeatedly conducted by the client and are expected to help him or her develop toward a "vital, values-based, flexible life."

The *avoidance circle* is about problems and a control and avoidance cycle, with reflections on life restriction and loss (loosing vitality and contact with one's values and becoming more preoccupied with problems), relief and struggle, entanglement and endless predictions, and evaluations of one's problems ("words, words, words"). The client loses contact with the present moment. Hayes assumes that such negative circular reflections result in "a narrow, struggle-based, inflexible life" (p. 197).

To take bold steps, Hayes again recommends using a worksheet and fitting 4 months of data on it, "allowing you to look at very large patterns of progress in each of the ten domains where you have done values work" (p. 191). By the reflections of the acceptance cycle, you do not become entangled in the "chatter" of your brain (but of course you may notice it) and get "out of your mind and into your life" as the book title promises. "You see that there is a distinction between you, the conscious driver of the bus, and the passengers you carry. You have room on the bus for them. You accept them. You defuse from them. However, then you turn your eyes back to the road and connect with that which you truly value. You drive in that direction. As a result, your life has grown slightly, and it has become slightly more vital

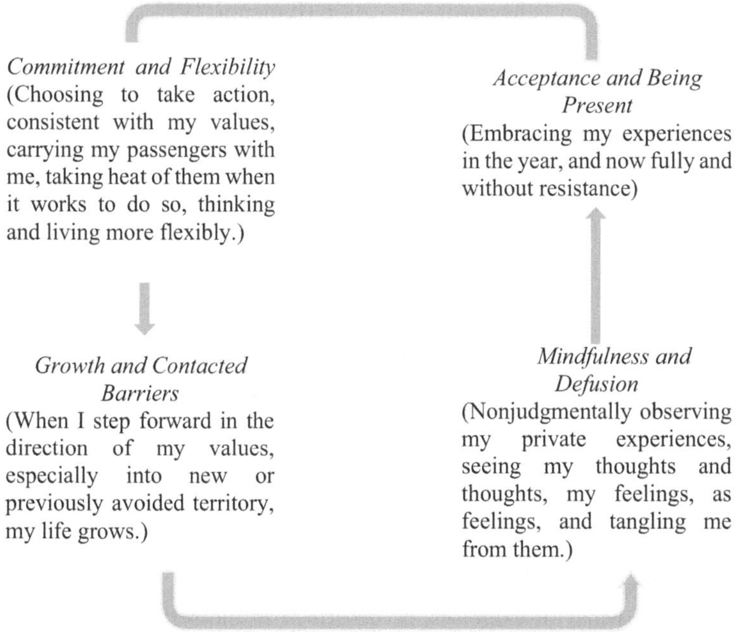

Fig. 6.5 *Acceptance cycle* (Modified figure, citations from Hayes 2005, p. 196)

and flexible. As you grow, however, you are likely to contact problems again. These problems are often not quite the same as old problems; rather, they are subtly different. They are new, and perhaps even more challenging" (Hayes, 2005, p. 197).

6.4.5.3 Scientific Evidence and Open Questions

Hayes (2005, p. 200 ff.) reports that the number of supportive controlled outcome studies has exploded. The Association for Contextual Behavioral Science lists more than 1000 randomized controlled studies on the effectiveness of methods[5] in the areas of anxiety, stress, obsessive–compulsive and OCD spectrum disorders, depression, smoking, substance abuse, stress, stigma and prejudice, chronic pain, willingness to learn new procedures, ability to learn new procedures, procedures, coping with psychosis, diabetes management, coping with cancer, coping with epilepsy, and employee burnout. However, as Hayes admits, the complete methods of his self-help book have not yet been evaluated in toto, and this might be difficult for all areas (p. 201).

Notably, as a psychological theoretical basis, ACT mainly refers to the classical learning theory of B. F. Skinner (1969) and language framing through conditioning. Even classic findings from alternative evidence-based learning theories such as

[5] https://contextualscience.org/act_randomized_controlled_trials_1986_to_present (date of last access: Jan 10th 2024).

Bandura's principles of behavior modification (Bandura, 1996; see *Sect. 6.5.1*) are not considered. The functional context is only reconstructed from behavior and context analyses in the subjective perception of the client. Newer international studies on human values; workable and empirically supported methods from psychological theories of reflection and clarification of problems and goals and their motivational psychological implications; the promotion of self-regulated learning; the improvement of result-oriented self-reflection and self-knowledge and self-development, as discussed at various points in this book; and self-concepts are neglected. Research from stress research on the decisive importance of external stressors and structures (see *Sect. 6.6*) is also not included. As a result, although the considerations and impulses are significant, they remain one-sided and too superficial at many points, for example, with regard to the difficulties of changing behavioral habits and concrete leadership-behavior (see *Sect. 6.5*) or stress and health management, where mindfulness methods only have very limited effects (see *Sect. 6.6*). I would like to see research, which compares the outcome of ACT methods to other methods in the fields mentioned.

In summary, the ACT approach is stimulating and can help individuals detach from difficult individual pains and emotions. However, the question is whether it is always appropriate to do this by mindful acceptance of the "chatter of our brain" and mental and behavior exercises, as described in the self-help book of Hayes (2002). Many sections are very stimulating to read and could help clients think and stimulate the use of worksheets. However, on the basis of my practical experience, I cannot imagine that it is realistic that a large proportion of clients will consistently carry out numerous exercises and worksheets without personal support and shared reflections and encouragement by a therapist or coach. Even then, the exercises might be far too extensive for many clients. I would encourage coaches and clients to make an individually appropriate selection of only a few of the exercises and explore them in more depth in psychoeducational discussions with clients on the basis of their experiences.

In addition, since we can find from studies on the problematic relationship between circular self-reflection or rumination and depression, it is important to ensure that clients learn and are accompanied to stop such endless negative "chatters of their mind" (see *Sect. 2.5.2*). It seems obvious that people who tend to brood or have depressive thoughts may fall into very intense, circling thoughts, which are difficult to stop without precise and careful psychological support from therapists or coaches. It could be especially problematic to stimulate clients to reflect on their own death and the associated life imbalances without therapeutic support. Why does Hayes not use the example of a speech of praise from friends on the next birthday? In the books on ACT, there are no references to side effects of this kind, and I have not found any references to such side effects in the studies cited or in a literature search with PsychInfo (a standard system for scientific literature search). A retrospective search and perhaps interviews with the conductors or participants of the existing studies would be important here. However, randomized studies in which a subgroup of clients is deliberately exposed to the risk of developing depressive episodes (even with therapeutic support) in my view are unacceptable and would not be accepted by any ethics committee.

6.5 Behavior Change, Social Interactions, and Conflict Analysis

Changing behavior is a very broad field. However, in my experience, clients rarely come with the intention of wanting to change a specifically defined behavior but rather with more general goals, such as improving their leadership skills, resolving conflicts with other people, preparing for job interviews, and addressing very specific concerns. In one coaching session, a client wanted support in her resolution from a domineering and torturous relationship with a narcissistic male friend (after several failed attempts at separation). As it turned out, she did not want to endure his rude dominating behavior even in public toward her for the umpteenth time and forgiven him again after insufficient reconciliation, only to be again humiliated. To achieve this, she wanted to change her behavior and reject it if he asked for forgiveness again. In the coaching, she wanted to clarify how she could do this.

Desired behavioral changes in coaching can be seen as learning tasks. The psychology of learning is a very large field of research and application with diverse theories and directions (Lefrançois, 2014) and many useful references to coaching. Learning by insight (Greif & Riemenschneider-Greif, 2018; Müller & Greif, 2022) and "Aha! experiences" (see *Sect. 5.4: Solution-Focused Counseling*), reflective learning (Argyris, 2002), self-regulated learning (Kluge & Hagemann, 2022), or transformative learning (Fisher-Yoshida & Yoshida, 2022) fits particularly well with coaching. Specifically, for behavior change, cognitive modeling is recommended as a very practical method whose effectiveness has been verified by evaluation studies. It is presented in the following.

6.5.1 Cognitive Modeling for Behavioral Change

The cognitive apprenticeship approach is a very generally applicable evidence-based method for behavior change (Collins et al., 1989). It is also referred to as *cognitive modeling* because it models and changes not only behavior but also internal cognitive processes (Reinmann-Rothmeier et al., 1994). It is a further development of Bandura's (1969) Model Learning. Somewhat simplified and adapted for coaching, the following steps must be performed in the modeling process:

1. *Behavior and Thoughts during Implementation:* Coaches explore and work out with clients the behavior that seems optimal in the situation. Then, they plan how exactly—step by step—it can be implemented. In doing so, not only are changes in behavior considered but also beneficial perceptions, thoughts, and feelings when acting (e.g., what should I pay special attention to, how do I cope with feelings of insecurity at the moment, or how do I deal with unexpected reactions of the people involved?).
2. *Support by Scaffolding:* The coach supports the client with reflexive suggestions. The coach and client name the important points to be considered and thus repeat

what the clients want to consider when acting. This helps the learners like a "scaffold" in the later implementation.
3. *Verbalization*: The clients repeat the solution and the process scaffold because this supports memorization and precise control of the process.
4. *Implementation and Reflection:* Clients observe and analyze their implementation in practice and, in a follow-up meeting, compare the implementation with the previously developed solution to possibly optimize it.
5. *Continuation and Exploration*: The clients continue practical implementation by themselves and explore on their own what they can improve.

The procedure can be described via an example of leadership behavior in a promotion interview with a sensitive employee who immediately "shuts down" when criticized and reacts wordlessly.

In *step 1* (*Behavior and Thoughts*), the coaching client (e.g., a manager) could use motivating words to initiate the conversation and make sure to look at the employee in a friendly manner and to seek eye contact. In addition, he or she can plan to pay attention to whether the employee reacts positively if only positive feedback on performance is given at first. Necessary points of criticism should only be made in the first conversation about a single, easily improvable performance and should be combined with a concrete suggestion for improvement, always asking the employee whether he or she has any alternative suggestions. The client also prepares encouraging words for the end of the conversation in the coaching session and plans to make a new appointment at the end after the employee has implemented the changes.

In *step 2* (*Scaffolding*), the sequence of necessary steps in the implementation of the new behavior of the manager is summarized and structured together with headings, e.g.:

1. Motivating and friendly welcome of the employee
2. Paying attention to the reactions of the employee
3. First, giving only positive feedback
4. Again paying attention to his or her reactions
5. Discussing only one easy point of criticism with improvements, and
6. Encouraging conclusions at the end and follow-up appointments

In *step 3* (*verbalization*), the client is then asked to repeat this process in his own words and write it down so that it can be better remembered.

In *step 4* (*implementation*), the client is asked to implement the process in the next meeting with the employee and to reflect on the implementation experience in a further coaching session.

With *step 5* (*continuation and exploration*), the practical implementations and optimizations are continued and optimized without coaching.

According to scientific research, cognitive modeling is one of the most effective learning methods and has proven itself in practice in companies internationally (Ebner et al., 2018; Greif & Kluge, 2004). To my knowledge, however, this method has rarely been used in coaching.

When coaching behavioral changes, it can be beneficial for the clients to reflect on their own values, strengths, or life goals beforehand. As a rule, coaches use the questioning techniques described above. In addition, further methods, which can be used in this broad field of coaching, are described below. The following presentation begins with a combination of methods for changing and sustainably implementing behavioral habits. Afterward, the focus was on communication behavior, especially the empty chair technique. It provides a transition to conflict management methods because it can be used to analyze and change communication behavior, especially in conflicts. At the end of the section, changes in leadership behavior with coaching support are discussed. All the methods listed here can be used for this purpose.

6.5.2 Habit Change

The significance and characteristics of habits were already analyzed in detail by William James (1892) in his classic "Principles of Psychology" and are still relevant today. He assumed that habits differ from other behaviors because they are activated by perceptions and are performed without conscious attention and without special effort. This has been found similarly in recent psychological and neuroscientific research. Additionally, from a current perspective (Gardner, 2015; Verplanken, 2018; Wood, 2019), habits are learned stimulus–response associations or sequences of actions as well as behavioral routines that are triggered by a stimulus as an impulse. As a result, our brain conserves energy.

6.5.2.1 Cues as Triggers of Unconscious Behavioral Habits

Authors such as Duhigg (2012) refer to these stimuli as "cues." They assume that the subsequent fixed behavioral routines, which we call habits, are learned because they have been followed (at least initially) by some kind of reward. These behaviors are learned consciously at the beginning, but later, they are no longer under conscious control but run automatically, such as the movements of our legs and feet when we walk. Duhigg refers to neuroscientific research, which states that when new behavior is learned, the frontal lobes of the human brain are activated, as in all consciously controlled processes. However, when the behavioral sequences become an automated routine, the frontal lobes remain passive. Instead, activation of the basal ganglia can now be observed, indicating processes that are regulated unconsciously (Yin & Knowlton, 2006). Thus, the brain conserves energy. In a sense, when the cue and trigger of a fixed habit are perceived, this leads to an effortlessly executed chain of behavior that is not consciously controlled.

Automated activation without the involvement of conscious volitional decisions, plans, and control also explains why people have a hard time overcoming "bad habits" through conscious volitional decisions and why they keep falling back into their habits if they do not inhibit automatic responses to cues or replace them with different cues for changed routines. Coaches need to know these implications and explain them to their clients if they wish to help them understand why it is so hard to change habits and how to do it and why relapses into old habits are to be expected. This generates new insights and increases the knowledge of the clients regarding how to overcome problematic behavioral habits in the future.

Stress can prevent planned changes from being implemented (Duhigg, 2012). Under stress, people "forget" what they have planned to do because coping with stress is a psychological priority. This is especially true for sticking to new work or schedule plans or priorities. Under stress, one falls back into the usual work routine or the former time pattern. If this happens more often, many give up with resignation on the planned changes.

6.5.2.2 Replacing Old Habits with New Ones

Wood (2019) distinguishes, as in everyday language, "good" and "bad habits." Exercising regularly is generally considered a "good habit." Smoking, overeating, and "constant daddling" using the mobile or frequently putting off important and urgent tasks for too long (procrastination) are usually called "bad habits" in surveys.

The following list shows examples of change requests of habits that have been mentioned in coaching sessions on the basis of my experience:

- Regularly perform relaxation or meditation exercises.
- More sports exercises should be performed on a regular basis.
- Healthier nutrition.
- Not going to the refrigerator before bedtime.
- Drinking water with every meal.
- Less "daddling" with the smartphone and spending this time more "wisely."
- Less time watching TV and more time reading "good books."
- Less time spent on emails and more time spent on self-directed, important tasks.
- Reduction of frequent procrastination in unpleasant but important tasks.
- Too long unimportant conversations and more time spent on important ones.
- Staying calm in stressful situations and having more composure in life.
- More time for family or friends.

What is the stimulus or cue that triggers them? To change old habits, it is advisable to identify the cues that activate them as precisely as possible (Adriaanse et al., 2009). To name just a few possible ones: Is it the television chair that invites us to sit down and from which we no longer get up for our scheduled workout jog, or the fatigue after work that seemingly paradoxically interferes with our performance of a relaxation exercise? Is it the inviting delicacies in the fridge that tempt us or, before going to bed, the need for something good to eat after such a hard day? Is it our thought: A beer in the evening cannot do any harm? Is it the smartphone that we like to put on the table that activates its activation? What does it do to us when we feel time pressure at work or during a presentation we are giving? Do we immediately react with stress and hectic? Our typical work routines and time management or procrastination often hide avoidance behaviors and inefficient behavioral habits that cost or waste time and end up making us so tired that we no longer have the energy to spend more time with family or friends, for example.

In my experience, it is important to "overlay" the cues for the old behavior patterns with psychologically powerful new cues, if possible. The new cues can serve as "reminders." In some cases, a "post it" slip of paper (stick to the refrigerator or on a notepad on the desk) is needed. A circle symbol on a PowerPoint slide can serve as a secret reminder to take a breath to calm down and to speak more slowly. Importantly, clients associate positive emotions, sensations, or expectations with new cues and behavior. It can be a stimulating creative task in coaching to brainstorm ideas for strong cues together and try them out until effective cues are found.

To replace a so-called "habit" with a "good habit," Wood (2019) recommends removing the triggering cue from view or covering it up, if possible, and practicing alternative behaviors in situations that involve self-rewards.

> Wood explains this with the example of the constant (in some cases already addictive) habitual glances at the smartphone for all signals for new messages or the active searching and entering of SMS messages, while one should actually perform other work tasks or even during the meal (Wood, 2019, pos. 3694 ff.). She recommends never putting your smartphone next to you on the table during a meal but instead putting it away here and in all other noninterference situations, turning it off and as inaccessible as possible, or even zipping it away in a bag. If you manage to do this, you should initially reward yourself with a previously planned reward.

In my experience, clients are fascinated to determine which cues trigger their unwanted habit and which new cues for desired behavior they can superimpose on it. My own example was the refrigerator, which I could not get past before going to bed without quickly grabbing something tasty. In my case, a "post it" on the fridge with a "No!" and a self-drawn ironic smiley face helped. As a "reward," when I looked at it in the evening, I always imaginated for a moment a feeling of "pride" that I had made it and that the next morning, I would not have to worry that the scales would show increased body weight. Such "imaginated rewards" often work well. However, it is important that they are very actively visualized mentally and emotionally, perhaps even when combined with a short mindfulness meditation. (I manage this on more than 90% of evenings but also allow myself a few exceptions—with good-tasting little yogurt cups having few calories kept in the refrigerator for this purpose.)

In our experience, few coaches are aware of how often the behavioral changes that their clients are seeking also involve changing habits. William James (1892) assumed that the vast majority of our everyday actions consisted of habits. Wood (2019, pos. 298 ff.) asked the students to log what they did and thought every hour every day. Sixty percent of the activities were classified as "habits" because, according to the self-observations, they were performed automatically and without thinking. A characteristic is also that when performing a behavioral routine, thoughts can wander off and be completely elsewhere.

According to Wood (2019, pos. 334 f.), almost any activity can become a habit: 88% of daily hygiene (showering and dressing, etc.), 55% of professional work activities, 44% while walking and exercising, and 48% of recreational and relaxation activities, such as sitting on the couch or watching TV (without truly looking, people often think of something completely different even when doing this). According to a corporate survey by Capgemini (2012) on problems in change management, 63.8% of respondents are convinced even that successful changes require overcoming habits first.

6.5.3 Psychoeducational Enlightenment of the Client

After futile attempts to change their "bad habits," many people at some point give up in frustration. Some feel ashamed of their supposed lack of willpower. The fact that, for many people, the difficulty of changing their habits leads to self-devaluation is expressed in the saying that, to do so, we have to overcome our "inner lazy bastard" (in Germany, it is called the "inner pig dog"). However, this metaphor basically leads into the wrong direction of thinking. When clients want to change their behavioral habits, it helps them understand why they have not succeeded thus far. Coaches briefly explain to them psychoeducationally how habits are activated by cues and then run after automation without any mental effort. After all, it is not at all an "inner pig-dog" that we have to overcome or a sign of "a weak will" but rather a positive strength and attempt of our brain to save energy. When we explain this to our clients, it can trigger a lasting "Aha! experience," which helps them expand their potential in changing their behavioral habits in the future.

Especially when clients feel ashamed of their perceived weakness of will, encouraging psychoeducational conversation is very beneficial. When clients talk about their supposed "bad habits" and futile attempts to break them, an enlightening conversation about why it is too difficult to change habits according to practical experience and scientific findings is a good idea. However, the conversation should not be lecturing but dialogical with questions about observations and the exchange of the client's reflections and the summary of information about interesting studies and findings. If the analysis of the problems is not based first on the individual examples of the clients but rather, in general, on a metalevel about the difficulties of all people and, if together, explanations for the difficulties are searched, this can stop the individual self-devaluation by comparison with others. This allows the clients to search for and try alternative approaches.

In my experience, a study by Tierney et al. (2011) on the difficulties of patients after cardiovascular disease to change their health behavior is very suitable as a starting point for questions that distract clients from their individual inadequacies. In this study, the patients were strongly advised by their doctor to exercise regularly and eat healthier food in the future, and they had made a firm commitment to do so (after all, it could be life-threatening for them if they did not change their health behavior). However, on average, they only stick for three months, as promised, to exercise regularly and eat healthier people in the future. To begin, I describe the study's purpose and ask clients for their estimates of how many months patients actually implement the health behaviors that are vital to them. Most estimate even less time, showing that they basically know that they are by no means alone in having difficulty changing behavior. Afterward, the results of the study can be reported briefly, and we can move on to questions and dialogs about how we can explain these difficulties and how we can overcome them.

The following example explains the procedure for changing habits. Depending on the field of knowledge, it has to be adapted.

1. Examples of Psychoeducational Enlightenment

The important basis of the psychoeducational intervention in this case is to explain the importance of the activation of behavior regulation by the basal ganglia as described above by cues. For this purpose, one can use an illustration of a cross-section of the human brain, as shown in Fig. 6.6. If the clients are interested, one can recommend good popular scientific literature, such as the book by Duhigg (2012) mentioned above, to them for further study. I also give them excerpts from my short practical guidelines we use in our coaching training (Greif, 2025, in prep.).

In the future, scientifically grounded videos will likely be used to complement psychoeducation. As with other complex services, informed clients are better able to critically reflect on coaching methods with coaches and to use the potential of coaching for themselves (Greif, 2015).

2. What Cues Activate the Old Habit?

To motivate clients to try out whether they can manage to stimulate changed behavior through new cues, it is necessary that they understand the meaning of cues for habits and can comprehend it with their own examples. First, we look for cues that activate undesirable habits. These do not have to be visible external stimuli

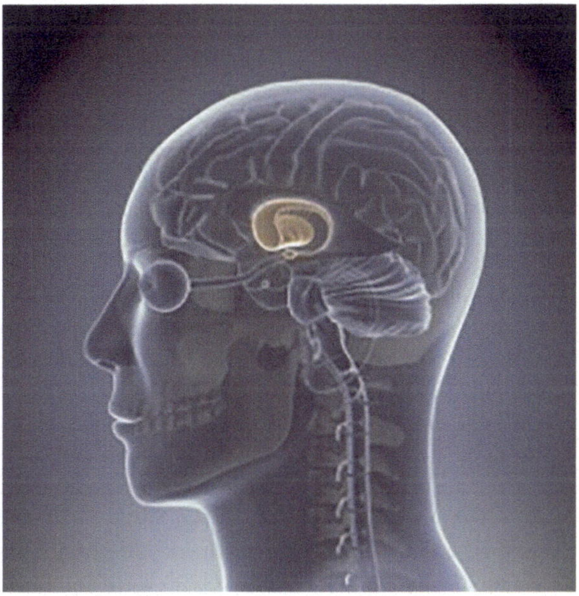

Fig. 6.6 Basal ganglia (license clipdealer, Media-ID: B:28192575)

but can also be sensations and thoughts that are triggered in certain situations. In coaching, clients are asked to imagine the situation as vividly as possible and ask if there is anything they pay particular attention to that might stimulate the habit. Clients can try to notice in future situations what the hypothetical triggers are. This requires good self-observation.

3. Planning the New Behavior

Next, it is a matter of planning new behaviors. As Oettingen (2014) describes this within her method of "Mental Contrasting," it is self-motivating for clients to imagine, in contrast, the consequences that will result from the desired changes and to visualize them very vividly. (Who would not then want to implement the behavior with positive consequences?) To prevent hasty giving up when faced with unexpected internal or external obstacles, it would also be beneficial if these obstacles are analyzed beforehand in the coaching session and if the use of resources to overcome them is preliminarily outlined.

4. New Cues for New Habits

Creatively finding new cues for new planned behavior can be fun for clients when guided in a playful way. Which reminders are effective and at the same time emotionally powerful enough to activate the desired behavior?

Storch and Kuhl (2012, p. 261 ff.) describe case studies of how self-motivation can be increased by associations with very positively experienced situations or stimulating thoughts, images, and imaginings. On the basis of my experience, I would additionally recommend not to stick rigidly to one way of self-motivation and especially not to a cue but rather to determine by trial and error whether the cue "works."

One of my own examples can serve as an illustration. I had plans to take a walk "in the fresh air" two or three times a week. As a cue and reminder, I put my running shoes in the hallway in the morning on the Day I planned to do that. However, that basically didn't motivate me very much. When I talked about this in a presentation at a coaching congress, Maggie Palmer suggested that I might be perhaps better motivating myself additionally with the old pop song sung by Nancy Sinatra, "These boots are made for walking". I like the song very much, and even when I thought of it just now while writing, I smile, immediately get into a good mood and want to go out into the fresh air …

It is psychologically interesting to explore with clients which suitable associations for their action intentions might evoke very positive feelings and help them motivate themselves and build up the necessary energy to carry out their intentions (see also *Sect. 9.2.4: "Affect Activation and Regulation for Emotion Regulation and Self-Motivation"*). Put illustratively, it is about clients creating a kind of "imagined movie scene," which is rousing and starts when they see the chosen cue. Once the new behavior has become a positively experienced new habit, they no longer need the entire movie. (I now have had the little dog "Paulchen." He is, with his enthusiasm for going outside, an extremely powerful "super cue," motivating me and my wife intensively to walk together even on rainy days.)

In the following, the subsequent accompaniment of the implementation in coaching is described. As mentioned, sustainable behavioral changes may be needed over a longer period of time.

6.5.3.1 Sustainable Implementation Through Shadowing Using Telephone or Messenger Systems

Often, prolonged amounts of practice are required for a new fixed habit to be automatically activated by the human brain and to result in lasting behavioral change. For example, it took students between 18 and 254 days to consistently and stably implement new eating habits (e.g., drinking water at least 95% of their meals) on a daily basis (Lally et al., 2010). Therefore, in addition to overlaying cues, coaching also requires implementation support. It ends only after the new action routine is stably implemented.

Observing and accompanying the implementation of planned behavioral changes is called "shadowing." In high-performance sports, it is common for the trainer or coach to observe or shadow his or her athletes during practice and in competitions and to talk through the observations with them afterward. In coaching, this method is rarely used (for a summary, see Greif, 2013b). It has been insufficiently researched but is estimated to be an extraordinarily effective practical intervention in coaching (Jarvis et al., 2006). *Section 9.3.3* lists existing studies on the use of shadowing in coaching. The results are very promising.

I already used shadowing in my first coaching sessions, e.g., during CEO speeches at company meetings and in executive events. When I had myself coached, I insisted on shadowing and knew from my own experience how beneficial this was.

Shadowing is followed by joint evaluation of observations and facilitative feedback by the coach. The practical effectiveness can probably be attributed to the fact that the coach's presence reinforces personal goal commitment and serves as a powerful cue to remind people of their intention to implement. Subsequently, very precise supportive behavioral feedback can be given.

Some think that the infrequent use of face-to-face shadowing is because clients do not like "coming out" that their coach is present in important situations. However, top managers coached by me did not try to conceal my role at all. When I was present, they publicly introduced me as "their coach". By the way, I myself also introduced one of my coaches quite openly in two situations that were important to me and quite delicate (with people and groups that were important to me and relatively conservative). In both situations, there were some astonished reactions at first but then very positive acceptance. In one case, I even received spontaneous recommendations for me and my competent achievements afterward.

What influence would it have on athletes' performance if their coaches left them alone in competition? In sports, even if the coach is present, it is the athlete who stands in the foreground with his or her achievements, and no one doubts that it is the athlete and not the coach who delivers them. The coach wins or loses with the champion and is usually easier to replace. Basically, it is similar to shadowing in coaching. Our clients deliver the performances. Especially given the difficulty of changing their behavioral habits, coaches should not leave their clients alone due to frustration and self-devaluations when they fail to implement their changes, which are difficult and appear easy.

However, the high costs of face-to-face shadowing, which can involve the coach being present for several hours, partly speak against it. A more cost-effective variant is therefore remote telephone shadowing or shadowing via a messaging system. In a telephone conversation after the implementation attempt, the clients are asked to describe whether the plan could be implemented and whether the hoped-for results were achieved or how the people in the environment reacted. It is important to carefully monitor clients' feelings and perceived inner resistance during the implementation process. Self-awareness can be made more difficult for the client because of his or her own involvement. However, through repeated self-observation and joint reflection, it can be improved. The clients learn to observe more closely and to pay attention to their self-perceptions. To avoid demotivating memories of negative feelings in the past, as described in *Sect. 6.4: Narrative Coaching*, the method of "self-distancing" (Kross & Ayduk, 2017) can be applied here.

To ensure that clients also notice and pay attention to small improvements or deteriorations, it is advisable to ask them to assess directly after the implementation attempt on a scale (from 0 to 10 or from "not at all" to "100%" or "completely perfect") how consistently the planned number could be implemented and to send this number to their coach via Signal, WhatsApp, SMS, or another messenger system. In a telephone conversation or coaching session, which observations the clients base their assessment on and to what they attribute the achieved or not yet achieved changes and what they plan to do afterward can be explored.

Accurate recall is easier if remote shadowing is performed shortly after the situation, if possible, on the same day or evening. An additional psychologically important advantage here is that experiences of failure and self-devaluation can be quickly absorbed in an early following coaching session. According to our experience, consistent implementation even of simple actions succeeds only in 40–50% of the first attempts. Unexpected events prevent planned execution (prioritized new tasks, unanticipated new situations or internal obstacles, etc.). Some clients give up very quickly in frustration when they fail. If the coaching conversation—as is common in most coaching sessions—follows only after a week or even later at the routinely scheduled appointment, it is hardly possible to overcome any demotivation. On the other hand, if the conversation follows quickly, "remotivation" is usually easy. In the simplest case, a new, unchanged attempt is planned in the next possible situation. This is especially important if the planned actions or changes are not appropriate or if the goals and plans need to be revised.

Remote shadowing, e.g., by phone, is repeated until the client is successful in implementation and goal achievement. In complex and unpredictable situations, this may require many repetitions. If the implementation is successful from the clients' point of view (with a rating of 7 or higher), the implementation support for future implementation attempts can be performed with a messenger system (Signal,

WhatsApp or SMS) instead of phone shadowing. This is particularly suitable if the change in habits is to be accompanied over a long period of time. For clients and coaches to invest as little time as possible for this purpose, it is sufficient to send the coach only the number with the rating for this task. If it makes sense, short keywords can also be added by the client (e.g., "Worked!" or "Nearly perfect!"). Coaches can respond briefly ("Congratulations!" "Great!"). Clients appreciate such encouraging brief feedback and report that they perceive the coach's presence and accompaniment shown in this way as very supportive. As a rule, talking with one another on the phone at scores of 6 and lower is recommended.

The time required is so short (often merely seconds or a few minutes) that clients and coaches can use it to accompany long implementation phases without any effort. In this way, it can support sustainable changes. When implementation is stable in more than 80% of cases and goal achievement is high, it is possible to move to longer intervals. To "fade out," after completion, clients are stimulated to reflect on what they can take away from this experience and make use of other changes they plan to implement. In this way, clients improve and expand their self-regulation skills.

Despite a longer implementation phase, clients may—after a longer time, spontaneously and involuntarily—often suddenly fall back into their previous behavioral patterns. As a precaution, you can therefore offer them to briefly ask again after 3–6 months via messenger how they are doing. Experience has shown that clients are very grateful for this and usually immediately restart their desired behavioral pattern after a brief refresher, e.g., by telephone coaching. However, people are not robots that always and forever act disciplined according to the program they have entered. They can consciously make new decisions and deliberately decide to return to old habits.

A case example is an entrepreneur whom I accompanied—as he wanted for several months daily (even during his vacation) to perform a breathing exercise with biofeedback for relaxation, which he liked and which reduced his blood pressure. The daily physiological values (heart rate variability and blood pressure measurements before and after exercise) could be statistically analyzed as a single longitudinal study because of the large number of measurements. They significantly improved HRV values (Greif & Palmer, 2022). However, as he reported in a recent coaching session, he stopped exercising after more than a year, even though it was doing him so much good. He immediately expressed strong feelings of guilt about being so inconsistent. We reflected together on what this was due to. For him, the psychoeducational explanation that such relapses are very common was great relief. Afterward, he found a simple and self-motivating way to refresh and immediately restart his exercises.

A guideline text on the rigorous implementation of behavioral changes in habits (Greif, 2024, in prep.) describes in more detail how to perform the method and accompaniment of the implementation. For complex changes and unpredictable situations, a modified approach is appropriate with a longer period of accompaniment using telephone shadowing, as described in another guideline on accompaniment of the implementation in case of complex changes.

6.5.4 Communication Behavior

Executives spend most of their work time communicating, approximately 60% of which is in meetings (Reichwald & Hensel, 2007), more and more of which is in videoconferences and, furthermore, in phone calls, with emails and WhatsApp, Signal, or other messenger systems. In particular, facing important talks at informational meetings or presentations in front of other executives or shareholders, some seek support in preparing through coaching. Coaching is also requested for the preparation of face-to-face or online meetings with smaller groups of employees to one-on-one meetings where important changes are involved. Clients find coaching particularly useful when it is difficult to convince employees to support changes or when conflicts are to be expected or are already virulent. Specific methods for conflict analysis and management are discussed in more detail below, both from the perspective of managers and others.

6.5.4.1 Verbal and Nonverbal Communication

Karl Bühler (1934) was one of the first to publish a scientific analysis of the basic features of human communication. He emphasized the tool character of language because it serves to "communicate something to another about the things," He distinguishes between "sender" and "receiver", which is still important today, as well as between different functions of the speech act:

Display: "The task was not completed."
Expressive statement: "I would be ashamed if I had not completed the task."
Appeal: "Admit it that you did not complete the task."

Communication is not only based on language. Even those who say nothing always convey extra information through facial expressions and gestures or glances. Watzlawick highlights the importance of never-ending nonverbal communication with his well-known phrase: "One cannot not communicate" (Watzlawick et al., 1967). Accordingly, Scholl et al. (2022) define "verbal and nonverbal communication" together very broadly as "the attempt to understand each other."

Borrowing from Bühler and Watzlawick, Schulz von Thun, a well-known author in Germany, distinguishes four sides of communication: factual content, self-disclosure, relationships, and appeal (Schulz von Thun et al., 2006). Catchy examples are used to explain the differences, which is probably why they have become very popular. Psychologically, it becomes interesting whenever the sides are different or even contradictory to each other, as they are delivered by the speaker or perceived by the listener. Thus, the sentence of a superior—"I appreciate your achievements of the last time very much"—can be accentuated nonverbally quite differently and, as a result, may also express the opposite to the content of the sentence. However, according to my literature searches, there is a lack of scientific research on whether the effects postulated by Schulz von Thun always or often occur in communication processes. Seen in this light, they should be regarded merely as speculative effects and should stimulate cautious and differentiated observations of self-contradictory communications.

6.5.4.2 Improving Communication in Coaching

A simple way to improve their communication in a future communication task is to ask clients to describe their task and situation. After that, the coach asks:

- Verbal: What do I want to say? How do I consider the listeners' point of view?
- Nonverbal: How do I express the message? How do I appear?
- Are there critical themes or statements that could trigger negative feelings and reactions in listeners? How do I deal with them?
- How can I calm down and activate myself in the situation? How can I activate and inspire myself and the listeners?

The essence of such simple methods of analyzing communication by describing and reviewing is that the client and the coach take the time to discuss everything carefully and prepare for different alternative scenarios. ("What do I do if…happens?") Describing and reviewing requires clients to be able to accurately imagine their own behavior and the communication processes that follow. The clients must subsequently be able to translate the mentally planned behavior into behavior. These are basically difficult requirements. Such methods are therefore only suitable for easy-to-realize communication tasks. More elaborate but more precise and informative are role-playing exercises. For this purpose, one begins as above with a description and review but then additionally asks the client to imagine the situation in his or her mind and to say the sentences that the client wanted to say. The coach plays the role of listener or role partner. Afterward, observations are analyzed and reflected upon together. The exercise can then be repeated.

Coaching communication analyses should be based on scientifically researched characteristics and communication models. An overview of communication in coaching by Scholl et al. (2022) can be recommended here as very suitable for coaching interventions. A basic assumption of this communication model is that nonverbal expression is linked to bodily sensations and signals to the participants what the speakers' feelings are about the theme and each other. Nonverbally and verbally expressed feelings can be analyzed with respect to three empirically well-researched basic dimensions:

1. Valence (positive versus negative feeling or friendly versus hostile when the feeling relates to other people).
2. Power (feeling strong or dominant versus weak or submissive).
3. Activation (active or excited versus passive or calm).

According to Scholl et al. (2022), these three dimensions shape and structure communication and mutual behavioral and personality perceptions. The different individual feelings can be arranged in a circle according to their similarity, as shown in Fig. 6.7. The circle can be divided into four circle segments, with each adjacent feeling being more similar than the feelings in the remaining segments.

If nonverbally and verbally expressed feelings correspond, this generally increases the credibility of the communication. If this is not the case, doubts of the listener may result, or this may be interpreted as irony or sarcasm. Coaches should pay attention to this in role-play exercises and sensitize their clients to it.

If nonverbally and verbally expressed feelings correspond, this generally increases the credibility of the communication. If this is not the case, doubts may result, or this may be interpreted as irony or sarcasm. Coaches should pay attention to this in role-play exercises and sensitize their clients to it.

The underlying symbolic-interactionist model (Scholl et al., 2022, p. 203 ff.) assumes that role identities (or self-concepts adapted for the interaction) are cocreated and negotiated in interaction processes: Can I make a good impression on the other person (impression management)? How do I see myself in this situation? How do I see him or her? Do our expectations match? How can I exert influence and achieve what I wanted?

To enable communication that is satisfying for both interaction partners, it is beneficial if the client puts himself or herself in the other person's shoes (perspective taking), in his or her feelings, how he or she sees me and what he or she wants to achieve in the interaction and where common ground exists. The empty chair exercise described in the following section is particularly suitable for this purpose. It can also be combined with role-playing exercises, improving verbal and nonverbal communication behavior.

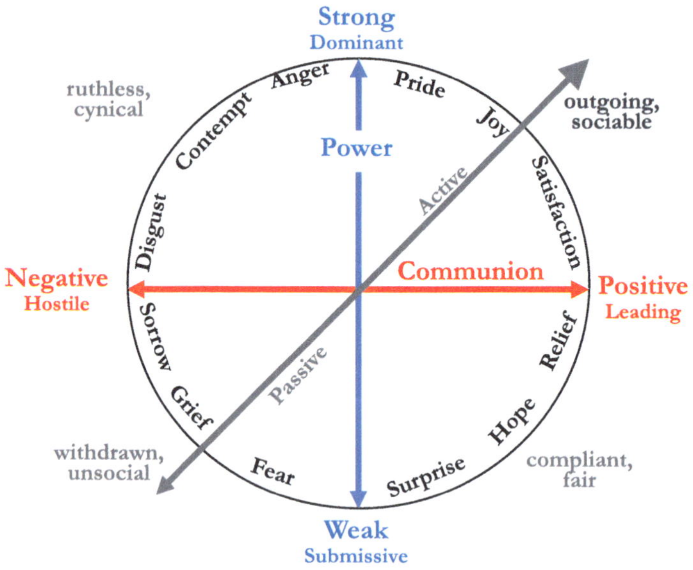

Fig. 6.7 Behavior and feelings (Modified from Scholl et al., 2022, p. 201)

6.5.5 *Empty Chair Exercise*

This exercise is classic and has its name because it is performed with two chairs, one of which, for an imaginary second person, remains empty. It is also called the two-chair exercise.

One person starts and performs their own behavior from memory on their own chair. Afterward, he or she switches to the empty chair and behaves like the imagined other person. The exercise was introduced in psychodrama by Moreno as "monodrama" (Rabel et al., 1996); however, it was not a behavioral exercise but was intended to dissolve rigid role structures. Schreyögg (1995, p. 266 ff., 2011) describes the use of the method in coaching and calls it "Imaginative Role Reversal." In Gestalt therapy, a variant is known as "chair work" according to Fritz Perls (Friedman, 1993; Kellogg et al., 2011). In addition to reenacting verbal and nonverbal communication behavior, it is possible to switch between external and internal dialog ("What did I feel and think in this chair?"). This change in perspective promotes understanding of the other person and reflection on how interactions with important partners can be improved. According to my observations, it already leads to behavioral changes when clients suddenly become aware in this exercise that they have provoked reactions in their counterpart through their behavior that they previously did not register, but they had to suffer the negative consequences …

The method is applicable to many themes:

- A better understanding of the effect of one's own behavior.
- Analyze inexplicable behavior of others (understand other people's perspective, improve social sensitivity/emotional intelligence).
- Self-confident behavior (in groups, in difficult situations) or self-assertion (especially in the face of bullying).
- Reducing communication problems with a specific person.
- Improving leadership behavior (communication of important tasks, recognition and appreciation, feedback, difficult team meetings, etc.).
- Behavior in promotion or goal-setting interviews (as a manager or as an employee).
- Behavior in conflicts with individuals or in groups, behavior in job interviews (career coaching).
- Rhetoric in presentations (coach plays "listener").

6.5.5.1 Sequential Steps of Empty Chair Exercise

1. *Initial situation*

   Explain the method, clients' goals, and description of the initial situation and participants (for a more detailed description and guidelines, see Greif, 2025, in prep.).

2. *Preparation*

   Set up two chairs facing each other ("Me" and "my counterpart"). The client alternately takes a seat on one of them. As described in the guidelines, the method can also be performed well online with PowerPoint slides and schematic figures, as shown in Fig. 6.8.
3. *Client on the chair "Me":* "What am I saying?"
4. *The client stands behind the chair "my counterpart":* "What does the other person feel/think?"—Empathize with the other person: "Now try to feel how what you said might have affected him or her. How did that person feel, what could he or she have been thinking?—How do you feel about your previous behavior now?" The coach can carefully add her own observations and impressions.
5. *Client sits down on the chair "my counterpart":* "What does the other person say?" (after recollection, in verbatim speech if possible)—"Does the behavior observed and acted out fit the hypotheses, thoughts, and hypotheses? How do you now feel about your previous behavior?"—The coach can carefully add his or her own observations and impressions. If it does not fit: were the hypotheses wrong? Which alternative explanation fits better? Or did the person control himself so well that it was not visible?)

Fig. 6.8 PowerPoint images for online performance of the empty chair exercise (Greif, 2025, in prep.)

6. *Client standing behind chair "Me":* "What do I feel/think now?" (Role change: The client says how he or she felt from her memory at that time in the situation the reaction of the counterpart and what has changed after the exercise.)
7. *Repetition of cycles 3 to 6:* "What am I saying?"—"What does my counterpart feel/think?"—"What is my counterpart saying now?"—"What do I feel?" (Continue alternating until the relevant part of the sequence has been played out or until the interaction phase ends or important interactions are clear to both the client and coach.)

Apparently, difficult or intense interaction situations take us emotionally and mentally so captive that it is difficult for us to ask ourselves how our behavior is perceived by the other person. If we do not reflect on our own behavior as a trigger for the other person's behavior, we quickly might think that the other person is behaving inappropriately or aggressively without cause. As a result, both interacting persons can feel indignant and offended because something is insinuated that was not meant that way at all but was not explicitly ruled out. Both therefore see themselves "in the right" to behave offensively or to withdraw offended. Experience has shown that role-play exercise very often promotes intensive new insights into the interrelationships in communication processes and leads to more sensitive behavior through changes in perspective.

The classic version of the psychodrama does not include behavioral exercises. They are often not necessary either if the clients have gained intensive new insight into the reactions of their counterparts to their behavior through the exercise or if, as an immediate consequence, they "cannot" maintain the previous behavior. (Since they do not want to violate the new insight, they have gained.) When important situations require precise behavior, they can be tested in the same scheme with a change of chairs. The *cognitive modeling method* described above is suitable as a basis for this purpose. Different scenarios can be simulated with alternative behavioral probes and repetitions while changing chairs.

It is remarkable that there is a lack of research on the effects of the Empty Chairs Exercise—as far as I could search in the psychological databases—although it has been around and recommended for a very long time. In the 1980s and 1990s, individual studies revealed that the use of exercise in the context of psychotherapy led to a reduction in anger and lowered blood pressure (Conoley et al., 1983) or to a decrease in strong feelings of sadness (Field & Horowitz, 1998). The theoretical expectations and observations in coaching described above regarding the perception of the role perspectives of the other person could well be tested by scientific research. It would be meritorious to begin such investigations. As long as they are missing, this classical method—despite best individual experiences on the basis of practical observations—can only be recommended with caveats and accompanied by careful observations about effects and possible side effects.

6.5.6 *Conflict Analysis and Management*

Conflicts with important people in professional or private life are a frequent theme in coaching. Examples include managers, who report conflicts with other management levels, with individual employees or sometimes even with their entire team. Employees have conflicts with other employees or their bosses. In private life, there are also conflicts with family, friends, or other people. To resolve conflicts, trained, independent mediators can mediate between parties (Montada & Kals, 2013; Brummans et al., 2022). However, before seeking such "official" intervention, clients often prefer to consult their coach.

6.5.6.1 What Are "Conflicts"?

Vollmer and Vetter (2022, p. 224), following De Dreu and Gelfand (2008, p. 6), define conflicts "as processes (…) that begin when an individual or group perceives differences between itself and another individual or group about interests, resources, beliefs, values, or practices that matter to them."

6.5.6.2 Conflict Resolution or Conflict Management?

Coaches should not create exaggerated expectations about the chances of conflict resolution. A "conflict solution" that fully satisfies all parties involved is rarely achievable. However, coaching can make it possible to analyze the conflicts and thus to understand them better, deal with the conflicts in a more reflective way, and change one's own behavior to de-escalate conflicts and look for improvements together with the other party that are sustainable for all sides. "Conflict management" is understood to include all methodically planned measures that are suitable for significantly reducing the risks and costs of conflict as well as the adverse effects for both sides. The term "management" refers to the fact that this is a longer, goal-oriented process that often includes many consciously planned measures for the containment of conflicts and ideally leads to their resolution.

6.5.6.3 Types of Conflicts

In general, a distinction is made between factual conflicts and personal conflicts. However, these two types of conflict are rarely completely independent of each other. In conflict dynamics, differences in opinion about an issue can very quickly give rise to personal animosities and mutual personal attacks. This can escalate to mutual enemy stereotypes and fundamental rejection of the other party's sources of information (e.g., as "fake news" or "lies").

Common distinctions in recent scientific theories (cf. Vollmer & Vetter, 2022) of conflict within groups are as follows:

1. Task conflicts (conflicts caused by different opinions about the interpretation of tasks and solution possibilities)
2. Relationship conflicts (involving incompatible behavior or disliked characteristics of individuals)
3. Process conflicts (differences of opinion about the procedures for achieving objectives, including responsibilities or resource allocation)

Task and process conflicts, according to available empirical studies, can have a positive influence on the quality of task completion because they stimulate working groups to discuss their different views. As a result, premature consensus solutions can be avoided. According to a summary of the research results of Behfar et al. (2008), team performance depends on mutual trust.

Relationship conflicts are particularly critical when the differences mutually lead to negative affective reactions or to discord. According to the studies available on this subject, they are difficult to resolve. Different types of conflicts can always quickly merge into one another (Vollmer & Vetter, 2022).

6.5.6.4 Win–Lose or Win–Win

Mixed-motive situations, where the goals and motives partly coincide but partly oppose each other, are often typical and very realistic (the so-called mixed-motive games). This seems to correspond most closely to the picture people have in their minds when they think of conflict (Halevy et al., 2012).

Fighting for one's own solution without compromise (win–lose: I win, the others lose) and enforcing one's own existing power is often risky even for the party that wins the game, at least in the long run. It is questionable whether the losing party will actively cooperate in the future. It may try to secretly undermine it.

Conflict avoidance is a very common behavior. However, when conflict resolution is required for good outcomes, avoidance results in both parties having disadvantages (Lose–Lose). Enforcement and avoidance, therefore, are generally unsatisfactory strategies. Expressed with game theory, conflict resolution is often a zero-sum game or win–lose situation (win–lose). In many cases, a compromise is probably the best achievable solution for all.

The ideal win–win solution, in which all parties can bring their interests together in such a way that they see themselves as winners (ideal combination of the interests of both parties), is usually hard to find, but it can be worth investing time in coaching and looking for it to avoid a compromise that is only half-heartedly supported by everyone because of the less than fully satisfactory results.

6.5.6.5 Conflict Management Methods

According to Vollmer and Vetter (2022, p. 228 f.), three methods of conflict management can be distinguished:

1. *Negotiation* (discussion of actual or perceived differences of interest, aiming at seeking a solution accepted by all parties involved)
2. *Mediation* (a mediator helps the parties find a solution, especially for relationship conflicts; see Montada & Kals, 2013; Brummans et al., 2022)
3. *Constructive controversy* (advocacy principle, rational argumentation, change of perspective, and integrative decision-making, aiming at a solution that is justified by objective data and socially supported)

Vollmer and Vetter (2022) explain these and other findings of general conflict research in their contribution to conflict management in coaching as background knowledge for coaches and clients. They emphasize that it is more promising to work preventively or prospectively in coaching at early stages of conflict emergence, if possible, and not only curatively when the conflicts have become virulent. They see the task of coaches in "generating understanding for the conflict situation" in their clients on this basis and guiding them to a comprehensive analysis to derive options for action, a suitable conflict management strategy and methods for dealing with the conflict. However, this requires an explanation of the advantages and disadvantages of different conflict management strategies in coaching. Some coaches, however, do not consider knowledge transfer in coaching to be acceptable in principle because this does not fit their understanding of the role of coaches. This attitude reaches its limits, however, at the latest when a client undifferentiatedly considers the win–lose strategy to be the best and wants to assert himself ruthlessly and antisocially in a conflict with a solution that is only advantageous for him or her and wants to instrumentalize the coach for an unethical goal.

Astrid Schreyögg (2002, pp. 92 ff.) emphasizes that clients can be successfully supported only by coaching in the analysis and management of their conflicts if, in the initial stages of conflict, only a certain hardening in the dispute has developed and groups with different points of view are emerging. Coaching is still possible when mutual typifications and first mutual accusations and insults or first aggressions begin. If, however, they prevail unlimitedly and are communicated to outsiders to generally damage the image of the opponents or if threatening strategies are practiced and finally even hit to harm and destroy the opponents, professional process counseling or mediation is needed, according to Schreyögg. In the end, only formal "power interventions" remain, e.g., by the company's board of directors (if it is not already involved in a problematic way) or, in the case of legal disputes, court proceedings are already to be expected.

The studies cited by Vollmer and Vetter and Schreyögg's suggestions on practical experience warn coaches to be rather cautious about their ability to resolve conflicts through coaching. In a guideline that we use in our coaching training (Greif, 2025, in prep.), we therefore focus on analyzing and reflecting on conflicts and jointly searching for ways to de-escalate conflicts and for starting points for developing cooperative solutions, which normally seem possible in the early stages of conflict dynamics. To better understand the perspective of the other side and to learn more sensitive communication behavior, exercises with the empty chair method described above can be used.

6.5.7 Leadership Behavior

In their contribution to the importance of leadership theories in coaching, Felfe and Elprana (2022, p. 532) provide a short summary of the task and superordinate goal "to direct employee behavior toward the fulfillment of the organization's goals." As different general management functions, they mention the following: formulating goals, organizing, deciding, and controlling. To the personnel leading, they count instructing, delegating, and motivating as well as training and education. They mention the following as typical management instruments and tools:

- "Goal setting
- Control systems or feedback discussions
- Assessment system or assessment interview
- Personnel development programs
- Instruction, training and education
- Team meetings, moderation, presentation
- Job descriptions and requirement profiles
- Planning and control, budgeting
- Instructions and regulations
- Time management techniques" (op. cit., p. 534)

A theme of coaching can be any of the leadership functions and tools listed by Felfe and Elprana. In addition to promoting reflection on these issues, the practical concern of managers is often to improve their communication behavior and leadership skills. In most cases, the behavior of employees or other persons is the first concern from the manager's point of view, followed by his or her own communication behavior. All the methods listed above in the *chapter on communication* for understanding the behavior of other people and for reflecting and changing one's own communication behavior are therefore important in the behavioral changes that managers seek in coaching. We do not need to describe the methods recommended for this again here and refer to the coaching methods already described.

When coaching executives, their particular tasks and goals must always be taken into account. In concrete terms, therefore, coaching can be about preparing planned discussions with employees or work teams, especially to convince them of necessary changes, in line with the concept of transformational leadership mentioned above. The conviction of the necessity of upcoming organizational changes and inviting them to actively participate, ideally even to inspire them, are crucial communications. Felfe and Elprana (2022) highlight the practical importance of this empirically well-confirmed leadership behavior for coaching. It is particularly important in *the coaching of change management. In a chapter* below, this is discussed in more detail.

Coaching can be useful as a companion to the practical use of all the above mentioned management tasks and tools after clients have become familiar with them in management seminars. For each new management task, coaching can help with planning and preparation and, for example, through telephone or online coaching via video, accompany the implementation. Coaching is particularly recommended for clients who are taking on a management role for the first time. Böning (2022) described the special features of coaching top managers. In his experience, they prefer highly experienced coaches with an entrepreneurial perspective and experience in corporate policy because they feel that only with them can they discuss the company's situation competently and safely.

Weihrauch et al. (2022) emphasize that an important orientation basis for leadership coaching is the concept of "good leadership." To this end, three cultures are reflected upon with the clients and put into practice:

1. Culture of excellence (open, hierarchy-free communication, problem-solving culture, constructive error culture and constructive dispute and conflict culture)
2. Culture of appreciation (trust, fairness, and appreciation)
3. Ethical leadership culture (Providing meaning and vision, setting common goals and agreeing on objectives, transparency through information and communication, fairness, autonomy and participation, role modeling, and others)

As the reproduced suggestions show, leadership coaching is extraordinarily multifaceted, depending on the position, organizational context, and situation of the clients. Scientific findings from general leadership research and the practical application of leadership methods (Kerschreiter et al., 2018) can help coaches take these particularities into account in their coaching tasks and address them in their individually adapted methodological approach in each case.

6.6 Stress Management, Burnout Prevention, and Health

Stress is generally the other side of the coin for all high-performance demands or a side effect when coping with complex, uncertain situations or conflicts. Clients who have initially come to coaching to improve their performance often address in the further course of coaching that they suffer from stress due to time pressure or too many tasks, technical breakdowns of the technology, constant action interruptions, unclear or contradictory instructions, and unfair behavior of their superiors as well as frictions and conflicts. In the following, methods for the analysis of the stress situation, reduction of stressors, relaxation and meditation, and empowerment of competences in stress management, which can be used in coaching, are explained.

Notably, health coaching rarely makes additional reference to stress management and burnout prevention (see the compendium by Sforzo et al., 2019), although there is overlap in symptoms and methods of assessing psychological and physical well-being and intervention methods. The disease itself can also trigger feelings of stress when its course is uncertain or when treatment is arduous. In this section, an arc is drawn between both fields, as shown below.

6.6.1 Coaching in Stress and Burnout Situations

6.6.1.1 What Is Stress?

Many definitions are based on the transactional stress model of Lazarus (1966). According to this model, feelings of stress are experienced not only in dangerous situations or when performance demands are high but also in the case of minor daily hassles. Stress feelings are the result of an interaction or transaction between the situation and the person's subsequent appraisals of the situation. "Stress" (more precisely, a "feeling of stress") is thereby generally regarded as an aversively experienced state of tension (Semmer et al., 2005) through negative feelings such as uncertainty, anxiety, frustration, and anger. The following expansion of the definition, which is based on Lazarus (Greif, 1991, p. 13), is suitable as a basis for an interview and analysis of the subjective feelings and thoughts of clients in the coaching conversation.

Stress Definition
The person experiences the situation as a subjectively intensive and unpleasant state of tension, which

- is nearby in time (or has already occurred) and
- lasts for a long time, which they fear they will not be able to fully control, although its avoidance is subjectively important for this person.

During the coaching session, the characteristics listed in the definition can be considered and explored individually with the client. If all of them apply, the situation can be classified as a *"stress situation."*

Now, according to a common definition, *"stressors"* can simply denote any *characteristics or conditions* that elicit *feelings of stress* (Semmer & Mohr, 2001).

Typical stressors are as follows:

- Time pressure
- Tasks that are too difficult
- Action interruptions
- Problems with work organizations
- Problems in cooperation and coordination
- Handling and trouble with difficult persons
- Environmental loads

- Accident risks
- Insecurity, responsibility
- Intensive emotional demands
- Monotony
- Excessively long working hours

According to the available evidence, prolonged situations, conditions, or characteristics that elicit stress feelings "without light at the end of the tunnel" over a long period of time or that are continuously repeated can have negative consequences for psychological well-being as well as cumulatively impair psychosomatic and somatic well-being (Semmer & Udris, 1993; Zapf & Semmer, 2004). According to the now "classic" longitudinal studies by Karasek and Theorell (1990), prolonged severe stress can increase the risk of myocardial infarction if it is associated with low decision latitude in action. However, to a certain extent, one cannot avoid or "buffer" the feeling of stress through greater decision latitude.

According to the *effort-reward-imbalance model* of Siegrist (1996), high demands of effort in work, which are not compensated in the long run by rewards (e.g., recognition) for the invested efforts, lead to stress and a weakening of the personal resources of the person. According to his surveys, the probability of coronary heart disease increases in this constellation.

6.6.1.2 What Is Burnout?

Freudenberger (1974) introduced the technical term "burnout" after he and others, who were originally very committed participants in the "Free Clinic Movement" and who felt completely emotionally exhausted and had no more energy. He suggested that this "burnout" occurs primarily in social particularly professions, in care work, because this work with people makes particularly intense emotional demands. In addition, he noted that burnout specifically affects those who have previously been very committed to their jobs. ("Whoever is burned out must have burned before.") According to the current state of research, however, burnout has been proven for numerous other occupational groups and without prior particularly committed activity, e.g., in the case of career starters (Burisch, 2010, p. 215 ff.).

Christina Maslach is one of the leading burnout experts. She distinguishes among three dimensions of the burnout experience (Maslach, 2017, p. 143 f.):

1. Exhaustion (lost energy and become depleted, debilitated, and fatigued)
2. Cynicism (negative or inappropriate attitudes toward clients or customers, having become irritable, lost idealism, and withdrawn)
3. Decline in professional efficacy (reduced personal accomplishment and productivity or capability, low morale, and an inability to cope)

Burisch (2015, p. 7, free translation) noted that burnout syndrome is difficult to distinguish from other syndromes. He highlights three core symptoms:

1. Emotional exhaustion
2. Subjective decline in performance
3. "Dehumanization" ("having negative or inappropriate attitudes, especially toward customers, employees, and colleagues")

Pines and Kafry (1978, p. 499) highlight "exhaustion" as the most important symptom in their definition and define burnout as "a general experience of physical, emotional and attitudinal exhaustion."

According to available studies, the main cause of emotional exhaustion in burnout is permanent overload due to stress. Burisch (2015, p. 76) names persistent stress, which is perceived as being without a way out, a "key phenomenon" in burnout but adds five levels that contribute to it (p. 10):

1. Individual level (wishes, needs, goals, abilities, personality traits, and attitudes, e.g., fixation on performance goals)
2. Interpersonal level (e.g., excessive performance expectations of supervisors)
3. Institutional level (e.g., an organizational culture with little recognition and consideration)
4. Societal level (such as societal conflicts).
5. Global level (such as global crises affecting one's own work)

6.6.1.3 Burnout and Mental Disorders

The symptoms of burnout and depression overlap in cases of severe burnout (Schonfeld & Bianchi, 2016). Therefore, coaches must be very careful with their clients not to cross the line to psychotherapy. To diagnose and treat depression, a qualification as a psychiatrist or psychotherapist and clinical experience are needed. Coaches who accept clients with burnout as clients must consult specialists or psychotherapists if there are indications of symptoms of depression (Greif, 2014a, 2014b). This also applies to anxiety disorders. They are less common but can also occur. Coaching can be used only as a preventive measure to prevent burnout in the case of persistent stress or initial emotional exhaustion symptoms in the early stages of burnout, as long as no symptoms have yet developed that would be classified as "mental disorders" according to the ICD-10 (2012).

6.6.2 Resource-Oriented Analysis of the Stress Situation and Burnout Risks

A stress analysis in coaching begins with the questions described above about the perceived situation. If the situation can be classified as a "stressful situation" according to the client's perceptions, it is recommended that the situation be explored in more detail, as explained in the guidelines for "resource-oriented stress analysis"

(Greif, 2025, in prep.). The clients are asked to describe which unpleasant ("aversive") sensations they experience in the situation and what they perceive as eliciting them. They should then state how strong these negative sensations are and how long they expect them to last and to recur in the future. It is also important to ask how long it takes them to calm down after the situation. If the clients describe that they feel emotionally exhausted, that the situations will continue for a very long time in the future, and that they need a very long time to calm down again, these would be alarming indications of burnout.

It is important psychologically not to dramatize the descriptions of the feelings but to receive them with interest, calmness, and understanding. Wherever possible, it should be respectfully acknowledged that the client has endured difficult situations. One can also ask how they have been able to cope. This, and the question of what gave them more energy after or during the stressful situation, quickly allows the analysis to move on to positive resources for coping with the situation. Did they use resources, e.g., their own potentials or other sources of strength and abilities, to cope with the situation, or were they supported by other people? What could be changed in the future?

To ensure that clients do not overlook important stressors, opportunities for improvement, or resources, a guideline for resource-oriented stress analysis (Greif, 2025, in preparation) contains checklists in which many stressors, starting points for improvement, and resources can be quickly flagged. Afterward, they are evaluated in more detail and summarized together in the coaching conversation—as in a professional conversation between experts, always supported by empathetic respect for the observations and achievements of the clients coping with the stress. In this way, a comprehensive picture of the stress situation emerges. Initial starting points for coping with demands, making greater use of resources, and improving the stress situation are revealed. The clients are always very grateful because normally, no one before has taken so much time to analyze their personal situation so thoroughly and with so much understanding.

If clients feel emotionally exhausted after continuous stress and find it difficult to recover, or if they are unable to recover at all, it would be necessary to clarify whether this might be a symptom of burnout. For diagnostic prescreening, coaches can use established standard questionnaires to assess burnout as well as depression questionnaires.

The classic burnout questionnaire is the Maslach Burnout Inventory (MBI). The fourth edition (Maslach & Jackson, 1981) contains subscales on (1) emotional exhaustion, (2) depersonalization, (3) personal accomplishment, (4) cynicism, and (5) professional efficacy.

Depression is often assessed by the Beck Depression Inventory (BDI) (revised edition Beck et al., 1996). Alternative answers are given for each question, and respondents are asked to choose between them. This allows us to assess the intensity of depression. For example:

0. I do not feel sad.
1. I feel sad.
2. I am sad all the time, and I cannot snap out of it.
3. I am so sad or unhappy that I cannot stand it.

The screening can provide preliminary, rough diagnostic information. However, it does not replace a qualified clinical diagnosis by specialists, licensed psychotherapists, or medical doctors. The coach must openly state that he or she is not qualified to treat burnout with depressive episodes. However, he or she can accompany the client in finding a licensed psychotherapist.

6.6.3 Reduction of Stressors

One approach to improving the situation of clients is to reduce stressors or improve the conditions that lead to feelings of stress in clients. This approach to stress prevention is called "structural changes" and is distinguished from the "behavioral changes" of stressed individuals (cf. Bamberg et al., 2011). Structural changes are considered fundamental and should be pursued as a priority. If the stressors are reduced, the causing conditions can be sustainably improved. Behavior change without reducing stressors is often just "curing the symptoms." The possibilities for structural change in coaching are first summarized below (Greif & Palmer, 2022). They are described in more detail in a guideline on reducing stressors (Greif, 2025, in prep.).

Stressors such as time pressure due to too little time to perform tasks or too many tasks or stress due to conflicts with people (customers, supervisors or other employees), error-prone computer programs, or technologies are often accepted as if they cannot be changed. Even superiors underestimate their influence on stress-related improvements in technology, work processes, and task organization. In coaching, problem areas can be identified, and starting points for improvement can be found. The proposed solutions are then developed with the client. In the process, the role of the coach temporarily changes to that of a consultant if he or she has the required knowledge and experience. The following two case studies illustrate the procedure. (Only the part of the coaching that relates to analysis and advice on decreasing the stress situation is shown.)

> The first case study involves a lawyer who performs legal consulting in his company. He points out that he is confronted with increasing requests for advice, which he can hardly cope with anymore. Moreover, he processes unfinished inquiries on increasingly longer working days and takes them home on weekends. As a result, he no longer has time for his family and becomes alienated, especially from his little daughter. In the coaching, we first analyzed the stress situation, resources, and goals. Then, we analyzed step-by-step (visualized using notes on a sequence of small cards) the exact process from the receipt of the request, the processing of the task, and the communication to the completion of the processing and the feedback reactions. The sequence shows that he receives requests by mail and starts to answer individual emails as quickly as possible. Short requests are answered immediately, and their processing speed is highly appreciated by the firm. However, his solutions usually immediately stimulate further communications and queries or corrections of the requests, which had been obviously formulated in a mistakable or misleading way. (Assumption: The quick answer also raises additional questions because the inquirers are still in the loop and online.)

Two changes have been made together as a solution to reduce the amount of work: (1) The lawyer has developed a short form with clarifying questions, which can be sent to the questioner. (2) Only a limited number of top urgent requests are answered immediately. Even if he has already processed the requests, he normally sends them out only at the end of his working day.

The changes have worked quite as expected, with no perceptible dissatisfaction of the inquirers. His response on the next working day was still considered very fast. The form reduces unnecessary additional interactions following misunderstandings. Rejections became less frequent, and the perceived quality of his legal advice even improved! He now managed to get home earlier in the evenings almost all the time and is happy because he very rarely had to take weekend work home. He profited much from implementation support (see *Sect. 9.3.3: Sustainable Implementation Support as a Metalevel Success Factor*). However, efficient clients must be careful not to immediately fill out the time they have gained with newly assumed tasks. This leads to a self-created vicious cycle.

In the second case study, I was consulted by a medical doctor at a clinic who headed the surgical department. It was a "goldmine" for the clinic, as he proudly said. However, as he himself feared, his constant stress amounted to burnout. He managed his work only with the last strength and already often felt emotionally exhausted. The equipment was outdated and required annoying extra work for the staff and for him. New equipment has long since been applied for, and the procurement applications have been reviewed by experts and approved by the hospital director. However, the responsible head of finance did not send them out but instead wanted to obtain further expert advice without pushing this forward quickly. The head of the surgical department felt helpless and angry at the same time. Not all positions in his department could be filled (here, too, the chief financial officer is putting the brakes on), and now his senior physician, who was completely stressed, was absent by illness. He himself had a cold and could hardly get up in the morning to go to work. After our stress analysis, the application of the MBI and a depression questionnaire revealed an acute burnout risk but no depression risk. He still has much (angry) energy to do something against unbearable conditions. Without going further into detail, quick "solutions" were worked out in the coaching conversations and accompanied by the coach in all steps. The first step involved talking to team members and gaining support for the next steps. The second step involved informing the chief financial officer and clinic director by an urgent email about the intolerable stress situation and the expected risks for the clinic. Without very quick measures as a result, it must be feared that the health of employees would deteriorate. This would end up being very expensive for the clinic. He shared that he himself is also already in poor health and will be out for at least a few days. It gave him strength that the employees were fully behind him and that the reaction of the director of the clinic followed immediately and shortly thereafter also the procurement promised by the chief financial officer. A doctor could even be quickly hired as a substitute. The delivery and installation of the new surgical equipment took time; however, "there was light at the end of the tunnel." This fits the definition of stress and that the stress feelings of everyone on the team could be reduced as expected. Overall, the coaching was completed in very few online videos and phone conversations and emails. The client's ratings with the evaluation sheet were consistently high, and his gratitude was very high.

Above the coaching definitions (see *Sect. 2.3*), it was noted that there are coaching concepts that reject any form of counseling in coaching. According to my definition, however, coaching is understood not only as the promotion of result-oriented reflections but also as counseling to improve the achievement of self-congruent goals or for conscious self-transformation and self-development (see Sect. 2.5*: Self-Congruent Goals, Self-Transformation, and Self-Development*). The consulting activity in the coaching is based on the concept of empowering the clients to help themselves. This means that coaches in both roles may share their own observations and make "reflective suggestions" (suggestions that provoke reflection and questioning of the suggestions). However, their clients' ownership of decisions about goals and solutions must always be respected and explicitly emphasized. In particular, stress management and health coaching require expertise and psychoeducative consulting interventions, as the case examples demonstrate.

For more complex problems, changes may require coaching, as in organizational change (see *Sect. 6.8*). If the resulting costs and savings opportunities for the company suggest action or additional support from experts and if the client can convince his or her superiors, the client's initiative can mobilize powerful energy. If the measures are successful, they can even be useful for one's career.

It is important not to try to do everything alone but to involve other people as early as possible who are probably also suffering from stressful situations. It is often important to estimate the costs for the company and to inform superiors and those responsible at an early stage. Structural changes through reductions in stressors by improving work design can lead to a substantial reduction in sickness-related absenteeism or even dismissal. Therefore, they are among the investments whose payback is, according to experience, easily verifiable and relatively certain. They can therefore communicate very well to supervisors in the organization. In coaching, difficult communications and negotiations can be prepared and possibly simulated, as in the case study on the surgical department above.

6.6.4 Activation of Resources and Coping Competencies

Recent stress theories emphasize the importance of a person's ability to cope with stressful situations. Personal resources are especially important when it seems impossible to improve the stress situation structurally. In coaching, one can then prioritize looking for resources that will help them cope with stress. In the following list, four types of resources and examples are given (see the guidelines on stress analysis and improvement in Greif, 2025, in prep.):

1. *Personal resources and strengths* (e.g., energy, willpower, skills, expertise, practical experience, learning skills, self-confidence, optimism, resilience, quick self-calming after stress, healthy sleep, regular exercise and healthy diet)
2. *Social resources* (e.g., mutual social support and a good team atmosphere, sympathetic supervisors, colleagues or coworkers, professional experts are available to help)
3. *Resources within the work activity* (e.g., discretion or latitude in carrying out the job, quieter work phases or recovery breaks after stressful phases, few action interruptions and minimal distractions from colleagues or incoming information, good working time organization)
4. *Organizational resources* (e.g., financial resources, access to knowledge in internal databases or on the Internet, appreciation of work performance, good

information about company policy, good general working atmosphere, influence on decisions about the organization of work, job security, positive future of the company)

As a first resource, clients can analyze in coaching which existing personal resources or "coping competencies" they can use or newly learn to better cope with the stressful situation. This may require behavioral changes that enable more efficient coping. For example, clients can create free space for themselves through better time management (especially through better control and shortening of "idle" conversations or through more efficient work processes).

In their large, classic longitudinal studies, Karasek and Theorell (1990) confirmed their assumption that stressful work demands lead to negative psychological and physiological stress consequences in the long term, where the decision latitude in their job performance is narrow and, furthermore, social support from colleagues and superiors in the workplace is weak (Shirom et al., 2009). The expansion of this decision latitude is thus a resource that enables clients, for example, to buffer particularly hectic work phases by taking short breaks or short quiet work phases. This can even increase work productivity. Social support from other people is another resource that has been shown to be particularly important. This includes not only concrete help but also opportunities to speak out and consult with sympathetic partners about what can be done. Coaches are undoubtedly also such a social resource. Empathetic listening and "moral" support from friends are helpful, and both can be encouraged in coaching.

The importance of *organizational resources* is often overlooked. Money can be used to finance expertise, training or coaching, or technical systems that do the work for you. In coaching, I often encourage clients to search the Internet or AI for knowledge that will help them. Accordingly, such resources can also be a theme in coaching.

6.6.5 Relaxation and Meditation

Relaxation or meditation techniques can be used to better cope with stressful situations. In practice, they are often seen as a separate group. However, similar to the improvement of coping skills and the use of other resources, they belong to the superordinate group of "individual behavioral changes."

A Google search with the keywords "stress, coaching and relaxation" (as of January 2021) returned more than 1.7 million entries. The search for "stress, coaching and meditation" resulted in more than 32 million entries. Many coaching providers recommend such methods on their websites as their main or even only intervention against stress. As stated above, it is problematic if stressful situations can continue to exert their negative effects unchanged. How does one manage to fight the permanent overwhelming stress caused by increasing time pressure with relaxation or meditation techniques? It does not get any lower.

I remember how outraged the attending nurses from hospitals in the USA reacted when a speaker in her presentation on burnout at the conference "Coaching in Leadership and Health care" (Institute of Coaching, Harvard Medical School Affiliate, 28-29th September 2018, Boston, USA), recommended practicing relaxation exercises in the evening against their exhaustion owing to constant exercise over time. The nurses felt that their rough hospital realities were not being taken seriously and only calmed down after I said that structural improvements (more staff and less overtime) were needed here first. (The speaker was relieved that she could now continue her presentation).

In addition to structural improvements and the activation of coping skills, relaxation and meditation techniques are very useful. There are different methods, which are propagated by separate associations and schools and have found ways into coaching methods. The classics are "progressive muscle relaxation" according to Jacobson (1925) and "autogenic training" according to Schultz (1928/1979). Today, relaxation suggestions with hypnotherapeutic methods, yoga exercises, and especially mindfulness meditations (Bosch & Michel, 2022) or biofeedback and many other methods are becoming increasingly popular. From the beginning until the present, there are firm beliefs that each preferred distinct method is suitable and best. However, with regard only to the effectiveness of the methods, this dispute is essentially obsolete. The different methods seem to have comparable physiological and psychological relaxation effects (Hamm, 2009).

Mindfulness exercises have their roots in the basic meditative practice and religious teachings of ZEN Buddhism. There are teachers who see this exercise with the awareness that their body functions as an introduction to this theology for their clients. Short meditations, each lasting only 3 min, are completely unacceptable against this background. Even if one were to meditate for an hour a day, this would at best be a preliminary exercise. It must therefore be openly stated that such short exercises are alienated to speak of "secularized" techniques, which have almost nothing in common with the original ZEN meditations.

After only 5 to 10 days, very short mindfulness meditations, such as the breathing exercise, can reduce emotional exhaustion caused by high work demands and improve job satisfaction (Hülsheger et al., 2013). These effects, which can be felt quickly by clients, probably explain why they are so readily used for self-calming when stress and emotional exhaustion are still "manageable." However, when clients can no longer generate energy for such short exercises or are unable to relax, this may indicate impaired self-calming abilities and severe burnout. Psychotherapists should be consulted in this case.

In coaching, clients in my experience can practice different variations of short-breathing exercises for self-calming:

1. Self-calming after a stressful situation comes down from stress (3 min, preferably in a quiet place or with a smartphone and mailing turned off, etc.)
2. Before expected stressful situations (e.g., before lectures and exams or in the morning as a meditative start before a stressful day)
3. In stressful situations (if they perceive their own stress reactions, they start a deep relaxing breathe, which is not recognizable to others)

The first option is probably the most common. You can also enter certain times with an abbreviation in your diary several times a day to bring some peace into your stressful day. The most demanding exercise is the third variant. It requires repeated practice until you are able to calm yourself with a deep breath and then succeed in doing so in a real stressful situation. (As a starter, it is a good exercise to perform it during stressful phone calls.)

The three variants of the method can be combined. However, excitement in stressful situations often prevents rigorous performance of the exercises over a longer period. Without implementation support through coaching, most forget what they have set out to do or do not manage to adjust to it, even if it would do them well. For clients to learn these techniques and use them routinely, experience has shown that the implementation support described above is necessary in coaching when they are learning new habits (see Sect. *9.3: Sustainable Implementation Support as a Metalevel Success Factor*).

According to my own practical observations, such breathing exercises can be recommended routinely with little effort for clients in addition to measures to reduce stressors and use resources. A single-case longitudinal study of a stressed entrepreneur over several months with additional stress reduction measures, breathing exercises, and biofeedback was conducted after daily measurements of heart rate variability and blood pressure (Greif & Palmer, 2022).

6.6.6 Health Coaching

Todorova (2022) described the role of coaches in health coaching and interdisciplinary collaboration with physicians in the treatment of obesity, diabetes, heart disease, hypertension, and high cholesterol. Coaches need careful professional training and practical experience in each of these areas so that they know exactly what to look for when following the doctor's treatment plan. Unlike in other coaching sessions, in some treatments, they have to be able to explain to the clients in detail and precisely when to take which medications and which additional exercises should be performed. For this task, it makes sense to qualify medical nurses or medical-technical assistants as coaches in the future.

The *"Psychoeducational enlightenment"* of the clients (see *Sect. 6.5.3*), concerning their behavior or feelings and intended to influence both, seems to be indispensable in health coaching. In the case of diabetes, for example, health coaches must be able to explain to clients in a motivating way not only information about medication and dosage but also how to perform measurements of blood glucose levels, dietary instructions and how they feel better afterward, and rules of conduct for emergency situations caused by hypoglycemia or hyperglycemia.

Health coaching is a field of work for coaches (Bamberg, 2022; Todorova, 2022) that is likely to grow strongly internationally with many specializations. In workplace health management (Badura et al., 1999; Bamberg et al., 2011), coaches can assist in the implementation of measures, specifically in the introduction of regulations for "healthy leadership" (Rudolph et al., 2020), through the coaching of executives. As Todorova (2022) explained, even during pandemics such as the COVID-19 pandemic, coaches can help families and single people cope psychologically with the often difficult situations they face.

However, too little attention has been given to the obvious links between health coaching and stress management coaching. Stress at work and burnout, as described above, can result in health problems. In addition, acute and chronic illnesses themselves are critical life events that can change and strain life situations to a very large extent. The approaches and methods described above can therefore help improve the stress situation in coping with illness and promote the support of families and social networks.

6.7 Team Coaching[6]

According to Jones (2022), most publications on team coaching address coaching sessions performed by independent or external coaches. Coaches usually take an eclectic approach that is systemic in nature. However, how coaches do that is unclear. She sees this as a future research task.

6.7.1 Team Coaching as Multilevel Coaching

A team consists of its individual members. Therefore, it is necessary to consider not only the team as a whole in coaching but also the individual members with their different ideas and characteristics. *Multilevel team coaching* (Greif, 2008, p. 287 ff.) takes this into account. It is an integrative approach based on West's team reflection concept (West & Anderson, 1996), which is mentioned in *Sect. 4.2*. It was further described as team coaching, tested in practice, and evaluated in case studies. A theoretical background is the multilevel systems theory of Mario von Cranach (1996). According to this theory, human actions are always organized on several levels. The levels are distinguished as individual, group, and organization. These levels are connected via interactions. Because all levels have their own special characteristics, none of them should be disregarded in coaching. The "multilevel work" of the coach consists of individual interviews with the team leadership and all team members as well as selected important key persons in the organizational context. The core is work at the group level.

According to the assumption of team reflexivity by West (2012), team productivity and innovativeness in complex group tasks improve when teams regularly reflect on their performance and how to improve it. As summarized by Dick et al. (2018), West and colleagues performed annual employee surveys with several hundred thousand UK health-care employees. Their *Team Reflectivity Questionnaire* includes three questions (cited from Dick et al., free translation) for this purpose that lend themselves well to team coaching interviews:

[6] I thank Christine Gockel for valuable suggestions on this section.

1. "Does your team have clear goals?"
2. "Do you work closely together to achieve these goals?"
3. "Do you meet regularly to reflect on your performance and discuss possible improvements?"

These three questions are answered "yes" by approximately 40% of the teams in hospitals. If hospitals predominantly have teams with positive agreement with the questions, the frequency of failure as well as bullying by patients and/or colleagues is significantly lower. As a remarkable "hard" criterion, lower patient mortality has been shown at the same time (Dick et al., 2018). The questions can also be used somewhat reformulated to evaluate reflections during team coaching. Questionnaires on "team climate" can be used to analyze additional areas of reflection, such as reflection on the team's vision, task-related reflexivity (frequent discussion of goals and improvement of working procedures), or constructive handling of conflicts. Their use and subsequent feedback of summarized responses are readily accepted by team members because the results provide concrete suggestions as to where team members feel there is room for improvement. Subsequent interventions at the group level are led by coaches or facilitators and consist of joint reflection exercises and plans to improve team climate (West, 2004). In the coaching field, this extraordinarily practical theory has received little attention because it is classified as a "team development" method rather than a coaching method. Since the focus of the method of West is on promoting "result-oriented reflections," it could very clearly, in our understanding and definition, also be considered "coaching" at the same time (see *Sect. 2.5: Coaching to Promote Result-Oriented Problem- and Self-Reflections* and Sect. *4.2: Group and Team Coaching*).

6.7.2 Performing Multilevel Coaching

After team coaching sessions of my own and supervised by me, as well as two longitudinal case studies of multilevel team coaching on student projects in psychology (Greif, 2008, p. 340 ff.), the following process has emerged (see the guideline text on team coaching in Greif, 2025, in prep.):

1. Preliminary interviews with clients and team management
2. Introduction of the coaches to the employees
3. Interviews with participants and questionnaires
4. First team meeting (with feedback from interviews and questionnaires)
5. Individual coaching sessions
6. Follow-up appointments
7. Interviews with participants and questionnaires
8. Conclusion and before/after comparisons

After the initial interviews, the multilevel work begins with the introduction of the coaches to the employees and a first draft, agreed with the management, of the team coaching process and the themes and questions to be discussed in the interviews with the participants. Suggestions for changes are strongly encouraged. The interviews are then performed with all of the participants. The interviews will focus on team members' work priorities and functions, goals and wishes, expectations and fears regarding team coaching, what they think is going well in the team and in the organizational context, and what should be improved. The planned process of team coaching is explained, and suggestions for change are included. Each team member can take advantage of confidential individual coaching sessions.

If possible, face-to-face coaching is preferable as the start of coaching at the group level. This requires at least half a day. Online coaching should take place in several shorter time blocks (quickly following each other on several days with many exercises in rotating pairs and subgroups). In addition, short online sessions on specific themes and exercises can be performed later in a very flexible way.

In terms of content, the first group meeting begins with a compilation of the goals and wishes of the participants (board, whiteboard, or a corresponding online tool) and the program with the recorded suggestions for change. For groups that know each other well, a round of introductions in which everyone says something about themselves that others do not yet know (hobbies, interests, experiences) has also proven useful. In teams with conflicts, it is not only advisable to lay down communication rules and discuss the advantages for the team climate and for reducing conflicts if team members learn to treat each other with respect and appreciation.

Rules of communication:

- Only one person talks at a time.
- The others listen and let what is said sink in.
- Respect the fact that the others have a different point of view than you do.
- Speak with appreciation about what you have heard—especially if you disagree or criticize.
- Accept that the coaches take care (in a friendly and appreciative way) that no one is criticized in a very general way.

The further course depends on the specific themes and goals to be worked on in the team coaching. Exercises can be performed with all together or with alternating subgroups or pairs, such as the following example exercise:

Example Exercise: What Do I Want from the Team and What Can I Contribute?

Form pairs to discuss two questions with each other:

1. What do I want from my colleagues on the team?
2. What can I offer the team so that we can work together in a better way?

In the plenary, they then present their ideas in turn (on a flipchart or whiteboard) and give appreciative feedback.

Afterward, they reflect together on what is likely to change positively in the team as a result of the suggestions that have been made. Finally, the implementation of the changes or wishes that have remained open are compiled and delegated to a subgroup.

If the team members plan to perform regular team reflections on improving tasks and cooperation processes (inspired by the interview questions on team reflexivity), it would be obvious for the coaches to moderate a session with reflections and suggestions on how these sessions should proceed. It is advisable to plan very concretely and close to behavior how this should be implemented in the future (e.g., with alternating teams of two in each case for preparing and moderating the sessions, planning for performing and recording the decisions, etc.). It is optimal if implementation starts immediately (possibly as a role-play simulation) and if the coaches supervise this and provide feedback and tips as needed. Afterward, the experiences are evaluated and possibly refined.

Multilevel team coaching can improve a group's self-confidence and motivation. It can also be useful for self-promotion in internal or external marketing. Dick et al. (2018) described scientifically reviewed methods for working with all work groups of an organization to formulate a coherent group vision and other team development interventions. It is important to clarify the decision-making and participation possibilities of employees from the perspective of the leader before they become the theme of the next meeting.

As part of multilevel work, it is advisable to perform individual coaching sessions with all team members and the team leader. The initial interview is a good start because it establishes a personal working relationship. Clients can also work on themes and goals in coaching that are not directly related to team coaching but are important to their work. Most often, however, the experience is reflected upon in the group coaching sessions. This is extremely helpful for coaches to identify different perceptions and interests more clearly. Since the coaching sessions are strictly confidential, only what the clients themselves want to bring up is brought up to the group. If the issues are conflictual, the coaching can discuss how this can be done in an appreciative way.

The team leader usually has the greatest need for coaching and wants to know what others think informally. However, confidentiality is especially important to maintain carefully here. It must be explained to the leader why it is impossible in professional coaching to break confidentiality. The leadership behavior in the team can be observed by the coaches if they wish this and open up very good learning opportunities.

6.8 Coaching During Organizational Changes

6.8.1 Coaching Needs and Method Overview

When managing organizational change, accompanying the coaching of executives, project managers, and core teams can be extremely useful. According to a survey of coaches by Bickerich and Michel (2022), there is a need for coaching in change management, especially in five areas:

1. Team and employee leadership
2. Self-presentation in the organization
3. Burnout prevention
4. Changes in positions or tasks
5. Change management (e.g., handling change resistance)

The first two topics require leadership and communication coaching, as explained in *Sect. 6.5*. Promising here is also the described coaching of the managers in promoting "Change Talks" in their teams with the method of *motivational interviewing* to consciously bring positive consequences of the changes to the front (see *Sect. 6.5: Motivational Interviewing*).

The third topic, *burnout prevention*, may seem surprising here. However, the often uncertain consequences of organizational changes and always additional tasks and challenges can overwhelm managers and employees. Unsurprisingly, many individuals experience intensive stress, and some even feel threatened by burnout. According to a survey by Kriegesmann et al. (2009), 23% complain of severe emotional exhaustion during organizational change, a core symptom of burnout. The coaching methods for improving *stress management and burnout prevention* described in *Sect. 6.6* are therefore very relevant in terms of organizational change. In addition, the reduction in structural stressors and increase in resources in the change process are prioritized over individual relaxation or coping behavior. According to my own coaching experiences, it would be optimal to call for additional resources (e.g., temporary employees or external help) from the responsible highest management levels at an early stage before those involved are no longer able to cope with the increased demands by performing well. These temporary extra resources can lead to an easing of stress during changes, which increases employees' motivation to participate. If the requirement for these resources is communicated convincingly in negotiations between project managers and management levels and if they are managed successfully during changes, the manager's reputation will rise. The communication of the requirements and the negotiations can be prepared in coaching.

A positive opportunity to manage change is that successfully implemented change projects increase the chances for career advancement of the change manager. Regarding the fourth topic, preparation for position and task changes, the *Career Coaching* mentioned in *Sect. 4.7* or the *Strengths Analysis* in *Sect. 6.4.4* can be used here. It is recommendable that those who are leading change for the first time are supported by coaching when taking on this new responsibility.

Harbert (2006) designed a coaching program to prepare change managers. She starts group sessions of future change managers from different areas. Using case studies, managers prepare for their tasks and roles in the change process with role reversal and self-reflection. Later, she encouraged peer coaching and reflection on the experience. She emphasized the multifaceted nature of the coach roles. The development of competence and the implementation of changes are to be accompanied for up to 6 months.

The fifth topic, change accompaniment, expands the view of employees, especially in the case of resistance to change. Multilevel coaching would be optimal here (see *Sect. 6.7.1: Team Coaching and Multilevel Coaching*).

6.8.2 Better Communication

One focus of coaching executives and project managers in managing change is to improve their communication. John P. Kotter described the principles and eight steps in his well-known theory on managing organizational change, especially communication tasks, very clearly (Kotter, 2007, p. 4):

1. "Establishing a Sense of Urgency
   (a) Examining market and competitive realities
   (b) Identifying and discussing crises, potential crises, or major opportunities
2. Forming a Powerful Guiding Coalition
   (a) Assembling a group with enough power to lead the change effort
   (b) Encouraging the group to work together as a team
3. Creating a Vision
   (a) Creating a vision to help direct the change effort
   (b) Developing strategies for achieving that vision
4. Communicating the Vision
   (a) Using every vehicle possible to communicate the new vision and strategies
   (b) Teaching new behaviors by the example of the guiding coalition
5. Empowering Others to Act on the Vision
   (a) Getting rid of obstacles to change
   (b) Changing systems or structures that seriously undermine the vision
   (c) Encouraging risk taking and nontraditional ideas, activities, and actions
6. Planning for and Creating Short-Term Wins
   (a) Planning for visible performance improvements
   (b) Creating those improvements
   (c) Recognizing and rewarding employees involved in the improvements
7. Consolidating Improvements and Producing Still More Change
   (a) Using increased credibility to change systems, structures, and policies that do not fit the vision
   (b) Hiring, promoting, and developing employees who can implement the vision
   (c) Reinvigorating the process with new projects, themes, and change agents
8. Institutionalizing New Approaches
   (a) Articulating the connections between the new behaviors and corporate success
   (b) Developing the means to ensure leadership development and succession"

In coaching, these easy-to-grasp principles can be communicated well to clients and used as a basis for preparing and improving their communications (see the guideline text on managing complex change in Greif, 2025, in prep.).

6.8.3 Managing Complex and Uncertain Changes

Organizational changes are rarely simple and completely predictable in their course. The more people, systems, tasks, and processes involved, the more complex they are, and the more unforeseen events can occur. Even in the case of supposedly routine changes, there can be major surprises when individual people involved—justifiably or not—behave critically or when an unusual technical breakdown occurs. Change management is therefore often a management of uncertainty (Greif et al., 2004; Stacey, 2010).

6.8.3.1 Which Processes Are Difficult to Manage

As Dörner (2003) explains psychologically in his studies on the "logic of failure," many people are unable to successfully solve complex uncertain problems because they use problematic simplification strategies. Coaching can help to recognize complexity and uncertainties at an early stage and to consider them carefully.

Particular difficulties arise when there is a time lag before effects occur in the processes or when—as in the case of virus pandemics—they grow exponentially after an initially still small increase. The failure to manage the starting COVID-19 pandemic in 2020/21 in many countries is an example and had severe consequences. Further interesting examples of exponential growth in organizational change are rumors of perceived or actual employee redundancies. If a person considered credible confidentially claims that redundancies are impending, this is very quickly passed around the organization in exponentially growing networks of conversations until almost all employees have heard it. Once such rumors are removed from the world, even if they are false, they hinder or prevent the necessary cooperation in implementing change. If any informal communications are spread, it is advisable to counter them with verifiable facts as early as possible and to communicate this through credible people.

With all these changes, small events can lead to exponentially increasing negative consequences. A new SAP program was introduced in the delivery warehouse of a building materials manufacturer. An unreliable printer needed to print the delivery papers and small mistakes in the programming led to a sharp increase in waiting times to several hours and overcrowding of the parking facilities at the site for the trucks that were to pick up the building materials. The forklift drivers had complained about the printer, but this was not taken seriously at first. The technicians claimed that the misprints were due to operator errors on the part of the forklift drivers and low competence because the printer ran correctly when they tested it. It was only when the first customers threatened to go to the company's competitors because the waiting times were unacceptable for them that a systematic check was made and it was determined that it was not operator error on the part of the workers but rather faulty programming of the printer by the company that had installed it.

It is therefore particularly important to be alert to whether the negative consequences of organizational change have gone undetected or are increasing exponentially and may spiral out of control. It is particularly easy to overlook consequences that occur only after a time lag. When accompanying changes, coaches can repeatedly provide impetus to conduct situation analyses and sensitively search for small effects with potentially large impacts. The earlier resistance is identified and problems are solved, the greater the chances of managing it constructively. As the example of supposedly incompetent forklift drivers shows, employee criticism should not be dismissed prematurely but taken seriously.

6.8.3.2 Manage Uncertainty

Managing uncertainty is a timeless issue in modern leadership approaches, especially in change management theories (Stacey, 2010). It affects not only companies but also public administrations and politics (Hartley, 2000). Uncertainty increases the complexity of management tasks because, in addition to known tasks, one must prepare for unknown problems whose complexity is also usually uncertain. The obvious question is whether the management of such uncertainty is possible.

Principles whose application leads to successful problem solutions despite complex and uncertain events have been scientifically researched. The following seven principles can be derived from this for practical application (Greif, 2013b, 140 ff.):

1. Expect the unexpected!
2. Keep analyzing the characteristics and changes of the task and the system as well as the environment!
3. Pay attention to many small signs and problems and learn how they affect outcomes, even if the individual effects are minimal!
4. Look for time-lagged influences (effects that appear only after a longer time interval) and nonlinear increases in negative effects!
5. Do not rigidly hold on to a solution that does not work! Change the solution, try new ones, and thereby improve effectiveness and flexibility in problem solving!
6. Do not let initial failures demotivate you and thereby tempt you to give up prematurely! Change the solution and persistently try again and again until it works!
7. Clarify your feelings and quickly try to reduce negative feelings after failure experiences! Calm down, keep activating your resources, motivation, and energy over a long period of time!

It is psychologically plausible that uncertainty elicits feelings of stress (Bordia et al., 2004). However, clients, supported by coaching, can learn to "expect something unexpected." It would be optimal for them to be so prepared that they observe with eager curiosity as to whether such a thing will happen because it is interesting, and they hope that they can learn new insights from it. They can use coaching as a space to report their observations and engage in interesting reflections. Coaching can also help them relieve stress and negative feelings, keep reanalyzing the situation, and flexibly modify previous solutions. When they no longer react to uncertainty as being "driven" but as proactive analysts and active managers, their management skills and self-confidence can also grow enormously as a model for their social environment.

Coaching can stimulate managers to enter into the employee's perspective to have insightful conversations with them and reduce concerns or find better solutions together. Resistance is often an indication of difficulties that can be recognized and overcome. Wherever possible, solutions should be sought that minimize the disadvantages for those affected as much as possible. In some cases, compensation for the disadvantages must be negotiated.

6.8.3.3 Pull Out All the Stops!

When coaching major organizational change, coaches need to be able to "pull all the levers" or "pull out all the methodological stops." The following case provides an example.

Multilevel Coaching for the Customer-Oriented Reorganization of an Industrial Service Provider

The coaching assignment was intended to support one of Europe's largest industrial service providers in a customer-oriented reorganization. After a fundamental restructuring of a corporate group into different companies, each of which focused on its core business, 9 decentral operating business units with approximately 30 business areas and approximately 150 profit centers had to be transferred into independent companies on the very large company site. Whereas previously internal corporate customers in the company had to order their services primarily from them, they were now to offer their services in free competition with other service providers and at market costs. Purchasing, for example, could no longer expect former Group companies to handle all their orders through them. They had to become better and more cost-effective than competitors on the entire market to avoid losing companies as customers. The formerly centralized maintenance department also had to learn in the short term how to survive in competition as an independent service company.

With the support of a management consultancy, the necessary analyses were to be carried out to work out the strategic options and a business model as well as an implementation plan in consultation with the divisions and limited partners of the new service companies and to negotiate these with the works council. In the end, the entire plan had to be presented to the limited partners in a workshop for a decision.

A new CEO had been assigned with the transformation. A young project manager was appointed as a special project manager for management. He first suggested me as his personal coach and then also for the new CEO and as a companion for the overall project because he valued my practical experience in coaching conflictual changes and was interested in taking scientific knowledge into account. My main tasks were to coach the CEO and the project manager as well as the core team and to accompany the processes until the final workshop and decisions were made. I had to pull out all my stops and conduct numerous individual coaching sessions as well as multilevel coaching sessions. In addition to my role as an individual and team coach, I was a member of the negotiation team for critical negotiations together with the external management consultancy. The following list reflects the most important tasks:

- Coaching of the CEO
- Coaching of the project manager
- Coaching of the core team (key employees from all work areas)
- Selection of the consultancy (not one of the large consultancies but a small consultancy specializing in industrial sectors with a very dedicated and competent team)
- Preparation and implementation of corporate client surveys by core team members
- Participation in the elaboration of the vision and strategy
- Preparation and accompaniment of talks with the managers of the subdivisions and the limited partners (owners)
- Preparation and accompaniment of talks and negotiations with the works council
- Preparation of the communication concept for employees (by the members of the core team)
- Preparation and implementation of communication events with the management level, strategy team and core team
- Conflict management
- Preparation and implementation of the final workshop (with individual coaching of the CEO and project manager as well as all core team members for the presentation of their subareas), in which the owners of the firms decided on the implementation of the changes and reorganizations

The job was enormous! I feel great co-responsibility for preserving the jobs of very many employees. I was already aware that when I accepted the job as a coach alone, I could easily be overwhelmed by the responsible tasks and different roles, lose my professional distance, and need someone outside the company to reflect on difficult situations and manage uncertain changes. I therefore negotiated the financing of a coaching for myself. Anke Finger-Hamborg took on this particular coaching task. To obtain a practical impression, she was also on site and participated in some coaching of the core team. She played a major role in enabling me as a coach to keep a professional distance and to reflect with her in a relaxed way on my roles, solutions in case of difficulties and unexpected events. The concept of "coaching the coach" is highly recommended for large projects after these experiences.

The strategic customer-oriented reorganization included the redefinition of core processes and their optimization, a socially acceptable reduction of jobs with the condition "no turmoil at the site," the customer-oriented redefinition of all products and services, the parallel introduction of an ERP system, and a reorganization of the management team. This reorganization was approved with minimal corrections in a meeting of the limited partners and owners of the firms after the presentations in the final workshop. Subsequent implementation achieved—in the period for which I was able to obtain data—over 85% of its target. However, not all growth targets could be achieved after later decisions by the limited partners.

The flexible management of many predictable and even more unpredicted difficulties by the project manager and the very well-composed core team as well as the management levels and the subsequent implementation to be determined by key performance indicators (KPIs) speaks for the commitment and competence of the stakeholders and the constantly present management consultants. From the perspective of the project manager and the other stakeholders, the coaching contributed significantly to the success of the complex change processes.

As in the case example, many of the above coaching methods are often used simultaneously in coaching large organizational changes: questioning techniques, vision development, communication and leadership with implementation support, conflict analysis and management, stress management, and multilevel coaching. Implementation support through shadowing can be carried out both through observations in various group situations with debriefings immediately following online and by telephone or mail. Coaches with expertise as business consultants have advantages and should be open and free to bring this in but always aware that the clients are the owners of the goals, decisions, and their implementation. The case study can therefore be seen as a prototype of a radical extension of the possibilities and potentials of coaches. It can be seen as a best practice example of posttraditional coaching.

Not only do large-scale organizational changes benefit from coaching. In many cases, coaching tasks are more narrowly focused on individual support for individual managers or project managers. They can already be conducive to success if they open a space for reflection for a calm and differentiated analysis of situations and events as well as self-calming and remotivating after frustrating experiences. In the long run, persistent but flexible improvements in solutions and plans can lead to differences between the success and failure of organizational change as well as a good and bad image as a leader.

6.9 Future Outlook on Coaching Methods Beyond Traditional Rules

In this chapter, coaching methods are analyzed in closer detail with the "scientific magnifying glass." Small and larger improvements and suggestions from scientific research are incorporated. Traditional principles and rules of coaching are not abandoned but rather questioned. Critical questioning is also necessary for scientific knowledge. Practitioners and scientists are encouraged to develop the principles and rules of coaching methods using the knowledge base and research of science together with careful observation of client responses and outcomes. Some traditional prohibitions are not useful. This results in fewer traditional prohibitions. The possibilities and potentials of coaches can be extended enormously in a permanent process of practical observation, reflection, and further development.

In my experience, coaches are very interested in learning about new coaching methods. In their Complete Handbook of Coaching Tools, Passmore et al. (2021) initially wanted to reflect only 50 methods; then, 100, 200, and finally more than 250 methods were used. A further sharp increase in coaching methods is predictable. It would be interesting to determine to what degree interest in new methods can be attributed. The constant search may lead to unconscious dissatisfaction with the methods used because they do not achieve the effects desired by the clients or fear that other coaches achieve more with new methods. Those who are completely satisfied with the methods they use will seek less. However, we should focus our attention not only on new methods, which are only perhaps more effective, but also on using practically and scientifically evaluated effectiveness methods more accurately and reliably. In supervising coaching exercises in continuing coaching education, I have often observed that some participants find it difficult to apply complex methods accurately, even though they have been given a guideline text and demonstration examples on how to do this. A very careful study of the reliability of intervention implementation in coaching methods (see *Sect. 7.2: Analysis of Coaching Processes*) was performed by Busch et al. (2022). "Fidelity matters!" is their central inference from significantly higher goal attainment and other positive effects in the group with more reliable use of methods. They point to similar findings in studies of reliability in health behavior (Borrelli et al., 2005). In the future, therefore, the reliability of the implementation of methods in coaching training, supervision, and research should be given more attention and, if necessary, improved. Little can be gained if coaches use methods only inaccurately.

Anyone looking for realistic prospects for the future is safe if she or he takes a close look at where new methods in demand are already expanding today. These include, for example, strengths coaching with picture cards or questionnaires. They come from evidence-based positive psychology and may also pave the way for the acceptance of questionnaire methods among coaches. Those who cautiously try them out as coaches will be surprised to see how interested their clients are in them and how they encourage self-reflection and comparisons to the means of other people in representative samples.

Methods that have been rarely used thus far, such as motivational interviewing, narrative coaching, or multilevel coaching, show promising results in their respective fields of application and should therefore also be increasingly tested and further evaluated in terms of their effectiveness. However, they require careful training and rigorous performance.

Gradually, there are an increasing number of tools for online coaching (Albrecht, 2023), even coaching bots as companions (Clutterbuck, 2022) or various e-coaching media (Berninger-Schäfer, 2022; Geissler, 2022). The initial hesitant acceptance among coaches indicated a very gradual change in the beginning. Who would have predicted that a pandemic such as COVID-19 would force many coaches to survive professionally and switch to online coaching as quickly as possible? Just before the pandemic, Melanie Maier's (2020) intensive surveys of coaches' media choices documented strong criticism of and resistance to online coaching. However, in publishing her work shortly after the onset of the COVID-19 pandemic, she added a paragraph indicating radical changes in coaches' opinions, which were spontaneously reported to her by her interview partners. The pandemic was obviously an event that produced the unanticipated disruptive leap in a coaching innovation. All coaching associations quickly offered introductions and counseling on how coaches could design their coaching with videos and online tools. Countless webinars were held for coaches, or continuing education courses were performed entirely online.

Like Clutterbuck (2022), we can predict that in the future, coaching will probably use not exclusively but also, much more often, online coaching methods, more IT and AI tools, and coaching bots. As he suggests, it is not a matter of either human or technology. The *future of digitization and AI in* coaching will be analyzed in detail below in *Sect. 10.2.* Often, how tools or bots are used is critical. In the future, we will need coaches with media expertise and competence to share their experiences and hypotheses with colleagues to coach their clients in the reflective use of their apps, tools, and AI systems.

The basic principle for coaches and their clients, which also applies to the future, is a reflective application of all methods and tools in coaching (Greif, 2017a).

6.10 Questions for Repetition and Remembering

1. Name three methods, which you did not know before and would like to learn. Justify your choice.
2. Which method is problematic from your point of view? What do you criticize about it?
3. For which method would you have ideas for a scientific evaluation study? Outline which research methods you could use and how you would design the study.

Chapter 7
Examining Coaching Effectiveness

7.1 Extended Evaluation Model

To evaluate coaching and its effectiveness, it is not enough to simply examine the achieved positive results and possible undesirable side effects (Schermuly & Graßmann, 2018). The prerequisites that clients and coaches bring with them in terms of their motivation and potential, as well as the processes through which the results are achieved, must also be considered. In addition, the conditions in the organizational context that are conducive or detrimental should be taken into account. In our extended evaluation model (Greif, 2017b; Greif & Jonas, 2021), we distinguish (simplified, with illustrative examples) the criteria shown in Table 7.1:

The focus of this chapter is on evaluating the results after the coaching sessions have ended. This is generally regarded as the core question of the effectiveness of coaching. The results such as satisfaction with the coaching or financial improvements can be evaluated from the perspective of the client as well as the coaches and the organization that commissioned the coaching. A distinction can be made between results that arise during the coaching process (possibly already in the first coaching meeting), short-term results (usually directly after the coaching has been completed), and long-term results (after several weeks or months).

The second subgroup is concerned with evaluating the quality of the coaching processes. Studies and methods for evaluating working alliances and the behavior of coaches or clients in the coaching process are described in detail in Chap. 8 below.

An inspiring book on the preconditions of coaching in organizations, building and sustaining a coaching culture in organizations that support the outcome of coaching, was published by Clutterbuck et al., 2018). However, only a few scientific evaluations of the effectiveness of coaching examine conducive or obstructive preconditions, particularly the organizational context conditions. One example of this is the study by Schnieders (2016) on the evaluation of the transfer climate. She adapted the "learning transfer system inventory (LTSI)" (Holton et al., 2000), which has been used successfully in training measures in organizations. As her

S. Greif, *The Future of Coaching*, https://doi.org/10.1007/978-3-031-96192-2_7

Table 7.1 Evaluation model for assessing coaching outcomes

(1) Preconditions		
Organization	*Coach*	*Client*
General acceptance of coaching methods	Good coaching training	Importance of the goal
Transfer climate	Experiential knowledge	Change motivation
(2) Processes		
Working alliance	*Behavior of the coaches*	*Behavior of the clients*
Mutual appreciation	Structured process guidance	Openness
Clarification of problems or goals	Emotional support	Reflexivity
(3) Results		
During the process	*Short term*	*Long-term*
Reduction of negative affects	Satisfaction with the coaching	Life satisfaction
New insights	Goal attainment	Career promotion
Clarity of problems or goals	Behavior changes	Financial improvements

comparative studies of training and coaching show, the factor structure of the LTSI is comparable in both fields according to confirmatory factor analyses. Notably, individual transfer motivation and self-efficacy confidence show the strongest correlations with the results in both samples, whereas for example, transfer support from superiors and colleagues or by organizational conditions favorable for transfer (suitable content, transfer design, application possibilities) has no significant effects.

7.2 How Effective Is Coaching?

7.2.1 *Qualitative and Quantitative Methods*

The number of qualitative and quantitative studies on the effectiveness of coaching has increased enormously in recent years. The study by Bachkirova et al. (2015) mentioned above is one of the few studies that use both types of methods. Her aim was to develop research methods to evaluate the effectiveness of coaching and mentoring offered to doctors by the London Deanary, a faith-based organization. A total of 120 clients were surveyed with ratings and a questionnaire on general self-efficacy before and after four coaching sessions. According to the results, more than 95% of the participants improved their self-efficacy, confirming that they could achieve positive changes in their work (significant, medium–strong effects). They also answered the open question on the changes they had perceived after coaching. In this context, a wide range of individual aspects were listed as positive changes. The largest group (32) mentioned greater confidence (e.g., "Substantially in-creased my confidence in the workplace in the context of being a new consultant joining a well-established senior team"), 22 emphasized problem-solving (e.g., "I can now confidently formulate strategies to help me achieve my goals"), and 17 new self-insights (e.g., "…gave me insight into the tools I possess myself to change my work and personal life"). Relatively few expressed negative effects, but 17 lacked solutions to problems ("…not all problems have a solution").

7.2.2 *Meta-Analyses Summarizing the Effects*

Studies in which changes before and after coaching are compared are particularly meaningful. To rule out the possibility that similar improvements have occurred spontaneously over time without coaching, comparisons with control groups are also needed, whereby assignment to the coaching or control group (or waiting group) should be randomized ("randomized controlled trials", RCT).

Kotte and Bozer (2022) summarized the results of five reviews with meta-analyses of published efficacy studies in which improvements were examined with before-after comparisons and randomized control groups (Burt & Talati, 2017; De Meuse et al., 2009; Jones et al., 2014; Sonesh et al., 2015; Theebom et al., 2014). The results show significant positive effects after coaching. However, they are strongest when subjective client assessments are used.

The number of studies included in the meta-analyses is still quite small and varies from 6 to 24 individual studies (with overlaps). The mean effect sizes in the meta-analysis by Sonesh et al. (2015) are basically very low ($g = 0.10$). In contrast, Theebom et al. (2014) reported medium to strong effects ($g = 0.66$). The differences in the effects between the individual studies are large. We cannot be satisfied with such unstable, often small results after coaching (Greif & Jonas, 2021). If we compare them with the results of meta-analyses on the effectiveness of training, the effect sizes are lower than those for scientifically based training methods (Ebner et al., 2018). As an intervention that can be "tailored" to the individual person and situation, coaching should actually be much more effective.

The authors of all the cited meta-analyses discuss various approaches to improve effectiveness. A classic standard approach in companies is routine evaluation through surveys of clients and employees or customers with questions on evaluation and suggestions for improvement. Accordingly, it would make sense in coaching to routinely ask clients for an evaluation and suggestions for improvement using suitable short survey methods and as coaches to evaluate the coaching sessions and think about improvements. In coaching, such an evaluation can be carried out very well at the end of the coaching but also after the coaching has reached intermediate goals or when difficulties arise in the process. Later in the chapter, we return to how such evaluations can be carried out in practice and how this can round off or improve coaching.

As discussed below in Chap. 8 on processes, it would also make sense to conduct special additional training courses for professional coaches in which they systematically improve their behavior on the basis of success factors in the coaching process. Manuals and training courses for psychotherapists to improve their resource activation (Flückiger & Wüsten, 2014) could serve as a model here. Their positive effects on the results of therapies have been proven by scientific evaluation.

7.2.3 *Negative Side Effects*

Schermuly and Graßmann (2018) state that coaching can have positive results for both clients and coaches but can also have effects or "side effects" that are perceived as unfavorable or undesirable. They are surprisingly common, as the following list of the most common side effects mentioned by clients according to their summary of the studies indicates:

- Reduced job satisfaction (39%)
- Reduction in the perceived importance of one's own work (29%)
- Triggering deeper problems that could not be addressed (23%)
- Decreased work motivation (22%)
- Reduced life satisfaction (22%)
- Worsening of the work–life balance (20%)
- Greater fluctuation in work performance (21%)

The side effects of health coaching should be evaluated with particular care and on a routine basis. It would be bad if clients were to suffer harm to their health due to careless behavior on the part of coaches.

7.3 Methods and Criteria for Evaluating Coaching

It is extremely useful for the marketing of coaching if, as a coach, you can refer to routine positive evaluations of your own coaching using methods that are also used in coaching research. If you do a good job as a coach, you need not be afraid of this. Nevertheless, especially in Germany, there is sometimes considerable resistance from coaches to such evaluations, as I experienced myself at a coaching conference organized by Uwe Böning and myself in Ekeberg (Germany). Scientific methods are loudly rejected by coaches and are generally criticized as being far from practice. The critics do not consider the fact that similar methods for evaluating or assessing customer satisfaction have long been used in practice in companies around the world for almost all products and services and are used to improve them and make them more attractive to customers. Many coaches believe that clients are against the use of scientific evaluation methods. However, as the participation of over 1200 clients in one of our studies with such methods developed in science for practical application (Kinder et al., 2020; see more results of this study below) proves, this is by no means the case! The clients willingly took up to 40 min to complete standard questionnaires and answer open questions about the goals and results of the coaching sessions.

7.3.1 Practical Rating Scales

There are numerous scientifically proven methods for evaluation that can also be used by individual coaching practitioners or providers. The results can be evaluated via peer supervision by coaches or peer counseling and used for improvement. The description of such practical rating scales is the focus below.

In practice, ratings for the subjective assessment of the degree of goal achievement and satisfaction with coaching are very common. To enable comparisons, it would be advantageous if the same or very similar questions and rating scales were used for evaluation throughout the coaching field (if possible, similar to those used in the training field). Table 7.2 shows a selection of such rating scales that we use as standards to evaluate the coaching of participants in our coaching training courses during their first coaching sessions with "real" clients and in our research studies. The complete scales can be downloaded from Greif (2023). To enable before-and-after comparisons, we use comparable questions at the beginning ("goal questionnaires") and for evaluation after the coaching sessions ("evaluation questionnaires"). The coaches also assess the coaching sessions from their perspective using analog ratings. Table 7.2 shows several ratings of our "goal questionnaire," which clients are asked to complete after the first coaching session. At the beginning, additional clients wrote down their goals in their own words in the questionnaire. To ensure that the coaching is about subjectively important goals, the client is asked in the first coaching session how important the goal appears to be, as recommended by Spence (2007) for goal attainment scaling. The exact percentage of goal achievement is a standard rating. It is advantageous to have these percentages assessed at the beginning before the coaching and then several times during or after the coaching to record changes. Table 7.3 shows the coaches' rating scales.

The assessment of how rigorously the planned measures have been implemented can be observed by the client in concrete detail. Experience shows that these assessments are lower (and presumably more realistic) than the sometimes quite optimistic goal attainment ratings.

For objective reasons, 100% goal attainment is rarely possible. The rating of satisfaction with goal attainment is therefore often a more appropriate assessment. When first completed at the beginning of coaching, the question should refer to satisfaction with goal attainment before the start of the coaching.

Tables 7.4 and 7.5 show some of the questions that clients and coaches are asked to answer to evaluate the coaching after completion or for an interim evaluation.

The proportion of coaching in the achievement of goals is probably flatteringly overestimated by satisfied clients for the coaches. (They often reach values of more than 70%.) The coach is involved only in the cocreation of goals in reflection and planning, whereas the client also implements plans in practice, which would undoubtedly constitute a larger proportion. However, such high percentages with high goal achievement provide marketing arguments for clients because they show how much clients value the support of their coaches.

Table 7.2 Goal questionnaire client <u>before</u> coaching

My goal or theme in keywords (as concrete as possible):

How strong is your desire to achieve this goal or clarify this theme?

Extremely week … Extremely strong

0	1	2	3	4	5	6	7	8	9	10

How determined are you to achieve this goal or work through the theme?

Extremely little … Extremely firm

0	1	2	3	4	5	6	7	8	9	10

Degree of goal achievement or theme clarification (in percent) *before* receiving coaching?

☐ %

How rigorously could the planned be implemented *before* receiving coaching?

Not at all … Completely

0	1	2	3	4	5	6	7	8	9	10

How satisfied were you with the level of goal achievement or theme clarification prior to coaching?

Extremely dissatisfied … Extremely satisfied

0	1	2	3	4	5	6	7	8	9	10

Comments on the current situation (in keywords):

The readiness to recommend the coach to other people is a question that has been adapted for coaching from modern customer satisfaction studies. It is based on what is probably the most popular customer loyalty question in companies internationally today. It was introduced by Reichheld (2003) with the purpose of asking the "ultimate" question that correlates best with customer loyalty and buying behavior (Reichheld & Seidensticker, 2006). Even if such an undisputable maximum correlation cannot be confirmed in research, this rating, which has been proven in many studies, is recommended. It can be used to compare coaching with other services. High values are very beneficial for the marketing of coaching methods or of the individual coach.

Table 7.3 Goal questionnaire coach before coaching

Goal or theme in keywords of the client (as concrete as possible):

How strong is the desire of the client to achieve this goal or clarify this theme according to the coach's estimation?

Extremely week — Extremely strong

0	1	2	3	4	5	6	7	8	9	10

How rigorously could the planned be implemented *before* receiving coaching according to coach evaluation?

Not at all — Completely

0	1	2	3	4	5	6	7	8	9	10

Degree of goal achievement or theme clarification (in percent) *before* receiving coaching according to coach evaluation?

[ ] %

How satisfied were you as coach with the level of goal achievement or theme clarification prior to coaching?

Extremely dissatisfied — Extremely satisfied

0	1	2	3	4	5	6	7	8	9	10

Comments on the current situation (in keywords):

7.3.2 *Standardized Scientific Questionnaires*

Standardized questionnaires, which have proven valuable in scientific research for many other interventions, can also be used for evaluation. Instruments whose statistical test quality criteria (reliability and validity) have already been tested are recommended. The following list contains several questionnaire scales that have been used in several coaching evaluations (Greif, 2013a; Greif & Jonas, 2021; Mühlberger et al., 2024):

- *Self-efficacy* (Schwarzer & Jerusalem, 1995): Improving the conviction that one can achieve the desired changes.
- *Basic psychological need satisfaction scales* (Deci & Ryan, 2000): The scales measure need fulfillment (e.g., after coaching) with three basic psychological needs: competence, autonomy, and relatedness.

Table 7.4 Evaluation of the coaching by the client

My goal or theme in keywords (as concrete as possible):

How important do you rate this goal or theme?

Completely unimportant — Extremely important

0	1	2	3	4	5	6	7	8	9	10

How rigorously could the planned be implemented *after* received coaching?

Not at all — Completely

0	1	2	3	4	5	6	7	8	9	10

Degree of goal achievement or theme clarification (in percent) *after* receiving coaching?

[ ] %

How satisfied were you with the level of goal achievement or theme clarification?

Extremely dissatisfied — Extremely satisfied

0	1	2	3	4	5	6	7	8	9	10

What proportion of the actual goal achievement or theme clarification was due to this coaching?

No part of the coaching — Completely through the coaching

0	1	2	3	4	5	6	7	8	9	10

How high is the probability that you will personally recommend the coach to your friends or colleagues?

Absolutely improbable — Extremely probable

0	1	2	3	4	5	6	7	8	9	10

Comments on the current situation (in keywords):

- *Volitional components inventory* (VCI) (Kuhl & Fuhrmann, 1998): Based on a neuropsychological theory of volition, the instrument measures modes of volition, self-control, and self-regulation (which have been improved through coaching).
- *PANAS scales for recording positive and negative affect* (Watson et al., 1988): Increase in positive affect and decrease in negative affect.

Table 7.5 Evaluation of coaching by the coach

Goal or theme in keywords of the client (as concrete as possible):

How important do you rate this goal or theme clarification for the client?

Completely unimportant — Extremely important

0	1	2	3	4	5	6	7	8	9	10

In your opinion as coach: How rigorously could the planned be implemented *after* receiving coaching?

Not at all — Completely

0	1	2	3	4	5	6	7	8	9	10

In your opinion as coach: Degree of goal achievement or theme elaboration (in percent)?

___ %

How satisfied were you as coach with the level of goal achievement or theme clarification?

Extremely dissatisfied — Extremely satisfied

0	1	2	3	4	5	6	7	8	9	10

In your opinion, as coach: what proportion of the actual goal achievement or theme clarification was due to this coaching?

No part of the coaching — Completely through the coaching

0	1	2	3	4	5	6	7	8	9	10

How high is the probability the client will indicate in the questionnaire that he or she personally recommends you as a coach to his or her friends or colleagues?

Absolutely improbable — Extremely probable

0	1	2	3	4	5	6	7	8	9	10

Comments on the current situation (in keywords):

- *Depression, anxiety, and stress scales (DASS)* (Lovibond & Lovibond, 1995): Reduction in depressive feelings, anxiety, and stress.
- *Psychological well-being* (Ryff & Keyes, 1995): Improvement in overall well-being or life satisfaction.
- The *self-access form* (SAF) identifies differences in accessing self-referential information (know who I am, what I think, want, need), which are positively associated with emotion regulation, adaptive functioning, well-being, and meaning in life (Quirin & Kuhl, 2018).

- *Emotional clarity* (Grant et al., 2002): Greater clarity about one's own feelings; subscale of the self-reflection and insight scale (SRIS); it is similar to scales on emotional intelligence. A problem is that the self-reflection subscale is correlated with ruminating and depression (see Greif & Berg, 2011).
- *Questionnaire on result-oriented problem, and self-reflection (RoPS)* (Greif & Berg, 2011): Depending on the focus of the coaching, self-reflections increase in this focus, e.g., with respect to goals, planned behavioral changes, self-management, or reflections on the situation. The scales do not correlate with the rumination and depression scales and therefore can be recommended as an alternative to the self-reflection subscale of the SRIS.
- *Transformational leadership* (Bass, 1990; Bass & Avolio, 1997): Improving leadership behavior, especially in the case of organizational change from the employees' perspective (idealized influence, inspirational motivation, intellectual stimulation, and individual consideration).

Several of these scales have been adapted to coaching and are integrated into our study, constructing factor scales for the practical evaluation of coaching described in the following subchapter. Mühlberger et al. (2024), in their theory-based coaching evaluation study, analyze the relationships between different important variables of "self-management competences (SMC)," referring to the neuropsychological theories of Kuhl et al. (2006) and Baumann and Kuhl (2021). They highlight that self-regulation is a very important outcome variable of coaching. It must be distinguished from self-control or self-discipline, which resemble an "inner dictatorship" and the suppression of one's own needs and emotions (Baumann & Kuhl, 2021, p. 1305). In contrast, self-regulation is understood as an empowering volitional competence pursuing self-congruent goals, which, like an inner democracy, accepts and integrates different feelings, preferences, and attitudes, including unconscious impulses. The basic variables that constitute SMC are self-regulation, self-control, volitional facilitation, and self-access.

7.3.3 Construction of Economic Factor Scales for the Practical Evaluation of Coaching

The following questionnaire scales have been compiled for routine practical evaluations of previous coaching interventions by clients and coaches. They were constructed with the data of our large online survey using XING (a German career-oriented social networking site), which involved 1217 clients and 326 coaches from German-speaking countries (Kinder et al., 2020). The scales were developed via exploratory factor analysis (EFA), item analysis, and confirmatory factor analysis (CFA) (Mühlberger et al., 2025a & 2025b, in prep.). The questionnaires for clients and coaches can be used not only in scientific research (they are available on request from the author). Coaches can also use them to evaluate the results of their coaching sessions.

The readiness of clients to cooperate in completing these scientific questionnaires refutes the prejudice of some coaches, who believe that such questionnaires would be rejected by their clients. In contrast, owing to this large project and our experience, they are very interested in their use. A practical approach in coaching is when clients and coaches fill in the questionnaires toward the end of the last session (if possible, in separate rooms). Afterward, they can be compared with each other. The resulting evaluations of the client and coach are often very similar. Once again, perceived similarities strengthen bonding. Major differences can stimulate important joint reflections and considerations about what has remained open and how to continue working on improvements after the coaching. In any case, such joint reflections are a final closing that rounds off the coaching very well. We conducted separate analyses for the samples of the clients and the coaches because we assume that the evaluation criteria observed by the clients and the coaches differ at least partially in their content.

7.3.3.1 A Short Excursion into Methodology: Scale Construction

Exploratory factor analysis (EFA) is an appropriate statistical method for the construction of questionnaire scales aimed at selecting items that measure statistically independent factors with low correlations among the resulting factor scales (for a description of the components of this traditional test construction method, see Urbina, 2014). If items that correlate with several factors are eliminated, factor scales with low correlation can often be constructed. The method creates a selection of items and scales for the factors that statistically represent the common correlations of all items as completely as possible. It is subsequently recommended to check the solution with robust classical item analyses, in which the correlation of the items with the total score of the scale (so-called item discrimination or item validity) is determined, and again, only those items are kept for the scale, which are highly correlated specifically with the total value to which it belongs and not with the different scales. All factor scales show high reliabilities (Cronbach's alpha; see Mühlberger et al. 2025a & 2025b, in prep.). The ultimate test is whether the factor scales show a good fit or correspondence with the empirical data via confirmatory factor analysis (CFA). CFA tests the goodness of fit of a structural model explaining the covariation between the items and among assumed latent variables or constructs (cf. Urbina, 2014, p. 191 ff.). In our CFA models, we used scales based on the previous EFA and short versions of existing standard scales together.

The standard fit criteria applied in our analyses are (cf. Hu & Bentler, 1999; Kline, 2023) a CHI-square value of $p = 0.5$ and higher (it is difficult to reach in large samples, as in our study), a comparative fit index (CFI), and a Tucker-Lewis index (TLI). A value of 0.90 is acceptable, and 0.95 or higher is good. A root mean square error of approximation (RMSEA) and a square root mean square residual (SRMR) of 0.08 are acceptable; 0.06 and lower are good. These fit criteria have reached acceptable values in the CFA, which results in the background for the following factor scales (see Mühlberger et al. 2025a & 2025b, in prep.).

7.3.3.2 Outcome Factor Scales for the Clients

Interestingly, clients can distinguish more factors than coaches are able to. This is entirely plausible. Even with maximum empathy, coaches cannot recognize every subjective perception of their clients. Table 7.6 shows the factors and selected items. The table shows the number of items that appear necessary to record the individual factors. Notably, the satisfaction scale already achieves a high level of reliability

Table 7.6 Summarized client scales (N = 1217 clients)

Outcome scale	*Item number*	*Item examples*	*Reliability*
1 Goal attainment	3	• I have been able to consistently do what was planned thus far. • Coaching was effective in helping me achieve my goals. • In your estimation, to what extent was the goal achieved? (Answer as a number from 0–100%).	0.80
2 Satisfaction	2	• How satisfied are you overall with the coaching? • How likely are you to recommend your coach to others? (0% to 100%).	0.87
3 Self-regulation: subscale self-determination	4	The coaching has helped me to … • … Recognize what I do voluntarily in many of the activities in my everyday life. • … Feel much more in harmony with myself. • … Feel freer in many situations to act the way I want to. • … Very often act in the awareness that I want what I do myself.	0.84
4 Self-regulation: subscale self-motivation	3	The coaching has helped me that I … • … Usually know exactly how I can increase my pleasure when my endurance wanes. • … Can focus on the positive aspects during a difficult activity. • … Usually know how I can find fun in something again when I get bored with it.	0.81
5 Self-regulation: subscale self-calming	3	The coaching has helped me that I … • … Can specifically reduce nervousness. • … Can quickly relax again even when I am in a state of great inner tension. • … Can release my tension when it becomes disturbing.	0.88
6 Self-control: subscale planning	4	The coaching helped me to… • … Make a time schedule when I have a lot of things to do (i.e., I define what I do and when). • … Go through the details mentally before I start doing something. • … Determine how I will proceed before I start a large task. • … Usually make a plan before I start something new.	0.90

(continued)

Table 7.6 (continued)

Outcome scale	*Item number*	*Item examples*	*Reliability*
7 Self-control: subscale anxious goal-orientation	4	• I often imagine what will happen if I don't do something on time to motivate myself. • I often imagine how bad I will feel if I don't get an unpleasant task done on time when I have to do it. • I draw my motivation from the fear of failure to make an extra effort. • I only get going by imagining how bad I will feel if I don't do something.	0.88
8 Self-awareness	4	The coaching helped me to… • … Keep a sensitivity for what I truly want when I am sad. • … a better sense what I want myself when I am under pressure. • … Keep in touch with my feelings when something has gone wrong. • … Don't lose access to my feelings under pressure.	0.89
9 Self-access	4	• When I'm in a bad mood, I sometimes don't truly know why. • Sometimes I'm not sure why I'm behaving this way or that way. • I realize that I don't actually know myself that well when I'm asked to describe myself as a person. • When I get out of a bad mood, I sometimes can't remember what actually led to it.	0.83
10 Need satisfaction and ability development	12	• The coaching helped me to get a clear picture of my roles. • The coaching helped me to choose the goals I pursue in such a way that they correspond to my deep desires and needs. • Coaching has helped me to face professional difficulties calmly because I can rely on my abilities. • Coaching has helped me to learn new and interesting skills.	0.92

with only two items, and these are a general satisfaction rating and the Net Promotor Question (see above). Unless otherwise specified, ratings from 0 to 10 were provided for the individual items (see the examples in Tables 7.2, 7.3, 7.4, 7.5 above).

The two scales for *goal attainment and satisfaction* correlate to $r = 0.55$ and are therefore rather high, so that they alternatively could be regarded as a common or two interrelated factors. However, we found plausible and interesting different correlations of the individual scales with other result factors and a better fit of the models if we measure them separately.

The scales *self-determination* and *self-motivation* are based on items from the scales of the volitional components inventory (VCI) of Kuhl and Fuhrmann (1998) mentioned above, adapted for the evaluation of coaching outcomes. An increase in both general factors and *self-access* is often aimed at a general long-term improvement *in self-management competence* through coaching (Mühlberger et al., 2024).

Self-calming is, according to Kuhl and Fuhrmann (1998), a specific way of self-regulation. It is very important in stressful or fearful situations to avoid experiencing a hectic mood and making mistakes or acting haphazardly under pressure, even in situations that increase negative affect. Planning behavior is seen by Kuhl and Fuhrmann (1998) as an individual's capacity for planning and is expected to be related to higher levels of achievement and goal attainment, as well as improved self-regulation.

The scale on *anxious goal orientation* is based on a classical division of two personality types by Heckhausen (1977), one of which is motivated primarily by hope of success, whereas the other is motivated by fear of failure. Dweck and Leggett (1988) reported that people who believe that their abilities are fixed and unchangeable are more inclined to be motivated by fear of failure than those who believe that their abilities could be developed through effort and practice. Therefore, coaching should help them change their fixed attitude and develop a more optimistic growth orientation.

According to Kuhl and Fuhrmann (1998), *self-awareness* is an important psychological prerequisite for positive development and successful action in difficult situations. The scale has been adapted from the VCI. The items of the *self-access form* by Quirin and Kuhl (2018) capture the basic factor described above, which is a prerequisite for appropriate self-reflection.

The last factor, *need satisfaction and ability development,* consists of 12 items. They include items from Deci and Ryan's (2000) scales on need satisfaction and refer to definitions of basic needs by Fiske (2009). The focus is on assessments of the satisfaction of needs and the development of personal skills through coaching. Only the four items with the greatest discriminating power are shown in the table. Other items related to opening up to new experiences, getting on better with people and getting to know them better, behaving in difficult or unexpected professional situations and finding solutions for problems in the workplace. This factor could therefore also be considered a positive growth factor. Notably, the different aspects are seen together as one coherent factor by the clients.

The ten factor scales used to evaluate the results of the coaching from the client's perspective depend on the focus of the coaching. The first two scales (goal achievement and goal, satisfaction) capture classic general assessments that are used not only for coaching but also for other services for evaluation directly after the end (or for interim evaluations). The scales for stress management and self-calming are particularly suitable for stress management and health coaching. Most of the remaining scales are used to record important, long-term improvements in self-management and self-regulation, self-access, and self-motivation. They are based on the neuropsychological theory of Julius Kuhl and coworkers (Kuhl & Beckman, 1994) and its assumptions about the arousal of affects and resulting actions of people with different personality traits in different affect-activating situations. The last Factor 10 also relates to long-term positive changes in the satisfaction of important needs and the development of the client's abilities, which are often sought in coaching. Here, the assumptions of Deci and Ryan's self-determination theory (Deci and Ryan, 2000) are the background.

To evaluate the outcomes of coaching from the coaches' perspective, it would make little sense to use scales comparable to those used with clients. We have therefore limited ourselves to constructing comparable factor scales with which the perceived goal attainment and satisfaction of the clients are assessed and, additionally, the challenges posed by the goals and the clients' expectations of coaching. Table 7.7 shows the scales.

A total of 308 coaches participated in our study (Mühlberger et al., 2025a & 2025b in prep.). They evaluated the processes and results of up to five complete coachings with their clients. To avoid placing too much burden on coaches, we have limited ourselves to only a few scales for an assessment of the results. Again, the first two factor scales, *goal attainment* rating and *satisfaction* of the client, correlate with $r = 0.68$ and show that they are not independent. The third factor refers to goals that are high and challenging and high expectations of the clients of the coaching. We assume that it is more difficult to attain such goals. Therefore, this factor could moderate goal attainment.

It would make sense to include further assessments here (see Table 7.3) and to compare especially the ratings of client *and* coach on goal attainment, rigorous implementation and satisfaction. The high similarity of the ratings of the client and coach could be interpreted as a sign of the high ability of the coach to perceive his or her clients' evaluations.

Table 7.7 Summarized coaches' scales (N = 308 coaches)

Outcome scale	*Item number*	*Items*	*Reliability*
1 Goal attainment	3	• My client has been able to consistently implement what was planned thus far. • The coaching was effective in helping my client achieve his or her goals. • In his or her estimation, to what extent was the goal achieved? (0–100%)	0.89
2 Satisfaction	2	• How satisfied do you think your client was overall with the coaching? (0–100%) • In your opinion, how likely is your client to recommend you? (0–100%)	0.87
3 Challenge and expectations	4	• The goal(s) that my client and I set were challenging. • How high were your client's expectations of the coaching? (very low, to very high) • How high were the goals your client set for themselves? (very low, to very high)	0.70

7.3.4 *Outcome Evaluation with So-Called "Hard" Criteria*

7.3.4.1 Economic Performance Indicators

The reported questions with rating scales or standardized questionnaire instruments are based on the subjective perceptions of the clients, coaches, or other persons. Critics therefore doubt their value and prefer so-called "hard" criteria, such as an increase in return on investment (ROI), which can be attributed to coaching. Depending on the sector and the organization's business objectives, other economic indicators (e.g., customer growth, productivity and efficiency) are also important. They are also known as "key performance indicators" (KPIs). In regard to improving the performance of individuals or teams, it may be possible to evaluate performance data recorded in the system. In occupational health management, reducing the number of sickness-related absence days of employees in work areas with and without health coaching support is of interest.

One methodological limitation of many surveys with KPIs in companies is that individual interventions, such as coaching, rarely lead to profit increases or improvements in other KPIs on their own. They often occur only in conjunction with other organizational or technological changes. One example project was the introduction of a new IT tool for customer advisory services at a major bank (Greif & Benning-Rohnke, 2015). Here, very strong KPI improvements were found when the operational data before and after the interventions were compared (customer growth of 105% and profit of 38%). However, it is not possible to determine what proportion of the improved figures was due specifically to coaching with implementation support. Prior to the coaching, several thousand consultants and managers with customer contact received training on how to approach customers using the tool. In addition, the goals were communicated in groups and individually defined with the line managers. However, the importance of coaching is partially supported subjectively by the participants and stakeholders, who attributed a large part of the success to coaching and, in particular, to the implementation support provided by coaches.

In many surveys in companies, as in the example, only combinations of measures that together result in changes in KPIs with subjective estimates of the influence of the individual measures implemented are possible. To determine how strong the effects of individual measures are, so-called field experiments, in which different interventions are tested in different areas of work, are needed. For example, to test the effectiveness of marketing measures, different campaigns are surveyed and compared across different regions. However, this is often not advisable in companies because it would be problematic to get managers and employees on board for different measures whose results are uncertain. This would probably increase the already latent resistance to change and lead to suboptimal results. It seems more practical here, as in the example, to do without the separability of the effects and to try to design a combination of measures that are likely to lead to optimal results. If the KPIs are collected in the long term, similar to a longitudinal study, step-by-step better combinations of measures can be designed and tested.

7.3.4.2 Physiological Measurements and Health Data

As mentioned in *Sect. 6.6* of this book, physiological measurements or health-related data can be used to evaluate *stress management and health coaching*. The following list gives examples:

- Pulse rate
- Blood pressure
- Blood sugar
- Cortisol
- Heart rate variability (HRV)
- Body weight
- Sleep quality (pulse and sleep movements)
- Exercise (e.g., jogging distance, heart rate during jogging)

Most values can be measured very easily with wrist measurements, e.g., wrist-watches with sensors or a blood pressure and pulse rate cuff. Some can be recorded directly with apps on smartphones. Diabetics can pass on their daily measurements to researchers. As a stress hormone, cortisol can be sent with urine, saliva, or hair samples to specialist laboratories for analysis. It is expected that the opportunities to carry out these and other measurements and to follow the course of their improvement or deterioration over a longer period will continue to increase. This provides very good opportunities to check the effectiveness of stress management and health coaching with "hard" measurements. Longitudinal studies with follow-up data over a longer period are important. Even longitudinal physiological measures and statistical analyses of individual clients are possible and meaningful. An example study with 76 biofeedback measurements (HRV) following breathing exercises accompanied by coaching over a period of 9 months (Greif & Palmer, 2022) revealed a statistically significant and strong increase in positive physiological effects.

7.3.5 Qualitative Methods

Rating scales, standardized questionnaires, and KPI data rarely provide information about the specific course of coaching or special features of individual cases. Additional qualitative studies are valuable here. They definitely are not dispensable. Some very simple qualitative methods are available. In their mixed-methods study, Bachkirova et al. (2015) asked clients to fill out questionnaires and describe in one word or sentence what was different for them after the coaching. The answers were evaluated using a qualitative content analysis and categorization of the topics mentioned. We also included this question in our large survey on coaching processes and the results mentioned above (Kinder et al., 2020).

7.4 Questions for Repetition and Remembering

(1) Which criteria and research methods are used to assess the effectiveness of coaching?
(2) How would you recommend evaluating the effectiveness of coaching?
(3) Are you satisfied with the effects achieved in your coaching or found in coaching research?
(4) Which "side effects" can coaching have on clients?

Chapter 8
Coaching Processes

8.1 What Are Processes?

The word "process" is borrowed from the Latin "processus" (progress) and "procedure" (to go forward, to advance). It refers to a sequence of events with a (positive or negative) development. In the coaching process, clients may have thoughts (e.g., new insights), feelings and responses, or actions triggered in a session (e.g., intentions to act, which are carried out after the coaching session), for example, through interactions with the coaches (e.g., questions in the session). Coaching outcomes (see *Chap. 7* on *the effectiveness of coaching*) are generated jointly by clients and coaches in interaction processes. They are, in technical terms, "cocreated" or "coconstructed" (Greif, 2017a, 2017b, 2017c). Instead of human coaches, the results can also be created in interaction processes with avatars (Berninger-Schäfer, 2022), coaching bots and AI systems (Clutterbuck, 2022).

The following definition of the term "coaching process" refers to both the procedures and interaction processes in the application of coaching methods by human coaches as well as by computers, AI programs, or other virtual systems.

Definition Coaching Process
"Coaching processes are all processes that are initiated in client interactions and actions before, during, or after contact with coaches or virtual systems."

8.2 Methods for the Analysis of Coaching Processes

The methods for analyzing the coaching processes describe and analyze what actually happens in coaching. They thereby provide information on what occurs specifically and precisely and enable conclusions to be drawn about how the results of the coaching process are cocreated by clients and coaches. These intangible or

S. Greif, *The Future of Coaching*, https://doi.org/10.1007/978-3-031-96192-2_8

difficult-to-record processes thus become accessible for scientific research and the (further) development of theories about success factors in coaching. They are also useful from a practical point of view. Coaches can use them to reflect on and improve their own behavior and that of their clients. They should be considered in the coaching training and supervision of coaches. However, their implementation is extremely time-consuming. It is necessary to convince coaches and clients to allow audio or video recording of coaching sessions. For some research methods, the voice recordings must be transcribed, or observers must be trained to reliably score and log the recordings qualitatively or with category systems for behavioral observations over many hours of work. All of these methods are not only time-consuming but also require the utmost precision and concentration. Studies using such methods can therefore be considered the "Champions League" of coaching research.

Very different methods are used in this field of research. The chapter begins with a description of the methods of behavioral observation as they have been used in psychology, especially in psychotherapy research. Qualitative methods of linguistics are then presented. Linguist Eva Graf (2015) analyzed transcripts of coaching conversations using linguistic methods (see below). Her goal is to capture the basic activities of coaching. The educator and communication researcher Harald Geissler (2016) developed another approach and differentiated a content category system to reconstruct the "grammar" or rules of coaching.

8.2.1 Behavioral Analyses of Coaching Video and Audios

Audio or video recordings of coaching sessions or logs of interactions with computer programs or the inputs in apps or messenger systems are required in the ideal case for the analysis and description of observed behavior in coaching processes.

In coaching, which is oriented toward model psychotherapy research, observational characteristics are researched to record general success factors in the behavior of coaches (Behrendt & Greif, 2022). For this purpose, observers are trained to register precisely defined characteristics of coaches' behavior. In this way, the following hypothetical success factors for result-oriented coaching were observed (Greif, 2008; Greif et al., 2012): (1) emotion and emotional support of the client by the coach, (2) emotion activation and calibration, (3) activation of result-oriented situations or reflections, (4) activation of result-oriented self-reflections, (5) goal clarification, (6) resource activation, and (7) implementation support. The first factor forms the basis for a good coaching relationship.

The Freiburg success factor model (Behrendt, 2006) includes the following factors: (1) rememberable experiences (holistically actualized experiences) and (2) giving process guidance, cooperatively accompanying, and (3) activating resources. In the more recent integrative meta-model, three general behavioral categories are distinguished (Behrendt et al., 2021, p. 103):

(1) Relationship-oriented behavior (that fosters effective working relationships and entails providing structured guidance, providing personalized support, and activating resources).
(2) Purpose-oriented behavior (which directly supports goal accomplishment and entails enhancing understanding, strengthening motivation, and facilitating implementation) and.
(3) Change-warranting behavior (which fosters comprehensive information processing that sustains change and entails the creation of memorable experiences).

In 109 video-recorded coaching sessions (an enormous number), observers have assessed coaches' behavior in terms of the success factors of the model (Mühlberger et al., 2023). Regression analyses were then used to explore which factors best predicted the outcomes achieved by clients 1 month after the end of coaching. Mediation effects were also analyzed. The results show that it is favorable for goal achievement if coaches lead the process in a structured manner, provide individualized support to clients, and activate clients' resources, thereby fostering an effective coach–client relationship. Behaviors observed to activate resources include (1) acknowledging clients and their achievements, (2) promoting self-efficacy, (3) encouraging the use of personal resources, and (4) framing problems as activating challenges.

For coaches' continuing education, the findings suggest that coaches learn how to perform the conversations in a structured way, listen carefully, and identify clients' concerns and resources. To activate and use resources, they must be transmitted in a descriptive way. The progress toward goals perceived by the clients is also important.

8.2.1.1 Fidelity Matters

Busch et al. (2022) performed an observational study of 42 coaches in which they examined the influence of the fidelity of the coaches' performance of the coaching methods on coaching outcomes and mechanisms of change. Coaches' intervention fidelity was observed in three sessions of each coaching. On the basis of these ratings, the sample was partitioned into two intervention groups ("high intervention fidelity" vs. "low intervention fidelity"). The results show that coaching was highly effective up to 4 months after the coaching intervention ended, independent of coaches' intervention fidelity, but the assumed change mechanisms of the coaching concept were only effective when there was a high degree of intervention fidelity. The authors conclude, therefore, that "fidelity matters" and should be more vigorously considered in coaching research in the future. It is remarkable how many coaches, despite specific training in these methods, do not adhere to how they are meant to be implemented.

8.2.1.2 Interaction Process Analyses

If only the behavior of the coaches is analyzed and the behavior of the clients is ignored, the interaction process analysis remains incomplete. The first study to analyze the interactions in terms of content and process was published by Ianiro et al. (2013). For this purpose, they video-recorded the first sessions of 33 coaching sessions and categorized the nonverbal and verbal behavior with a coding program by trained observers. The program also analyzes which behavior of one person follows which of the others. In their evaluation, they draw on basic social psychological and clinical psychological research, according to which a person's interaction behavior can be classified as either "friendly" or "unfriendly" and as "dominant" (in my opinion, "self-confident" is more accurate) and "nondominant" (or "unconfident"). According to their hypotheses, friendly but at the same time confident behavior of the coach (shown nonverbally and verbally) increases the probability of goal achievement after coaching. It also encourages clients to behave in a self-confident and friendly manner. Not surprisingly, the combination of unfriendly and self-confident behavior has particularly unfavorable effects.

Section 6.3 (*Questioning Methods*) summarizes the reactions of clients to different types of questions. Research has begun, but much more research is needed. Fuhrmann (2017) developed a category system for an analysis of interactions in coaching, which waits to be applied in research. Fingas, Busch et al. (under review) at the University of Hamburg, Germany, studied the observed interactions of coaches, which stimulate specific types of client behavior (e.g., planning behavior). We anticipate that this area of research, which is extremely important for the advancement of effective coaching interactions, will develop substantially.

It is not easy to convince clients and coaches to release videos or audio recordings of coaching sessions for research, even if anonymity is guaranteed. However, this is possible. After all, it is quite interesting for clients to be able to discuss the analyses with their coach after the coaching session has ended and to see how they have activated their resources in the interactions, for example. This process is apparently particularly important but difficult for the clients to observe for themselves during active interactions. Coaches benefit greatly from participating in such research because it allows them to perceive, reflect, and improve their own behavior more realistically.

8.2.2 Qualitative Linguistic Methods

Linguistics can be seen as the core discipline in the study of language and communication (Fleischhacker & Graf, 2023, p. 3). Qualitative linguistic methods are a special inductive, descriptive-phenomenological approach. Fleischhacker and Graf (2023) provide an overview of their application to coaching process research and review 46 contributions. The linguistic approach views coaching "as talk-in-interaction" and "professional helping interaction." The constructivist perspective "conceptualizes coaching as emerging in situ, which means that both coach and client create coaching as a communicative event via their mutually depending (non) verbal contributions to the coaching conversation that eventually allow for learning and development in clients" (op. cit. p. 3).

Linguistic analysis is not deductive and is guided by theoretical preassumptions about interactions. It inductively analyses these interactions in a bottom-up manner and tries to identify "recurring communicative practices and language strategies to tackle important tasks in coaching (e.g., building the working alliance or establishing the coaching realm)" (op. cit. p. 21). An example finding is a heuristic meta-model of the "basic activities of coaching." The result is a mapping of four major constituents of coaching: (1) defining the situation, (2) building the relationship, (3) coconstructing change, and (4) evaluating the coaching (op. cit. p. 16).

Until now, such findings have remained rather abstract and general. The authors conclude that the "limited number of researchers and studies (many of them are case studies), as well as the diversity of linguistic findings prevent the drawing of robust conclusions (for theory building and modeling) at this point" (op. cit. p. 23).

8.2.2.1 Questionnaire Methods

Most research on coaching processes is based on questionnaires. They are easy to apply and require little time from the respondents. However, descriptions of these processes are based on individual subjective perceptions. As F. Schmidt and Thamm (2008) reported in our first study, the questionnaire scales correlate very poorly with the behavioral observations of the same processes by trained observers. Correlations are also low between coaches and clients. Nevertheless, as individual interpretations, the subjective perceptions of clients and coaches are of great psychological importance, especially if respondents see the processes differently. It is plausible that these perceptions correlate more highly with subjectively assessed levels of goal achievement and satisfaction with coaching of the same person, also collected via questionnaires, or with further perceptions of outcomes than do some of the behavioral observations described above in *Chap. 7* on *the effectiveness of coaching*.

8.2.2.2 Working Alliance

In an international survey of 1895 pairs of clients and coaches from 34 countries by de Haan et al. (2016), coaching success (subjectively rated) is best predicted by the perceived "working alliance" in coaching along with self-efficacy beliefs:

> The 'working alliance inventory' (WAI) was developed by Horvath and Greenberg (1989) and has since been used in psychotherapy studies but is also increasingly used in coaching research. According to the underlying theory of Bordin (1979), the success of counseling or therapy depends more on the strength of the joint interaction and less on the nature of the working relationship. With WAI, three components are to be covered (adapted to coaching):

(1) *Goal:* (e.g., 'My coach and I worked together toward goals that we agreed on.' 'My coach and I agreed on what was important for me to work on.' 'My coach and I developed a shared understanding of what changes would be good for me.')
(2) *Task:* ('Coaching made it clearer to me how I could change.' 'What I did in coaching opened up new perspectives on my problem.' 'I believe that what I did in coaching will help me achieve the changes I am looking for.')
(3) *Bond*: ('My coach and I respect each other.' 'I believe my coach likes me.')

In the large online survey using XING, described above in *Chap. 7 on the effectiveness of coaching* involving 1217 clients from German-speaking countries, clients' responses to questions on the subscale 'tasks' subscale showed the strongest correlations with their rated goal achievement and questions on satisfaction with coaching (Kinder et al., 2020). However, the title 'tasks' of the second scale might be somewhat misleading. If you look at the questions, they rather refer to a process alignment between coach and client, in the sense of a jointly created clarity about the intended changes and goals.

Grassmann et al. (2019) conducted a meta-analysis summarizing 27 coaching studies on the correlations between working alliances and outcomes (27 samples and 3563 coaching processes). They reported a moderate but stable mean correlation of $r = 0.41$ between a good working alliance and various coaching outcomes. The highest correlations they found were with resulting coaching satisfaction ($r = 0.64$), perceived effectiveness ($r = 0.58$), and self-efficacy ($r = 0.32$). The practical recommendation for coaches is to review the working alliance regularly in their coaching sessions as they go through the process. They should be aware that their clients' views may differ from theirs. If they check with the questionnaire several times in the process, they can initiate improvements in the working relationship at an early stage.

8.2.2.3 Strengthening Self-Efficacy

Self-efficacy is the subjective expectation that one is able to achieve an aspired goal through one's own performance. Stronger self-efficacy is often studied in coaching research only as an outcome of coaching. However, it can also be considered a precondition or process factor as a favorable motivational condition and "driver of future performance" (Sitzmann, 2013). De Haan et al. (2016) found in their Europe-wide research that there is a relationship between both clients' and coaches' self-efficacy expectations that promotes coaching success.

Common scales for general self-efficacy have been constructed by Schwarzer and Jerusalem (1995). A typical statement is "I can always manage to solve difficult problems if I try hard enough." However, such general statements are rarely appropriate. It usually depends on the specific situation and task with which a problem can be solved. It makes a difference, for example, whether the task is to resolve a conflict with other people or to perform interviews between a manager and an employee or to solve technical problems. Depending on the subject matter of the coaching, the assessment of self-efficacy is very specific to what is being advanced in the coaching process. For example, in a conflict coaching session, clients might be asked to rate: "In my coaching, I am working on improving my ability to manage conflicts of my team." In contrast, in coaching with a manager to conduct employee performance interviews, one would ask them to assess a different self-efficacy, e.g., "In my coaching, I am working on how to improve performing performance interviews with my team members."

8.2.2.4 Activating Result-Oriented Self-Reflections

One characteristic of coaching is that "self-reflections" are activated in the process, as explained in Sect. 2.5.2. However, constantly thinking about oneself is psychologically problematic. This symptom could indicate depressive rumination. For example, Anderson et al.'s (1996) self-reflection scale SRIS-SR, which was initially used in coaching research, correlates with depression and anxiety, as previously noted by Grant et al. (2002). This is plausible, as items of the scale such as "I frequently take time to reflect on my thoughts" describe a person who often reflects on his or her own thoughts and not on solutions to existing problems in specific situations and possible positive changes.

In *Sect. 2.5.2*, therefore, a strict distinction was made between aimless rumination and result-oriented reflections. Result-oriented reflection occurs whenever a person derives conclusions from it for his or her future feelings, thoughts, and actions. Therefore, items referring to result-oriented rumination may not only ask about the frequency of rumination but also mention the results achieved, e.g., "The last time I thought about myself and my goals, I developed a plan on how to achieve my goals." In the coaching process, the coach can stimulate such reflections (see the questioning methods and other methods in *Sect. 6.3*). An example of a question about this in a process questionnaire would then be, "In coaching, my coach has stimulated me to reflect on myself and my goals, and I have developed a plan for how to achieve my goals." We can assume that the affirmative response to such questions correlates with corresponding coaching results.

Like in the questions about self-efficacy, in self-reflections, the respective object that is activated in the coaching process must be addressed explicitly. Self-reflections can refer to extremely different areas. Only if the respective reflections stimulated in the coaching are addressed in the questions can high correlations with the results addressed in them be expected. This also applies to questions about stimulating "problem reflections" in the coaching process (see *Sect. 2.5.2* above for the differentiation of result-oriented and circular self-reflections).

8.2.3 Construction of Reliable Factor Scales on Processes

The Work Alliance Inventory (WAI) is a popular instrument and one of the most commonly applied questionnaires in coaching research. However, Horvath and Greenberg (1989) mentioned very early that the subscales of the WAI correlate very highly among themselves. In one study, the Goal and Task scales even correlated with $r = 0.92$, Bond and Goal = 0.84, or Task and Bond = 0.79. Therefore, these scales could be considered parallel tests measuring a single identical construct, and similar correlations can be expected between the individual scales and outcome criteria. In other studies, these intercorrelations are lower (in the study by Kinder et al., 2020, $r = 0.61$, 0.59, and 0.52), but they remain statistically too high for scales measuring different constructs that are clearly independent of each other. Carefully constructed questionnaire scales can be expected to have correlations below $r = 0.30$ among themselves and, consequently, relate differently to separable characteristics. To improve the practical separation of the theoretically distinguished characteristics, it would be necessary to perform factor analyses and item analyses of all items. It is recommended that all questions that correlate with several factors at the same time be subsequently sorted. Basically, the WAI would have to be reconstructed.

Diller et al. (2022) published a study in which entrepreneurs coached clients. Their results show that, in addition to task and goal agreement between clients and coaches as assessed by the working alliance questionnaire, closeness, perceived empathy, and perceived need supportive behavior correlate with coaching success (applying similar success scales as those in Kinder et al., 2020). Future coaching research should therefore, in their opinion, go beyond working alliance research.

There are numerous questionnaire scales on subjective perceptions of coaching processes that can be used in coaching process research, which are expected to correlate with coaching outcomes. According to the research mentioned above (Kinder et al., 2020), questions about the satisfaction of the clients are most strongly related to a scale capturing "trust" (e.g., "My coach is very competent in his coaching activities." "My coach was very concerned about my well-being."), as well as a scale for empathy, which correlates simultaneously with perceived goal achievement. This fits the practically and theoretically founded assumption that a relationship perceived as supportive and as appreciative is important as a basis in coaching.

All in all, it would make theoretical sense and be practically useful to combine all interesting questionnaires with the scales used thus far in coaching process research in a joint analysis. This would allow us to determine which process factors can be distinguished by clients and coaches. A joint analysis of several scales is currently in progress in our research group on the abovementioned dataset of 1217 clients and their 326 coaches (Mühlberger et al., 2025a and 2025b). However, since answering all complete questionnaires would have demanded too much time from the clients and coaches, only a few questions of the scales could be selected at a time. Typical items from the following questionnaire scales were included:

- *Working alliance* between coach and client (WAI, adapted version after Hatcher and Gillaspy, 2006) scales *Goal. Task, Bond.*
- *Trust* (adapted questions from Mayer et al., 1995).
- *Empathy.* The empathy scale is composed of eight questions adapted to coaching—including four on *Cognitive State Empathy* (Shen, 2010), three on *Identifying Emotions of Others*, and one question on *Interactive Empathy* (Kellett et al., 2006).
- *Affect Calibration* (adapted from Greif, 2008).
- *Resource Activation and Implementation* (adapted from Greif, 2008).

- *Self-Access Form* (Quirin and Kuhl, 2018).
- Stimulation of *Problem and Self Reflections* (Greif & Berg, 2011).

"We definitely need better Working Alliance Scales in Coaching" is the working title of a paper (Mühlberger et al. 2025a and b, in prep.) we are preparing for publication on the basis of the data of our large study described in *Chap. 7* above. The analysis aims to (1) construct independent and reliable process scales and (2) integrate additional items from the relevant similar and different process scales mentioned above, assessing trust, empathy, affect calibration, resource activation and implementation, self-access and self-reflection, which are missing from the working alliance scales. We used a combination of exploratory factor analyses, item analyses, and confirmatory factor analyses (cf. Urbina, 2014). This allows the creation of factor scales that statistically represent the correlations among the items as completely as possible. Only those items that are highly correlated with only the sum value of the scale are included in the scale. In this way, we were able to construct scales with high reliability (Cronbach's Alpha) that correlate with each other lower than those used in the Working Alliance Studies.

If we survey only the individual subjective perceptions of clients or coaches, it can be assumed that people in general (with exceptions) can distinguish only a few characteristics in a differentiated and reliable way. This has already been shown in research on personality traits. For example, while Cattell and Eber (1964) constructed a 16 PF questionnaire that is still in use today to measure 16 personality factors, the questions measured only 6 factors reliably and separably (Greif, 1970). Several are similar to the so-called "Big Five" personality factors found later, which can be reliably distinguished and measured with questionnaires after comprehensive statistical analyses of personality traits (Goldberg, 1993). In coaching research today, various questionnaire instruments with many scales are used to analyze processes in coaching. However, their statistical relationships have rarely been analyzed together. According to the initial analyses from our XING survey, they are highly correlated with each other. Apparently, only five to seven separable factors can be reliably captured in each case—in a sense, the "Big Five to Seven" of distinguishable subjective success factors in coaching.

Tables 8.1 and 8.2 summarize the preliminary results of exploratory factor analyses of process questionnaires and the correlations of the resulting reliable and relatively independent process factor scales with the outcome factors *goal attainment and satisfaction* (Mühlberger et al. 2025a and 2025b, in prep.). Four factors can be distinguished in the client process questionnaires, as shown in Table 8.1. The number of items that can be captured by separable and reliable scales after exploratory factor analyses and item analyses is indicated. The complete set of scales and items is accessible online in a report by Mühlberger et al. (2025a). For reliability, Cronbach's alpha coefficients are reported. In the table, the last two columns show the correlations (all highly statistically significant) with the two strongest separable outcome factors (according to factor and item analyses of the outcome items).

Process Factor 1 relates to *mutual respect, esteem, and bond* and refers to basic attributes of the working relationship in coaching. The scale consists of three items.

Table 8.1 Summarized client process scales (N = 1217 clients)

Process factor	Item numbers	Items	Reliability	Correlation with Goal attainment	Correlation with Satis-faction
1 Mutual esteem, respect and bond	3	• My coach and I respect each other. • I believe that my coach would have taken care of me even if we didn't agree. • The coach was appreciative.	0.72	0.43	0.68
2 Competent coach	5	• The coach acted with assurance. • I am convinced of my coach's abilities. • My coach has a great deal of knowledge about what is required in coaching. • My coach is very competent in his coaching activities. • I knew that my coach was true to his word.	0.85	0.47	0.77
3 Clarification, planning, and resource activation	16	• The coach worked with me to clarify and precisely describe the goals I want to achieve with the coaching. • My coach and I developed a shared understanding of what changes would be good for me. • The coach helped me to develop a plan on how I could achieve my goal. • The coach worked with me to think concretely about how I could use my strengths more effectively or overcome weaknesses. • The coach actively encouraged me to think about my themes and draw concrete consequences from them. • The coaching made it clearer to me how I can change myself.	0.92	0.59	0.62
4 Empathic coach	9	I had the impression that my coach… • Understood how I get on in my situations. • Understood my reactions to certain situations. • Realized how I was feeling. • Encouraged me to talk about my feelings.	0.91	0.50	0.64

Table 8.2 Summarized coaches' process scales (N = 308 coaches)

Process factor	Item numbers	Items	Reliability	Correlation with Goal attainment	Correlation with Satis-faction
1 Mutual esteem, respect, and bond	4	• I like/liked my client. • My client and I respect/respected each other. • I like/liked my client, even if we were not of the same opinion. • As a coach, I was appreciative.	0.72	0.27	0.25
2 Clarification, planning, resource activation	9	• As a coach, I worked … • To ensure that the client actively • Addresses his or her themes and derived concrete conclusions from them. • Toward getting the client to think about how he or she can better organize his or her daily life and find concrete ways to improve it. • That the client becomes clearer about his or her needs and motives and derives conclusions from this. • That the client thinks specifically about how to use his or her strengths more effectively or overcome weaknesses. • To ensure that the client clarified and precisely described the goals he or she wanted to achieve with the coaching. • That the client prioritized which goals he or she chooses first. • As a coach, I encourage the client to choose goals that are achievable but challenging for him or her. • As a coach, I worked with the client to analyze his or her potential and competencies for goal attainment. • As a coach, I helped the client to develop a plan on how to achieve the desired goal.	0.85	0.38	0.33
3 Goal alignment	3	My client and I … • Worked toward goals that we agreed on. • Agreed on what was important for him or her to work on. • Had a common understanding of what changes would be good for him or her.	0.82	0.19	0.33

Two of these come from the Bond subscale of the WAI. The third was constructed by us. It seems to be psychologically plausible that the correlation with the outcome scale *Satisfaction* with the coaching correlates substantially and more strongly than with *goal attainment*.

Factor 2 *competent coach* refers to a special kind of respect, namely, respect for the abilities and competencies of the coach. In addition, the client trusts the coach as being true of his or her words. It seems plausible that extraordinarily high correlations with the satisfaction factor can be found here. It might be of interest here that the result scale on satisfaction also contains the classical customer rating that refers to the extent to which the client recommends the coach to other people.

Factor 3 *Clarification, planning, and resource activation* has 16 items. This scale correlates most highly with the degree of goal achievement. Notably, these different facets of reflection and clarification of themes and goals, planning, and resource activation belong together in the perceptions of the clients. This corresponds with assumptions from psychological expectations about the basic success factors of coaching. The item on shared understanding of the goal (subscale goal) and two others on clarity about the changes and opening up new perspectives (subscale task) originate from the WAI. Most items are from the questionnaire on supporting result-oriented problem- and self-reflections in the coaching process. This shows that clients perceive that the stimulation of such reflections is important. This finding supports our theoretical assumption that the promotion of result-oriented problem- and self-reflection is a core of the coaching process and definition of coaching (see *Sect. 2.5* above and *Sect. 9.2.5* on our integrative theory below). The fact that items from different WAI scales belong to this broad factor shows that the psychological differentiation of the Goal and Task scales is questionable.

Factor scale 4 *empathic coach* describes a coach from the client's perspective who understands their situation and feelings. Nearly all the items were taken from an empathy questionnaire constructed by our team. Like Factors 1 and 2 do, it correlates most highly with client satisfaction with the coaching.

The process factors correlate very highly with the outcome factors *of goal attainment* and *satisfaction*. All factors show correlations between r = 0.60 and 0.77 with *satisfaction* (the highest correlation reaches Factor 2 *competent coach*). The correlations with *goal attainment* are lower but still in a high range between r = 0.43 and 0.59 (the highest correlation shows the broad Factor 3 *Clarification, planning, and resource activation*). Therefore, they could be seen as subjective success factors of coaching as perceived by the clients. However, the level of correlation between subjective perceived processes and subjective effects is presumably overestimated, especially as the process and outcome factors are surveyed directly one after the other. It would be necessary to survey the process factors during or directly after the process and the outcome factors only at the end after a lag of time. In the absence of such studies, the factors can be regarded only as hypothetical success factors.

Table 8.2 presents the analyses for the first five process factor scales found in the sample of the coaches. There are similarities but also interesting differences in the process factors of the clients.

For Factor *1 mutual esteem, respect, and bond*, the first three items come from the WAI (bond subscale) and refer to basic attributes of the working relationship in coaching. As with the clients, the third is a self-constructed item. The factor is almost identical to process Factor 1 for the clients. The correlations of r = 0.25 with the outcome factor satisfaction evaluated by the coach (including an estimation of the clients' satisfaction) are significant but relatively low. For the clients, the value for satisfaction reached r = 0.68. This raises the question of whether coaches might underestimate the obvious psychological connection between mutual appreciation and the bond for the satisfaction of clients with the coaching.

Factor 2 *clarification, planning, and resource activation* comprises coaching behavior, which is fundamental for coaching. According to today's practical experience and the theoretically based assumptions presented in this book, they should be realized in addition to *esteem and bond* in the working relationship with the client for successful coaching. In particular, this includes encouraging result-oriented reflections to clarify the client's own needs, themes, and problems that have been brought into the coaching, clarifying and prioritizing the goals that the client wants to achieve, planning by the client for implementation, and using his or her own strengths to achieve the goals. It makes sense that these different behavioral routines belong together from the coach's point of view and therefore correlate with each other and form a common subjectively perceived success factor. The first four items come from the questionnaire on promoting the result-oriented problem- and self-reflection, the following three from our questionnaire on the success factor goal clarification, and the last two are our questions on resource activation and implementation support. Some of the items in this factor scale are comparable to those in Factor 3 in terms of the client process factors. As with the clients, this factor also achieves the relatively highest correlation with the outcome factor *goal attainment*, with r = 0.38. However, it only remains in the medium range compared with the extraordinarily high value of r = 0.92 for this factor, as rated by the clients.

Process Factor 3 *goal alignment* consists of three items from the WAI goal subscale on this issue. It is plausible that these three very similarly formulated questions form a common process factor among coaches. At r = 0.19, the scale correlates significantly, but weakly, with *goal attainment* and moderately highly, at r = 0.33, with *satisfaction* with the coaching by the coach and client.

Process factors that correlate substantially with the results that coaching aims to achieve can be regarded as hypothetical success factors. In the previous tables, we used only simple correlations. However, the highest correlations are only within a medium range. This means that, in contrast to the clients, we were unable to find any strong success factors among the coaches. This may be because most coaches realize and systematically activate the process factors in their self-perception to a high degree. We can find only small variances here between coaches. This range restriction reduces the possibility of statically allowing high correlation coefficients. However, the greater variance in the comparable success factors among the clients and the sometimes extraordinarily high correlations with *goal achievement and satisfaction* may indicate that there might be differences perceived by the clients that are not perceived by the coaches. It is possible that their self-image does not allow them to be not perfect in the coaching relationship or their coaching behavior.

It would also be conceivable that coaches in the process are focused on completely different factors that correlate more strongly with the outcome factors. From my supervision jobs, I know that coaches very often contemplate finding the best approach and intervention method, which can support the client. They often feel slightly insecure but are sometimes enthusiastic if they intuitively ask questions in the process or find special interventions, which have decisively advanced the coaching process. The intuitive feeling during the process of having found good questions and a suitable intervention for the respective client could therefore be a success factor that has a variance in coaching and correlates much higher with *goal attainment and satisfaction*. In any case, further research is necessary.

More interesting and psychologically informative than simple correlations are structural equation models (SEMs), in which the relationships among the process factors and their relationships with the outcome factors are modeled simultaneously. We calculated such models for this purpose and checked their fit with our data (Mühlberger et al. 2025a and 2025b) using the criteria summarized above in Sect. *7.3.3 Construction of Economic Factor Scales for the Practical Evaluation of Coaching*. They are summarized in our integrative theory in *Sect. 9.4*.

8.2.4 Future Research Needs

Boyatzis et al. (2022, p. 8 f. quoted in excerpts) see a need for research on coaching processes in the following seven fields:

(1) "Critical moments (or micromoments) during the coaching process and how they affect outcomes.
(2) Coaching process and outcomes, including psychophysiological and neurobiological variables.
(3) On the role of various approaches to artificial intelligence and coaching bots.
(4) Mediating or moderating role of the relationship quality between the coach and the client and coach and their supervisor.
(5) Moderating or mediating effects of other physiological variables, such as sleep, nutrition, and exercise.
(6) Use and training of special equipment for measuring physiological variables.
(7) Acute experiences such as trauma, posttraumatic growth, and burnout."

The themes raised in the list are important and should be considered in the future. However, the methods of behavioral observation and interaction process analyses of success factors in coaching as well as linguistic analysis of transcripts, as summarized above in this chapter, should be added. Such studies are of interest to coaching practitioners because they describe and analyze concrete behavior in the coaching process and coaching outcomes. From my point of view, this laborious domain is the "Champions League" of coaching research, which may be worthy of worldwide competition and awards. In addition, in the field of research using questionnaires, studies that go beyond the WAI scales with a broader and deeper analysis of the subjective perceptions of the processes by the clients and coaches are needed. They can also be applied as a routine without much effort by coaching practitioners.

Physiological and neuroscientific measurement methods are very promising for the future because they can capture internal biological processes in humans that are not directly observable, as well as the inner results of these processes, using measurements that have also established their value in the field of healthcare. In stress management and health coaching, some studies have used these methods. These include classic measurements, such as heart rate, heart rate variability, blood pressure, or electrodermal activity (not consciously controllable changes in electrical skin resistance due to sweat gland secretion, activated by the autonomic nervous system; it is not only used in lie detectors) or the measurement of the release of cortisol as a stress indicator (in blood, urine, or hair samples). However, it is not advisable to record processes and effects, for example, in the case of feelings of stress, exclusively by physiological measures, such as cortisol measurements. Using hair samples, the course of cortisol release over several months can be determined very reliably in laboratories (hair grows approximately 1 cm per month, cf. Stalder et al., 2012). However, the relationship between physiological and psychological measurements is complex and has not yet been fully explored. For example, Miller et al. (2016) reported that diurnal variations in positive affect are more closely associated with cortisol release than are those in negative affect. Therefore, it is advisable to always record subjective feelings in parallel. In any case, the subjective perception of negative or positive affective states is important psychological information.

For general cardiological health, not only blood pressure measurements but also heart rate variability (HRV) measurements can be used very easily without much expertise. It can be recorded with continuous pulse measurements today even by many digital wristwatches. A single case study of several months of stress management coaching reported significant improvements in daily blood pressure and HRV values after relaxation methods (Greif & Palmer, 2022). For further health measures, see *Sect. 6.6 Stress Management, Burnout Prevention, and Health.*

Depending not only on the object and field of application but also on the theoretical basis and coaching method, special qualitative and quantitative methods must be used to analyze the processes and results in the respective special coaching approach. Innovative coaching methods, as well as today's coaching research, are too often based on small and limited practice and research circles. It makes little sense for each researcher to prefer and propagate his or her own regional criteria and measurement methods without attempting to gain a broad, international overview of existing research in the field. An example is the important research on critical moments (or micromoments) during the coaching process, cited in the first place on the above list of future research subjects by Boyatzis et al. (2022).

In particular, those moments in the coaching process that elicit new insights from the client are considered important in this context. Notably, references to classical research in Gestalt psychology on new insights and "Aha! experiences" are rarely taken into account, as they were already conducted and published by Köhler (1921) and Maier and Fredrick (1931) and are still the basis of modern neuroscientific research (cf. Beeman & Kounios, 2015). If we refer to these theories and research, interesting research questions can be derived with implications for practice, process, and outcome research in the field of coaching (Müller & Greif, 2022). "Aha! experiences" tend to be very fast processes that unfold with strong positive emotions and very strong certainty. This finding fits with laboratory studies with interviews and neurophysiological measurements with functional magnetic resonance imaging by Subramaniam et al. (2009), according to which very strong and fast activation in the dorsal anterior cingulate cortex is detectable during these moments. The Times of London, in a report on this research, called the activated area the "E-spot" (for Eureka) of the human brain. The Gestalt findings may stimulate more detailed research into whether and how new insights are activated that evoke rapid, strongly positive feelings and are associated with an immediately experienced subjective certainty that this insight is very helpful. It also raises the relevant question of how problematic fixations on habitual solutions that do not work can be overcome (Müller & Greif, 2022).

As the neglect of relevant research and research methods in related fields shows, scientifically based coaching needs investigations for a broader, international overview of existing research concerning the subject area. To provide impulses and suggestions for expanding coaching through the current wealth of scientific evidence, we have published our *International Handbook of Evidence-Based Coaching* (Greif et al., 2022b). It contains more than 70 short articles by authors from the scientific and coaching communities on the state of the art of theories, research, and practice that appear to be of interest to coaching. Coaches and scientists can quickly identify relevant research, research methods, and applications and receive suggestions for further reading.

Themes of the handbook in brief:

(1) *General themes, coaching process, research, and profession:* Definitions and concepts—science and practice—pseudoscience and charlatanry—gender and micropolitics—coaching relationship—diagnostics—success factors in the coaching process—interactions in the coaching process—ethics—professionalization—forms of contracts—quality of service—state of coaching research—team coaching research—health coaching research—supervision for coaches—system theories—behavior modification—brain-focused coaching—understanding and comprehension—e-coaching—future of AI in coaching—coaching and sustainability.

(2) *Individual characteristics and changes:* Insights through coaching—defense mechanisms—mindfulness—affects and action regulation—burnout—embodiment—emotional intelligence—emotion regulation—feedback—motivational interviewing—gender theory—health—decision making—complex problem solving—culturality—career—crises—learning—mentalization—motivation and goal commitment—motivation, will, and implementation—side effects—personality development—mental disorders—resilience—self-development—

self-reflection—meaning—language and meaning—stress and stress management—transformative learning—transference and countertransference—growth and security orientation—perception and judgment—values—goals.

(3) *Leadership and teams:* Failure in groups—leadership coaching—leadership theories—interaction dynamics in groups—team coaching—problems of teamwork—implicit leadership theories—interaction—communication—conflict management—bullying—roles—top management.

(4) *Organization and society:* change processes—dynamics in family businesses—power and micropolitics—organizational metaphors—organizational context—organizational culture—coaching and sustainability.

In addition to opening up more to the stimulating variety of related scientific theories and research, coaching needs a common discourse about which research methods in the subject areas can be recommended as standard criteria. As the example of the WAI scales shows, coaching research should use research instruments that have been constructed with more methodological rigor. Another point that has been too little considered in coaching research is that progress in application-oriented intervention methods is hardly possible if each researcher uses different research instruments for evaluation. Comparisons between processes and the effectiveness of each intervention method used by both human coaches and AI coaching bots and AI apps require at least partial use of the same research methods. This does not imply that different research methods may not be used at the same time. To determine which intervention methods we can best analyze and compare coaching processes and results, we need the best possible research instruments and at least a partial agreement on standard measurements and qualitative data. In this way, transparent competition between intervention methods will also be possible in coaching, as today is being established in the general health research sector, at least in part, by independent researchers.

8.3 Questions for Repetition and Remembering

(1) Which research results on coaching processes match your experience, and which are new findings for you?

(2) If you were to perform a study on coaching processes: What criteria or research methods would you use for this?

(3) How do you see the chances that practitioners will observe and study coaching processes and results more carefully and meaningfully in the future?

Chapter 9
Result-Oriented Coaching

9.1 Integrative Theory Framework

"Result-oriented coaching" (Greif, 2008, 2013b; Greif et al., 2022a; Greif & Schubert, 2015) is not a closed theory but an integrative "theory framework" open to improvement and enlargement of its scientific explanatory power. For this reason, it is placed at the end of this book as an integrative approach. The conceptual framework incorporates the definitions developed in Chap. 2, many of the individual concepts and theories described above, especially evidence-based assumptions and methods, and combines them. The following presentation updates the basic concepts and assumptions. It also takes into account recent scientific findings.

9.1.1 Opening to Improvement but Not Eclectic

Result-oriented coaching uses basic terms such as "result-oriented problem and self-reflection" and "self-congruence of goals." For this purpose, these terms are theoretically underpinned and defined (see Sect. 2.5.2 for these basic terms). In the following, these definitions are supplemented and included in empirically testable assumptions with reference to scientific theories and research in the theory framework. Since the initial elaboration of the basic definitions and assumptions (Greif, 2008), the results of many recent studies have been taken into account, references have been made to further scientific theories, and current intervention methods have been incorporated (see Chaps. 5 and 6). Through these definitions and appropriately reformulated assumptions, eclecticism in coaching can be overcome without losing openness to corrections and extensions of theory and methods.

In positive psychological coaching and some other coaching concepts, sometimes all possible effective interventions and methods are combined without theoretically based selection, following the motto "We use all interventions that cultivate scientifically proven

S. Greif, *The Future of Coaching*, https://doi.org/10.1007/978-3-031-96192-2_9

positive feelings, behaviors, or cognitions" (see Green & Palmer, 2019, p. 3). However, this can promote arbitrariness in the selection of findings and methods. One method is used today and another tomorrow, without careful consideration of whether the methods fit together systemically and in their basic terms and psychological-theoretical bases. Within positive psychological concepts, however, there are also approaches aimed at systematizing the effects of coaching, such as the *integrative cognitive–behavioral coaching* model *(ICBC)*, which compiles different types of methods in a systematic overview. (Dias et al., 2017; Green & Palmer, 2019, p. 199 ff.)

Eclecticism is not only a problem in scientific theories and the intervention methods promoted. It is also problematic when coaches base their coaching concept only on mixed concepts and assumptions as well as superficially pragmatically selected methods. According to the pattern, "I adopt everything that somehow works, regardless of whether it fits with my conception of coaching and with my other methods." Openness therefore leads to arbitrariness. Like scientists do, coaches should constantly think through their technical terms and assumptions in terms of their coherence and whether they fit with their beliefs and ideas about coaching and experience. This is especially true when new methods with the terms used in them and their expected outcomes are adopted. Have they been scientifically verified, or how can I support them with my own observations? Do the terms have unintended secondary meanings? (An example is the not very humane term "operating temperature" in Schmidt–Tanger's NLP method mentioned above in Sect. 5.9. In its technical meaning, it means "heating up" the client as if he were an old diesel engine to increase his or her willingness to change). Practitioners should also always ask themselves how their repertoire of methods fits together. Are there methods that have problematic side effects? Theoretical and methodological openness may not lead to eclectic or arbitrary additions of assumptions and methods. If eclecticism is to be overcome, the essential point is to integrate matching or suitably redefine basic terms and assumptions from precise practical observations and empirically grounded theories and scientific findings as a basis.

9.1.2 Integrative Theory

Figure 9.1 summarizes the basic theoretical framework of result-oriented coaching. The underlying constructs and their general interrelationships are shown graphically in the figure. The individual assumptions are additionally explained verbally below.

The assumptions in Fig. 9.1 refer to coaching sessions that focus on definable concrete goals of the clients, e.g., desired behavioral changes. The four boxes shaded in darker gray and numbered at the top of the figure reflect the constructs naming the expected outcomes of coaching. The lighter boxes below denote constructs describing the behaviors of the coach that, following existing evidence, are generally conducive to achieving these outcomes. These factors are called general success factors.

The model excludes specific success factors that require special knowledge and behavioral interventions on the part of the coach. Such specific factors are needed,

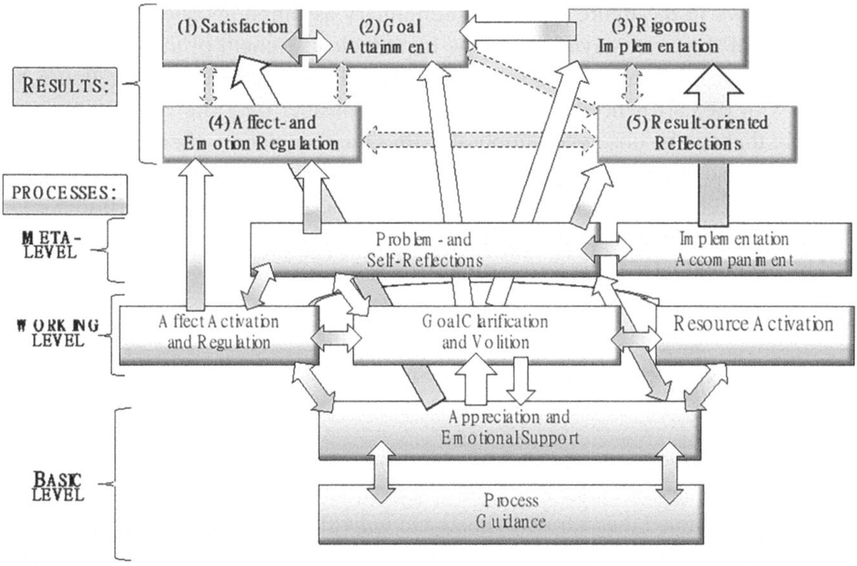

Fig. 9.1 General success factors (observed behavior of the coach) and coaching results

for example, for coaching that does not focus on concrete goals, such as the narrative coaching described in Sect. 6.4.1 with its specific requirements, which opens a space for self-reflection on questions of meaning or clarification of self-identity. Specific success factors are also necessary for special coaching tasks and interventions, such as in career development (see Kauffeld et al., 2022) or in health coaching, including specifically coaching to support preventive behavior in pandemics (see Todorova, 2022), or for coaching certain individuals who require particularly sensitive behavior on the part of the coach, such as clients with mental disorders (see Möller, 2022) or safety-oriented clients (see Böhm et al., 2022). A slightly different coaching behavior is also suggested for coaching certain groups of people, such as top managers (Böning, 2022), and special companies, such as family companies with their specific conflict dynamics (see Schlippe, 2022), coaching exceptional situations, such as crises (see Sperling et al., 2022), or problematic behavior in the environment, such as bullying (see Zapf & Beitler, 2022). Assumptions about coaching methods for more complex themes or problems, e.g., coaching complex management processes in organizational change or transformation, are described in Sect. 6.8.

In the figure, the constructs are shown as boxes, and the assumptions are shown as arrows. The assumptions and the model are tentative because they are based on only a small number of studies to date. Further research, as it becomes available, will likely lead to corrections of the assumptions of the theory of result-oriented coaching. However, even preliminary hypotheses should be formulated in a way that is transparent, open to criticism, and verifiable. Practitioners can compare them with their observations in their coaching sessions. Scientists can be encouraged to conduct research.

The arrows in the figure represent preliminary assumptions about correlations. The width of the arrows symbolizes the hypothetical strength of the relationships. Many relationships are reciprocal or "circular." This is reflected in the figure by arrows with two arrowheads. Since the results consider only the consequences of coaching that can be observed temporally after the completion of coaching, arrows without reverse effects have been drawn at this point. However, this does not mean that coaching outcomes do not have retroactive effects. For example, an initial high level of satisfaction immediately after the last coaching session is likely to be lowered by the client later if the long-term goal has not been achieved in the end.

9.1.3 Systemic Relationships

In the assumption of result-oriented coaching, not only linear effects but also circular feedback effects are formulated, as shown by the double-headed arrows in Fig. 9.1. In general, it is assumed that intraindividual and individual-to-organizational processes are, in principle, self-organizing. The *self-organization theory of synergetics* is used here as a general systems theory (cf. Greif et al., 2004; Kriz, 2022). Furthermore, specifically for team and multilevel coaching, reference is made to Mario von Cranach's (1996) multilevel systems theory (see above Sect. 6.7.1). It assumes that, in organizations, different structures emerge as systemic levels of individuals, groups, and organizations, which are in complex interrelationships with each other.

9.2 General Coaching Results

At the top of Fig. 9.1, five expected important general results of goal-oriented coaching are listed:

(1) *Satisfaction* (satisfaction with coaching and coach)
(2) *Goal attainment* (attainment of self-congruent and/or adopted goals)
(3) *Rigorous implementation* (e.g., following through on planned behavior changes by sticking to one's plan to exercise or relax on a regular basis over an extended period of time)
(4) *Improving affect and emotion regulation* (resulting in both a decrease in negative affect and emotions in everyday situations and an increase in positive affect and emotions used for self-motivation)
(5) *Result-oriented reflections* (awareness of individual strengths or self-regulation abilities, clearer self-concept or reflective analysis of interaction problems in the environment and solutions, how they can be overcome in similar future situations or opportunities, and how they can be used to achieve important goals)

In most coaching studies, outcomes are measured with subjectively perceived ratings (see Chap. 7 above). In our online survey of 1217 clients and 326 coaches described earlier (Kinder et al., 2020; Mühlberger et al., 2024, 2025a, 2025b, in prep.), we used standard ratings to assess client and coach satisfaction, the likelihood of recommending the coach, and perceived goal attainment. We collected subjective ratings of change implementation and goal attainment, as well as several other scales and individual questions, such as self-efficacy, result-oriented self-reflection, self-regulation, and well-being. As the factor analyses mentioned in Chap. 7 show, the individual subjective ratings of satisfaction, coach recommendation, goal attainment, and implementation are statistically closely related for both clients and coaches. Therefore, they can be measured as a common factor with a common questionnaire scale. Analogous to the general intelligence factor, it can be called the general perceived outcome factor (cf. Sternberg & Grigorenko, 2002). However, if we separate the satisfaction and subjective goal attainment ratings, we can find partly different relationships with different success or process factors, which are theoretically plausible and show a satisfactory fit with the data in our structural equation model (see below, Sect. 9.4). For example, there are stronger statistical relationships between subjectively perceived *Bonds and Appreciation* of the coach and *Satisfaction*, whereas the relationship is closer between a common factor of *Goal Clarification, Planning and Resource Activation* with *Goal Attainment*. As outlined in Chap. 8, the close correlations between satisfaction and goal attainment would also presumably be partially reduced if the latter are captured by objectifiable observations (in the case of behavioral changes, e.g., by ratings of trained observers), by performance data (e.g., performance improvement, for accomplishing more tasks and/or improving the quality of services or reaching higher satisfaction of the customers of the clients, and in the health domain by, e.g., improving physiological measurements and other health criteria), or last, but not least, by increasing economic results. In Fig. 9.1, we have therefore separated *Satisfaction* and *Goal Attainment* into two highly correlated result factors.

9.2.1 Satisfaction

Satisfaction is a very important subjective rating of the clients and/or customer, who ordered and paid for the coaching service. Coaching studies often survey only general satisfaction with coaching as well as with the coach. In addition, respondents are asked to indicate the likelihood that they would recommend the coaching service and/or coaches to others.

9.2.2 Goal Attainment

In the present model, we focus on assumptions about the achievement of definable specific goals. These include an infinite number of different intended behavioral changes of any kind, such as improved performance, a reduced number of errors, more sensitive communication behavior, more systematic studies for exams or other tasks, as well as more calmness, composure, and mindfulness, as well as more time for family and friends, regular exercise, healthier diets, etc.

9.2.3 Rigorous Implementation

Subjectively rated behavior observations of support for the implementation of planned changes also correlate strongly with positive ratings for Factor 1 *Satisfaction* and Factor 2 *Goal Attainment*. However, when a coach or observer asks in more detail to what extent concrete changes were actually implemented accurately and consistently, a very different picture often emerges. Frequently, the first implementation attempts are hindered or prevented by unforeseen external or internal events (in my experience, especially stress or changes in priorities or unexpected behavior of other people). Only if the implementation attempts are evaluated, analyzed, and recorded by the client over a longer period of time (see the method of *shadowing* for changing habits in Sect. 6.5.2) can a more reliable assessment of the rigorous implementation be made. These are normally systematically recorded in our coaching training. Notably, the subjective ratings of the extent to which the planned changes were implemented after *shadowing* (on a scale of 0 to 10) are significantly lower than the ratings of goal achievement. This seems plausible because they are more concretely related to observable behavior aspects and because they are constructively discussed with the coach.

9.2.4 Improvement in Affect and Emotion Regulation

As described above in Sect. 6.6, the importance of coaching to promote relaxation, mindfulness, and meditation has increased enormously. To evaluate whether this was achieved, the PANAS scales (Watson et al., 1988) mentioned above, which have been tested in many health areas, can be used to evaluate the increase in positive affect and decrease in negative affect after coaching. For the assessment of emotional regulation, further questions serve to determine whether clients are more successful after coaching in reducing nervousness in a very deliberate way, in being able to relax again quickly even in a state of strong inner tension, or in being able to relax tensions when they become disturbing. Example scales can be found in our above-mentioned study (Mühlberger et al., 2025a, 2025b, in prep.). However, it would also be interesting in future coaching research to use instruments, which are used in general research on the regulation of emotions (cf. Gross, 2008).

9.2.5 Result-Oriented Reflections

A central construct of result-oriented coaching and a specific defining characteristic of coaching (Greif, 2008; Greif et al., 2022a) is the promotion of *result-oriented reflections*. They are activated in the coaching process and therefore can be classified as *general success factors* (see below). At the same time, increasingly intensive result-oriented reflections may be observed after the coaching. Clients have learned to think systematically about the situation before acting without falling into circular ruminations. This enables them to find balanced solutions or to reduce hasty actions.

As a result of coaching, awareness of individual strengths may improve, questions of meaning, self-concept and identity, or problems in the environment and how they can be overcome can be clarified, and possibilities and how they can be used to achieve specific goals. Result-oriented reflections on problems in the social environment and on structures and processes in the organization to which the client belongs are also on the rise. Therefore, two types of reflections were distinguished in Sect. 2.5.2: *Self-Reflections* and *Problem Reflections*. We constructed *scales for the result-oriented problem reflection and self-reflection*. Research results from evaluation studies of coaching effectiveness published by Greif and Berg (2011) show that coaching can have very strong effects in this regard. However, the content of self-reflection varies greatly depending on the subject of the coaching. For example, a manager may have reflected on his or her leadership behavior during coaching, whereas a student may have reflected on consistently following his or her study plans for the next exam. The self-reflection scales should therefore be very specific to these topics. An example question might be "During the coaching session, I reflected on my leadership behavior and identified areas for improvement" or "I reflected on the fact that I have not consistently followed my study plans for the exam thus far and have decided to do a better job of following them in the future."

9.3 Coach Behavior: General Success Factors

The model in Fig. 9.1 focuses on *general success factors* in the coaching process and their interactions and effects. The model is based on existing *observational studies on the behavior of coaches*, which have a positive influence on the described results and on practical observations (Behrendt & Greif, 2022; Greif et al., 2012). In the model in Fig. 9.1, success factors are differentiated into basic level, working level, and metalevel factors:

Basic Level

- *Process Guidance* (structuring of the coaching process and the individual sessions by the coach).
- *Appreciation and Emotional Support* (verbal and nonverbal appreciative behavior of the coach and his or her emotional support of the client as the basis of a constructive working relationship).

Working Level

- *Goal Clarification and Volition* (Clarification of the client's own goals and those set by others, motivation, planning, and volitional decision-making to implement the plans).

- *Resource Activation* (activation of clients' strengths and potentials, social support from other people and use of existing technical or other resources).
- *Affect Activation and Regulation* (awareness of the client's own affects and feelings, use and promotion of self-regulation, to support the intended changes).

Metalevel

- *Problem Reflection and Self-Reflection* (encouraging result-oriented problem reflection and self-reflection that can help overcome obstacles or solve problems).
- *Accompaniment of the Implementation* (accompanying the implementation trials through shadowing or other methods, if possible, until the intended changes are stabilized sustainably).

In the following, assumptions are formulated about the effects of coach behavior that implements these success factors. As mentioned above, success factors that are not captured by the behavioral observations of coaches in the coaching process by trained observers (see Chap. 8) but rather by subjective surveys, such as questionnaire scales, differ in being subjectively perceived factors. The initial findings are presented below in Sect. 9.4.

9.3.1 Basic Level Factors

The basis of coaching is created by the coach in interaction with the clients through two basic success factors: (1) *process guidance* and (2) *appreciation and emotional support* by the coach. The first factor was introduced into coaching research by Peter Behrendt (Behrendt & Greif, 2022). The second factor refers to the classic basic variable of psychotherapy and counseling by Rogers (1972). Both factors are related to each other and are presumably mutually dependent. Without process guidance, coaching does not progress, and without mutual *appreciation and emotional support* from the coach, there is usually no beneficial coaching relationship. In the theoretical model mentioned above (Behrendt et al., 2021) and in their large observational study (Mühlberger et al., 2024), they are summarized as "relationship-oriented coach behavior." In addition, resource activation is also listed. The present model of result-oriented coaching in Fig. 9.1 is classified as an independent success factor at the working level, as explained below.

9.3.1.1 Process Guidance

Coaches generally guide coaching conversations normally by asking questions. ("Who asks, leads.") They begin coaching with introductory questions about the themes that clients want to work on in the session and whether they want to report current information about them. Then, depending on the theme, specific follow-up questions or different methods can be suggested and used. At the end, the results of the session are summarized, and any plans until the next session are formulated. As these examples show, process guidance does not mean that coaches make decisions about structuring the process without the clients. In contrast, their way of leading is directed by close consideration of the needs and goals of their clients. Clients usually expect coaches to carry out this structuring task for both, using their professional conversational and methodological skills to their benefit.

Basic Assumptions on Process Guidance
Clients expect coaches to guide the entire coaching process in a structured way, aligning it closely with the themes and goals they want to work on. Structured *process guidance* increases the likelihood of satisfactory processing and *goal attainment* for clients.

9.3.1.2 Appreciation and Emotional Support

Process guidance without mutual appreciation and emotional support by the client and coach (second basic level factor) is problematic. The interaction process analyses of Ianiro et al. (2013) confirm this additional assumption and expand the picture because they have observed nonverbal behavior. In their study, goal attainment is highest at the end of coaching following nonverbally displayed, confident yet friendly behavior by the coach. Without the observable friendliness of the coach, goal achievement is the weakest.

In his Person-Centered Psychotherapy, Carl Rogers (1972) viewed "unconditional" appreciation and empathy as "basic variables" for the training of therapists and counseling. "Unconditional" here does not mean accepting everything that the person seeking advice says or does but rather valuing the client overall as a person and clearly communicating this appreciation to him or her. "Empathy" in general terms refers to understanding and empathizing with the feelings, thoughts, and actions of others. Emotional support requires empathy, but doing so additionally requires that one clearly supports the person seeking advice not only rationally but also with demonstrated warm feelings.

Bordin (1979, p. 252) proposed "that the working alliance between the person who seeks change and the one who offers to be a change agent is one of the keys, if not *the* key, to the change process." One of the prerequisites of successful psychotherapy is deeper bonds of trust. To capture these and other characteristics (see Chap. 8 in this book), the "Working Alliance Inventory" (WAI) has been developed. Typical questions on the bond subscale include "I feel that my therapist appreciates me" and "My therapist and I respect each other." As described above, the questionnaire is increasingly used in the coaching field (Grassmann et al., 2019). In result-oriented coaching, mutual respect and appreciation and emotional support are seen as fundamental success factors and prerequisites for a supportive working relationship in coaching (Behrendt & Greif, 2022; Greif, 2008) or prerequisites for a satisfying working relationship in coaching.

Presumably, mutual trust in coaching develops very quickly in the first contact. However, as case studies and indications from (weak) negative correlations with outcome criteria show, it can be problematic if the coach focuses only on establishing mutual appreciation in the sessions and neglects progressing on the working level of the interaction process, such as goal clarification and resource activation (Greif & Schubert, 2015; p 73 ff.; Mühlberger et al., 2025a, 2025b).

Basic Assumption on the Success Factor Appreciation and Emotional Support
Without the mutual appreciation and emotional support of clients and coaches, coaching is unlikely to achieve positive effects. It has an effect on client *satisfaction* and promotes the *success factors at the working level.*

In Fig. 9.1, this assumption is reflected by the arrow from the basic success factor *Appreciation and Emotional Support* to the outcome factor *Satisfaction*. The perceived appreciation and support by the coach enables the client to openly address his or her goals, motives, and volitional decisions in coaching (success factor *goal clarification and victimization*), to talk about his own affects and emotions (success factor affect activation and regulation), and to find resources that promote the achievement of goals (success factor *resource activation*). The realization of these success factors at the working level, in turn, opens the clients to frank *problem reflection* and *self-reflection*. This strengthens the trusting coaching relationship, as symbolized by the arrows with retroactive effects. If, however, coaches focus exclusively and solely on the success *factors of appreciation and emotional support* and neglect the remaining factors, it can be expected that they will generally be able to achieve only an (short-term) increase in their clients' *satisfaction*. This is hardly sufficient for implementing difficult behavioral changes or goals of their clients.

The results of the study of coaching behavior of Busch et al. (2022) show that empathic behavior predicts goal attainment 4 months after the end of the coaching. However, this can be found only in the group of coaches, who adhere very strictly to the rules of conduct for coaching as conveyed in the study (see Chap. 7, "High intervention fidelity counts"). Therefore, they conclude that "empathic behavior is vital for establishing a trusting coach–client relationship and essential for effective communication." However, this in addition could depend on the fidelity with which the coaches perform the necessary intervention behavior. Without intervention at the working level, fidelity empathy may not stimulate difficult changes.

9.3.2 Working-Level Factors

The working level is so named because the corresponding factors are repeatedly worked through until this has led to practicable plans of changes that can be implemented. Three interdependent success factors are distinguished, which can be used by coaches: (1) *goal clarification and volition, (2) resource activation, and (3) affect activation and regulation.*

9.3.2.1 Goal Clarification

When coaching is about achieving concretely definable goals, *goal clarification* as a success factor is at the center of the working level, as shown in Fig. 9.1. This clarification is systematically worked out and repeatedly perfected by the clients, supported by their coaches. As a rule, plans are immediately drawn up for actions that lead to the achievement of goals.

Clarifying goals and planning actions to achieve these goals is a standard method in coaching (see especially the goal-oriented approaches in Sects. 5.1 and 5.3.2). Many coaches assume that *goal clarification* is already sufficient to activate clients to implement the planned actions to attain their goals. However, in an extensive review with meta-analyses of 422 studies with a total of 82,107 study participants on a variety of different goals, Sheeran (2002) reported that clarified goals are implemented on average in only approximately 50% of the cases. The motivation researchers Gollwitzer et al. (1996) therefore assume in their theory that "implementation intentions" strengthen motivation when they are added to goal clarification and planning. They consist of conscious, volitional decisions to carry out the planned actions. In coaching, this can be achieved by asking clients to make additional conscious and firm volitional decisions to implement changes after goal clarification and planning (Greif, 2013b). As Sheeran (2002) demonstrated on the basis of existing research, this significantly increases the likelihood of implementation. In Fig. 9.1, the success factor is therefore referred to as a combination of *goal clarification and volition.*

Assumptions About the Effects of the Success Factors of Goal Attainment and Volition

If clients want to achieve concrete goals, systematic *goal clarifications* promoted by questions from the coaches and conscious *volitional decisions to implement* the intended actions have a positive influence on the *rigorous implementation* of the planned changes and *goal attainment*. When this is successful, *satisfaction* with coaching increases. However, if the goals are not achieved in the long run, *satisfaction* can be expected to decrease.

Especially in the case of goals that are complex and difficult to implement, especially when the plans do not achieve the intended results, the coaching process usually requires repeated result-oriented reflection on why the plans did not work and how they might need to be improved. Clients can then change their goals and plans and renew their improved implementation intentions with a firm decision of will. In Fig. 9.1, this is represented by an arrow with two arrowheads pointing to the success factor of *problem reflection and self-reflection.*

9.3.2.2 Resource Activation

To implement their goals and plans, clients need resources as follows:

1. *Personal potentials and strengths*
   - Values and attitudes
   - Motivation
   - Personality traits
   - Knowledge and experience
2. *Support from other people*
   - Family and friends
   - Colleagues and superiors
   - Counselors
   - Coaches
3. *Accessible knowledge*
   - In the internet & Artificial Intelligence systems
   - Technical literature
   - Continuing education
   - Skills/competencies
4. *Computer software and technical systems*
5. *Time*
6. *Money*

In coaching, the resources that can be used by the clients to achieve their goals can be identified and consciously activated in resource-oriented situation analyses with the clients. When clients realize that they can use previously unused resources to achieve their goals, this changes their plans (they may also change their goals). It is therefore recommended that clients become aware of the resources they can use to achieve their goals before the final *goal classification* and development of solutions or plans with solution paths and actions. In Fig. 9.1, this circular mutual promotion of the success factors *goal clarification and volition and resource activation* is expressed by an arrow with two arrowheads. For a more detailed performance of resource-oriented situation analyses, solution development, and planning, reference can be made to specific guideline texts in my collection (Greif, 2025, in prep.).

> Flückiger and Wüsten (2014) created a manual to guide psychotherapists and counseling to perform resource activations. Examples of coaching behavior in this regard include whether they use questions to explore clients' strengths and competencies as resources that can be used to achieve goals or whether clients are guided to reflect intensively on past successes and consider whether they can use what they did then in a modified way in this case. This behavior of coaches can be assessed by trained observers. (Greif et al., 2010)

For many clients, resource activation is an intangible, abstract construct at the beginning of coaching. In coaching, they are concerned with themselves and the implementation situation, not with the coach's behavior in identifying and strengthening their resources. Questions in questionnaires such as "The coach analyzed with me my possibilities and competencies to achieve the goal" refer to this. The questionnaire scale with this question correlates with goal attainment (Kinder et al., 2020).

Assumptions About the Effects of Situation Analysis and Resource Activation in Coaching
When clients want to achieve concrete goals, systematic resource-oriented situation analysis and resource activation positively influence *goal clarification and turnover*, action planning, and, as a consequence, the resulting factors *rigorous implementation* and *goal attainment*.

9.3.2.3 Affect Activation and Regulation

In coaching, situation analysis can awaken emotions that have been experienced in the context of goal attainment attempts. In his neuropsychotherapy, Grawe (2006) assumes that *resource activation* is more successful when it is based on "problem actualization" (it is partly similar to the "resource-oriented situation analysis" described above). This activation is often accompanied by emotions. In a sense, the negative emotions re-experienced in therapy reinforce the desire to find solutions and can support the activation of the resources found for this purpose. Generalizing and transferring this to coaching, we can therefore expect a mediating effect of the activation of emotions on the activation of resources.

In psychotherapy, strong anxiety or other emotions and their management are often central themes of therapy. When emotions are very intense and when they determine the client's entire life, especially when they can be considered a symptom of a mental disorder according to the International Classification of Diseases (WHO, 2019, ICD-11), treatment by coaches who do not have psychotherapeutic training and licensure is not allowed. As Borsum (2008) demonstrated in a comparison of audio recordings of psychotherapy and coaching, affects and emotions take up significantly more time in psychotherapy than in coaching.

The neuropsychological theory of Kuhl (2001, p. 431 f., free translation) understands an "affect" as the basal "result of a central, nonconscious mechanism" that "generates hormonally and neurochemically mediated physical states." The foremost elementary affects are *pleasure* and *displeasure*. Pleasure sensations reward and pave the way for behavior. Displeasure, however, inhibits behavior. Following Gray (1987), Kuhl assumed that positive and negative affects are activated by different neurobiological systems. However, Kuhl does not view them as completely exclusive pairs of opposites. Therefore, in some situations, both types of affect can be ambivalently activated.

"Emotions," as distinct from affects, are affects additionally "associated with knowledge" (Kuhl, 2001, p. 618 ff.). Thus, a feeling of "joy" is associated with "knowledge" about the event that activated this positive affect in the past. Emotions are thus complex positive or negative affects associated with a person's experiences. The influence of emotions on behavior is also complex. In the case of a generalized feeling of anxiety that was originally triggered by certain experiences and situations (e.g., a fear of dogs due to a painful dog bite in childhood, which since then is recalled again and again every time the person meets a dog), psychotherapists therefore conduct a precise exploration of the triggering stimuli in the situation (a "problem actualization" sensu Grawe).

As highlighted in Frijda's (2008) comprehensive review of the psychology of emotions, emotions stimulate actions that are by no means always useful to the actors and have positive consequences. An example would be the angry swearing of a car driver at other road users, which is listened to by his fellow passengers, who are embarrassed by it. Emotions activate behavior, but as Frijda (2008) shows by the example of typical behavioral patterns for feelings such as "sorrow" and "depressiveness," the behavior is not always functional. In coaching, it is therefore advisable to explore whether dysfunctional consequences are triggered by emotions.

Gross (2008) developed a process model for emotion regulation and distinguished five strategic starting points for planning changes in emotions:

(1) Selecting another situation (e.g., avoiding a fear-inducing situation)
(2) Changing the situation (e.g., shielding from danger)
(3) Distracting attention (e.g., directing one's gaze to something else)
(4) Cognitive change (e.g., consciously reevaluating a stressful situation in positive terms as an "interesting challenge")
(5) Modulation of response (e.g., deep breathing in and out to self-calm in the situation)

Kuhl (2001) explored the relationships between affect and mental processes in detail. One of his basic assumptions describes a modulating effect of strong negative affect on access to the self and one's own feelings. "If one succeeds in actively regulating negative affect back below a critical threshold, then one feels oneself more strongly again, i.e., becomes quite literally 'more self-aware' and then has the extended overview of one's many experiences, possibilities for action, creative ideas, and meaningful insights" (Kuhl, 2005, p. 12, free translation). The focus of self-reflection expands. Storch and Kuhl (2012, p. 73 ff., free translation) use case studies to describe the need to reduce strong negative affect through self-calming so that a person can integrate "potentially painful experiences into the growing self." If another person has the intention to implement a new action but only associates this with weak positive feelings, it would be conducive to "self-motivation" if they activated strong positive feelings associated with their intention.

Storch and Kuhl (2012, p. 261 ff.) use a case example to describe how self-motivation is increased by associations with very positively experienced situations or stimulating thoughts, images, and imaginings. As an introduction to the method, clients are told why it is motivating to associate stronger positive emotions with those associated with the implementation of their intention to act. Clients are then encouraged to look for and use appropriate opportunities that activate positive emotions. (See also the case study on self-motivation in Sect. 6.5.2)

To weaken strong negative affects activated by a situation, one can, for example, practice consciously breathing in and out calmly once to calm oneself in the situation and mentally saying "calm" to oneself. Storch and Kuhl (2012, p. 240 ff.) mention as further possibilities a conscious distraction by remembering positive experiences or other interventions. The distraction strategy listed above in Gross (2008) fits in with this approach.

According to Kuhl's (2005) neuropsychological theory, conscious self-reflection has a direct backlash effect on strong affect. According to his assumption, the activation of conscious reflections (as measurable by activity in the frontal left cortex) weakens strong (negative but also positive) affects. This can be used in coaching, as the following case study shows. I have already mentioned other aspects of the case study above.

My client, a student, had hesitantly told me that he had failed the written exams in his Masters in Environmental Management at London University. His studies were financed by his parents, who were not wealthy, which put much pressure on him. In coaching, he sought help to retake the exam because he was very afraid of failing it again. This fear was clearly visible in his facial expressions and insecure speech. To reduce his strong affect through deliberate self-reflection, I asked him to describe as accurately as possible his feelings of anxiety before and during the exam situation. This self-reflection task immediately changed his behavior. He paused, straightened his upper body, and began to talk thoughtfully about his feelings. I asked him if he noticed that his behavior and feelings changed as a result of conscious self-reflection and briefly explained that this was consistent with the premise of neuropsychological theory and that by consciously self-reflecting on his feelings of anxiety, he could reduce the intensity of his feelings during the exam. We practiced reflecting on his feelings several more times in coaching. To support him emotionally, we talked on the phone before his 3-hour exam in London (written answers to open-ended questions), and I reminded him of the prearranged task to begin consciously reflecting on his feelings when he entered a panic situation and to think about how he could describe his feelings to me the evening after the exam. In addition, he had reason to panic! The testing staff had given him the wrong year's questions, and a staff member had to return and find the right ones. Nevertheless, my client was able to use the conscious reflection method to significantly reduce and stop his emerging feelings of panic. This left him enough time to answer the exam questions very successfully.

Of course, this was not the only theme of this coaching. The focus was on motivating the students to memorize (e.g., using mind maps) the extensive learning content and to write answers to possible questions—also in English. This required realistic time planning and, above all, the activation of new energies to persevere during the preparation period of several months. An internship in an ecological project helped him a lot. As described above, we deliberately planned it so that even if he did not pass the exam, he would still be able to experience a professional perspective in his desired career field.

As in the case study, scientifically accurate neuropsychological findings can inspire a precise approach to coaching. The three different assumptions discussed above are again summarized in the following formulations for a better overview.

Assumptions on Affect and Emotion Regulation in Coaching

(1) If positive and negative affects and emotions are remembered and reconstructed via "resource-oriented situation analysis," the search for their triggers and for strategic starting points for planned changes in emotions can be structured. This is expected to increase the motivation to activate resources for the implementation of planned changes.

(2) Consciously reflecting on and verbalizing experienced negative affect and emotions moderates their momentary intensity and allows for calmer self-reflection with access to the self and important feelings.

(3) Coaching can encourage clients to motivate themselves through practice, reduce unwanted negative affect and emotions, and improve their affect and emotion regulation through sustained practice.

Approved questionnaire scales can be used to record the expected results (see Sect. 7.3). Specifically, to reduce negative affect or improve positive affect, the PANAS scale (Breyer & Bluemke, 2016), which is commonly used in many fields of application, can also be used in coaching (Greif, 2013a).

9.3.3 *Success Factors at the Metalevel*

9.3.3.1 Promotion of Result-Oriented Reflections

Not all types of self-reflection have positive psychological effects. Self-reflections in the form of aimlessly circling ruminations are problematic. Some individuals tend to do this and suffer tremendously from it (Kuhl et al., 2000). We therefore distinguish between "aimless circling" and "result-oriented" reflections. In coaching, clients' ongoing circular ruminations about problems or about themselves should be stopped and not stimulated.

In our definition of "coaching" above in Sect. 2.5.2, we also distinguished and defined "problem reflections" and "self-reflection." "Problem reflections" are reflections on an undesirable initial state in the environment and how to achieve a desirable goal or end state. "Self-reflections," on the other hand, are reflections on images or actions related to real and ideal self-concepts or self-discrepancies and how to reduce them. Examples of problem reflections include thinking about a stressful or unproductive work situation and how to change it. Examples of self-reflections are thoughts about one's own problematic behavior or personal weaknesses and how to change them. Reflections are not just about behavior and feelings. They also include new knowledge and insights, a perceived better understanding of a problem situation, or one's own strengths that do not result in direct action.

Encouraging Result-Oriented Reflections in Coaching

(1) Stopping circular rumination:

In coaching, aimless circular rumination can be reduced by practicing techniques such as "thought stopping" with implementation support and intentionally planned distractions from ruminative thoughts through activities that are rewarding for the client. This can reduce depressive thoughts, feelings of helplessness, and anxiety. Overall energy levels during performance are likely to improve.

(2) Promotion of result-oriented reflection:

Result-oriented problem reflection and self-reflection can be promoted by using reflexive questioning techniques that focus on how to achieve desirable goals or changes and/or images and actions related to developing a more positive real and ideal self-concept for the client. Clients can learn to focus their reflections and actions in a more result-oriented way.

Grant et al. (2002) used a specific self-reflection scale in their studies of coaching effectiveness within their "Self-Reflection and Insight Scales" (SRIS). It contains questions on the frequency of self-reflection ("I do not often think about my thoughts" and "I rarely spend time in self-reflection" each to be reverse scored). Here, even individuals who tend to engage in long circular self-reflections or ruminations can score high on the scale. It is therefore basically not surprising that this scale is correlated with rumination, anxiety, and depressiveness (Grant et al., 2002; Greif & Berg, 2011; Lovibond & Lovibond, 1995). The scale is therefore unlikely to capture the increase in facilitative self-reflection that coaching seeks to achieve.

We constructed a questionnaire for results-oriented problem reflection and self-reflection whose scales (Greif & Berg, 2011) do not correlate with rumination, anxiety, or depression. In studies with randomized control groups, strong significant effects have been found after coaching (Röhrs, 2011; Schmidt & Thamm, 2008; Webers, 2008). An example of a result-oriented problem reflections is "When I thought about a specific problem last time, I developed a new way of looking at it that resulted in concrete practical consequences for me." As in this example, the question asks whether the reflection led to a result (imagined or practical). This makes the question format slightly more complicated but is necessary to rule out fruitless rumination.

In a study evaluating blended couple coaching for small business owners and their spouses (copreneurs) to help them psychologically detach from work, Busch et al. (2022) used items from our questionnaire on result-oriented self-reflection (e.g., "During the coaching, I thought about my personal needs, goals, and norms, and I made a plan for how to reach them."). The results show that self-reflection predicted *satisfaction* ($r = 0.52$) and *goal attainment* ($r = 0.46$) during coaching.

To capture the observable behavior of coaches in promoting result-oriented problem reflection and self-reflection, we constructed observation scales and created a manual for observer training (Greif et al., 2010). However, the application of these methods is quite laborious. Less work is needed here in qualitative case studies in which transcripts of dialogs from a few coaching sessions are analyzed together with the consequences (Greif & Schubert, 2015). Interestingly, an interaction process study investigated how often clients show self-reflective behavior in coaching conversations after coaches' reflection-enhancing questions (Fuhrmann, 2017).

In the case of the student who had failed his Master's degree at London University, the student was full of shame because his parents had financed expensive university education abroad, and it was the first time that he had disappointed his parents by failing. Because this was so disappointing to him, he underwent coordinated therapeutic and medical treatment with a psychiatrist in tandem with the coaching. The constant brooding took away his motivation and time for learning. To prevent him from fixating for months on the exam (which could only be repeated after a year), I helped him find and complete a voluntary internship of several months in his chosen field of environmental management. (With the intended side effect, he could determine if he could work in this field with his bachelor's degree). In addition, he practiced the 'thought stop' technique and was able to significantly reduce his brooding phases (with implementation support through telephone shadowing, see Sect. 6.5.3 above). He was able to consciously stop his reflections and deliberately postpone them until the next coaching session. In the sessions, he learned to focus his reflections in a calm and 'result-oriented' way. This went increasingly well, especially as he also reported on the content of the exam texts and papers he had prepared in the meantime at each coaching session. My (not pretended) interest in the professional field of environmental management increased his motivation to learn and to explain to me what he had learned. He passed the exam with distinction!

9.3.3.2 Result-Oriented Reflection as a Meta-Success Factor

As mentioned above (see Sect. 2.5), Stelter (2013, p. 412) coaching opens a "reflective space," giving "time for self-reflection" about new possibilities for action and the search for meaning. Furthermore, the subject of reflection can also include individual values, strengths and weaknesses, conflicts with other people, etc., as well as the consequences of the COVID-19 pandemic or uncertain changes and crises in posttraditional society, the digital revolution, climate change, or wars. Reflections can refer to the general consequences or to the resulting personal situation and future developments as well as to the self-concept and personal search for the meaning of one's own striving and living (see the methods in Sect. 6.4). In problem reflections, general solutions to problems can be thought through self-reflections, personal consequences, and possibilities. In coaching, reflections increase on the specific issues that are discussed in each case. Through these reflections, important new insights can emerge (Greif & Riemenschneider-Greif, 2018; Müller & Greif, 2022). Afterward, concrete goals or changes can be developed. However, reflections that, as a result, lead to more clarity of thought about the object of reflection are already important goals.

Result-Oriented Problem Reflection and Self-Reflection, More Clarity, and New Insights
Encouraging result-oriented problem reflection and self-reflection increases the likelihood that clients will develop greater clarity about the subject of their reflections and gain new insights. When goals are derived from this, they are formulated in a more considered way. Optimism, self-efficacy beliefs, and motivation improve when the self-concept includes more positive self-evaluations or when the client has developed a concrete plan to begin positive self-development.

The assumption of the importance of self-reflection can be extended by Kuhl's (2001) neuropsychological theory and his assumption that "self-access" is a prerequisite for people to consciously think through and explicate their self-representations or self-concepts. Quirin and Kuhl's (2018) research provides evidence that people differ in their self-access and in the extent to which they can identify their self-congruent needs, values, and goals. In their research, Quirin et al. (2011) show that self-access appears to in turn increase feelings of congruence. This allows individuals to recover from negative impressions and experiences so that they can speak. Applied to coaching, it would be reasonable to assume that coaching improves self-access and self-congruence when self-reflective questions are repeatedly asked or when other methods are used to promote reflection on one's needs, values, and goals.

Assumptions of Self-Access in Coaching
Clients differ in the ease of their self-access. If self-access is habitually difficult for clients, it is more difficult to stimulate self-reflection in coaching. Through coaching, it can be facilitated, and self-congruence can be improved if result-oriented self-reflection on one's needs, values, and goals is repeatedly stimulated through reflective questions and other methods.

Interventions that support reflections partly overlap with the psychoanalytical *mentalization* concept of Fonagy and Target (Fonagy et al., 2002; in the field of coaching, see Taubner & Kotte, 2022). The authors assume that the ability to mentalize starts to develop in early childhood and is influenced by the quality of the relationship and attachment to one's own parents and is transferred to the interpretation of the relationship to emotionally significant persons in adulthood. As Thomsen (2024) elaborates, it addresses not only conscious self-reflection but also implicit thoughts and feelings about oneself and the opinions and reflections that are expected of the client by relevant reference persons in his or her environment. Noneffective mentalization is assumed to be a possible result of insecure primary attachment experiences and can be found in regressions in the relationship trying to please everyone or conflicts with the supervisor through unrealistic expectations. As Taubner and Kotte (2022) assume, in coaching, it is possible to support the client in developing a deeper understanding of his or her behavior and the perspectives of other people in conflicts. In practical applications, mentalizing as a method in coaching is very demanding because it is not easy to take all facets into account. Very far-reaching, differentiated, psychological conclusions are drawn from the client's self-explorations and small psychological clues. The prerequisite for this is an empathic relationship and an open exploratory attitude on the part of the coach. Thomsen (2024) constructed a *Reflective Functioning at Work Interview* (RFWI) based on the model of interview methods in psychotherapy research on mentalization. In the interviews, the interviewees' relationships with their superior manager and another reference person were explored and analyzed using a complex assessment procedure. In an individual coaching case study, she describes how difficult it is for the coach to realize the requirements of the mentalization method. It remains to be seen whether coaches use this method of exploration and reflection, which, according to initial findings in psychotherapy, is promising but challenging. Promoting *result-oriented self*-reflection according to the definitions and assumptions above is probably easier to implement in practice. However, perhaps this is a challenge that coaches face.

9.3.3.3 Assumptions on How to Change Habits

Here, we return to a summary of how habit change can be supported in coaching. This integrates the assumption into the theoretical framework of result-oriented coaching. The practical procedure is explained in detail in the *Methods section* (Sect. 6.5.2).

Experiences of failure in implementing desired changes in one's own "bad habits" can lead to strong self-devaluation. They not only are frustrating and demotivating but can also cause resignation. (Such failures are particularly critical when clients have not succeeded despite coaching, "even though the coach tried so hard with me.") Therefore, the priority is to explore such experiences with understanding and to activate all the resources of the clients so that they are able to plan and successfully implement achievable changes.

(1) As a first step, coaches can enlighten their clients psychoeducationally, considering the psychological and neuroscientific findings described in the methods chapter (see Sect. 6.5.3 in this book) on this topic, about why habit change is difficult not only for them but also for many people in general, and how they can overcome these difficulties with the support of the coach. Clients can develop new insights in an appreciative dialog with their coaches—perhaps even combined with a powerful "Aha! experience". They may realize that habit activation occurs unconsciously through cues and that it is important to remember that simply trying to force oneself to implement the desired new behavior is not optimal. Failure usually leads to self-devaluation. Alternatively, they can try to see if change will be more successful if they find new emotionally positive

cues for the desired behavior and develop the expectation that this will give them the potential to perform this difficult task better in the future. Higher "self-efficacy expectations" strengthen their motivation to begin the desired change in their habits.

(2) To increase the likelihood of practical implementation of the planned behavioral changes in the second step, the cues that activate the old habits (the refrigerator with the tempting delicious food or the mobile phone on the table inviting online encounters, etc.) should be identified in coaching, as described in Sect. 6.5.2. Clients can consciously pay less attention to these cues, move them out of sight, or distract themselves from them.
(3) This generally helps increase the probability of the desired implementation if the new behavior is very carefully planned and vividly visualized with emotionally positive consequences. It is important to consider and plan precisely how possible internal or external obstacles can be overcome (cf. Oettingen, 2014).
(4) In the fourth step, it is important to find cues for the planned new habit that the client can associate with the strongest possible positive feelings or expectations and that promote self-motivation. These should be used to overlay the old cues with as strong an emotionally positive feeling as possible. A calendar entry in the smartphone may serve as a reminder but would not necessarily be emotionally self-motivating. The smiling Post-It on the fridge mentioned in Sect. 6.5.2, which encourages a friendly pause, or a cue that starts an individually strongly stimulating "movie in the mind cinema" with emotionally positive thoughts about how to get past the fridge and not have to fear the scale the next morning because of too many snacks before going to bed, is preferable. As described in the Method for Changing Habits (Sect. 6.5.2), cues should be tested and changed until individually effective cues are found.

The following box summarizes the assumptions about changing behavioral habits in coaching.

Assumptions About Changing Behavioral Habits in Coaching

When intentions to abandon fixed behavioral habits or implement new ones fail, it often evokes self-devaluation and resigned, giving up on those behavioral changes.

When the number of self-devaluations is reduced, self-efficacy beliefs increase, and the likelihood of implementing the desired changes increases when the coaches:

(1) Enlighten clients psychoeducationally about current scientific findings on habit change, showing that it is normal for many other people to be unable to change their habits and how this can be explained and overcome.
(2) Identify cues with the client and motivate the client to consciously pay less attention to them or avoid anything that activates and maintains problematic behavior.

(3) Plan and visualize concrete new behaviors that can replace the old habit with emotionally positive consequences, considering ways to overcome internal and external barriers.
(4) Stimulate clients to create and practice new cues to remind them to perform new behaviors that are associated with strong positive emotions and are self-motivating.
(5) Plan and visualize concrete new behaviors that can replace the old habit with emotionally positive perceived consequences, considering ways to overcome internal and external obstacles, and
(6) They encourage clients to create and practice new cues to remind them to perform new behaviors that are associated with strong positive emotions and are self-motivating.

The accompanying of the behavioral changes is subsequently recommended until the new behavior is stably executed in more than 80% of the cases. The assumptions are reflected in the following section.

9.3.3.4 Accompaniment of the Implementation as a Metalevel Success Factor

A central success factor, which is classified as a higher-order factor at the metalevel in Fig. 9.1, is implementation support. This factor addresses long-term support for clients during implementation through shadowing (for the theoretical basis and implementation of these methods, see Sect. 6.5.2). Shadowing in coaching means that the coaches accompany their clients as directly as possible in their implementation attempts (face-to-face, telephone call directly after implementation, or WhatsApp/SMS directly afterward or joint use of AI tools for this purpose) and support them until they implement their plans and change stably (in more than 80% of situations) and sustainably (as long as they want to, even indefinitely) and achieve their associated goals (e.g., regular exercise to stay physically healthy and fit). As shown in Sect. 6.5.2, we assume that this strongly increases the degree of goal achievement of the coaching.

This success factor is rarely found in observational studies of coaching. This is probably because outside of sports, where it is a natural part of coaching, there are only a few business coaches who use shadowing to accompany implementation. As described above, some coaches feel that shadowing is not part of their coaching role. They argue that implementation should be the sole responsibility of the client, because otherwise the client will fear that they are no longer making the changes on their own but will owe them to the coach. In sports coaching, shadowing is a standard method. High-performance athletes, contrary to the prejudice of some business coaches, do not attribute their performance primarily to their coach but rather to their own abilities and efforts. What would be the result if coaches left their athletes alone in competition and did not analyze their performance and its optimization together with the athlete?

Result-oriented coaching does not prohibit extensions of methods in coaching, which, like shadowing, are obviously useful for clients. Shadowing is, according to previous experience and research, very effective and fits fully the coaching definition (see Sect. 2.5.2) as a promotion of result-oriented self-reflection and counseling of persons (in the sense of a "help for self-help") can be and are theoretically integrated. In my experience, similar to sports coaching, clients are proud when they are able to overcome an unwanted habit and understand how they can do the same with other behavioral changes on their own. Why should coaches not support their clients during the difficult implementation phase, with their frustration and self-devaluation, when their plans have not worked successfully? If coaches just try to work through failure in the next session after a week or two, trying to recreate what clients do not want to be reminded of is difficult and sometimes psychologically almost impossible.

The effectiveness of shadowing as implementation support is demonstrated by high implementation rates and goal achievement levels when it is consistently applied in the coaching of other participants and external clients in our coaching training, as are the results of two studies with students on reducing procrastination when studying for exams (Greif, 2020). I first became aware that it is even possible to achieve a 100% implementation rate with coaching and implementation support when we conducted further training of shift leaders with transfer coaching to perform a difficult information session with their employees about the critically perceived changes in their leadership role (Greif & Scheidewig, 1998). Very impressive results in changes in the leadership behavior of officers in the German Armed Forces Application study were also obtained in the German Armed Forces (Kaufel et al., 2006; Scherer et al., 2004). In a project of a large bank (N > 600) to introduce a new tool for customer acquisition, a customer growth of 105% and an increase in profit of 20% were achieved in a before-after comparison. It is not possible to determine what proportion of the results were due to the tool, the team discussions and target agreements, or the coaching and shadowing. However, participants and stakeholders predominantly attributed the results to shadowing during implementation. However, further research is needed to demonstrate the effectiveness of implementation support with shadowing. The following summarizes the assumption.

Assumptions of the Effects of Implementation Support in Coaching
If the implementation of the planned changes (after a *clarification of goals* and a conscious decision of will as well as *resource activation and planning*) is systematically accompanied by telephone and WhatsApp/Signal/SMS shadowing until stable implementation in more than 80% of the cases, the probability of *sustainable implementation and goal achievement* increases markedly.

In Fig. 9.1, this assumption is reflected by circular arrows to other success factors and a broad direct arrow to the outcome criteria of *implementation* and *goal achievement*.

9.4 Models of Success Factors by Subjective Questionnaires

On the basis of the data from our large studies described in Sects. 7.3.3 and 8.2.3 (Mühlberger et al., 2025a, 2025b, in prep.), we constructed economical but reliable questionnaire scales that can be used for practical evaluation of outcomes and processes as rated by clients and coaches. We found that clients and coaches partly differ in the factor scales they distinguish for their evaluations. However, in constructing the models for clients and coaches, we focused on using comparable factor scales for the processes as perceived by clients and coaches.

The following two models show the resulting structural equation models (SEMs). The goodness of fit of both SEMs is acceptable. Figure 9.2a shows the model for clients (χ^2/df = 3.82, CFI = 0.94, TLI = 0.94, RMSEA = 0.05, SRMR = 0.04), and Fig. 9.2b shows the model for coaches (χ^2/df = 1.99, CFI = 0.93, TLI = 0.93, RMSEA = 0.06, SRMR = 0.07). Both models statistically predict *satisfaction* and *goal attainment* quite well.

As Fig. 9.2a, b shows, a broad factor, *clarification, planning, and resource activation*, is at the core of the relationships in both models. It includes items from the *Goal* and *Task* scales of the traditional *Working Alliance Scales* (WAI, Hatcher & Gillaspy 2006) along with ratings of resource activation that were neglected in the

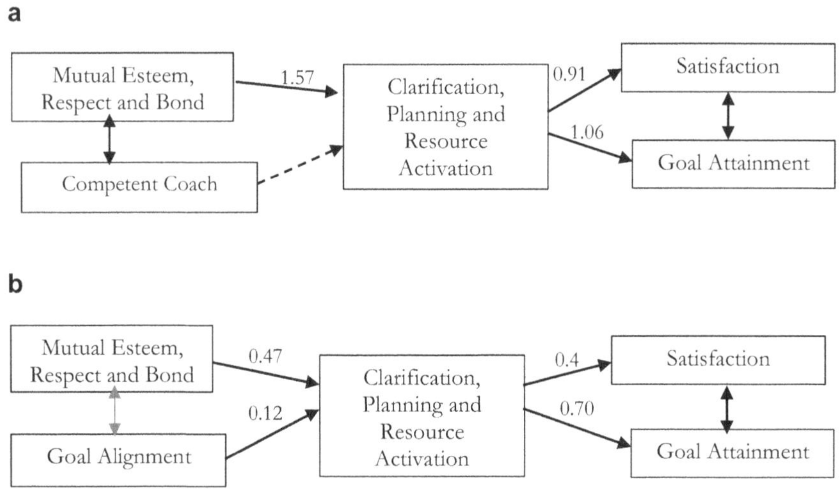

Fig. 9.2 (**a**) Structural equation model of the clients (N = 1217)—Prediction of *satisfaction* and *goal attainment* (questionnaire scales). (**b**) Structural equation model of the coaches (N = 308)—Prediction of *satisfaction* and *goal attainment* (questionnaire scales)

WAI. This factor can be interpreted as the subjectively perceived complex *success factor* at the working level. Interestingly, the broad process factor of *clarification, planning, and resource activation* is itself apparently influenced by Mutual Esteem, Respect and Bond, and Empathic Coach. This comparable factor in both models can be classified as a *subjective success factor* at the basic level (comparable to differentiating levels in the model shown in Fig. 9.1).

As Fig. 9.2a shows, clients also perceive the coach's competencies as another basic factor related to *clarification, planning, and resource activation*. To my knowledge, this factor has not been identified in existing research on coaching process factors, although it is obvious that clients evaluate their coach's competencies and that positive evaluations may have an influence. However, the relationship between the process factors *competent caching and planning and resource activation* is not significant and is therefore shown as a dashed arrow. Unlike clients, it is plausible that coaches do not emphasize their own competence as a supportive factor (see Fig. 9.2b). For them, however, *goal alignment*, which refers to the agreement of goals with the client, is important as another basic factor that moderates the complex central factor at the working level.

The two models show that subjective *satisfaction* and *goal achievement* can be statistically predicted by short factor scales for measuring the subjective success factors in the process. However, the correlations are probably overestimated because they were collected at the same point in time after the end of the coaching. It would be more appropriate to collect the process factors during the coaching and the resulting factors after the end of the coaching. In addition, we should remain aware that subjective perceptions in general are often positively exaggerated, especially in emotionally intensive personal cooperation in coaching. It would be a challenging task for the future to collect behavioral and questionnaire data together and integrate them into a common model, as we have succeeded in doing in our research on stress in the workplace (Semmer et al., 1996).

9.5 Problems and Open Questions

The concept of *result-oriented coaching* is not a closed theory but rather a "theoretical framework" that is open to expansion and change. The concept includes not only assumptions whose validity has been tested in the field of coaching but also assumptions from experimental psychological and applied neuroscientific research, especially from research in psychotherapy and industrial and organizational psychology. New assumptions based on related research can be added to the framework. It is crucial for inclusion that the assumptions fit or explicitly redefine the definitions and can be integrated into a common framework. They should also be supported by scientific theory and research. It is essential that they expand the explanatory content of the integrative concept and its practical usefulness. "Result-oriented" was chosen as the programmatic name of the concept because an expansion of practical usefulness should be linked to more and better results of coaching interventions.

The concept is open to methods that expand the scope of coaching and the tasks and roles of coaches. For example, assumptions about the use of psychoeducational interventions and implementation support extend the common roles of coaches. These extensions are covered by the definition of coaching and fit into the self-image of coaches who enable clients to gain new insights and provide "help for self-help," i.e., support in activating the clients' individual, social, and other resources for the self-active implementation of desired changes and the further development of their potentials and self-determination.

As discussed in Chap. 8, a variety of quantitative and qualitative analytic methods can be used to test the validity of assumptions about the conditions, processes, and outcomes of coaching and the effectiveness of interventions. Randomized control group research designs are important when the methods of analysis used are sensitive and meaningful to the expected effects. However, their results can often be better understood and interpreted in practice when supported by qualitative evidence from participants in interviews and case studies. To verify whether coaching leads to positive results in the long run, more longitudinal analyses are recommended in the future, especially individual case studies that document and analyze coaching sessions and results over a longer period of time.

If the positive psychology program (preferably version 2.0, which does not exclude negative emotions, see Sect. 5.3.1 above) is used for comparison, then the theoretical framework of result-oriented coaching is also an evidence-based coaching concept that is similarly open to new effective intervention methods. An important difference, however, is that for each change, the basic concepts should be defined, and the assumptions should be formulated precisely (as scientifically verifiable as possible). This avoids the eclecticism of some positive psychology methods. If coaching methods are merely listed next to each other in a common scheme, their relationships with each other remain uncertain, and the question of which methods can be preferred or combined for which theme or goal remains unanswered. After all, methods based on different theories and constructs are by no means mutually exclusive. More specifically, we need not only "more" but above all "more systematic" research in the field of coaching.

One problem is that the amount of research needed to test the assumption in the field of coaching is already very large and continues to grow with each expansion. Research can no longer be performed by individual scientists. The open theory framework with its assumptions can be seen as a (likely never completed) research program that invites researchers from all disciplines and fields of application to test and further develop the assumptions in their field (by no means only in the coaching field but also adapted in other person-oriented intervention fields and in applied basic research). It seems difficult to replicate all the assumptions in the coaching application field with as many relevant samples as possible (especially executives and other professionals). Some reviewers believe that only studies conducted with professionals are meaningful and are against using students in coaching research. However, this would preclude research with survey instruments that take much time to administer to clients. The time required to complete long questionnaires and other instruments is so great that only research groups that can invest much of their time (e.g., in exchange for free coaching) are eligible. Therefore, in a forthcoming publication, we test the effectiveness of the described combination of methods (goal clarification, resource activation, planning, formulation of an intention to act, and implementation support) for students in different disciplines to consistently implement their study plans for exams and reduce their procrastination. In parallel, we are collecting and analyzing shorter before-after surveys in the field of coaching professionals with and without implementation support for multiple behavioral changes (for preliminary results, see Greif, 2020).

9.6 Questions for Repetition and Remembering

The following questions address the theoretical framework for result-oriented coaching:

(1) What results can or cannot be achieved by the coach's process guidance and appreciation/emotional support and empathy?
(2) How is result-oriented self-reflection stimulated, and what is its significance for the processes and results of coaching?
(3) How can clients improve their emotion regulation?
(4) How can coaching achieve the rigorous implementation of planned behavioral changes to overcome "bad habits"?

Chapter 10
Perspectives

10.1 Future Development of Coaching

10.1.1 Future of Coaching

10.1.1.1 Future Expectations of Coaching Practitioners

In their 2022 survey, the International Coaching Federation (ICF) asked 14,591 coaches (77% ICF members) from 153 countries about their greatest concerns and opportunities (ICF, 2023a). A large majority of the coaches reported negative effects on their income in the first years of the COVID-19 pandemic. However, after they invest in training, given their mix of services and use of online media, the development increasingly recovers. Even positive assessments predominated. Most coach practitioners are confident that growth will continue in the future. A total of 74% of the respondents predict that their mix of methods will include audio–video communication and that 56% of the respondents will engage in person coaching in person (these are two independent estimates, which do not add to 100%). This differs from pre-COVID-19 times, when most of the coaching was done in a physical presence. This shows that the pandemic has brought about disruptive changes in coaching.

By far, the greatest business concerns according to the 2022 survey are inflation and the costs of goods and living (65%). Problems related to the reputation of coaching are the second greatest concern of 51% of coaches. This suggests that criticism of the quality of coaching and its application has become so strong that it is alarming. Unfortunately, how this can be responded to and what significance more scientifically based coaching can have in this regard are not addressed here. Regarding internal concerns, the responding coaches named especially increasing operating costs (35%), keeping up with technological changes (33%), own reputation and brand management (29%), and reduced income (28%).

Gross and Stephan (2015) noted the importance of the image of the coaching profession for future growth. Coaching is an intangible service and is practiced

S. Greif, *The Future of Coaching*, https://doi.org/10.1007/978-3-031-96192-2_10

confidentially, quasi "in secret." This makes coaching an obvious projection surface for insinuations and image-damaging criticism and discrimination (Greif, 2017c). In addition, there are self-appointed coaches and charlatans who make promises that they do not and cannot keep. I am often asked by potential clients or journalists how to recognize a reputable coach. It is in the interest of coaching associations and coaches with high professional standards as well as cautious clients to address these or other criteria and to apply them strictly in their certification by coaches. A "healthy distrust" of fantastic promises must also be promoted by clients and associations to avoid unintentionally becoming a "cocharlatan" (analogous to the coalcoholic who does not openly address the alcoholism of persons in his environment and thus tolerates or indirectly supports it). Coaching associations set quality standards for coaching training and coaches to prevent such image-damaging practices. However, I am not aware of many expulsion proceedings against members for charlatanism or professional ethical misconduct in the associations.

In terms of opportunities, increased awareness of the benefits of coaching (58%) and increased adoption of coaching within organizations (43%) are seen by Gross and Stephan (2015) as the most important in the coming years. In addition, some respondents see a higher demand for coaching (38%) and a or hope that credible data on the return on investment (ROI) and return on expectations (ROE) from coaching (34%) will be obtained (probably by scientific studies).

10.1.1.2 Future of Coaching as a Profession

Bennett (2006, p. 241 f.) has conducted an interdisciplinary literature review on the criteria that should be realized for a discipline to be recognized as a "profession." He subsequently lists 11 criteria that coaching should fulfill as a profession (shortened and summarized):

(1) Identifiable and distinct skills (widely accepted skills as required for skilled coaching).
(2) Education and training required to acquire proficiency (minimum initial and ongoing training required to coach).
(3) Recognition outside the community as a profession (by other established professions such as a profession and federal government).
(4) Developed, monitored, and enforced codes of ethics by a governing body, making the profession a self-disciplined group (established codes of ethical conduct and systems for monitoring ethical interventions conducted by coaches).
(5) Public service, motivated by altruistic service rather than financial gain.
(6) Formalized organizations (e.g., widely accepted established professional organizations that represent the profession).
(7) Evaluation of merit (credentialing) and self-regulating, encouraging diversity of thought, evaluation, and practice (e.g., accepted requirements for coaches; systems for accessing competence; systems for monitoring and regulating service delivery by coaches; means of encouraging a wide array of thought).

(8) A community of practitioners (e.g., forums for practitioners to develop relationships and exchange ideas related to the practice of coaching; publications that support the establishment of the community of practice) should be established.
(9) Status or state of recognition associated with membership in the profession (e.g., recognition by those served and the general public as a profession).
(10) Public recognition from outside the practicing community that the profession is distinct and actually in existence.
(11) Practice is founded on theoretical and factual research and knowledge (e.g., defined body of knowledge; defined theoretical foundation; ongoing evidence-based theoretical and practical research).

In her sociological analysis of the status of coaching as a profession, Fietze (2017) discusses classical profession models. She describes four basic characteristics of a profession according to the sociological discussion (op. cit. p. 8):

(1) "The development of professional expertise with recourse to scientific findings,
(2) the clear definition of the scope of activities,
(3) the assertion of an exclusive area of competence for the defined scope of activities in the form of a monopoly, which is normally safeguarded formally and legally by a protected title;
(4) the formation of associations and a corporative self-administration of their bodies of knowledge, their orientation toward ethics and standards, and their profession-specific practices."

Several of the characteristics listed by Bennett (2006) and Fietze (2017) are similar. An important difference is formally and legally the protected title of the profession. The title "coach" is often discussed as critical vulnerability; it is not legally protected, and even charlatans cannot be forbidden from using the title "coach."

In their review of the future of coaching as a profession, Lane et al. (2010, p. 379) refer to the criteria and evaluation of Bennett (2006) and conclude that "there is a long way to go before coaching can be defined as a profession in the narrowest sense," since "none of these criteria is fully realized in the professional field of coaching, either nationally or internationally." Several "obstacles or conditions hinder the establishment of coaching as a profession in the traditional (narrow) sense. We would argue that it might not even be in the best interests of coaching or its clients to pursue the traditional route to legitimization" and argue "that it might not even be in the best interests of coaching or its clients to pursue the traditional route to legitimization" (op. cit. p 389).

In my view, it is questionable whether all criteria are reasonable. For example, we can doubt whether the skills that coaches need are "distinct" or something unique or whether they are merely based on contextually applied general abilities, skills, and social competencies. Fietze (2017, p. 10) refers to the traditional distinction between coaching and expert consultation as an example of the area of competence of coaching and the distinction between coaching and passing on knowledge. As discussed above in Sect. 1.2, this fixation, in my view, is premature and would reduce the further development of the profession to traditional rules, which were propagated at the beginning of coaching. I would also doubt whether any profession will ever succeed in defining a firmly defined "body of knowledge" and a "theoretical foundation" on the basis of scientific evidence. It would be more appropriate to search for knowledge that always remains open for discussion, improvement, and extension of its scientific explanatory power (as demanded for the assumptions and intervention methods in the theoretical framework of *result-oriented coaching* in Chap. 9 below).

According to Fietze (2017), the classical model of professions is to exert power in their defined scope of activities. However, doubts emerge if the standard of professional autonomy can be lifted today under the general conditions of digitalization and deregulation (op. cit. p. 14 f.). Tietze therefore favors the weaker term "professionalism" instead of the idea of developing a "profession." Here, the evaluation of professional performance becomes the center, understood as lifelong learning and competence acquisition. Moreover, it would be more important than a fixed canon of knowledge if the coaching associations in cooperation with scientists would define and regularly, after several years, repeatedly redefine the application of scientifically based self-evaluations and external evaluation instruments for the analysis and improvement of coaching results and processes (see Chaps. 7 and 8 in this book) and demand their use not only in scientific studies but also in coaching practices. In this way, this would, in a certain sense, promote the production of new knowledge and quality improvement.

10.1.2 Future of the Coaching Market

Coaching is considered one of the services with exceptionally high growth rates. Gross and Stephan (2015) conducted surveys to analyze market development in Germany. They document a rapid increase in supply and demand. The increase in the market entry of corporate customers was still less than 10% in 1994. By 2010, it had already risen almost linearly to over 90%. Over the course of 5 years, the average growth per year was 40% or more. The economic crisis of 2008 did not lead to a feared collapse in demand, and even after slumps following the COVID-19 pandemic, the demand for coaching recovered quickly.

The ICF conducts global surveys of coaches at regular intervals. In a global study in 2022, 14,591 respondents from 153 countries across major regions worldwide participated (ICF, 2023b). It can be estimated that there are approximately 109,200 professional coach practitioners worldwide, an increase of 54% from the comparable estimate for 2015. A total of 13,320 managers/leaders use coaching skills. However, this is only a very rough estimate. The estimated total global revenue from coaching in 2022 was 4564 billion US dollars (2088 in North America and 1421 in Western Europe). It grew by 60% between 2019 and 2022. The increase in the number of active coach practitioners was the main factor driving the increase in total annual revenue.

The estimated annual revenue or income from coaching is 52,800 US dollars and rose by 12% between 2019 and 2022 (per-hour coaching session $244 and 9% increase, ranging from $277 in Western Europe to $114 in Latin America and the Caribbean). More than 53% reported less than $30.000 in annual revenue from coaching. On average, active coaches had 12.2 clients and spent 11.9 hours per week working as coaches.

The growth in the number of coaches has been rapid. The greater the number is, the more obvious the question is whether the increase will stagnate or decline in the future. According to their coach survey, Middendorf and Salamon (2018) suspected that the market would stagnate, at least in Germany. According to the ICF survey, however, this is by no means to be anticipated. However, during the COVID-19 pandemic, there was a temporary slump in demand and revenue.

My personal forecast for the future is that the coaching market will completely recover after the decline caused by the COVID-19 pandemic and will continue to expand in the future. My forecast is based on my individual observations and discussions with colleagues and intuitive estimations. (It is said that people are quite good at such intuitive estimates…) I like to encourage the readers formulating their own predictions and to observe, which of them come true in the future. In my view, a general expansion in the classic business coaching fields can be expected with a high degree of certainty, especially in countries where coaching has not been very widespread in companies thus far. In North America, Western Europe, and Australia, I expect the use of coaching to increase in fields of application that have been relatively underdeveloped to date, such as health coaching or reflection on questions of meaning and the development of one's own values and strengths (see the methods in Sects. 6.6 and 6.4), AI-Coach-Bots, and AI-augmented coaching (see the following chapter). In addition, there is undoubtedly a great deal of untapped market potential for coaches who specialize in new specific target groups or themes. Those who know the needs of potential customers and are inventive should find their market!

10.2 Consequences of Digitization and Artificial Intelligence[1]

10.2.1 Clients First: Future Problems and Chances in their Working and Private Life and Resulting Coaching Demands

When the consequences of digitalization and *artificial intelligence (AI)* in the coaching field are analyzed, only their application in coaching sessions and their direct impact on coaching practices and coaches are usually evaluated. However, it is much more important to first examine their general consequences for clients in their working and living environments. These changes will significantly influence the

[1] I thank Michèle Rieth for her valuable suggestions for this chapter!

content and themes of future coaching sessions. Coaches need to prepare and understand what is coming for their clients to be able to support them in coping with this transformation of their work and life.

Considering the foreseeable changes due to digitalization and AI in the working and living environment of clients in the "Second Machine Age" (Brynjolfsson & McAfee, 2014), this results in many concrete starting points for future coaching themes. The following list reflects some of them. Some have already become apparent at an early stage (Brynjolfsson & McAfee, 2014; Greif, 2017a. p. 59 ff.):

Humans and Technology

- Efficiency and optimization of the human-technology system
- Addictive use and psychological dependence on mobile and other systems
- Reduction in human social contacts
- Reflection on the future of working with smarter technology
- Reflective use of intelligent systems and apps

Work Changes and Digital and AI Qualifications

- Fear of uncertain work changes due to digitization
- Job changes and digital qualifications
- Planning and implementation of digital transformation
- Monitoring and maintenance of complex digital systems
- Stress and time pressure when performing tasks with new digital systems
- Stress due to the complexity of permanently accumulating data volumes ("big data") and interpretations, especially in the attractive new profession of data analyst ("data scientist") digital and AI qualification. The volume of data will also increase for all people working with AI or using it in their private life.

Click- and Cloudworking, Increase in Home Work, and Extreme Flexibilization of Employment

- Winning and successfully processing orders
- Organization of work and rest at home
- Existential anxiety and stress because there are not enough orders
- Self-employed digital upskilling
- Winning standing orders
- Job search and applying for employment

Unemployment

- Coping with professional existential anxieties
- Dealing with resistance to change and protests
- Negotiation of redundancy plans
- Outplacement, career coaching and qualifications for new jobs
- Job coaching for reintegration into working life
- Establishment of job coaching in industrialized and developing countries

The fear of many people losing their jobs to robots and AI was recognized early on. An example is the publication of McClure (2018), with the theme "You're fired says the robot." The fear of not being able to learn how to use AI systems competently is also a widespread phenomenon. There are now special questionnaires to investigate the fear of AI with scales assessing learning and job replacement fears (Wang & Wang, 2022).

It is conceivable that these and other yet unforeseen new threats and work change topics will further increase the demand for coaching in the future. Coaches who take up these themes could therefore be among the "crisis winners" of digitization and AI. However, coaches would have to "redadapt" and even "reinvent" their future coaching in line with the pulse of the times and acquire the necessary additional professional qualifications to be able to serve these themes competently and professionally.

For clients with the fear that they will not be able to understand and learn AI systems, coaches need methods for overcoming fear, circling ruminations, and learning to transform them into result-oriented, positive reflections about their potentials and chances, as described above in Sects. 2.5 and 6.4; support their client's planning of their learning, especially for familiarization with AI systems; and support them during learning difficulties. When complex computer systems are used, well-proven methods of error training (Keith & Frese, 2008), exploratory learning from errors (Greif, 1994, see below), and the methods described above for implementation support (see Sect. 9.3.3) can be used. They have already proven their worth in overcoming the uncertainties and fears of new technologies.

If clients fear being replaced by AI systems and losing their job, specialized career coaching would be necessary, again with methods to reduce anxiety and encourage people to be open to change and to develop their own potential and use it confidently. Since clients may well lose their jobs, it would be necessary to encourage them to seek professional career counseling in addition to coaching, as recommended in career coaching (Kauffeld et al., 2022).

In any case, it is necessary for coaches to expand their traditional role, acquire AI expertise, work with psychoeducational methods, act as learning motivators, and work with AI tools in coaching clients to show how they can be used. Of course, coaches cannot promote everything that is required in such transformations. They should support their clients in finding information and training opportunities for the specific requirements themselves and in finding the best experts. The coach's task is to support the clients and their situation with their potential and external resources holistically in the background and in the long term until the clients are able to successfully continue with the various tasks in a self-regulated manner.

Stefan Stenzel (HR expert in leadership development) in the technology company SAP (market leader in enterprise application and ERP software to run companies in all industries) and an expert for SAP's international coaching.[2] In his book about the future of the coaching business (Stenzel, 2022), he also calls for more field competence among coaches about the changing business world. In particular, he highlights the consequences of the future developments of hardware and processors,

[2] I thank Stefan Stenzel for valuable contributions to these paragraphs.

Big Data, demographics, and ethical challenges. Coaching must adapt to a changing environment and a changing market in order to remain attractive for the coming generation of "AI natives." Stenzel describes the consequences of demographic change for coaching (e.g., with regard to various diversity characteristics), and also the social (psychological) changes that are taking place (analysis of the *volatility, uncertainty, complexity, and ambiguity (VUCA)* learning, identity, reflexive life-style), and the innovations in business and companies (e.g., platforms, HR systems, new employment relationships and skills, careers, leadership). He sees a consistent analysis process in three steps: (1) what does the change mean for the client (managers or employees), (2) for the "service coaching," and (3) for the coach themselves and the coaching.

Stenzel (2024a) asks what the remaining differences between humans and machines will be. For Stefan Stenzel (2024b), the fact that ChatGPT or another model of generative AI will at least be able to hold coaching-like conversations in the future is actually only a question of the ever-increasing computing power and even more specialized algorithms that will come about as so-called agents. In view of these new developments in coaching, Stenzel calls for a conceptual "reset" of coaching.

10.2.2 History and Future: Humanistic Design of Working Conditions

The design of humane work is a classic subject of historical scientific analysis and discussion. Learning from history means looking back at the beginnings and especially at undesirable developments in history and how attempts were made to overcome them. The following short summary focuses on the basic models and questions about the division and design of labor and technology and their consequences for the development of humans, beginning with the first industrial revolution to the digital revolution of our time.

(1) The Division of Labor and its Consequences for Human Development

Among the historical foundations of today's economic systems are Adam Smith's (1723–1790) analysis of the division of labor as the cause of economic productivity and the wealth of nations (Smith, 1776). Using the example of pin manufacturing, he shows how productivity increases when the various subtasks are simplified and divided among different workers and how workers specialize in perfecting their respective tasks: one worker pulls the wire, another cuts it, another creates the cap and one the needle point, and one polishes the needle. The division of labor became the model and driving force of industrial manufacturing in Great Britain and other countries. However, it was accepted by Smith (1776, Book V, p. 981 ff.) that people who spend their whole lives performing only a few simple operations "of which the effects are nearly always the same" become, as he drastically puts it, "as stupid and ignorant as it is possible for a human creature to become." These people lose their ability to carry out complex tasks autonomously and their motivation to invest effort and engage in innovative activities. Interestingly, Adam Smith himself regarded these consequences as negative. As he argues, the consequence is a decrease in motivation to perform, ossification of the mind, and inability to participate in a reasonable conversation and to form a judgment about the great questions and interests of one's country. However, he thinks that this must be accepted because of the general benefits of production and wealth. He demands, however, that the government take precautions against these negative consequences by means of the general schooling of children and other public educational institutions.

(2) Tayloristic Division of Labor by Scientific Management

Frederick Winslow Taylor (1856–1915), an American engineer and management theorist, followed the principle of the division of labor to increase efficiency. He is considered the "Father of Scientific Management" because he used time and motion studies to investigate the most efficient method or "one best way" to perform working tasks. Management should use these findings to select and train suitable workers. The resulting separation of head and hand work (managers are responsible for planning and supervision, and workers are responsible for only practical execution) has been heavily criticized by unions and scientists. One example is the dedicated criticism of one of the founders of applied psychology, Erich Stern:

> "In the Taylor system, the division of labor is carried to extremes; it appears to be dominated purely by the idea of increasing the performance of man in the same way as that of the machine. (…) Here, labor appears to be completely detached from man, who must increasingly become a machine. (…) *For us, it is not the task but the human being that is in the foreground;* we want to restore for him, as far as it is possible under the present conditions, the joy of work." (E. Stern, 1921, p. 92, free translation, emphasis as in the original).

(3) Hawthorne effect: Satisfying relationships of the employees

During the "Great Depression" from 1929 until 1933, there were increasing conflicts with timekeepers and problems caused by workers' performance restraint and problems with production figures. Worldwide attention has been given to social psychological investigations led by Elton Mayo (Harvard School of Business in Boston) at the Hawthorne plant of Western Electric in Cicero, Illinois, USA (Roethlisberger & Dickson, 1939). The first experiment focused on the simple question of what effect brightness had on work performance. In the series of trials, the paradoxical effect was that performance improved permanently even when brightness was reduced to moonlight. Roethlisberger and Dickson attributed this to the kindness of the experimenters. This "Hawthorne effect" has subsequently led to the assumption, which is considered generally valid, that improving interpersonal relationships and job satisfaction leads to increased job performance. In addition to the division of labor, the authors therefore recommended a friendly management style to increase performance.

However, as more detailed research in the 1970s shows, the Hawthorne effect is a myth (Rice, 1982). Far from being friendly, the experimenters were disciplining the employees and gave constant performance feedback.

Noncooperating employees were eliminated from the experiments. This was probably particularly effective because the working conditions and compensation in the experiments were very privileged and because the employees did not want to lose these privileges.

Although there are correlations between job satisfaction and performance, they are small. After a meta-analysis of the results of 74 studies, Iaffaldano and Muchinsky (1985) estimate that the correlation is only $r = 0.17$. Low satisfaction, however, is correlated with absenteeism from work and the likelihood of quitting. Even performance pay, job satisfaction, and good human relations are seen as important target criteria.

(4) Group Dynamics and Humanistic Organizational Development

After his emigration from fascist Germany, the Jewish social psychologist Kurt Lewin and his American colleagues were actively engaged in research and application for the development of a humanistic psychology and a democratic society in the United States. His research on the positive effects of the democratic leadership style of teachers in comparison with the authoritarian style or laissez-faire behavior is well known (Lewin et al., 1939).

Lewin became responsible for conducting psychological educational campaigns to improve the implementation of new American laws against racial segregation. He founded the National Training Laboratories for Applied Behavioral Science in Bethel, USA, and performed the so-called T-Groups (French & Bell, 1995). Lewin's concepts formed the basis for the later humanistically oriented concepts of organizational development, with emphasis on need fulfillment and promotion of the development of the potentials of the members of the organization and their participation in the decisions concerning them.

(5) Humanistic Job Design

Important historical roots of today's humanistic concepts of work and organization are provided by the research of the Tavistock Institute in Great Britain in the coal mining industry beginning in 1949 (Trist & Bamford, 1951). As Cherns (1989) described, the psychoanalytically influenced social psychologists of the Tavistock Institute had to look for new jobs after World War II. During the war, they had resettled soldiers. They took on a project assignment from the National Coal Board to study the effects of mechanization and division of labor in the mining industry. During this research, they realized that the miners of one pit found an interesting way of combining traditional group work with the new mining technology of the time. This apparently reduced the division of labor and disintegration of work groups introduced by management with mechanization. They examined and compared the two different forms of work organization and reported that the combined solution with less division of labor resulted in lower absenteeism rates, fewer accidents, and higher productivity. These results and experiences gave rise to the Tavistock Institute's "Sociotechnical Systems Approach" (Trist & Bamford, 1951) and the concept of semi-autonomous work groups. Their conclusion was that, when new technologies are introduced, it is not enough to merely optimize the organization of work in technical terms. The social and technical systems must be optimized together. The goal is a better "fit" between the two. The work group is given responsibility for complete task domains. This is intended to increase the flexibility of the entire sociotechnical system and, through job enlargement and enrichment and more complex and meaningful tasks, achieve more humane job design.

In the course of the 1970s, humanistic concepts of work structuring were strongly received, especially in West Germany and Switzerland. The improvement of the "Quality of Working Life" and the "Humanization of Work" were the dominant themes in the labor sciences. They were included in the reform program of the West German Social Democratic Party, which was in power at the time. In 1974, the Ministry of Research and Technology Development of the Feral Republic of Germany launched the research program for the *Humanization of Working Life* (later renamed *Work and Technology* after the change of government in 1989). With an annual budget of more than 100 million DMs and numerous in-company application projects—always with the participation of works councils and accompanying research—it is one of the largest research and implementation programs in the world. Initially, controversial, it has undoubtedly contributed to the development of multidisciplinary research on humanization. In West Germany, research in the fields of work sciences, including work psychology and its practical application, has benefited the most from this program. Semi-autonomous work groups have been tested, among others, in the automotive industry (Ulich et al., 1973). How human–computer interaction can be designed humanely and how complex systems can be trained efficiently is shown by a project on redesigning complex office systems as *growing systems* (the complexity of the software program is increased step by step as decided and regulated by the users) in combination with a training concept for exploratory learning from errors (Greif, 1994; showing the strongest effects in the meta-analysis of different error training evaluation studies by Keith & Frese, 2008). It is also of interest for designing and training employees to master the increase in complexity of AI systems, as discussed below. Most of the projects, however, have remained short-term existing experiments.

Parallel to these developments in Western Germany, Winfried Hacker (1973) carried out highly regarded projects on "personality-enhancing work design" behind the "Iron Curtain" in the former German Democratic Republic (GDR). They showed that more complex work tasks and increased individual decision latitude at work can promote the development of abilities and work motivation and, at the same time, increase productivity. However, the introduction of semi-autonomous work groups was not permitted in the GDR's party-led political hierarchical system.

Industrial and Organizational Psychology in the United States and other Western countries has continuously enhanced its humanistic value orientation. In the 1960s and 1970s, Kurt Lewin's students propagated a departure from the Taylorist idea of the human being, according to which workers can only be motivated to perform through reward and punishment ("carrot and stick") (McGregor, 1960). Oriented to classical humanism, their ideal conception of the human being was the person who strives for self-actualization in work and through his or her achievements. They extended Lewin's concepts of democratic leadership and participative group decision-making (Likert, 1961) with concepts for the general expansion of employee participation and more democracy in organizations.

(6) Future Challenge: Control by AI Superintelligence?

Geoffrey Hinton, the so-called "Godfather" of AI and Winner of the Nobel Prize in Physics 2024, has warned in several interviews[3] that the extraordinary learning capabilities of AI will lead in the future to the most fundamental technological revolution in human history. The challenge is that in the long run (in approximately 20 years), AI will become smarter than humans. This will result in the existential threat that AI superintelligence might take over control. Therefore, much more scientific AI safety research and experiments are needed. Since no government of the world can risk allowing AI to take control, all governments should support such research and mandate that companies spend money on controlling AI safety. At the same time, Hinton noted that AI can be extremely useful, especially anywhere where it is applied for better predictions. His examples include medical doctors who use it for better diagnosis and treatment of their patients or companies that apply it to improve their production or services.

The domination of humans by AI systems is the ultimate threat to human living conditions. Various approaches that attempt to prevent or at least reduce these risks and other problematic consequences are presented below.

(7) Approaches for the Future of the Ethical and Humanistic Applications of AI Systems

For the vision of a humane future development and use of AI systems, the clarification of ethical questions is needed. *UNESCO's Business Council for Ethics of AI*, a collaborative initiative between UNESCO and companies, launched October principles to "develop due diligence and supervision mechanisms to identify, prevent and mitigate risks and be accountable for the way they address the impact of AI on human rights, the rule of law, and inclusive societies"[4] (UNESCO, 2021).

"It is strategic for UNESCO to work with companies that develop or use AI in different sectors, identifying good practices that take into account and respect ethical standards. The Recommendation can act as a guide to help these companies identify possible risks in their services and how to avoid them, as well as contribute to moving toward intelligent regional regulation that ensures an adequate competitive environment, for the benefit of everybody."

[3] An example is the you tube interview on BNN Bloomberg (26.6.2024) https://www.youtube.com/watch?v=mqjX8AzfJ_A (last retrieved 7.11.24).

[4] https://www.unesco.org/en/artificial-intelligence/business-council (last retrieved 18.10.2023)

In 2024, the European Parliament decided on a very detailed regulation for the use of AI.[5] "The *EU AI Act* is intended to promote the uptake of human-centric and trustworthy AI and to ensure a high level of protection of health, safety, fundamental rights, democracy, and rule of law from harmful effects of AI systems while supporting innovation and the functioning of the internal market.18.10.2024" In summary, four risks are emphasized:

- "Unacceptable risk is prohibited (e.g., social scoring systems and manipulative AI).
- Most of the text addresses high-risk AI systems, which are regulated.
- A smaller section handles limited risk AI systems, subject to lighter transparency obligations: developers and deployers must ensure that end-users are aware that they are interacting with AI (chatbots and deepfakes).
- Minimal risk is unregulated (including the majority of AI applications currently available on the EU single market, such as AI-enabled video games and spam filters—at least in 2021; this is changing with generative AI)."

The AI Act prohibits the following types of AI systems:

- S*ubliminal, manipulative, or deceptive techniques*.
- *Exploiting vulnerabilities* related to age, disability, or socioeconomic circumstances.
- *Biometric categorization systems* infer sensitive attributes (race, political opinions, etc.), except for labeling or filtering of lawfully acquired biometric datasets or when law enforcement categorizes biometric data.
- *Social scoring*, i.e., evaluating or classifying individuals or groups on the basis of social behavior or personal traits.
- *Assessing the risk of an individual committing criminal offenses* solely on the basis of profiling or personality traits, except when used to augment human assessments on the basis of objective, verifiable facts directly linked to criminal activity.
- *Facial recognition databases are constructed* by untargeted scraping of facial images from the Internet.
- *Inferring emotions in workplaces or educational institutions,* except for medical or safety reasons.
- *"Real-time" remote biometric identification* in publicly accessible spaces for law enforcement (exceptions: searching for missing persons, abusing victims, preventing substantial and imminent threats to life, identifying suspects in serious crimes)

The purpose of this regulation is to improve the functioning of AI in the European market by laying down a uniform legal framework in accordance with Union values, to promote human-centric and trustworthy AI, and to support innovation, protecting "natural persons, undertakings, democracy, the rule of law and environmental

[5] https://artificialintelligenceact.eu/the-act/ (last retrieved 5.11.24)

protection, while boosting innovation and employment and making the Union a leader in the uptake of trustworthy AI."

State monitoring systems of human behavior, such as those introduced in China, are very clearly prohibited in the EU. Companies such as Apple have reacted very quickly to this regulation. This can be seen, for example, in the fact that the introduction of AI for voice input into the iPhone 2024 was initially halted in Europe, and adjustments were made. Future experience will reveal whether the EU's detailed regulations can effectively reduce the risks of using AI without impairing technological innovation in international competition and promote human-centric and trustworthy AI.

Another important basis for regulating the introduction and use of AI has been published by the *Ethics Council of the Government of the Federal Republic of Germany* (for further background, see also Wong & Simon, 2020; Jacobs & Simon, 2022). This analysis and report "Humans and Machines" (Deutscher-Ethikrat, 2023) are also very detailed (287 pages). A current project. They formulate risks and opportunities that are associated with AI and recommendations for policymakers and AI developers. The basic standards are closer to scientific ethical approaches. Judith Simon, a professor of ethics in information technology at the University of Hamburg, is a member of the German Council. She highlights that increasing the expansion of abilities using AI can be seen as a basic positive ethical criterion. She says, "that entrusting tasks to AI should essentially be aimed at broadening human abilities and authorship and not decrease them."[6]

Symbiosis of Humans and AI and Joint Growing Systems

The history of the division of labor and its significance for the humane organization of work has always been a historical battle to overcome the inhumane consequences of the division of labor and the use of machines or computers. With adaptive learning AI systems, which process large amounts of data in a barely controllable way, this struggle is facing a new round and the challenge of being controlled by AI systems. Replacing the work of humans with AI systems for economic reasons and abandoning their control by users rather than fighting for humane applications is a simple but problematic strategy with similar negative consequences for the human development of abilities and the dequalification or even enslavement of humans by AI systems, as well as for higher educated employees and managers. However, opportunities also open up for sovereign selection and the use of AI systems by users, who are concerned that they can master the systems and enforce their decisions and, in particular, assemble and use them in a way that does not restrict their values and personality development but rather expands them as much as possible. The ideal model involves the coevolution of productivity and the expansion of people's self-regulation, abilities, opportunities, and resources together with their AI systems.

[6] https://www.deutschland.de/en/topic/culture/german-ethics-council-risks-of-artificial-intelligence (last retrieved 1.11.2024)

For such solutions, the traditional model of the division of labor between humans and machines or computers no longer fits. A more appropriate metaphor for this joint evolution would be the *model of a symbiosis of humans and AI systems* (Greif, 2017a). The term "symbiosis" (Greek "syn": together and "bios": life) refers to a useful and inseparable coexistence of two "partners" with possibilities for coevolution, as can be observed in the plant and animal world.

First, comparable practical examples of such symbioses between humans and computer systems can be found not only in the field of data science but also in many scientific research projects in which scientists are using the newest edition of specialized complex information and big research data-processing software systems. Scientists who are truly good in this field do not simply use preset standard program solutions but rather inform themselves about the state of research on the weaknesses and limitations of the programs and control and test each important solution with appropriate criteria. In this way, both young and old experts gradually develop their expertise and are held in high esteem when they are able to master highly complex programs and big sets of data. Therefore, this might be a model for the future mastering of AI.

The abovementioned coevolution of souverain mastering of complex software systems by the concept of *growing systems* provides another practical example as a possible precursor of how people can select software modules and decide, not immediately to use the complete systems, but increasing and controlling the complexity step by step and thus mastering it and developing their capabilities with confidence. If the complexity of systems and data exceeds the capabilities, this leads to stress, errors, and overload. If, on the other hand, complexity gradually increases only after the person decides that the current level of complexity has been competently mastered, our research on learning complex software systems not only shows that overload is prevented. Compared with that of the control group, learning performance is significantly and strongly improved, and the transfer of what has been learned to master other complex systems increases (Greif, 1994). These results support the idea of designing and teaching complex AI systems and datasets as "growing symbiotic systems." Coaches with AI knowledge and skills would be ideal partners of their clients in such coevolution processes. They can support their client's successful long-term self-motivation and learning, similar to career coaching. The positive opportunity is to screw the joint productivity of sovereign humans with learning AI tools and joint learning to incredible heights.

As mentioned above, Judith Simon highlights the expansion of abilities and authorship using AI as a central positive ethical criterion and therefore prevents any diminishing of human action capability and authorship and any diffusion of responsibility.[7] Unfortunately, however, there will probably always be people who allow themselves to be dominated by a technology or AI and reduce their developmental abilities or who become psychologically dependent on the tools and want to use

[7] https://www.deutschland.de/en/topic/culture/german-ethics-council-risks-of-artificial-intelligence (last retrieved 1.11.2024)

them almost constantly. To put it harshly, this would be a kind of "self-enslavement." An existing example can be when a person is constantly on the alert and being controlled by mobile phone messages. In Sect. 6.5, coaching methods are discussed in the context of changing such "bad habits." They can also be applied to reflect on and reduce problematic excessive uses of AI.

10.2.3 Use of E- and AI in Coaching

Kluge and Hagemann (2016) outlined fields of application and future developments of new media in digital transformation as well as personnel development, including coaching. They call for more research on the suitability for different groups of people and tasks. In synchronous and asynchronous distance coaching, online and e-coaching technologies have steadily increased in popularity in coaching in recent years, stimulating more research (Berninger-Schäfer, 2022; Geissler, 2022, 2025; Kanatouri, 2020; Terblanche, 2023, 2024; Tavis & Woodward, 2024; Terblanche et al., 2022a, 2022b).

Clutterbuck (2022) described the future possibilities of using artificially intelligent chatbots that are capable of learning and adapting in coaching. According to his assessment, "friendly" chatbots that can imitate "emotionally intelligent" behavior and learn to behave in communication in a way that is individually adapted to the client's preferences are particularly suitable. As mentioned above, according to the snapshot study of the International Coaching Federation (ICF, 2023a), the majority of coaching practitioners expressed uncertainty about the future of AI. Forty-six percent agreed with the proposition that "AI will make it easier to run their coaching business."

Strong and Terblanche (2020) analyze the criteria they believe emotionally intelligent coaching chatbots must meet compared with human coaches. In doing so, they view effective natural coaching dialogs and other human capabilities as models for the construction of chatbots. Currently, in 2024, existing chatbots had limited and defined capabilities. However, new and better coach bots are being created at an exponential rate. When they are available, they will replace human coaches, according to Strong and Terblanche.

Different ways of Using AI in Coaching

AI can be used in various ways in coaching. One main distinction is (1) the use of AI systems as a complete replacement for human coaches or (2) the use of AI to support or supplement coaching by coaches, also referred to as "AI-augmented coaching." Rasool (2024, p. 90 ff.) differs more precisely between four frameworks of AI-curated coaching: (1) AI-informed (coach is informed by an AI but enacts and manages the coaching process without AI), (2) AI-guided (coach uses AI suggestions to guide the coaching process), (3) AI-delivered, supervised (the coaching process is delivered by an AI coach but is moderated and supervised by a human coach), and (4) AI-delivered, unsupervised (the coaching process is delivered by an AI coach but is not moderated and supervised by a human coach; the AI manages boundaries or violations autonomously, where a human coach is eventually requested to intervene).

Different Predictions of Future Development: AI-Augmented Coaching or Takeover by AI-Coaching Bots?

The COVID-19 pandemic was an unanticipated disruptive change that led to revolutionary changes in the field of coaching. The pace of change was very rapid. Coaching associations immediately began to upskill their members through online fast-track courses. Coaching continuing education courses were converted. (Our continuing coaching training was already complete online after 2 weeks in April 2020 and received best feedback from participants). Internet coaching platforms are competing with coaching associations. They offer online and AI tools, recruit coaches, and promise client referrals. If we look at these developments, it seems to be a safe prediction that AI in coaching will result in disruptive changes for the whole field of coaching. It is even possible that the coaching business is almost completely taken over by AI coaching bots. If AI in coaching has accelerated as quickly as COVID-19 has in the past, coaches urgently need AI training just as quickly.

Rauen (2018a), as speaker of the German Coaching Federation at a coaching congress, dared to make the prediction that, in the future, simple coaching tasks would be taken over completely by intelligent systems. For human coaches, only the area of complex coaching would remain. However, empirically verifiable AI systems in the future may also be able to coach complex problems autonomously.

A current research question is whether social support from chatbots can achieve empathy, emotional bonding, and commitment comparable to those of human coaches. As Strong and Terblanche (2020, p. 57) state, the trust and credibility of the bot emerges if it demonstrates expertise and transfers knowledge on a par with or better than humans do, but it is questionable if this can replace credible empathy and bonding with human coaches or inspiring human motivation. The friendly feedback I receive on my behavior from health apps or AI systems does not affect me much emotionally.

It would be plausible and empirically testable to investigate whether hormonal responses involving the release of oxytocin, the so-called cuddle hormone, can be measured in interactions with coaches in which strong feelings of trust and empathy are experienced. The hormone plays an important role in establishing and maintaining social bonds with other people and in reducing stress (Guastella & MacLeod, 2008; Heinrichs et al., 2009; Kosfeld et al., 2005). I would not expect even the friendliest and empathetic feedback from an AI bot to generally lead to comparable responses for all individuals (although there may be some strange exceptions). Credible Feedback from people motivates and strengthens me a lot. After observing similar reactions from my clients to my personal appreciation and enthusiasm for what they achieve, I cannot imagine that this intensive common emotional experience can be replaced by AI feedback in the same motivating and bonding way for most of my clients. People can be very sensitive about who gives them feedback and try to figure out why the feedback was phrased positively or negatively. Of course, as Terblanche (2024) mentioned, an AI bot is able to simulate empathetic behavior, and there will be people who prefer such reliable AI comments. But we know that this behavior was programmed by the AI developers.

Terblanche et al. (2022) compared the coaching goal attainment efficacy of human coaches and an AI coach. They used two longitudinal randomized control trial studies and measured increases in clients' goal attainment over a 10-month period. The mean scores of goal attainment (mean of several measures) show strong and significant effects in comparison to those of the control groups; however, goal attainment remains low (approximately 41%). As argued above in Chap. 7, *the* effectiveness of human coaching is often not very high. Low results are relatively easy to surpass. Coaching bots can replace human coaches in a cost-effective way. Terblanche et al. (2022) reported that the always accessible and cost-effective AI chatbot is used much more frequently than expensive human coaching. They see this as a major advantage of AI coaching and an opportunity to spread and "democratize" coaching. In my opinion, however, it is problematic to prematurely equate "cost-effective" with "democratic." Only equal participation in rights and privileges for all people, which does not discriminate against any groups of people, can be democratic. That must be checked. Cheap AI bots could potentially have adverse effects.

Terblanche et al. (2022) believe that human coaches can build on their particular strengths and that, in the coming years, humans will not be outperformed by AI bots in the areas of emotional intelligence, empathy, uniquely human forms of intelligence, the transfer of learning, and higher-order complex sense-making. AI coaches that focus on narrow goal-oriented coaching and are based on fundamental, proven theories (perhaps with more "intervention fidelity" than many human coaches; see Chap. 8 Busch et al., 2022) may very well rival human coaches in that specific coaching (see also Terblanche, 2024).

David Clutterbuck (2022) sees AI tools merely as "assistants" to coaches. My prediction is that AI systems and tools will not largely replace human coaches in the foreseeable future of this decade. There will certainly be attempts to replace coaches with lower-cost intelligent chatbots. According to my personal forecast, there will be many customers and companies that test and use such systems. However, similar to the field of using AI in medical diagnoses and therapies, "demanding" customers who want the best possible coaching service, especially for very important or critical themes, and coaching clients who are looking for security and who value credible emotional support and inspiring motivation from experienced persons, will prefer AI-augmented coaching by empathetic human coaches, even if this cost more. The future will show if this prediction is true.

Another expectation is that, especially in companies that fund coaching for their employees, there will be increased pressure to use coaching bots instead of human coaches to reduce costs (Koch, 2020). As described above in terms of opportunities for professional and private use of AI by clients, I see better alternatives, as coaches can also keep costs low by using supporting tools and evolve with increasing skills to create a personal–empathic coaching relationship with their clients and to support their clients by autonomously using the best possible comprehensive AI knowledge and tools in realizing their goals, clarifying their situation, and clarifying questions of the meaning of their life. The prerequisite is that the coaches and clients handle the tools confidently and carefully reflect and decide how to use them.

Obstacles to the Use of AI in Coaching and Reservations of Coaches
Today, a major obstacle to the use of AI, as mentioned above, is that it does not guarantee data privacy. Sensitive personal questions and data should therefore be entered only after the data privacy of the system becomes more transparent and the system's answers and knowledge files are safe from being leaked. In some cases, a transitional solution until the systems guarantee confidentiality is for coaches, instead of the client, to call up the AI under their name and enter anonymized data and questions into the AI in joint coaching sessions. The AI's answers can then be discussed together.

The reservations of many coaching practitioners about the use of e- or AI coaching methods have been very strong and polarized in recent years and remain so today. In discussions at conferences or in group meetings in associations, I have seen coaches as late as 2022, 2023, and early 2024, who fundamentally reject online coaching and AI tools in coaching because, in their opinion, they prevent the development of an empathic coaching relationship or even because coaching is impossible with them. Some even think that this would be the "demise of coaching" (Coachilly Magazine, 2023).

Who would have dared to predict that the startling slogan "digitize or die" would become reality so quickly for the professional existence of coaches. Shortly before the outbreak of the COVID-19 pandemic, Melanie Maier conducted very intensive surveys of coaches in her dissertation (Maier, 2020) on the evaluation of coaches of various online media in coaching rather than face-to-face coaching. She documented many negative evaluations, up to and including widespread rejections. As she told me, after she completed her surveys and the COVID-19 pandemic broke out, several coaches whom she had interviewed spontaneously told her later that they had largely changed their dismissive attitudes. During the COVID-19 pandemic, they had no choice but to use previously rejected online media to continue their coaching business. In the process, they realized that these media were not at all as problematic as they had previously thought.

However, it is becoming increasingly difficult to rationally justify blanket rejection as well as unrestricted acceptance in the face of growing empirical knowledge and scientific research. What is required is a differentiated questioning and analysis of which specific tools are used in which specific way. The advantages and disadvantages of AI depend on its quality and use, which can be very different. They are to be clarified by ethical analyses and scientific studies, as to which specific online and AI tools with and without presence coaching can worsen or perhaps even improve the coaching relationship and effectiveness (see the outlook by Terblanche, 2024).

Controlling AI by Prompts
Getting an AI system to do exactly what you want is a challenging task. The good news is that knowledge of computer programming languages is not necessary. The AI system can be controlled and directed by verbal commands, so-called *prompts*, which generate a response or start a task performed by the AI (Podesser, 2023).

Companies hire prompt designers (also called prompt engineers) and pay them well, e.g., to perform a business strategy for the company using SWOT analysis, create a marketing strategy, and advertise using a special marketing model but also to develop or optimize technological solutions. The job of a prompt designer is seen as one of most attractive modern jobs. Harald Geissler, a provider of online coaching training in Germany, sells the training and customization of prompts for an AI bot that coaches can use with their clients.[8] Colin Button designed more than 50 ChatGPT prompts for coaches early.[9] They can be used, e.g., for creating a session plan for a client with a goal, on the basis of one of several different coaching models (e.g., the GROW model) and interactive worksheets for the client. Coaches who become familiar with prompt design will undoubtedly be in demand in the future.

Using AI in Coaching Is Not Always Useful

In my experience and research, a simple online coaching tool that generally promotes the coaching relationship is the accompaniment of the implementation of the changes desired by the clients by means of short online messenger communication using WhatsApp or Signal. In contrast to the use of AI tools for this task, there are no data protection problems if it is used, as described in *Habit Changes* in Sects. 6.5.2 and 9.3.3, if no explanations of the content are communicated or if a request to talk about it is answered by the phone or in a meeting. As the example shows, different media can certainly be combined. AI tools do not always provide the simplest solution. Our quick method for evaluating and communicating the success of the implementation works very well and efficiently when changing behavioral habits during coaching. Many clients spontaneously report that they experience the implicit presence thereby shown by the coaches as very positive, even during difficult phases of implementation. Of course, it would also be very easy to construct an AI bot instead of using the messenger. However, it is likely important for the psychological commitment of the clients that the bot alerts clients to the coach's attentive implicit presence to keep the coach informed and to point out when direct contact between the client and coach would be beneficial.

Coaching as a Reflective Space for the Use of AI

The sociologist Giddens (1991, pos. 42) described how, in posttraditional, modern societies, traditional customs, and habits are dissolving and how permanent complex global changes influence individual social life down to the most personal individual experiences. Everything is constantly questioned. Knowledge is seen only as hypothetical (pos. 68). To be able to develop a coherent self-identity despite these uncertainties, he sees the need for an institutionalization of reflexivity (pos. 111). Stelter (2013) draws on Giddens' analysis and sees the importance of coaching as opening a "reflexive space" to think about new possibilities for action and for the search for meaning in one's life. In their analyses, Giddens and Stelter were unable to determine the importance of digitalization to the use of AI systems. Will the

[8] https://www.online-coaching-lernen.de/ausbildung/kompaktkurs-ki-coaching/ (retrieved 1.2. 2024.

[9] https://www.thinkific.com/blog/chatgpt-for-coaches/ (retrieved 2.2.2024)

reflective space created through coaching also end up being created solely together with AI systems and not with humane coaches or other humans? Wouldn't it be inherently paradoxical for clients to use AI systems in coaching to reflect on their use of AI systems? If the AI reliably and verifiably informs our clients and us coaches about vulnerabilities and problematic uses of AI and stimulates us to perform our own reflections and stimulate sovereign decisions, the apparent paradox is resolvable. Additionally, to promote result-oriented self-reflection as well as to clarify the use of AI tools in the professional and private spheres as coaches and clients, AI tools may well be used in addition, as long as they do not limit our sovereignty and self-regulation abilities and resources but rather expand them. Greif and Rauen (2022) describe the increasing importance of coaching as a reflexive space for the expected changes brought about by the digital revolution. The following statement summarizes the particular importance of coaching in the expected changes:

Increasing Importance of Reflection on Digitalization and AI in Coaching

Through complex and uncertain societal changes and through digitalization and AI, the importance and use of coaching as a reflexive space together with coaches is increasing. As long as the sovereign reflections and decisions of individuals are not impaired but self-regulation, abilities, and resources are expanded, AI tools adapted to clients using prompt design can be applied in addition to conversations with human coaches.

Augmentation of the Success Factors of Coaching Through AI

Harald Geissler has developed "triadic coaching" and coach training in Germany,[10] where the participants learn to formulate prompts for ChatGPT in coaching processes supervised by human coaches. He assumes that the *general success factors* of coaching, described above in Sect. 9.3, are applicable to this AI-augmented coaching (Geissler, 2025). He has started research and ratings of the prompts and behavior observation of these factors for a concrete interaction protocol of a coaching session. He asked me to perform ratings and discuss the differences and similarities with traditional human coaches. For this purpose, I developed the following speculative model of the general success factors of AI-augmented coaching (Fig. 10.1).

In Fig. 10.1, the success factors in which behavior can be observed by both the human coach and the AI with comparable results or where a combination seems to be useful are marked with +AI. The success factors at the basic level are particularly evident in the factor of *process guidance*, where the human coach has the AI carry out subprocesses. However, showing credible appreciation and emotional support is a job where the human coach can be more successful. *With respect to the working*

[10] https://www.coachdb.com/de/coach-ausbildung/online-coaching-lernen.html (last retrieved 15.11.24).

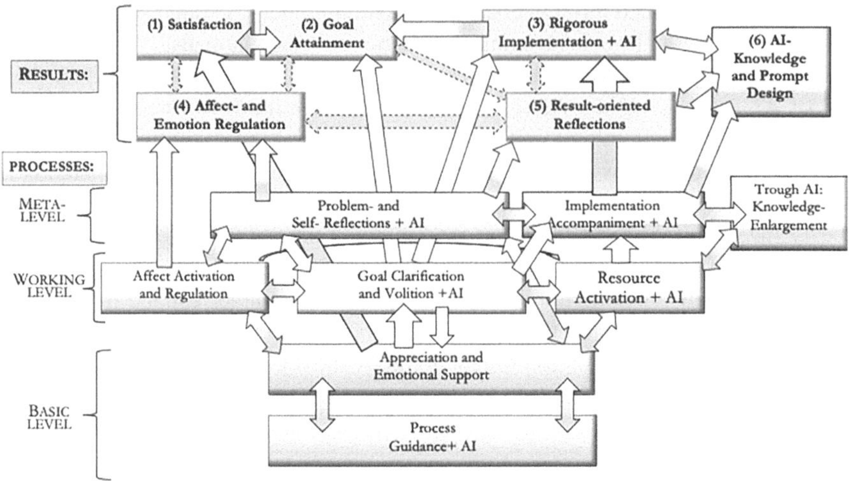

Fig. 10.1 General success factors of AI-augmented coaching (observed behavior of coach and AI) and coaching results

level factors, this also applies to the factor *affect activation and regulation*. Questions exploring resources and *resource activation and goal clarification* can be supported very well by questions of the AI system in addition to the coach. (Supporting the formulation of a firm volitional implementation, the model of a human coach might be a little better.)

AI can also contribute to success factors at the metalevel. In particular, the stimulation of *problem reflections and self-reflections* through systematic questions asking individuals to reflect precisely on problems in the environment or situation of the client or questions or on the real and ideal self-image of the client can be performed in exercises with specialized AI procedures. Since a realistic clarification of a problem situation and the development of the self-concept and clarification of the identity of the client are crucial for his or her future development, I would not recommend delegating this fully to the AI, at least supervision and support by an empathic and experienced human coach in my view is always necessary.

As mentioned above, the task of *Accompaniment of the Implementation,* acceleration can be supported by AI tools. However, the commitment to rigorously implement difficult behavior changes (e.g., habits) might be greater if the AI system always informs the coach and if the coach from time to time reacts by empathy after frustrating situations and enthusiasm after successes.

In traditional coaching, the coach rarely directly promotes *knowledge enlargement* by imparting knowledge. This is where the AI comes out on top. (As emphasized several times, in posttraditional coaching, human coaches should also impart knowledge in a psychoeducative way to help people help themselves.)

The wealth of knowledge that AI systems can draw on is immeasurable. In my view, this can be the decisive difference between traditional and AI-augmented coaching. Clients who use AI-augmented coaching will be impressed by their knowledge enlargement and will not care that such transfer of knowledge is against the basic rules of traditional coaching (see Sect. 1.2 above). If clients decide whether they want to use new knowledge or be thrown back on their own knowledge by a traditional coach who does not use AI and even withholds his or her own experience, fearing the ability to break the traditional rule, not to influence their client too much, will probably decide in favor of AI-augmented coaching (or even the AI Coach Bot). In my opinion, competition with these systems can be won only by human coaches if they expand their AI knowledge and augment the knowledge of their clients by using AI systems and tools in addition to passing on their own experiential knowledge in a psychoeducational way. Like a sports coach, business coaches can provide empathetic and motivating feedback and accompany the implementation with personal commitment for the success of their clients. In doing so, they can act as role models of how to use AI tools and communicate authentically that the clients who use AI remain the owners of their goals and paths and always make decisions, i.e., retain control over the entire interaction coaching and change processes.

10.3 More Guidance Through Science and Practice-Based Coaching!

The development of concepts, assumptions, and methods in coaching has been driven by inspiring personalities and their concepts from the beginning until today. Some of them were mentioned: Gregory Bateson with his systemic analyses, Sir John Whitmore with the GROW concept, Steve de Shazer with Solution Focused Coaching, Albert Ellis with Cognitive Behavioral Psychotherapy and the analysis of irrational beliefs, Antony Grant with Goal-Oriented Coaching, David Drake with Narrative Coaching, and Martin Seligman with Positive Psychological Coaching. Grant has conducted many scientific research studies in the coaching field and is one of the founders of evidence-based coaching. Seligman has also stimulated coaching research. The situation is similar for more recent concepts. We find authors who claim to restructure coaching or propagate new universally applicable methods. However, if you read their publications and review their short literature lists, you will notice that they do not cite any research studies but rather only general popular literature and arguments of well-known personalities. As a result, today's leadership in development is based primarily on the individual experiences and opinions of individual authors. This coaching literature is therefore not evidence-based through scientific research but rather "eminence-based" in essence.

These authors may not see themselves as "eminences" in the literal sense. Perhaps they could, however, in their next publication, disseminate less supposed certainty but themselves point out the uncertainty of some of their assumptions and open questions and possibilities for independent critical examination through precise practical observations or scientific research. Readers, too, might ask such questions about the concepts and assumptions propagated, especially in the case of contributions from which they want to take something for their practice.—Of course, this also applies to all assumptions and conclusions in this book! Critical reflections and references to open questions can be found for each chapter. In the questions at the end of the chapters, this is often explicitly invited.

If we are inspired by the words—or better yet, the actions—of competent people, that is perfectly OK. However, basically, it would be an anachronism if we left the future of coaching to individual expert authorities and their concepts, assumptions, and methods shaped by personal experience. The themes and goals of our clients are as diverse as life can be. For example, anyone who tries to activate all clients to solve all their problems using only de Shazer's miracle question should think about and carefully observe with which problems and people this does not work well. Additionally, the concepts and methods of almost all other mentioned professional authorities are not universally applicable "for everything." The coaching methods of Tony Grant, which are most closely aligned with scientific research, and positive psychological coaching, as well as result-oriented coaching or the approach of ACT, draw on many authors and their research and methods and consider a wide variety of coaching themes and goals and the psychological differences between different clients.

Today, more than ever before in the history of science, scientific research and findings are based on the research of many scientists and on competing investigations to support their assumptions. Even famous scientists who have received a Nobel Prize for their research (often several together) always emphasize that they did not make achievements alone. If we orient ourselves with alert criticism to scientific findings and research found by many scientists, the risk that we behave anachronistically decreases. Scientific research never stands still. New research has always faced challenges and keeps us alert.

Science orientation implies openness to discourse and criticism and is always prepared to question assumptions and findings when research shows that the previous assumption cannot be maintained or when the data collected can be mapped or predicted more accurately by other models. This is not easy for coaches and associations because, at first glance, marketing coaching seems easier if you advertise coaching services without any limitations. However, you will not convince critical customers by exaggerating or concealing unresolved effects. Realistic and verifiable descriptions are more intelligent. Openness to criticism and change naturally also applies to my own assumptions and models reproduced in this book. Compared with my first draft theory on result-oriented coaching (Greif, 2008) and the first German-language version of this book (Greif, 2021), new research findings were included in this book, which led to modifications and additions in the definitions and assumptions. As a theoretical framework open to improvement, the theory invites critique, corrections, and extensions of its scientific explanatory power.

More guidance in future development belongs to coaching, which is scientifically and practically grounded and is not a prediction but rather expresses hope. The hope is that the further development of coaching in the future will be based more on broad scientific and practical foundations. However, coaching is not feasible without sound practical knowledge, skills, and experience. Scientists do not make decisions about what should happen in individual coaching sessions in practice. Clients are the "owners" of the themes, goals, and decisions in the coaching process.

Coaches guide clients through the process. According to the problem-solving conception of science mentioned above (Greif, 1993), science basically has, among other tasks, a kind of service job in guiding and helping to solve important practical problems. For these scientific services to be seen and used, we need exchange and dialogs between scientists and practitioners. Ilona Holtschmidt, one of the Heads of the Research Committee of the German Coaching Association (DBVC), initiated a research dialog forum for coaches, and together, we held a first online evening on "Health Coaching: Latest Research and Practice" in February 2021. The exchange was very lively. Since then, these online dialog events have become regular good practices. One was in 2024 by Michael Bauer, a young German researcher, on AI and organizational transitions and the role of coaching. This was followed in March 2021 by a dialog evening with me and coaches from the Munich chapter of the International Coaching Federation (ICF) on the topic of "More science into coaching," initiated and codesigned by Felix Müller, a practitioner, who is very interested in science and a coauthor. The concept of the evening corresponds to the mentioned service function of science: The coaches brought questions and topics into the dialog to which they wanted answers or amounts from science. Such dialogs can be the beginning of building bridges across the gap between science and practice. (In a sense, the rope that is shot over the abyss to later pull the first supporting bars on it to the other side). Among the world's most active and best providers of scientifically oriented dialogs, conferences, and training events are the Institute of Coaching (IOC) based at McLean Hospital (Belmont, MA), the Centre for Coaching at Henley Business School (Henley-on-Thames, United Kingdom), and the International Centre for Coaching and Mentoring Studies at Oxford Brooks University (United Kingdom). In December 2024, Nicky Terblanche presented and discussed the current state of research on AI in coaching online at the IOC.

> A concrete practical step in expanding cooperation between scientists and practitioners can be joint publication. Well-placed publications are definitely good for the reputation of not only scientists but also practitioners. In my experience in such coproductions, the exchange and discourse about common and different practical observations and assumptions are always very challenging. I have always learned something new, as have my cooperation partners. Together, observations are analyzed and integrated and formulated into the shared analyses and assumptions. In this context, theories can be used and developed jointly by scientists and practitioners as socially constructed "thinking tools".
>
> As a next step after such dialogs, collaboration in a practice-based research project would be obvious. The great advantages of cooperating with practitioners are their field contacts, their knowledge of how to use them, and often the management of the implementation. As a scientist, I contribute to my literature research as well as my experience and knowledge about planning, conducting qualitative or statistical analyses of research and publications.

"Reflective practitioners" (Schön, 1983) review their own practice again and again—similar to scientists—to improve it. They can use scientifically based research instruments for self-evaluation to analyze the processes and results, or they can bring their coaching into evaluation studies to evaluate the effectiveness of their coaching, which are conducted by scientists (see above Chap. 7). It is one of the standards of science to conduct such evaluations independent of influence by unnamed sponsors. Adherence to this standard must be explicitly stated in most journals today. In addition, compliance with ethical standards of research and data protection must be verified. In all good journals, at least two independent reviewers check the quality of the article regarding whether relevant literature has been taken into account, whether it was methodologically up-to-date and carefully documented, and whether the results are scientifically and practically significant. Effectiveness studies in the coaching field that have been conducted and published according to the quality criteria of science are generally carefully reviewed and reliable. However, as emphasized in all presentations and publications on the state of research evaluating the effectiveness of coaching, more studies are needed, especially more research on the effectiveness of individual methods or groups of methods and new target groups and fields of application (see above Sect. 7.2). In the important future field of coaching, scientists independent of sponsors must take on more guidance for the coaching profession. However, the same applies here: In coaching, the clients are the owners of the evaluation of the themes, goals, and decisions, and the coaches guide and structure the processes. Science depends on cooperation with coaches and their clients to evaluate processes and effectiveness. However, this can succeed very well, as large and many small bridges expand between science and practice.

It has already been stated in the opening chapter that coaching today is designed primarily by practitioners on the basis of their practical experience or concepts, assumptions, and methods, which are usually very loosely connected to scientific theories and research-based findings. This will also be true in the future. This book describes bridges between science and practice that are very substantially created, many that are small, and many that are under construction. Theories are scaffolding and research and are similar to additional building materials with which such bridges can be built. The sweeping and forward-looking bridge designed by artist Michael Griem for this book and shown above in Fig. 1.1. is still under construction but must be completed together!

My Closing Chord
Practice and research!
Research and practice!
Practice and research!

10.4 Questions for Repetition and Remembering

(1) What are your forecasts for the market development of coaching in this decade? In which practice areas will demand flatten or increase?
(2) What consequences do you expect from digitalization and the use of artificial intelligence for coaching methods and for coaching themes due to changes in clients?
(3) How do you see the future impact of scientific findings and research on coaching practices?

References

Acar, F. E., & Kiliıc, A. (2011). Secondary-school teachers' questioning activities in learning-teaching process. *Education, 132*(1), 173–184.

Adriaanse, M. A., de Ridder, D. T. D., & de Witt, J. B. F. (2009). Finding the critical cue: Implementation intentions to change one's diet work best when tailored to personally relevant reasons for unhealthy eating. *Personality and Social Psychology Bulletin, 35*(1), 60–71.

Albrecht, E. (2023). *Die besten Online-Coaching-Methoden*. managerSeminare.

Alkaissi, H., & McFarlane, S. I. (2023). Artificial hallucinations in ChatGPT: Implications in scientific writing. *Cureus, 15*(2), e35179.

Anderson, E. M., Bohon, L. M., & Berrigan, L. P. (1996). Factor structure of the private self-consciousness scale. *Journal of Personality Assessment, 66*(1), 144–152.

Anthony, W. S. (1966). Working backward and working forward in problem-solving. *British Journal of Psychology, 57*(1–2), 53–59.

APA. (2006). Evidence-based practice in psychology – APA presidential task force on evidence-based practice. *American Psychologist, 61*(4), 271–285.

Argyris, C. (2002). Double-loop learning, teaching, and research. *Academy of Management Learning & Education, 1*(2), 206–218.

Athaluri, S. A., Manthena, S. V., Krishna, V. S. R., Kesapragada, M., Yarlagadda, V., Dave, T., & Duddumpudi, R. T. S. (2023). Exploring the boundaries of reality: Investigating the phenomenon of artificial intelligence hallucination in scientific writing through ChatGPT. *Cureus, 15*(4), e37432. https://doi.org/10.7759/cureus.37432

Austin, J. T., & Vancouver, J. B. (1996). Goal constructs in psychology: Structure, process, and content. *Psychological Bulletin, 120*(3), 338–375.

Bachkirova, T., Linet, A., & Reading, E. (2015). Evaluating a coaching and mentoring programme: Challenges and solutions. *International Coaching Psychology Review, 10*(2), 175–189.

Badura, B., Ritter, W., & Scherf, M. (1999). *Betriebliches Gesundheitsmanagement – ein Leitfaden für die Praxis*. Ed. Sigma.

Bähre, M. (2001). *Coaching – Das systemische Konfliktgespräch*. Diplomarbeit im Fachgebiet Arbeits- und Organisationspsychologie der Universität Osnabrück.

Bamberg, E. (2018). Gesundheit im Coaching. In S. Greif, H. Möller, & W. Scholl (Eds.), *International handbook of evidence based coaching: Theory, research and practice. Cham: Switzerland: Springer Nature* (pp. 235–243). Springer.

Bamberg, E. (2022). Health in coaching. In S. Greif, H. Möller, W. Scholl, J. Passmore, & F. Müller (Eds.), *International handbook of evidence based coaching: Theory, research and practice* (pp. 419–428). Springer Nature.

Bamberg, E., Ducki, A., & Metz, A.-M. (Eds.). (2011). *Gesundheitsförderung und Gesundheitsmanagement in der Arbeitswelt – Ein Handbuch*. Hogrefe.

S. Greif, *The Future of Coaching*, https://doi.org/10.1007/978-3-031-96192-2

Bamberger, G. G. (1999). *Lösungsorientierte Beratung*. Beltz.

Bandler, R., & Grinder, J. (1975). *The structure of magic: A book about language and therapy* (Vol. 2 vols). Science and Behavior Books.

Bandler, R., & Grinder, J. (1979). *Frogs into princes. Neuro linguistic programming*. Real People Press.

Bandler, R., & Grinder, J. (2014). *Neue Wege der Kurzzeit-Therapie* (15th ed.). Junfermann.

Bandler, R., Roberti, A., & Fitzpatrick, O. (2013). *The ultimate introduction to NLP – How to build a successful life*. Harper Collins & Kindle.

Bandura, A. (1969). *Principles of behavior modification*. Holt, Rinehart & Winston.

Bandura, A. (1994). *Lernen am Modell. Ansätze zu einer sozial-kognitiven Lerntheorie*. Klett-Cotta.

Barrett, K., O'Connor, M., & McHugh, L. (2019). A systematic review of values-based psychometric tools within Acceptance and Commitment Therapy (ACT) [article]. *Psychological Record, 69*(4), 457–485. https://doi.org/10.1007/s40732-019-00352-7

Bass, B. M. (1990). From transactional to transformational leadership: Learning to share the vision. *Organizational Dynamics, 18*(3), 22–48.

Bass, B. M., & Avolio, B. J. (1997). *Full range leadership development: Manual for the Multifactor Leadership Questionnaire (MLQ)*. Mind Garden.

Bateson, G. (1981). *Ökologie des Geistes. Anthropologische, psychologische, biologische und epistemologische Perspektiven*. Suhrkamp.

Baumann, N., & Kuhl, J. (2021). PSI theory in action: The assessment of self-competences as an aid in counseling and therapy. In J. F. Rauthmann (Ed.), *Handbook of personality dynamics and processes* (pp. 1297–1316). Elsevier. https://doi.org/10.1016/B978-0-12-813995-0.00051-0

Beck, A. T., Steer, R. A., Ball, R., & Ranieri, W. (1996, December). Comparison of beck depression inventories-IA and -II in psychiatric outpatients. *Journal of Personality Assessment, 67*(3), 588–597.

Beeman, M., & Kounios, J. (2015). *The eureka factor: Creative insights and the brain*. Penguin.

Behfar, K. J., Peterson, R. S., Mannix, E. A., & Trochim, W. M. K. (2008). The critical role of conflict resolution in teams: A close look at the links between conflict type, conflict management strategies, and team outcomes. *Journal of Applied Psychology, 93*(1), 170–188.

Behrendt, P. (2006). Wirkung und Wirkfaktoren von psychodramatischem Coaching – Eine experimentelle Evaluationsstudie. *Zeitschrift für Psychodrama und Soziometrie, 5*(1), 59–87.

Behrendt, P., & Greif, S. (2022). Success factors in the coaching process. In S. Greif, H. Möller, W. Scholl, J. Passmore, & F. Müller (Eds.), *International handbook of evidenced based coaching: Theory, research and practice* (pp. 877–888). Springer Nature.

Behrendt, P., Mühlberger, C., Göritz, A. S., & Jonas, E. (2021). Relationship, purpose, and change – An integrative model of coach behavior. *Consulting Psychology Journal: Practice and Research., 73*(2), 103–121.

Bennett, J. L. (2006). An agenda for coaching-related research: A challenge for researchers. *Consulting Psychology Journal: Practice and Research, 58*(4), 240–249.

Berninger-Schäfer, E. (2022). *Online coaching*. Springer.

Bertalanffy, L. v. (1948). Zu einer allgemeinen Systemlehre. *Biologia Generalis, 195*, 114–129.

Bickerich, K., & Michel, A. (2018). Change-Prozesse als Anwendungsfeld im Coaching. In S. Greif, H. Möller, & W. Scholl (Eds.), *Handbuch Schlüsselkonzepte im Coaching* (pp. 75–84). Springer.

Boehnke, K., & Hanke, K. (2022). Values and their importance in coaching. In S. Greif, H. Möller, W. Scholl, J. Passmore, & F. Müller (Eds.), *International handbook of evidence-based coaching* (pp. 959–970). Springer Nature.

Boer, D. (2014). *Short Schwartz's Value Survey – deutsche Fassung*. https://www.goethe-university-frankfurt.de/51799161/ssvsg_scale.pdf (last access 4.12.2020).

Böhm, A., Mühlberger, C., & Jonas, E. (2022). Growth- and security-orientation in coaching: Success through motivational fit. In S. Greif, H. Möller, W. Scholl, J. Passmore, & F. Müller (Eds.), *International handbook of evidence based coaching: Theory, research and practice* (pp. 407–418). Springer Nature.

Böning, U. (2022). Business coaching in top management. In S. Greif, H. Möller, W. Scholl, J. Passmore, & F. Müller (Eds.), *International handbook of evidence based coaching: Theory, research and practice* (pp. 123–136). Springer Nature.

Boniwell, I. (2015). *Strengths cards*. Positran.

Bono, J. E., Purvanova, R. K., Towler, A. J., & Peterson, D. B. (2009). A survey of executive coaching practices. *Personnel Psychology, 62*(2), 361–404.

Bordia, P., Hobman, E., Jones, E., Gallois, C., & Callan, V. J. (2004). Uncertainty during organizational change: Types, consequences, and management strategies. *Journal of Business and Psychology, 18*(4), 507–532.

Bordin, E. S. (1979). The generalizability of the psychoanalytic concept of the working alliance. *Psychotherapy: Theory, Research & Practice, 16*(3), 252–260.

Borrelli, B., Sepinwall, D., Bellg, A. J., Breger, R., DeFrancesco, C., Sharp, D. L., et al. (2005). A new tool to assess treatment fidelity and evaluation of treatment fidelity across 10 years of health behavior research. *Journal of Consulting and Clinical Psychology, 73*(5), 852–860.

Borsum, F. (2008). *Vergleich von Coaching und Psychotherapie – Vergleich und Abgrenzung von Wirkfaktoren und Inhalten*. Diploma thesis, Work and Psychology Unit, University of Osnabrück, Germany.

Bosch, C., & Michel, A. (2022). Mindfullness in coaching. In S. Greif, H. Möller, W. Scholl, J. Passmore, & F. Müller (Eds.), *International handbook of evidence based coaching: Theory, research and practice* (pp. 627–636). Springer Nature.

Boyatzis, R. E. (2008). Leadership development from a complexity perspective. *Consulting Psychology Journal, 60*, 298–313.

Boyatzis, R. E., & Akrivou, K. (2006). The ideal self as the driver of intentional change. *Journal of Management Development, 25*(7), 624–642.

Boyatzis, R. E., Hullinger, A., Ehasz, S. F., Harvey, J., Tassarotti, S., Gallotti, A., & Penafort, F. (2022). The grand challenge for research on the future of coaching. *The Journal of Applied Behavioral Science*, 002188632210799.

Boylston, A. (2014). William Watson's use of controlled clinical experiments in 1767. *Journal of the Royal Society of Medicine, 107*, 246–248.

Brandon, S. E. (2014). *Towards a science of interrogation* (Bd. 28, pp. 945–946). Wiley.

Breyer, B., & Bluemke, M. (2016). *Deutsche version der Positive and Negative Affect Schedule PANAS (GESIS Panel)*. Leibniz Institute for the Social Sciences. http://zis.gesis.org/kategorie/showScaleFromRobots/title/*?forwardedSkalaTitleURL=%2Fskala%2FopenScale%2F556%2FDeutsche+Version+der+Positive+and+Negative+Affect+Schedule+PANAS+%28GESIS+Panel%29 (last access 6.10.2017).

Brummans, B. H. J. M., Higham, L., & Cooren, F. (2022). The work of conflict mediation: Actors, vectors, and communicative relationality. *Human Relations, 75*(4), 764–791.

Brynjolfsson, E., & McAfee, A. (2014). *The second machine age*. Norton.

Bühler, K. (1934). *Sprachtheorie: Die Darstellungsfunktion der Sprache*. Fischer.

Burghardta, S., Koranyib, S., Magnuckic, G., Straussa, B., & Rosendahla, J. (2018). Non-pharmacological interventions for reducing mental distress in patients undergoing dental procedures: Systematic review and meta-analysis. *Journal of Dentistry, 69*, 22–31.

Burisch, M. (2010). *Das Burnout-Syndrom – Theorie der inneren Erschöpfung* (4. Aufl). Springer.

Burisch, M. (2015). *Burnout erkennen, verstehen, bekämpfen Informationen für Führungskräfte (Broschüre)*. CConsult, VBG Versicherung.

Burt, D., & Talati, Z. (2017). The unsolved value of executive coaching: A meta-analysis of outcomes using randomised control trial studies. *International Journal of Evidence Based Coaching and Mentoring, 15*(2), 17–24.

Busch, C., Dreyer, R., & Janneck, M. (2022). Blended health coaching for work-linked couples: Coaches'intervention Fidelity and Empathy Matter! *Coaching Theorie Praxis*. https://doi.org/10.1365/s40896-022-00065-9.

Busch, C., Romana, D., & Janneck, M. (2021). Blended recorvery and burnout coaching for small-business copreneurs. *Consulting Psychology Journal: Practice and Research, 73*(1), 65–87.

Carver, C. S., & Scheier, M. F. (1998). *On the self-regulation of behavior*. Cambridge University Press.

Cassidy, T., Jones, R. L., & Potrac, P. (2016). *Cassidy, Jones and Potrac, understanding sports coaching: The social, cultural and pedagogical foundations of coaching practice, Routledge, 2008* (3rd ed.). Routledge.

Cattell, R. B., & Eber, H. J. (1964). *The sixteen personality factor questionnaire*. Institute for Personality and Ability Testing.

Chalmers, A. F. (2013). *What is this thing called science?* (4th ed.). Hackett.

Cherns, A. (1989). Die Tavistock-Untzersuchungen und ihre Auswirkungen. In S. Greif, H. Holling, & N. Nicholson (Eds.), Arbeits- und Organisationspsychologie. *Internationales Handbuch in Schlüsselbegriffen*. Psychologie Verlags Union.

Chomsky, N. (2017). *On language: Chomsky's classic works: Language and responsibility and reflections on language (reprints)*. The New Press (Google Play).

Clutterbuck, D. (2007). *Coaching the team at work*. Nicholas Brealey International.

Clutterbuck, D. (2022). The future of AI in coaching. In S. Greif, H. Möller, W. Scholl, J. Passmore, & F. Müller (Eds.), *International handbook of evidence based coaching: Theory, research and practice* (pp. 369–380). Springer Nature.

Clutterbuck, D., Megginson, D., & Bajer, A. (2018). *Building and sustaining a coaching culture*. Kogan Page.

Coachilly Magazine. (2023). *Controversial AI in coaching: Empowerment or demise?* https://coachilly.com/controversial-ai-in-coaching-empowerment-or-demise/ (last retrieval 13.10.2023).

Cohen, J. (Ed.). (1988). *Statistical power analysis for the behavioral sciences*. Erlbaum.

Collins, A., Brown, J. S., & Newman, S. E. (1989). Cognitive apprenticeship: Teaching the crafts of reading, writing and mathematics. In L. B. Resnick (Ed.), *Knowing, learning, and instruction: Essays in honor of Robert Glaser* (pp. 453–495). Lawrence Erlbaum Associates.

Conoley, C. W., Conoley, J. C., McConnell, J. A., & Kimzey, C. E. (1983). The effect of the ABCs of Rational Emotive Therapy and the empty-chair technique of Gestalt Therapy on anger reduction. *Psychotherapy: Theory, Research & Practice, 20*(1), 112–117.

Cooke, R., & Sheeran, P. (2004). Moderation of cognition-intention and cognition-behaviour relations: A meta-analysis of properties of variables from the theory of planned behaviour. *British Journal of Social Psychology, 43*(2), 159–186.

Cousineau, D., & Chartier, S. (2010). Outliers detection and treatment: A review. *International Journal of Psychological Research, 3*, 58–67.

Cranach, M., & v. (1996). Toward a theory of the acting group. In E. H. Witte & J. H. Davis (Eds.), *Understanding group behavior. Volume 2: Small group processes and interpersonal relations* (pp. 147–187). Lawrence Erlbaum Associates.

DBVC. (2012). *Definition coaching*. Verfügbar unter: http://www.dbvc.de/der-verband/ueber-uns/definition-coaching.html (last access 23.8.2019).

De Dreu, C. K. W., & Gelfand, M. J. (2008). Conflict in the workplace: Sources, functions, and dynamics across multiple levels of analysis. In C. K. W. De Dreu & M. J. Gelfand (Eds.), *The psychology of conflict and conflict management* (pp. 3–54). Lawrence Erlbaum.

De Haan, E., Grant, A. M., Burger, Y., & Eriksson, P.-O. (2016). A large-scale study of executive and workplace coaching: The relative contributions of relationship, personality match, and self-efficacy. *Consulting Psychology Journal: Practice and Research, 68*(3), 189–207.

De Meuse, K. P., Dai, G., & Lee, R. J. (2009). Evaluating the effectiveness of executive coaching: Beyond ROI? *Coaching: An International Journal of Theory, Research and Practice, 2*(2), 117–134.

De Shazer, S., & Dolan, Y. (2007). *More than Miracles - The State of the Art of Solution-focused Brief Therapy*. Haworth.

Deci, E. L., & Ryan, R. M. (2000). The "what" and "why" of goal pursuits: Human needs and the self-determination of behavior. *Psychological Inquiry, 11*(4), 227–268.

Deci, E. L., & Ryan, R. M. (2008). Self-determination theory: A macrotheory of human motivation, development, and health. *Canadian Psychology/Psychologie Canadienne, 49*(3), 182–185.

Deplazes, S. (2015). *KaSyCo – KategorienSysteme zur Analyse von Coachingprozessen.* Dissertation Dr. phil., Kassel: University Press.

Derks, L. A. C. (2000). Butterflies in a box. *NLP World: The Intercultural Journal on the Theory and Practice of Neuro-Linguistic Programming, 7*(3), 1–15.

Deutscher-Ethikrat. (2023). *Mensch und Maschine – Herausforderungen durch Künstliche Intelligenz.* Deutscher Ethikrat.

Dias, G. P., Palmer, S., & Nardi, A. E. (2017). Integrating positive psychology and the solution-focused approach with cognitive-behavioral coaching: The integrative cognittive-behavourla coaching model. *European Journal of Applied Positive psychology, 1*(3), 1–8.

Dick, R. V., Wegge, J., & Stegmann, S. (2018). Analyse und intervention bei der Gruppen- und Teamarbeit. In S. Greif & K.-C. Hamborg (Eds.), *Enzyklopädie der Psychologie. Band Psychologische Interventionsmethoden – Methoden der Arbeits, Organisations- und – Wirtschaftspsychologie* (pp. 275–327). Hogrefe.

Diller, S., Brantl, M., & Jonas, E. (2022). More than working alliance. *Coaching | Theorie & Praxis, 8*, 1–17.

Donley, J. E. (1911). Psychotherapy and re-education. *The Journal of Abnormal Psychology, 6*(1), 1–10.

Doran, G. T. (1981). There's a S.M.A.R.T. way to write management's goals and objectives. *Management Review, 70*(11), 35–36.

Dormandy, K., & Grimley, B. (2024). Gatekeeping in science: Lessons from the case of psychology and neuro-linguistic programming. *Social Epistemology*. https://doi.org/10.1080/02691728.2024.2326828

Dörner, D. (1979). *Problemlösen als Informationsverarbeitung*. Kohlhammer.

Dörner, D. (2003). *Die Logik des Mißlingens. Strategisches Denken in komplexen Situationen* (10th ed.). Rowohlt.

Drake, D. (2010). Narrative coaching. In E. Cox, T. Bachkirova, & D. A. Clutterbuck (Eds.), *The complete handbook of coaching* (pp. 120–131). Sage.

Drake, D. (2017a). *Narrative coaching: The definitive guide to bringing new stories to life* (2nd ed.). CNC Press, Kindle Edition.

Drake, D. (2017b). Working with narratives in coaching. In T. Bachkirova, G. Spence, & D. Drake (Eds.), *The SAGE handbook of coaching* (pp. 291–309). Sage.

Drake, D., & Stelter, R. (2014). Narrative coaching. In J. Passmore (Ed.), *Mastery in coaching. A complete psychological toolkit for advanced coaching* (pp. 65-96). Kegan Page.

Dreyer, P. (2010). Interview mit Herrn Sakurai, CEO von "Coach 21", Japan, *Ekeberger Coachingtage 2010*. Ekeberg, Struxdorf, Schleswig Holstein, Germany.

Dreyer, P. (2013). Interkulturelles coaching: Japan – Coaching unter Kirschblüten. *Training aktuell, August*, 27–29.

Duhigg, C. (2012). *The power of habit: Why we do what we do in life and business*. Random House, Kindle.

Dweck, C. S., & Leggett, E. L. (1988). A social-cognitive approach to motivation and personality. *Psychological Review, 95*, 256–273.

Ebermann, D. (2018). Interview mit Dr. Wolfgang Loos – Die Rolle des Coachs ist in der Öffentlichkeit angekommen. *Coaching Magazin, 4*, 14–20.

Ebner, K., Greif, S., & Kauffeld, S. (2018). Humanressourcen und Personalentwicklung. In S. Greif & K.-C. Hamborg (Eds.), *Methoden der Arbeits-, Organisations- und Wirtschaftspsychologie. Enzyklopädie der Psychologie, B/III/3* (pp. 145–214). Hogrefe.

Ebner, K., & Kauffeld, S. (2019). Laufbahngestaltung durch Karrierecoaching: Abgrenzung, Methodeneinsatz und Forschungsstand. In S. Kauffeld & D. Spurk (Eds.), *Handbuch Karriere und Laufbahnmanagement* (pp. 759–784). Springer.

Ellis, A. (1993). *Grundlagen der Rational-Emotiven Verhaltenstherapie*. Pfeiffer.

EMCC. (2018). *EMCC global competence framework – glossary V2*. European Mentoring and Coachjing Centre. https://emccdrive.emccglobal.org/api/file/download/uKy7MLlofV6NoR4grJpySLZNGpbYoGntuZSeu9zf (retrieved 23.3.2022).

Engel, A. M., & Kuhl, J. (2022). Affective change for action control and self-growth in coaching. In S. Greif, H. Möller, W. Scholl, J. Passmore, & F. Müller (Eds.), *International handbook of evidenced based coaching: Theory, research and practice* (pp. 27–38). Springer.

Erickson, M. H., Rossi, E. L., & Rossi, S. I. (1976). *Hypnotic realities: The induction of clinical hypnosis and forms of indirect suggestion*. Willey (Kindle version).

Felfe, J., & Elprana, G. (2022). Leadership theories as knowledge base in coaching. In S. Greif, H. Möller, W. Scholl, J. Passmore, & F. Müller (Eds.), *International handbook of evidence-based coaching* (pp. 531–541). Springer Nature.

Festinger, L. (1978). *Theorie der kognitiven Dissonanz*. Huber.

Field, N. P., & Horowitz, M. J. (1998). Applying an empty-chair monologue paradigm to examine unresolved grief. *Psychiatry: Interpersonal and Biological Processes, 61*(4), 279–287.

Fielder, J. H., & Starr, L. M. (2008). What's the big deal about coaching contracts? *The International Journal of Coaching in Organizations*.

Fietze, B. (2017). Is coaching on its way to becoming a profession? A profession-centric sociological assessment. In A. Schreyögg & C. Schmidt-Lellek (Eds.), *The professionalization of coaching - a reader for the coach* (pp. 23–46). Springer.

Fingas, S., Busch, C., Dreyer, R., & Lehmann-Willenbrock, N. (under review). *Zooming in: Exploring fine-grained behavioral dynamics in copreneur workplace coaching*.

Finke, J. (2004). *Gesprächspsychotherapie. Grundlagen und spezifische Anwendungen*. Thieme.

Fisher-Yoshida, B., & Yoshida, R. (2022). Transformative learning and its relevance to coaching. In S. Greif, H. Möller, W. Scholl, J. Passmore, & F. Müller (Eds.), *International handbook of evidence-based coaching* (pp. 935–948). Springer Nature.

Fiske, S. T. (2009). *Social beings: Core motives in social psychology*. Wiley.

Fledderus, M., Oude Voshaar, M. A. H., ten Klooster, P. M., & Bohlmeijer, E. T. (2012). Further evaluation of the psychometric properties of the Acceptance and Action Questionnaire–II. *Psychological Assessment, 24*(4), 925–936. https://doi.org/10.1037/a0028200

Fleischhacker, M., & Graf, E.-M. (2023). New ways of investigating coaching: Linguistic research on executive, business and workplace coaching – A systematic scoping review. *Coaching: An International Journal of Theory, Research and Practice*, 1–29.

Flückiger, C., & Wüsten, G. (2014). *Ressourcenaktivierung: Ein Manual für Psychotherapie, Coaching und Beratung* (2nd ed.). Huber.

Fonagy, P., Gergely, G., Jurist, E. L., & Target, M. (2002). *Affect regulation, mentalzation and the development of the self*. Karnac books.

Franke, R. (2023). Coaching und KI. *Coaching-Magazin, 16*(4), 46–48.

Frankfurt, H. (2005). *On bullshit*. Princeton University Press.

Frankl, V. E. (1970). *The will to meaning: He foundations and applications of logotherapy*. Plume/Penguin.

French, W. L., & Bell, C. H. (1995). *Organization development*. Prentice Hall.

Freud, S. (1939). *Die Traumdeutung* (Erstausgabe 1899/1900). Leipzig: Deuticke.

Freudenberger, H. J. (1974). Staff burn-out. *Journal of Social Issues, 30*(1), 159–165.

Friedman, N. (1993). Fritz Perls's "layers" and the empty chair: A reconsideration. *Gestalt Journal, 16*(2), 95–119.

Frijda, N. H. (2008). "The Psychologists" point of view. In M. Lewis, J. M. Haviland-Jones, & L. F. Barrett (Eds.), *Handbook of emotions* (3rd ed., pp. 68–87). Guilford Press.

Fuhrmann, L. (2017). *Entwicklung eines Kategoriensystems zur Analyse von Interaktionsprozessen im Coaching*. M. Sc. Psychologie, Universität Hamburg.

Gabriel, G. (2004). Definition. In J. Mittelstraß (Eds.), *Enzyklopädie Philosophie und Wissenschaftstheorie* (2nd., Bd. 1, pp. 439–442). Metzler.

Gardner, B. (2015). A review and analysis of the use of "habit" in understanding, predicting and influencing health-related behaviour. *Health Psychology Review, 9*(3), 277–295.

Geissler, H. (Ed.). (2008). *E-Coaching*. Schneider.

Geissler, H. (2009). Die inhaltsanalytische "Vermessung" von Coachingprozessen. In B. Birgmeier (Ed.), *Coachingwissen – Denn sie wissen nicht, was sie tun?* (pp. 93–128). Verlag für Sozialwissenschaften.

Geissler, H. (2016). *Die Grammatik des Coachens: Eine empirische Rekonstruktion*. Springer.

Geissler, H. (2022). E-coaching: An overview. In S. Greif, H. Möller, W. Scholl, J. Passmore, & F. Müller (Eds.), *International handbook of evidence-based coaching: Theory, research and practice* (pp. 269–280). Springer Nature. https://doi.org/10.1007/978-3-030-81938-5_22

Geissler, H. (2025). *KI-Coaching - Wie man Künstliche Intelligenz im und für Coaching nut zen kann*. Springer. https://doi.org/10.1007/978-3-658-47141-5

Geissler, H., & Rödel, S. (2023). *Praxishandbuch professionelles online-coaching: Mit Online-Materialien. E-Book inside*. Beltz & Kindle.

Giddens, A. (1991). *Modernity and self-identity: Self and society in the late modern age*. Blackwell (Kindle Edition 2013).

Glasman, L. R., & Albarracín, D. (2006). Forming attitudes that predict future behavior: A meta-analysis of the attitude-behavior relation. *Psychological Bulletin, 132*(5), 778–822.

Goldberg, L. R. (1993). The structure of phenotypic personality traits. *American Psychologist, 48*(1), 26–34.

Gollwitzer, P. M., Kuhl, J., & Heckhausen, H. (1996). Das Rubikonmodell der Handlungsphasen. In J. Kuhl & H. Heckhausen (Eds.), *Enzyklopädie der Psychologie, Bd 4, Motivation, Volition und Handlung* (pp. 531–582). Hogrefe.

Gorell, R., & Jones, G. (2012). *50 Top tools for coaching: A complete toolkit for developing and empowering people* (2nd ed.). Kogan Page.

Graf, E.-M. (2015). Kommunikative Basisaktivitäten im Coaching-Gespräch: Ein linguistischer Beitrag zur Coaching-Prozessforschung. *Coaching | Theorie & Praxis, 1*(1), 5–14.

Graf, E.-M., Dionne, F., & Spranz-Fogasy, T. (2020). How to investigate the local and global change potential of questioning sequences in executive coaching? A call for interdisciplinary research. *Scandinavian Studies in Language, 11*(1), 214–238.

Graf, E.-M., & Spranz-Fogasy, T. (2018). Welche Frage, wann und warum? – Eine qualitativ-linguistische Programmatik zur Erforschung von Frage-Sequenzen als zentrale Veränderungspraktik im Coaching. *Coaching | Theorie & Praxis, 4*(1), 17–32.

Grant, A. M. (2003). What is evidence-based executive, workplace, and life coaching? *Keynote address presented at the first evidence-based coaching conference*. University of Sidney, Australia, July 2003.

Grant, A. M. (2006). Workplace and executive coaching: A bibliography from the scholarly business literature. In D. R. Stober & A. M. Grant (Eds.), *Evidence based coaching handbook* (pp. 367–388). Wiley.

Grant, A. M. (2011). Is it time to REGROW the GROW model? Issues related to teaching coaching session structures. *The Coaching Psychologist, 7*(2), 118–126.

Grant, A. (2022). Goals in coaching practice. In S. Greif, H. Möller, W. Scholl, J. Passmore, & F. Müller (Eds.), *International handbook of evidence based coaching* (pp. 391–406). Springer Nature.

Grant, A. M., Franklin, J., & Langford, P. (2002). The self-reflection and insight scale: A new measure of private self-consciousness. *Social Behavior & Personality: An International Journal, 30*(8), 821–836.

Grant, A., & O'Connor, S. (2022). Goals in coaching practice. In S. Greif, H. Möller, W. Scholl, J. Passmore, & F. Müller (Eds.), *International handbook of evidence based coaching* (pp. 391–406). Springer Nature.

Grassmann, C., Schölmerich, F., & Schermuly, C. C. (2019). The relationship between working alliance and client outcomes in coaching: A meta-analysis. *Human Relations, 73*(1), 35–48. https://doi.org/10.1177/0018726718819725

Graßmann, C., & Schermuly, C. C. (2021). Coaching with artificial intelligence: Concepts and capabilities. *Human Resource Development Review, 20*(1), 106–126. https://doi.org/10.1177/1534484320982891

Grawe, K. (2006). *Neuropsychotherapy: How the neurosciences inform effective psychotherapy*. Erlbaum.

Gray, J. A. (1987). *The psychology of stress and fear* (2nd ed.). University Press.

Green, S., & Palmer, S. (2019). *Positive psychology coaching in practice*. Routledge.

Greif, S. (1970). Untersuchung der deutschen Übersetzung des 16 PF Fragebogens. *Psychologische Beitrage, 12*(2), 186–213.

Greif, S. (1991). Streß in der Arbeit – Einführung und Grundbegriffe. In S. Greif, E. Bamberg, & N. Semmer (Eds.), *Psychischer Streß am Arbeitsplatz* (pp. 1–28). Hogrefe.

Greif, S. (1993). Mensch-computer Interaktion, psychologische Theorien und innovatives Problemlösen. In W. Bungard & T. Herrmann (Eds.), *Arbeits- und Organisationspsychologie im Spannungsfeld zwischen Grundlagenorientierung und Anwendung* (pp. 145–166). Huber.

Greif, S. (1994). Fehlertraining und Komplexität beim Softwaredesign. *Zeitschrift für Arbeitswissenschaft, 48*(1), 44–53.

Greif, S. (2002). Vorwort zum Handbuch coaching. In C. Rauen (Ed.), *Handbuch coaching* (2nd ed., pp. 11–16).

Greif, S. (2007). Geschichte der Organisationspsychologie. In H. Schuler (Ed.), *Lehrbuch Organisationspsychologie* (4th ed., pp. 21–58). Huber.

Greif, S. (2008). *Coaching und ergebnisorientierte Selbstreflexion*. Hogrefe.

Greif, S. (2011). Qualitative oder quantitative Methoden in der Coachingforschung – Methodenstreit zwischen unversöhnlichen Wissenschaftsauffassungen? In Y. Aksu, E.-M. Graf, I. Pick, & S. Rettinger (Eds.), *Coaching, Beratung und Supervision – Multidisziplinäre Perspektiven vernetzt* (pp. 37–52). VS Verlag für Sozialwissenschaften.

Greif, S. (2013a). Conducting organizational based evaluations of coaching and mentoring programs. In J. Passmore, D. B. Peterson, & T. Freire (Eds.), *The Wiley-Blackwell handbook of the psychology of coaching and mentoring* (pp. 445–470). Wiley Blackwell.

Greif, S. (2013b). Putting goals to work in coaching: The complexities of implementation. In S. David, D. Clutterbuck, & D. Megginson (Eds.), *Beyond goals: Effective strategies for coaching and mentoring* (pp. 125–149). Gower.

Greif, S. (2014a). Coaching bei Stress und Burnout: Nicht ohne Diagnostik. In H. Möller & S. Kotte (Eds.), *Diagnostik im Coaching. Grundlagen, Analyseebenen, Praxisbeispiele* (pp. 217–232). Springer.

Greif, S. (2014b). Coaching und Wissenschaft – Geschichte einer schwierigen Beziehung. *Organisationsberatung, Supervision, Coaching, 21*(3), 295–311.

Greif, S. (2015). Evaluation von Coaching als schwer bewertbare Dienstleistung. In A. Schreyögg & C. Schmidt-Lellek (Eds.), *Die Professionalisierung von Coaching* (pp. 47–70). Springer.

Greif, S. (2017a). Researching outcomes of coaching. In T. Bachkirova, G. Spence, & D. Drake (Eds.), *The SAGE handbook of coaching* (pp. 569–588). Sage.

Greif, S. (2017b). Digitale transformation und Industrie 4.0. In S. Greif (Ed.), *Managementkonzepte und coaching beim change management* (2nd ed., pp. 59–73). Europäische Fernhochschule Hamburg GmbH.

Greif, S. (2017c). Hard to evaluate: Coaching services. In A. Schreyögg & C. Schmidt-Lellek (Eds.), *The Professionalization of coaching – A reader for the coach* (pp. 47–68). Springer.

Greif, S. (2018). Woran erkennt man pseudowissenschaftliche Theorien und weshalb sie im Coaching problematisch sind – am Beispiel NLP. *Organisationsberatung, Supervision, Coaching (OSC), 25*(3), 371–387.

Greif, S. (2019a). *Leittext Konsequente Umsetzung*. https://www.researchgate.net/publication/336923145_Leittext_Konsequente_Umsetzung (last access 12.2.2020)

Greif, S. (2019b). *Zielfragebögen zu Beginn des Coachings*. Osnabrück, retrieved from https://www.researchgate.net/publication/334131539_Zielfragebogen_zu_Beginn_des_Coachings (last access 3.7.2019).

Greif, S. (2020). How to bridge the intention-action-gap. In J. Passmore (Eds.), *Global coaching conference*. London, May 21st 2020 (Online).

Greif, S. (2021). *Was it coaching? Wissenschaftliche Grundlagen und praktische Methoden*. Kindle: Online und Print on Demand, Hardcover: tredition (Hamburg).
Greif, S. (2022a). Motivation, will and implementation. In S. Greif, H. Möller, W. Scholl, J. Passmore, & F. Müller (Eds.), *International handbook of evidence based coaching: Theory, research and practice* (pp. 649–664). Springer Nature.
Greif, S. (2022b). Pseudoscience and charlatanry in coaching. In S. Greif, H. Möller, W. Scholl, J. Passmore, & F. Müller (Eds.), *International handbook of evidence-based coaching* (pp. 755–772). Springer Nature.
Greif, S. (2023). *Coaching evaluation questionnaires – Before and after the coaching*. https://www.researchgate.net/publication/376071828_Coaching_Evaluation_Questionnaires-Before_and_after_the_Coaching
Greif, S. (2025, in prep.). *Coaching tools – Based on science and practice*.
Greif, S., & Benning-Rohnke, E. (2015). Konsequente Umsetzung von Zielen durch coaching. *Coaching | Theorie & Praxis, 1*(1), 25–35.
Greif, S., & Berg, C. (2011). *Result-oriented self-reflection – Report on the construct validation of theory-based scales*. University of Osnabrück, unpubl. paper, retrieved from https://www.researchgate.net/publication/264973092_Result-oriented_self-reflection_-_Report_on_the_construct_validation_of_theory-based_scales (last access 4.7.2019).
Greif, S., & Bertino, M. (2022). Burnout: Characteristics and prevention in coaching. In S. Greif, H. Möller, W. Scholl, J. Passmore, & F. Müller (Eds.), *International handbook of evidenced based coaching: Theory, research and practice*. Cham.
Greif, S., Finger, A., & Jerusel, S. (Eds.). (1993). *Praxis des Selbstorganisierten Lernens. – Einführung und Leittexte. Reihe Soziale Kompetenz*. IG Chemie-Papier-Keramik & Bund-Verlag.
Greif, S., & Jonas, E. (2021). Evaluation von Coaching-Prozessen und -ergebnissen. In C. Rauen (Ed.), *Handbuch coaching* (4th ed., pp. 347–372). Hogrefe.
Greif, S., & Kluge, A. (2004). Lernen in Organisationen. In H. Schuler (Ed.), *Enzyklopädie der Psychologie. Organisationspsychologie 1 – Grundlagen und Personalpsychologie* (pp. 751–825). Hogrefe.
Greif, S., & Kurtz, H.-J. (1998). *Handbuch Selbstorganisiertes Lernen* (2nd ed.). Verlag für Angewandte Psychologie.
Greif, S., & Palmer, S. (2022). Stress and stress management in coaching. In S. Greif, H. Möller, W. Scholl, J. Passmore, & F. Müller (Eds.), *International handbook of evidence based coaching: Theory, research and practice* (pp. 863–874). Springer.
Greif, S., & Rauen, C. (2022). Self-reflection in coaching. In S. Greif, H. Möller, W. Scholl, J. Passmore, & F. Müller (Eds.), *International handbook of evidenced based coaching: Theory, research and practice* (pp. 839–850). Springer Nature.
Greif, S., & Riemenschneider-Greif, F. (2018). Wie im Coaching neue Einsichten entstehen – Anregungen für eine theoriegeleitete Erforschung innerpsychischer Prozesse. In R. Wegener, M. Loebbert, A. Fritze, & M. Hänseler (Eds.), *Coaching-Prozessforschung* (pp. 116–140). Vandenhoeck & Ruprecht.
Greif, S., Runde, B., & Seeberg, I. (2004). *Erfolge und Misserfolge beim change management*. Hogrefe.
Greif, S., & Scheidewig, V. (1998). Selbstorganisiertes Lernen von Schichtleitern. In S. Greif & H.-J. Kurtz (Eds.), *Handbuch Selbstorganisiertes Lernen* (2nd ed., pp. 347–362). Verlag für Angewandte Psychologie.
Greif, S., & Schubert, H. (2015). Ergebnisorientiertes Reflektieren im Coaching. In A. Ryba, D. Pauw, D. Ginati, & S. Rietmann (Eds.), *Professionell coachen – Das Methodenbuch: Erfahrungswissen und Interventionstechniken von 50 Coachingexperten* (pp. 54–80). Beltz.
Greif, S., Schmidt, F., & Thamm, A. (2010). *Rating of coaching success-factors. Observation manual*. Osnabrueck: Work and Organizational Psychology Unit, University of Osnabrück, Germany (unpubl. paper).

Greif, S., Schmidt, F., & Thamm, A. (2012). Warum und wodurch Coaching wirkt – Ein Überblick zum Stand der Theorieentwicklung und Forschung über Wirkfaktoren. *Organisationsberatung Supervision Coaching, 19*(4), 75–390.

Greif, S., Möller, H., Scholl, W., Passmore, J., & Müller, F. (Eds.). (2022a). Coaching definitions and concepts. In S. Greif, H. Möller, W. Scholl, J. Passmore, & F. Müller (Eds.), *International handbook of evidenced based coaching: Theory, research and practice* (pp. 1–12). Springer Nature.

Greif, S., Möller, H., Scholl, W., Passmore, J., & Müller, F. (Eds.). (2022b). *International handbook of evidence based coaching: Theory, research and practice*. Springer Nature.

Griffith, C. R. (1926). *Psychology of coaching: A study of coaching methods from the point of psychology* (reprinted in 2019 by Lang). New York: Scribner.

Grimley, B. (2008). NLP coaching. In S. Palmer & A. Whybrow (Eds.), *Handbook of coaching psychology: A guide for practitioners* (pp. 193–210). Routledge/Taylor & Francis Group. http://search.ebscohost.com/login.aspx?direct=true&db=psyh&AN=2007-18824-011&site=ehost-live

Grimley, B. (2013). *Theory and practice of NLP coaching. A psychological approach*. Sage.

Grimley, B. (2016). What is NLP? The development of a grounded theory of neuro-linguistic programming, (NLP), within an action research journey. Implications for the use of NLP in coaching psychology. *International Coaching Psychology Review, 11(2)*, 166–178. http://search.ebscohost.com/login.aspx?direct=true&db=pbh&AN=118250925&site=ehost-live

Gros, S. (2010). *Provokation in der Beratung Haltung, Anwendung und Wirkungsweise Eine empirische Erhebung bei Anwendern Ing*. In M. C. A. B. W. H. A. Wien (Ed.).

Gross, J. J. (2008). Emotion regulation. In M. Lewis, J. M. Haviland-Jones, & L. F. Barrett (Eds.), *Handbook of emotions* (3rd ed., pp. 497–512). Guilford Press.

Gross, P.-P., & Stephan, M. (2015). Der Coaching-Markt. *Coaching | Theorie & Praxis, 1*(1), 15–24.

Guastella, A. J., & MacLeod, C. (2008). A critical review of the effects of oxytocin on human behavior. *Psychological Bulletin, 134*(6), 1123–1144.

Güntner, A. V., Kauffeld, S., & Passmore, J. (2022). Motivational interviewing as a tool for coaching in the workplace. In S. Greif, H. Möller, W. Scholl, J. Passmore, & F. Müller (Eds.), *International handbook of evidence-based coaching* (pp. 665–680). Springer Nature.

Gureje, O. (2018). ICD-11 chapter on mental and behavioral disorders: Heralding new ways of seeing old problems. *Epidemiology and Psychiatric Sciences, 27*(3), 209–211.

Hacker, W. (1973). *Allgemeine Arbeits- und Ingenieurpsychologie. Psychische Struktur und Regulation von Arbeitstätigkeiten*. VEB Deutscher Verlag der Wissenschaften.

Hacker, W. (2014). *Allgemeine Arbeitspsychologie Psychische Regulation von Wissens, Denk- und körperlicher Arbeit* (3rd ed.). Hogrefe.

Häcker, H. O., & Stapf, K.-H. (2009). Psychologische Beratung. In H. O. Häcker & K.-H. Stapf (Eds.), *Dorsch Psychologisches Wörterbuch* (15th ed., p. 127). Huber.

Haken, H., Wunderlin, A., & Yigitbasi, S. (1995). An introduction to synergetics. *Open Systems & Information Dynamics, 3*(1), 97–130.

Halevy, N., Chou, E. Y., & Murnighan, J. K. (2012). Mind games: The mental representation of conflict. *Journal of Personality and Social Psychology, 102*(1), 132–148.

Hamm, A. (2009). Entspannungsverfahren. In M. Hautzinger & P. Pauli (Eds.), *Psychologische Methoden* (Bd. 2, Psychologische Interventionsmethoden, Enzyklopädie der Psychologie, pp. 223–270). Hogrefe.

Handler, G. (2007). *Konzept zur Entwicklung integrierter Beratung – Integration systemischer Elemente in die klassische Beratung*. Deutscher Universitäts-Verlag.

Hanke, K., & Boehnke, K. (2018). Werte und ihre Bedeutung im coaching. In S. Greif, H. Möller, & W. Scholl (Eds.), *Handbuch Schlüsselkonzepte im coaching*. Springer.

Hansson, S. O. (2013). Defining pseudoscience. In M. Pigliucci & M. Boudry (Eds.), *Philosphy of pseudoscience* (pp. 61–78). The University of Chicago Press.

Harbert, S. (2006). Rolle und Aufgaben von Coaching im Veränderungsmanagement bei McKinsey. *Organisationsberatung – Supervision – Coaching, 3*, 211–217.

Hartley, J. (2000). Leading and managing the uncertainty of strategic change. Publication date. *Managing Strategic Implementation, 4*(7), 109–122.

Härtl-Kasulke, C., & Kasulke, O. (2018). *75 Bildkarten positive psychologie: Stärken stärken*. Beltz.

Hatcher, R. L., & Gillaspy, J. A. (2006). Development and validation of a revised short version of the working alliance inventory. *Psychotherapy Research, 16*(1), 12–25.

Hautzinger, M. (2006). *Rategeber Depression – Informationen für Betroffene und Angehörige*. Hogrefe.

Hautzinger, M. (2022). Behavioral modification and its relevance in coaching. In S. Greif, H. Möller, W. Scholl, J. Passmore, & F. Müller (Eds.), *International handbook of evidence-based coaching* (pp. 65–76). Springer.

Hayes, S. C. (2005). *Get out of your mind and into your life (the new acceptance and commitment therapy)*. New Harbinger Publications. Kindle-Version.

Hayes, S. C. (2023). Vision of excellence Award & how do we know what our clients need from us? In *Institute of coaching annual conference – Coaching in leadership & healthcare conference*.

Hayes, S. C., Barnes-Holmes, D., & Roche, B. (2001). *Relational frame theory: A post-Skinnerian account of human language and cognition*. Plenum Press.

Hayes, S. C., Strosahl, K. D., & Wilson, K. G. (2011). *Acceptance and commitment therapy* (2nd ed.). Guilford Publications, Kindle-Version.

Heckhausen, H. (1977). Achievement motivation and its constructs: A cognitive model. *Motivation and Emotion, 1*, 283–329.

Heinrichs, M., von Dawans, B., & Schächinger, H. (2009). The social dimension of stress reactivity: The role of oxytocin. *Psychoneuroendocrinology, 34*(1), 1–10.

Herrmann, T. (1979). *Psychologie als Problem*. Klett.

Hobsbawm, E., & Ranger, T. (1992). *The invention of traditiion*. Cambridge University Press.

Holton, E. F., III, Bates, R. A., & Ruona, W. E. A. (2000). Development of a generalized learning transfer system inventory. *Human Resource Development Quarterly, 11*(4), 333–360.

Horvath, A. O., & Greenberg, L. S. (1989). Development and validation of the working alliance inventory. *Journal of Counseling Psychology, 36*(2), 223–233.

Hu, L., & Bentler, P. M. (1999). Cutoff criteria for fit indices in covariance structure analysis: Conventional criteria versus new alternatives. *Structural Equation Modeling, 6*(1), 1–55.

Hülsheger, U. R., Alberts, H. J. E. M., Feinholdt, A., & Lang, J. W. B. (2013). Benefits of mindfulness at work: The role of mindfulness in emotion regulation, emotional exhaustion, and job satisfaction. *Journal of Applied Psychology, 98*(2), 310–325.

Hüther, G. (2004). *Die Macht der inneren Bilder*. Vandenhoeck & Ruprecht.

Hüther, G., Heinrich, M., & Senf, M. (2020). *Education for future: Bildung für ein gelingendes Leben*. Goldmann, Munic, Kindle-Edition.

Iaffaldano, M. T., & Muchinsky, P. M. (1985). Job satisfaction and job performance: A meta-analysis. *Psychological Bulletin, 97*(2), 251–273.

Ianiro, P. M., Schermuly, C. C., & Kauffeld, S. (2013). Why interpersonal dominance and affiliation matter: An interaction analysis of the coach-client relationship. *Coaching: An International Journal of Theory, Research & Practice, 6*(1), 25–46.

ICD-10. (2012). *GM-Version – Kapitel V – Psychische und Verhaltensstörungen (F00–F99)*. http://www.dimdi.de/static/de/klassi/icd-10-gm/kodesuche/onlinefassungen/htmlgm2012/block-f30-f39.htm (last access 8.5.2013).

ICF. (2020). *2020 ICF Global coaching study – Final report*: International Coaching Federation Retrieved 31.1.2022 – https://coachingfederation.org/research/global-coaching-study

ICF. (2021). *ICF professional coaching core competencies: International Coach Federation*, https://coachingfederation.org/core-competencies (retrieved Oct. 26th 2021).

ICF. (2023a). *2023 ICF coaching snapshot: Future of coaching*. International Coach Federation (ICF).

ICF. (2023b). *Global coaching study 2023 Final Report*. International Coaching Federation (ICF).

Jack, A. I., Rochford, K. C., Friedman, J. P., Passarelli, A. M., & Boyatzis, R. E. (2019). Pitfalls in organizational neuroscience: A critical review and suggestions for future research. *Organizational Research Methods, 22*(1), 421–458. https://doi.org/10.1177/1094428117708857
Jacobs, M., & Simon, J. (2022). Reexamining computer ethics in light of AI systems and AI regulation. *AI and Ethics*.
Jacobson, E. (1925). Progressive relaxation. *The American Journal of Psychology, 36*, 73–87.
James, W. (1892). *Principles of psychology*. Henry Holt.
Jarvis, J., Lane, D., & Filler-Travis, A. (2006). *The case for coaching*. cipd Books.
Jones, R. J. (2022). Team coaching research: The state of play. In S. Greif, H. Möller, W. Scholl, J. Passmore, & F. Müller (Eds.), *International handbook of evidence based coaching* (pp. 915–924). Springer Nature.
Jones, R. J., Woods, S. A., & Guillaume, Y. (2014). A meta-analysis of the effectiveness of executive coaching at improving work-based performance and moderators of coaching effectiveness, *Paper presented at the British Psychological Society Division of Occupational Psychology Annual Conference, 06/01/14–08/01/14, https://eprints.worc.ac.uk/2967/(retrieved 14.10.2014)*. Brighton.
Kaiser, F. (2018). *Wofür braucht man Coaches, wenn man Freunde hat?* Bachelor Wirtschaftspsychologie, Ruhr-Universität Bochum, Bochum.
Kanatouri, S. (2020). *The digital coach*. Routledge (Kindle).
Kanfer, F. H., & Philipps, J. S. (1970). *Learning foundation of behavior therapy*. Wiley.
Kanning, U. P. (2014). Mythos NLP. *Skeptiker, 27*(3), 118–127.
Kanning, U. P. (2019). Jenseits der Vernunft – Fragwürdige Ansätze im Coaching. *Organisationsberatung, Supervision, Coaching*.
Karasek, R., & Theorell, T. (1990). *Healthy work: Stress, productivity, and the reconstruction of working life*. Basic Books.
Katz, D., & Kahn, R. L. (1966). *Social psychology of organizations*. Wiley.
Kaufel, S., Scherer, S., Scherm, M., & Sauer, M. (2006). Führungbegleitung in der Bundeswehr – Coaching für militärische Führungskräfte. In W. Backhausen & J.-P. Thommsen (Eds.), *Coaching. Durch systemisches Denken zur innovativen Personalentwicklung* (pp. 419–438). Gabler.
Kauffeld, S. (2001). *Teamdiagnose*. Verl. für Angewandte Psychologie.
Kauffeld, S., Güntner, A. V., & Ebner, K. (2022). Career coaching. In S. Greif, H. Möller, W. Scholl, J. Passmore, & F. Müller (Eds.), *International handbook of evidence based coaching: Theory, research and practice* (pp. 137–150). Springer Nature.
Kauffman, C., Bonniwell, I., & Silberman, J. (2010). The positive psychology approach to coaching. In E. Cox, T. Bachkirova, & D. A. Clutterbuck (Eds.), *The complete handbook of coaching* (pp. 158–171). Sage.
Keith, N., & Frese, M. (2008). Effectiveness of error management training: A meta-analysis. *Journal of Applied Psychology, 93*(1), 59–69.
Kellett, J. B., Humphrey, R. H., & Sleeth, R. G. (2006). Empathy and the emergence of task and relations leaders. *The Leadership Quarterly, 17*(2), 146–162.
Kellogg, S., Roediger, E., & Jacob, G. (2011). Veränderungen durch Stühlearbeit (transformational chairwork): Eine Einführung in psychotherapeutische Dialoge. In *Fortschritte der Schematherapie. Konzepte und Anwendungen* (pp. 74–85). Hogrefe.
Kerschreiter, R., Heinitz, K., May, D., & Wesche, J. S. (2018). Führungsdiagnostik, Führungsinstrumente und Führungskräfteentwicklung. In S. Greif & K.-C. Hamborg (Eds.), *Enzyklopädie der Psychologie. – Band Psychologische Interventionsmethoden – Methoden der Arbeits-, Organisations- und – Wirtschaftspsychologie* (pp. 215–273). Hogrefe.
Kersting, M., & Klehe, U.-C. (2018). Personalauswahl und -beurteilung: Eine integrative Perspektive. In S. Greif & K.-C. Hamborg (Eds.), *Methoden der Arbeits-, Organisations- und Wirtschaftspsychologie, Enzyklopädie der Psychologie, B/III/3* (pp. 81–144). Hogrefe.
Kilburg, R. R. (1996). Toward a conceptual understanding and definition of executive coaching. *Consulting Psychology Journal: Practice and Research, 48*(2), 134–144.

Kinder, N., Mühlberger, C., Schiemann, S. J., Stollberg, J., Jonas, E., & Greif, S. (2020). Was macht erfolgreiches Coaching wirksam? 1.217 Klienten beantworten Fragen der Wissenschaft. *Coaching-Magazin, 2020*(1), 42–49.

Kline, R. B. (2023). *Principles and practice of structural equation modeling (methodology in the social sciences) (English edition) [Print Replica] Kindle Edition* (5th ed.). Guilford Press e-book.

Klonek, F. E., Güntner, A. V., Lehmann-Willenbrock, N., & Kauffeld, S. (2015). Using motivational interviewing to reduce threats in conversations about environmental behavior. *Frontiers in Psychology, 6*(1015).

Klonek, F. E. & Kauffeld, S. (2012). "Muss, kann ... oder will ich was verändern?" Welche Chancen bietet die Motivierende Gesprächsführung in Organisationen. *Wirtschaftspsychologie, 4–2012*, 58–71.

Kluge, A., & Hagemann, V. (2016). Wirtschaftspsychologie neue und soziale Medien in der Fertigung und der Personalentwicklung. *Wirtschaftspsychologie, 2016*(1), 3–19.

Kluge, A., & Hagemann, V. (2022). Learning as the basis for coaching. In S. Greif, H. Möller, W. Scholl, J. Passmore, & F. Müller (Eds.), *International handbook of evidence-based coaching* (pp. 543–552). Springer Nature.

Koch, A. (2020). *Online-training unter Preisdruck.*

Köhler, W. (1921). *Intelligenzprüfungen am Menschenaffen* (2. Aufl.). Berlin: Springer.

Kosfeld, M., Heinrichs, M., Zak, P. J., Fischbacher, U., & Fehr, E. (2005). Oxytocin increases trust in humans. *Nature, 435*(7042), 673–676.

Kotte, S., & Bozer, G. (2022). Workplace coaching research – Charted and uncharted territories. In S. Greif, H. Möller, W. Scholl, J. Passmore, & F. Müller (Eds.), *International handbook of evidence-based coaching – Theory, research and practice* (pp. 971–981). Springer Nature.

Kotte, S., & Zimmerman, J. (2022). Coaching supervision. In S. Greif, H. Möller, W. Scholl, J. Passmore, & F. Müller (Eds.), *International handbook of evidence-based coaching – Theory, research and practice* (pp. 187–197). Springer Nature.

Kotter, J. P. (2007). Leading change why transformation efforts fail. *Harvard Business Review, January*, 2–9.

Kozlowski, S. W. J., & Ilgen, D. R. (2006). Enhancing the effectiveness of work groups and teams. *Psychological Science in the Public Interest, 7*(3), 77–124.

Kriegesmann, B., Kley, T., & Kublik, S. (2009). *Innovationstreiber Mitbestimmung? (InnoMit) Bestandsaufnahme, Konzepte & Handlungsperspektiven - Projekt im Auftrag der Hans-Böckler-Stiftung im Forschungsschwerpunkt "Strukturwandel – Innovation und Beschäftigung" – Zwischenbericht für den Projektbeirat am 2. Juli 2009.* Bochum.

Kriz, J. (2014). *Grundkonzepte der Psychotherapie* (7th ed.). Beltz PVU, Kindle Edition.

Kriz, J. (2016). *Systemtheorie für Coaches – Einführung und kritische Diskussion.* Springer.

Kriz, J. (2018). Nicht alles ist "systemisch". *Organisationsberatung, Supervision, Coaching, 25*(4), 515–524.

Kriz, J. (2022). Systems theories as basis for coaching. In S. Greif, H. Möller, W. Scholl, J. Passmore, & F. Müller (Eds.), *International handbook of evidence based coaching: Theory, research and practice* (pp. 889–900). Springer Nature.

Kross, E., & Ayduk, O. (2017). Self-distancing: Theory, research, and current directions. *Advances in Experimental Social Psychology, 55*, 81–136.

Kuhl, J. (2001). *Motivation und Persönlichkeit. Interaktionen psychischer Systeme.* Hogrefe.

Kuhl, J. (2005). *Eine neue Persönlichkeitstheorie (PSI-Theorie Light).* Unpublished report.

Kuhl, J., & Beckman, J. (1994). *Volition and personality.* Hogrefe & Huber Publishers.

Kuhl, J., & Fuhrmann, A. (1998). Decomposing self-regulation and self-control: The volitional components inventory. In J. Heckhausen & C. S. Dweck (Eds.), *Motivation and self-regulation across the life span* (pp. 15–49). Cambridge University Press.

Kuhl, J., & Kazén, M. (2003). Handlungs- und Lageorientierung: Wie lernt man, seine Gefühle zu steuern? In J. Stiensmeier-Pelster & F. Rheinberg (Eds.), *Diagnostik von Motivation und Selbstkonzept* (pp. 201–219). Hogrefe.

Kuhl, J., Baumann, N., Perrig, W. J., & Grob, A. (2000). Self-regulation and rumination: Negative affect and impaired self-accessibility. In *Control of human behavior, mental processes, and consciousness. Essays in honor of the 60th birthday of August Flammer* (pp. 283–305). Erlbaum. http://search.ebscohost.com/login.aspx?direct=true&db=pdx&AN=0140193&site=ehost-live

Kuhl, J., Kazén, M., & Koole, S. L. (2006). Putting self-regulation theory into practice: A user's manual. *Applied Psychology, 55*(3), 408–418. https://doi.org/10.1111/j.1464-0597.2006.00260

Lakatos, I. (1981). Science and pseudoscience. In S. Brown (Ed.), *Conceptions of inquiry: A reader* (pp. 114–121). Methuen.

Lally, P., Jaarsveld, C. H. M., Potts, H. W. W., & Wardle, J. (2010). How are habits formed: Modelling habit formation in the real world. *European Journal of Social Psychology, 40*(6), 998–1009.

Landmann, M., Perels, F., Otto, B., & Schmitz, B. (2009). Selbstregulation. In E. Wild & J. Möller (Eds.), *Pädagogische psychologie* (pp. 49–70). Springer.

Lane, D. A., Stelter, R., & Stout-Rostron, S. (2010). The future of coaching as a profession. In E. Cox, T. Bachkirova, & D. A. Clutterbuck (Eds.), *The complete handbook of coaching* (pp. 377–390). Sage.

Lawrence, P. (2017). Managerial coaching—A literature review. *International Journal of Evidence Based Coaching and Mentoring, 15*(2), 43–65.

Lazarus, R. S. (1966). *Psychological stress and the coping process*. McGraw Hill.

Lefrançois, G. R. (2014). *Psychologie des Lernens* (4. Aufl.). Springer.

Lewin, K., Lippitt, R., & White, R. K. (1939). Patterns of aggressive behavior in experimental created "social climates". *Journal of Social Psychology, 10*, 271–299.

Likert, R. (1961). *The new patterns of management*. McGraw Hill.

Lindeman, M. M. (2005). Measuring values with the short Schwartz's value survey. *Journal of Personality Assessment, 85*(2), 170–178.

Linder-Pelz, S. (2010). *NLP coaching – An evidence based approach*. Kogan Page.

Linley, A., & Dovey, H. (2012). *Technical manual and statistical properties for Realise2*. Coventry: Centre of Applied Positive Psychology, http://www.capp.co/Portals/3/Files/Realise2_Technical_Manual_V1.3_Dec_2012.pdf (last access 1.10.2019).

Linley, P. A., Woolston, L., & Biswas-Diener, R. (2009). Strengths coaching with leaders. *International Coaching Psychology Review, 4*(1), 37–48.

Locke, E. A., & Latham, G. P. (2002). Building a practically useful theory of goal setting and task motivation. *American Psychologist, 57*(9), 705–717.

Loebbert, M. (2016). *Wie Supervision gelingt – Supervision als Coaching für helfende Berufe*. Springer.

Lomas, T., & Ivtzan, I. (2016). Second wave positive psychology: Exploring the positive–negative dialectics of wellbeing. *Journal of Happiness Studies: An Interdisciplinary Forum on Subjective Well-Being, 17*(4), 1753–1768.

Looss, W. (1991). *Coaching für Manager. Problembewältigung unter 4 Augen* (3rd. ed. 1993). Landsberg/Lech: moderene industrie.

Lovibond, S. H., & Lovibond, P. F. (1995). *Manual for the depression anxiety stress scales*. Psychology Foundation of Australia.

Luhmann, N. (1995). *Social systems, Stanford*. Stanford University Press.

Lundahl, B., & Burke, B. L. (2009). The effectiveness and applicability of motivational interviewing: A practice-friendly review of four meta-analyses. *Journal of Clinical Psychology, 65*(11), 1232–1245.

Lyobomirsky, S., King, L., & Diener, E. (2005). The benefits of frequent positive affect: Does happiness lead to success? *Psychological Bulletin, 131*(6), 803–855.

Macho, S. (2016). *Wissenschaft und Pseudowissenschaft in der Psychologie [Science and pseudoscience in the psychology]*. Hogrefe. http://search.ebscohost.com/login.aspx?direct=true&db=pdx&AN=0322643&site=ehost-live

MacKie, D. (2014). The effectiveness of strength-based executive coaching in enhancing full range leadership development: A controlled study. *Consulting Psychology Journal: Practice and Research, 66*(2), 118–137.

Maier, M. (2020). *Bewertungskriterien der Medienwahl im Coaching – Entwicklung und Einsatz eines Instrumentes zur Analyse von Akzeptanzfaktoren für die Umsetzbarkeit zentraler Coach-Aktivitäten in ausgewählten Coachingmedien des Online- und Präsenz-Coachings aus der Sicht von Coaches.* Helmut-Schmidt-Universität/Universität der Bundeswehr Hamburg, Hamburg, Germany.

Maier, N. R., & Fredrick. (1931). Reasoning in humans. II. The solution of a problem and its appearance in consciousness. *Journal of Comparative Psychology, 12*, 181–194.

Maslach, C. (1982). *Burnout, the cost of caring*. Prentice-Hall.

Maslach, C. (2017). Finding solutions to the problem of burnout. *Consulting Psychology Journal: Practice and Research, 69*(2), 143–152.

Maslach, C., & Jackson, S. E. (1981). The measurement of experienced burnout. *Journal of ccupational Behavior, 2*(2), 99–113. https://doi.org/10.1002/job.4030020205

Maurer, I. (2009). *Führungskräftecoaching*. Tectum.

Mayer, R. C., Davis, J. H., & Schoorman, F. D. (1995). An integrative model of organizational trust. *Academy of Management Review, 20*(3), 709–734.

McCay, S., & Kemp, T. (2019). Neuroscience and coaching. In S. Green & S. Palmer (Eds.), *Positive psychology coaching practice* (pp. 57–70). Routledge.

McClure, P. K. (2018). You're fired, says the robot: The rise of automation in the workplace, technophobes, and fears of unemployment. *Social Science Computer Review, 36*(2), 139–156. https://doi.org/10.1177/0894439317698637

McCracken, L., & Morley, S. (2014). The psychological flexibility model: A basis for integration and progress in psychological approaches to chronic pain management. *Journal of Pain, 15*, 221–234. https://doi.org/10.1016/j.jpain.2013.10.014

McGregor, D. (1960). *The human side of enterprise*. McGraw Hill.

Megginson, D., & Clutterbuck, D. A. (Eds.). (2005). *Techniques for coaching and mentoring*. Butterworth-Heinemann.

Megginson, D., & Clutterbuck, D. A. (2008). *Coaching und mentoring – Individuelle Beratung für individuelle Berufskarrieren*. Spektrum.

Megginson, D., & Clutterbuck, D. A. (Eds.). (2009). *Further techniques for coaching and mentoring*. Elsevier.

Menne, A. (1973). Definition. In H. Krings, H. M. Baumgartner, & C. Wild (Eds.), *Handbuch philosophischer Grundbegriffe, Band 1–6* (pp. 268–274). Kösel.

Merrill, K. A., Steinmetz, J. E., Viken, R. J., & Rose, R. J. (1999). Genetic influences on human conditionability: A Twin study of the conditioned eyeblink response [article]. *Behavior Genetics, 29*(2), 95–102. http://search.ebscohost.com/login.aspx?direct=true&db=pbh&AN=11304805&site=ehost-live

Middendorf, J. (2004). Wertehierarchie. In C. Rauen (Ed.), *Coaching tools* (pp. 173–178). managerSeminare.

Middendorf, J. (2018). *16. Coaching-Umfrage Deutschland 2017/2018*. Frechen – www.BCO-Koeln.de: Büro für Coaching und Organisationsberatung (BCO) mit Unterstützung des Roundtable der Coachingverbände.

Middendorf, J. (2020). *18. Coaching-Umfrage 2019/2020*: BCO: Büro für Coaching und Organisationsberatung und Round Table Coaching.

Middendorf, J., & Salamon, L. (2018). *16. Coaching-Umfrage: Der Markt stagniert*. wirtschaft + *weiterbildung, 05_2018*, 34–37.

Miller, W. R., & Rollnick, S. (1991). *Motivational interviewing: Preparing people to change addictive behavior*. Guilford.

Miller, G. A., Galanter, E., & Pribram, K. H. (1960). *Plans and the structure of behavior*. Henry Holt and Co.. https://doi.org/10.1037/10039-000

Miller, K. G., Wright, A. G. C., Petersonb, L. M., Kamarcka, T. W., Andersona, B. A., Kirschbaumc, C., et al. (2016). Trait positive and negative emotionality differentially associate with diurnal cortisol activity. *Psychoneuroendocrinology, 68*, 177–185.

Moberger, V. (2020). Bullshit, pseudoscience and Pseudophilosophy. *Theoria, 86*(5), 595–611.

Möller, H. (2022). Mental disorders in coaching. In S. Greif, H. Möller, W. Scholl, J. Passmore, & F. Müller (Eds.), *International handbook of evidence based coaching: Theory, research and practice* (pp. 577–586). Springer Nature.

Möller, H., Giernalczyk, T., & Hinn, D. (2022). Individual and collective defense mechanisms. In S. Greif, H. Möller, W. Scholl, J. Passmore, & F. Müller (Eds.), *International handbook of evidence based coaching: Theory, research and practice* (pp. 459-471). Springer Nature.

Montada, L., & Kals, E. (2013). *Mediation: Psychologische Grundlagen und Perspektiven* (3rd. ed.). Beltz. Kindle Edition.

Moshagen, M., Hilbig, B. E., Erdfelder, E., & Moritz, A. (2014). An experimental validation method for questioning techniques that assess sensitive issues. *Experimental Psychology, 61*(1), 48–54. https://doi.org/10.1027/1618-3169/a000226

Mühlberger, C., Behrendt, P., & Jonas, E. (2023). *Guide, support, and activate resources! Three dimensions of relationship-oriented coach behavior that foster goal attainment.* Unpublished paper.

Mühlberger, C., Zerle, G., Möller, J., Diller, S. J., Greif, S., Kinder, N., & Jonas, E. (2024). Zooming in on the self in workplace coaching: Self-regulation and its connection to coaching success. *Journal of Occupational Psychology, 98*, 1–25. https://doi.org/10.1111/joop.12543

Mühlberger, C., Greif, S., Zerle, G., & Jonas, E. (2025a, in prep.). *Report on "Analysis of Working Alliance Scales in coaching research"* (Working Title).

Mühlberger, C., Greif, S., Zerle, G. & Jonas, E. (2025b, in prep.). *We definitely need better Working Alliance Scales in coaching research* (Working Title).

Müller, F., & Greif, S. (2022). Insights through coaching. In S. Greif, H. Möller, W. Scholl, J. Passmore, & F. Müller (Eds.), *International handbook of evidence based coaching: Theory, research and practice* (pp. 471–485). Springer Nature.

Münsterberg, H. (1915). *Business psychology*. La Salle Extension University.

Neenan, M., & Dryden, W. (2002). *Life coaching - A cognitive-behavioral approach.* Brunner-Routledge.

Ng, V., Cao, M., Marsh, H. W., Tay, L., & Seligman, M. E. P. (2017). The factor structure of the Values in Action Inventory of Strengths (VIA-IS): An item-level exploratory structural equation modeling (ESEM) bifactor analysis. *Psychological Assessment, 29*(8), 1053–1058.

Nowak, C. (2017). Systemisch – was denn sonst! *Organisationsberatung, Supervision, Coaching, 24*(4), 477–487.

O'Halloran, P. D., Blackstock, F., Shields, N., Holland, A., Ross, I., Kingsley, M., et al. (2014). Motivational interviewing to increase physical activity in people with chronic health conditions: A systematic review and meta-analysis. *Clinical Rehabilitation, 28*(12), 1159–1171.

Oettingen, G. (2014). *Rethinking positive thinking: Inside the new science of motivation.* Penguin.

Offermanns, M. (1998). *Das systemische Konfliktgespräch – Ein Personalentwicklungsinstrument für Leiter von Veränderungsprojekten.* Diplomarbeit im Fachgebiet Arbeits- und Organisationspsychologie der University of Osnabrück, Germany.

Offermanns, M. (2004). *Braucht Coaching einen Coach? Eine evaluative Pilotstudie.* ibidem.

Palmer, S., Szymanska, K., & Whybrow, A. (2008). Cognitive behavioural coaching: An integrative approach. In S. Palmer & A. Whybrow (Eds.), *Handbook of coaching psychology: A guide for practitioners* (pp. 86–117). Routledge/Taylor & Francis Group.

Palmer, S., Tubbs, I., & Whybrow, A. (2003). Health coaching to facilitate the promotion of healthy behaviour and achievement of health-related goals. *International Journal of Health Promotion and Education, 41*(3), 91–93.

Palmer, S., & Whybrow, A. (Eds.). (2018). *The handbook of coaching psychology: A guide for practitioners* (2nd ed.). Routledge (Kindle Edition).

Passarelli, A. M. (2015). Vision-based coaching: Optimizing resources for leader development. *Frontiers in Psychology, 6*.

Passmore, J. (2011a). MI – balance sheet techniques. *The Coaching Psychologist, 7*(2), 151–153.

Passmore, J. (2011b). Motivational interviewing – A model for coaching psychology practice. *The Coaching Psychologist, 7*(1), 36–40.

Passmore, J. (2011c). Motivational interviewing techniques reflective listening. *The Coaching Psychologist, 7*(1), 50–53.

Passmore, J. (2012a). MI techniques: Recognising change talk. *The Coaching Psychologist, 8*(2), 107–110.

Passmore, J. (2012b). MI techniques: The typical day. *The Coaching Psychologist, 8*(1), 50–51.

Passmore, J. (2013a). MI techniques: Agenda mapping. *The Coaching Psychologist, 9*(1), 32–35.

Passmore, J. (2013b). Motivational interviewing: Reflecting on ethical decisions in MI. *Coaching Psychologist, 9*(2), 112–116.

Passmore, J., Brown, H., Csigas, Z., & the-European-Coaching-and-Mentoring-Research-Consortium. (2017). *The state of play in european coaching & mentoring – Executive report*. Henley Business School and EMCC International.

Passmore, J., Brown, H., Greif, S., & Rauen, C. (2018). *Coaching in Germany*. Henley Business School.

Passmore, J., Day, C., Flower, J., Grieve, M., & Moon, J. J. (Eds.). (2021). *We coach! The complete handbook of tools, techniques, experiments and frameworks for personal and team development*. Libri Publishing.

Passmore, J., & Fillery-Travis, A. (2011). A critical review of executive coaching research: A decade of progress and what's to come. *Coaching: An International Journal of Theory, Research and Practice, 4*(2), 70–88.

Passmore, J., Peterson, D. B., & Freire, T. (2013). The psychology of coaching and mentoring. In J. Passmore, D. B. Peterson, & T. Freire (Eds.), *Wiley-Blackwell handbooks in organizational psychology* (pp. 1–11). Wiley-Blackwell.

Passmore, J., & Whybrow, A. (2008). Motivational interviewing: A specific approach for coaching psychologists. In S. Palmer & A. Whybrow (Eds.), *Handbook of coaching psychology: A guide for practitioners* (pp. 160–173). Routledge/Taylor & Francis Group.

Peterson, C., Stephens, J. P., Park, N., Lee, F., & Seligman, M. E. P. (2010). Strengths of character and work. In P. A. Linley, S. Harrington, & N. Garcea (Eds.), *Oxford handbook of positive psychology and work* (pp. 221–231). Oxford University Press.

Pigliucci, M. (n.d.). Pseudoscience and the Demarcation Problem. In J. Fieser & B. Dowden (Eds.), *Internet encyclopedia of philosophy a peer-reviewed academic resource*.

Pines, A., & Kafry, D. (1978). Occupational tedium in the social services. *Social Work, 23*(6), 499–507.

Podesser, S. (2023). *Prompt design – How to talk to AI*. Kindle.

Pourmansour, J. (1997). *NLP und Zahnarztangst? – Eine Studie zur Effektivität der NLP-Intervention University of Muenster*. Muenster, Germany.

Proksch, S. (2016). Questioning techniques. In S. Proksch (Ed.), *Conflict management* (pp. 69–77). Springer.

Purdie, J. (2010). *Life coaching for dummies*. Wiley – Kindle Edition.

Pusba, L. (2022). Brain-focused coaching. In *International handbook of evidence based coaching: Theory, research and practice* (pp. 77–97). Springer Nature.

Puspa, L., Ibrahim, N., & Brown, P. T. (2018). Increase in gamma band qEEG activity during executive coaching: Some preliminary observations and possible implications. *Major Issues and Other Topics Related to Mental Health, Neuroscience, and Cyber-psychology*, 90–97.

Puspa, L., Ibrahim, N., & Brown, P. T. (2019). "Wanting" and "liking" brain mechanisms in coaching: A qEEG study using the CARE coaching model. *Biomolecular and Health Science Journal, 02*(02), 89–95.

Quinlan, D., Swain, N., & Vella-Brodrick, D. A. (2012). Character strengths interventions: Building on what we know for improved outcomes. *Journal of Happiness Studies, 13*, 1145–1163.

Quirin, M., Bode, R., & Kuhl, J. (2011). Recovering from negative events by boosting implicit positive affect. *Cognition and Emotion, 25*, 559–570.

Quirin, M., & Kuhl, J. (2018). The self-access form – development and validation in the context of personality functioning and health. *Journal of Individual Differences, 39*(1), 1–17.

Rabel, G., Erlacher-Farkas, B., & Jorda, C. (1996). Die wichtigsten im Monodrama verwendeten psychodramatischen Techniken. In *Monodrama. Heilende Begegnung. Vom Psychodrama zur Einzeltherapie* (pp. 118–128). Springer.

Raddatz, S. (2018). *Beratung ohne Ratschlag: Systemisches Coaching für Führungskräfte und BeraterInnen* (10th ed.). Verlag Systemisches Management.

Rapp, F. (1973). Methode. In H. Krings, H. M. Baumgartner, & C. Wild (Eds.), *Handbuch philosophischer Grundbegriffe* (Vol. Band 4, pp. 913–929). Kösel.

Rasool, J. (2024). *Coaching 5.0: Industry 5.0 Coaching*. Kindle.

Rath, T. (2014). *Entwickle deine Stärken: mit dem Strengths Finder 2.0*. Redline.

Rauen, C. (2001). *Coaching*. Hogrefe.

Rauen, C. (Ed.). (2007). *Coaching-Tools II. Erfolgreiche Coaches präsentieren Interventions techniken aus ihrer Coaching-Praxis*. managerSeminare.

Rauen, C. (Ed.). (2012). *Coaching-Tools III. Erfolgreiche Coaches präsentieren Interventions techniken aus ihrer Coaching-Praxis*. managerSeminare.

Rauen, C. (Ed.). (2013). *Coaching-Tools. Erfolgreiche Coaches präsentieren 60 Interventions techniken aus ihrer Coaching-Praxis* (8th ed.). managerSeminare.

Rauen, C. (2018a). Quo vadis, Business Coaching? *Keynote, DBVC Coaching-Kongress 2018*. Dorint Hotel Sanssouci, Potsdam, 2.11.2018, https://www.youtube.com/watch?v=8R44ytfufZc (last access 24.2.2021).

Rauen, C. (2018b). Quo vadis, Business Coaching?, *DBVC Coaching-Kongress 2018*. Dorinth Hotel Sancoussi Potsdam.

Rauen, C. (2019). *Definition Coaching* Verfügbar unter: https://www.coaching-report.de/definition-coaching.html (last access 26.8.2019).

Reichheld, F. F. (2003). The one number you need to grow. *Harvard Business Review, 81*(12), 46–54.

Reichheld, F. F., & Seidensticker, F.-J. (2006). *Die ultimative Frage. Mit dem Net Promoter Score zu loyalen Kunden und profitablem Wachstum*. Hanser.

Reichwald, R., & Hensel, J. (2007). Kommunikation als Teil der Führungsaufgabe. In A. Zerfaß, M. Piwinger, & U. Röttger (Eds.), *Handbuch Unternehmenskommunikation* (pp. 649–659). Gabler.

Reinmann-Rothmeier, G., Mandl, H., & Prenzel, M. (1994). *Computerunterstützte Lernumgebungen: Planung, Gestaltung und Bewertung*. Publicis-MCD-Verlag.

Rice, B. (1982). Legenden sterben langsam. Die Geschichte des Hawthorne-Effekts. *Psychologie Heute, 9*, 50–55.

Roethlisberger, F., & Dickson, W. (1939). *Management and the Worker*. Harvard University Press.

Rogers, C. (1942). *Counseling and psychotherapy: Newer concepts in practice*. Houghton Mifflin.

Rogers, C. (1951). *Client-centered therapy: Its current practice, implications and theory*. Constable.

Röhrs, B. (2011). *Selbstkonzept und Selbstreflexion im Multidirektionalen Feedback*. ibidem.

Rosinski, P. (2003). *Coaching across cultures: New tools for leveraging national, corporate, and professional differences*. Brealey (Kindle Edition).

Rosinski, P., & Abbott, G. N. (2006). Coaching from a cultural perspective. In D. R. Stober, A. M. Grant, D. R. Stober, & A. M. Grant (Eds.), *Evidence based coaching handbook: Putting best practices to work for your clients* (pp. 255–275). Wiley.

Roth, G. (2019). *Warum es so schwierig ist, sich und andere zu ändern: Persönlichkeit, Entscheidung und Verhalten* (revised ed.). Klett Cotta and Kindle.

Roth, G., & Ryba, A. (2016). *Coaching, Beratung und Gehirn: Neurobiologische Grundlagen wirksamer Veränderungskonzepte* (2nd ed.). Klett-Cotta.

Rückerl, T., & Rückerl, T. (2008). *Coaching mit NLP-Werkzeugen*. Wiley-VCH.

Rudolph, C. W., Murphy, L. D., & Zacher, H. (2020). A systematic review and critique of research on "healthy leadership". *The Leadership Quarterly, 31*(1), 101335.

Ryff, C. D., & Keyes, C. L. M. (1995). The structure of psychological well-being revisited. *Journal of Personality and Social Psychology, 69*(4), 719–727.

Sarkar, S., & Pfeiffer, J. (2006). *The philosophy of science – An encyclopedia*. Routledge.

Scherer, S., Scherm, M., Kaufel, S., & Pfeifer, M. (2004). Coaching in der Bundeswehr. *Personalführung, 37*(11), 44–51.

Schermuly, C. C. & Graßmann, C. (2018). A literature review on negative effects of coaching – What we know and what we need to know. *Coaching: An International Journal of Theory, Research and Practice*.

Schlippe, A. V., & Schweitzer, J. (2019). *Gewusst wie, gewusst warum - Die Logik systemischer Interventionen*. Vandenhoek & Ruprecht.

Schmelz, M. (2009). *Auslandsentsendungen – ein Ansatz zum Einzel- und paarcoachings*.

Schmidt, G. (2022). *Einführung in die hypnosystemische Therapie und Beratung* (10th ed.). Carl-Auer and Kindle.

Schmidt, P., Bamberg, S., Davidov, E., Herrmann, J., & Schwartz, S. H. (2007). Die Messung von Werten mit dem "Portraits Value Questionnaire". *Zeitschrift für Sozialpsychologie, 38*(4), 261–275.

Schmidt, F., & Thamm, A. (2008). *Wirkungen und Wirkfaktoren im Coaching. – Verringerung von Prokrastination und Optimierung des Lernverhaltens bei Studierenden*. Diplomarbeit, Fachgebiet Arbeits- und Organisationspychologie, Universität Osnabrück, Deutschland.

Schmidt-Lellek, C. (2020). Perspektiven für das Coaching nach der Corona-Krise. *Organisationsberatung, Supervision, Coaching*, 1–15.

Schmidt-Tanger, M. (2006). Hirnforschung – Und das NLP hat doch Recht. *Kommunikation & Seminar, 03/2006*.

Schmidt-Tanger, M. (2014). Coachen statt klönen - Emotionale Relevanz und Status im Coaching, *Kongress Coachig heute: Zwischen Königsweg und Irrweg*. Erding (20.–21.2. 2014): Hochschule für angewandtes Management.

Schnieders, T. (2016). *Einflussfaktoren auf den Transfererfolg von Coaching im Vergleich zum Training. Eine vergleichende Analyse anhand des deutschen Lerntransfer-System-Inventars*. Dissertation im Fachbbereich Human wissenschaften, University of Osnabrück.

Scholl, W., Lackner, K., & Grieger, K. (2022). Communication as a method and as a topic in coaching. In S. Greif, H. Möller, W. Scholl, J. Passmore, & F. Müller (Eds.), *International handbook of evidence-based coaching* (pp. 199–212). Springer Nature.

Schön, D. A. (1983). *The reflective practitioner*. Basic Books.

Schonfeld, I. S., & Bianchi, R. (2016). Burnout and depression: Two entities or one? *Journal of Clinical Psychology, 72*(1), 22–37. https://doi.org/10.1002/jclp.22229

Schreyögg, A. (1995). *Coaching. Eine Einführung für Praxis und Ausbildung* (7th ed. 2012). Frankfurt/Main: Campus.

Schreyögg, A. (2002). *Konfliktcoaching – Anleitung für den Coach*. Campus.

Schreyögg, A. (2004). Supervision. In *Ein Integratives Modell. Lehrbuch zu Theorie und Praxis* (4th ed.). VS – Verlag für Sozialwissenschaften.

Schreyögg, A. (2005). *Coaching von Doppelspitzen*. Campus.

Schreyögg, A. (2011). Imaginativer Rollentausch. In C. Rauen (Ed.), *Coaching tools* (7th ed., pp. 205–207). managerSeminare.

Schreyögg, A. (2022). Transfereence and countertransference and their significance for coaching. In S. Greif, H. Möller, W. Scholl, J. Passmore, & F. Müller (Eds.), *International handbook of evidence-based coaching – Theory, research and practice* (pp. 925–934). Springer Nature.

Schultz, J. H. (1928/1979). *Das autogene Training* (17. Aufl.). Stuttgart: Thieme.

Schulz von Thun, F., Ruppel, J., & Stratman, R. (2006). *Miteinander reden: Kommunikationspsychologie für Führungskräfte* (6th ed.). Rowohlt.

Schunk, D. H., & Greene, J. A. (2018). Historical, contemporary, and future perspectives on self-regulated learning and performance. In D. H. Schunk & J. A. Greene (Eds.), *Handbook of self-regulation of learning and performance* (2nd ed., pp. 1–15). Routledge/Taylor & Francis Group.

Schwartz, S. H. (1994). Are there universal aspects in the structure and contents of human values? *Journal of Social Issues, 50*(4), 19–45.

Schwartz, S. H. (2007). *Basic human values: An overview*.

Schwarzer, R., & Jerusalem, M. (1995). Generalized self–efficacy scale. In J. Weinman, S. Wright, & M. Johnston (Eds.), *Measures in health psychology: A users portfolio. Causal and control beliefs* (pp. 35–37). NFER–NELSON.

Seligman, M. E. P. (2007). Coaching and positive psychology. *Australian Psychologist, 42*(4), 266–267.

Seligman, M. E. P. (2011). *Flourish*. Simon & Schuster.

Seligman, M. E. P., & Csikszentmihalyi, M. (2000). Positive psychology: An introduction. *American Psychologist, 55*, 5–14.

Semmer, N., McGrath, J. E., & Beehr, T. A. (2005). Conceptual issues in research on stress and health. In C. L. Cooper (Ed.), *Handbook of stress medicine and health* (2nd ed., pp. 1–44). CRC Press.

Semmer, N., & Mohr, G. (2001). Arbeit und Gesundheit: Konzepte und Ergebnisse der arbeitspsychologischen Stressforschung. *Psychologische Rundschau, 52*(3), 150–158.

Semmer, N., & Udris, I. (1993). Bedeutung und Wirkung von Arbeit. In H. Schuler, H. M. I. Brandstätter, W. M. I. Bungard, S. M. I. Greif, E. M. I. Ulich, & B. M. I. Wilpert (Eds.), *Lehrbuch Organisationspsychologie* (pp. 133–165). Huber.

Semmer, N., Zapf, D., & Greif, S. (1996). "Shared job strain": A new approach for assessing the validity of job stress measurements. *Journal of Occupational and Organizational Psychology, 69*(3), 293–310.

Sforzo, G. A., Kaye, M. P., Harenberg, S., Costello, K., Cobus-Kuo, L., Rauff, E., et al. (2019). Compendium of health and wellness coaching: 2019 addendum. *American Journal of Lifestyle Medicine, 14*(2), 155–168.

Sheeran, P. (2002). Intention-behavior relations: A conceptual and empirical review. In W. Stroebe & M. Hewstone (Eds.), *European review of social psychology* (Vol. Bd. 12, pp. 1–30). Wiley.

Shen, L. (2010). On a scale of state empathy during message processing. *Western Journal of Communication, 74*(5), 505–524.

Shirom, A., Armon, G., Berliner, S., Shapira, I., & Melamed, S. (2009). The effects of job strain on risk factors for cardivascular disease. In C. L. Cooper, J. C. Quick, & M. Schabracq (Eds.), *International handbook of work and health psychology* (3rd ed., pp. 49–75). Wiley-Blackwell.

Shum, H.-Y., He, X.-D., & Li, D. (2018). From Eliza to XiaoIce: Challenges and opportunities with social chatbots. *Frontiers of Information Technology & Electronic Engineering, 19*(1), 10–26.

Siegrist, J. (1996). Adverse health effects of high-effort/low-reward conditions. *Journal of Occupational Health Psychology, 1*(1), 27–41.

Simon, F. B., & Rech-Simon, C. (1999). *Zirkuläres Fragen – Systemische Therapie in Fallbeispielen: Ein Lehrbuch*. Carl Auer.

Sitzmann, T. G. (2013). A meta-analytic investigation of the within-person self-efficacy domain: Is self-efficacy a product of past performance or a driver of future performance? *Personnel Psychology, 66*(3), 531–568.

Skinner, B. F. (1969). *Contingencies of reinforcement: A theoretical analysis*. Appelton-Century-Crofts.

Slagter, M., & Wilderom, C. (2018). Team coaching and effective team leadership. In S. Greif, H. Möller, & W. Scholl (Eds.), *Handbuch Schlüsselkonzepte im coaching. Springer reference psychologie* (pp. 505–602). Springer.

Smedslund, G., Berg, R. C., Hammerstrøm, K. T., Steiro, A., Leiknes, K. A., Dahl, H. M., et al. (2011). Motivational interviewing for substance abuse. *Campbell Systematic Reviews, 2011*(6, complete issue, https://doi.org/10.4073/csr.2011.6).

Smith, A. (1776). *An inquiry into the nature and causes of the wealth of nations*. Collier and Son.

Sonesh, S. C., Coultas, C. W., Marlow, S. L., Lacerenza, C. N., Reyes, D., & Salas, E. (2015). Coaching in the wild: Identifying factors that lead to success. *Consulting Psychology Journal: Practice and Research, 67*(3), 189–217.

Spence, G. B. (2007). GAS powered coaching: Goal attainment scaling and its use in coaching research and practice. *International Coaching Psychology Research Review, 2*(2), 155–167.

Sperling, J., Augustin, A., & Wegge, J. (2022). Crises as a problem in coaching. In S. Greif, H. Möller, W. Scholl, J. Passmore, & F. Müller (Eds.), *International handbook of evidence based coaching: Theory, research and practice* (pp. 233–244). Springer Nature.

Spranz-Fogasy, T., Graf, E.-M., Ehrenthal, J., & Nikendei, C. (2019). Requesting examples in psychodiagnostic interviews: Therapists' contribution to the sequential co-construction of clients' change. *Communication & Medicine, 16*(2), 129–141.

Stacey, R. D. (2010). *Complexity and organizational reality: Uncertainty and the need to rethink management after the collapse of investment capitalism* (2nd ed.). Routledge/Taylor & Francis Group.

Stalder, T., Steudte, S., Miller, R., Skoluda, N., Dettenborn, L., & Kirschbaum, C. (2012). Intraindividual stability of hair cortisol concentrations. *Psychoneuroendocrinology, 37*, 602–610.

Steger, M. F., Frazier, P., Oishi, S., & Kaler, M. (2006). The meaning in life questionnaire: Assessing the presence of and search for meaning in life. *Journal of Counseling Psychology, 53*(1), 80–93.

Steinke, I. & Steinke, J. M. (2019). *Was it Coaching?* Die Ursprünge von Coaching und.

Steinmetz, H., Isidor, R., & Baeuerle, N. (2012). Testing the circular structure of human values: A meta-analytical structural equation modelling approach (PSYNDEXshort). *Survey Research Methods, 6*(1), 61–75.

Stelter, R. (2013). Narrative approaches. In J. Passmore, D. B. Peterson, & T. Freire (Eds.), *The Wiley-Blackwell handbook of the psychology of coaching and mentoring* (pp. 407–425). Wiley-Blackwell.

Stelter, R. (2014). Third-generation coaching: Reconstructing dialogues through collaborative practice and a focus on values. *International Coaching Psychology Review, 9*(1), 51–66.

Stelter, R. (2018). *The art of dialogue in coaching: Towards transformative change*. Routledge.

Stelter, R. (2022). Meaning as a topic in coaching. In S. Greif, H. Möller, W. Scholl, J. Passmore, & F. Müller (Eds.), *International handbook of evidence-based coaching* (pp. 553–564). Springer Nature.

Stelter, R., Nielsen, G., & Wikman, J. M. (2011). Narrative-collaborative group coaching develops social capital—A randomised control trial and further implications of the social impact of the intervention. *Coaching: An International Journal of Theory, Research and Practice, 4*(2), 123–137.

Stenzel, S. (2022). *Die Zukunft des Coaching-Business – Neuausrichtung an der Lebens- und Arbeitswelt des Klienten von morgen*. Springer Gabler.

Stenzel, S. (2024a). *Coachbots werden uns zu besseren Menschen bzw. Coaches machen.* Unterschiede zwischen Mensch und Maschine, die auch zukünftig einen Unterschied machen sollten. Positionen, 2/2024; https://www.dgsv.de/wp-content/uploads/2024/04/Positionen_1-2024.pdf

Stenzel, S. (2024b). *ChatGPT kann auch coachen!? – Rechenpower und Algorithmen statt Sinn und Bedeutung*. Organisationsberatung, Supervision, Coaching (OSC), 31, 2024, pp. 97–112.

Stern, W. (1903). Angewandte psychologie. *Beiträge zur Psychologie der Aussage, 1*, 4–45.

Stern, W. (1921). *Angewandte psychologie*. Teubner.

Sternberg, R. J., & Grigorenko, E. L. (2002). The general factor of intelligence: How general is it? .

Stierlin, H. (1994). *Individuation und Familie: Studien zur Theorie und therapeutischen Praxis.* Suhrkamp.

Stober, D. R. (2006). Coaching from the humanistic perspective. In D. R. Stober & A. M. Grant (Eds.), *Evidence-based coaching handbook: Putting best practices to work for your clients* (pp. 17–50). Wiley.

Stober, D. R., & Grant, A. M. (Eds.). (2006). *Evidence-based coaching handbook: Putting best practices to work for your clients*. Wiley.

Storch, M., & Kuhl, J. (2012). *Die Kraft aus dem Selbst*. Huber.

Stout-Rostron, S. (2022). Culturality in coaching. In S. Greif, H. Möller, W. Scholl, J. Passmore, & F. Müller (Eds.), *International handbook of evidence-based coaching* (pp. 245–256). Springer Nature.

Strelzig, J. (2015). Interview with Gunther Schmidt. *The International Society of Hypnosis Newsletter, 39*(2), 12–14.

Strikker, H. (2016). Coaching-Kompetenzen für Mentorinnen und Mentoren – Neues Wissen mit Lebenserfahrung verbinden. In R. Wegener (Ed.), *Coaching als individuelle Antwort auf gesellschaftliche Entwicklungen* (pp. 215–224). Springer.

Strong, N., & Terblanche, N. (2020). Chatbots as an instance of an artificial intelligence coach A perspective on current realities and future possibilities. In R. Wegener, S. Ackermann, J. Amstutz, S. Deplaze, H. Künzli, & A. Ryter (Eds.), *Coaching im digitalen Wandel* (pp. 51–62). Vandenhoeck & Ruprecht.

Sturt, J., Ali, S., Robertson, W., Metcalfe, D., Grove, A., Bourne, C., et al. (2012). Neurolinguistic programming: A systematic review of the effects on health outcomes. *British Journal of General Practice, 62*, 757–764.

Subramaniam, K., Kounios, J., Parrish, T. B., & Jung-Beeman, M. (2009). A brain mechanism for facilitation of insight by positive affect. *Journal of Cognitive Neuroscience, 21*(3), 415–432.

Sue-Chan, C., & Latham, G. P. (2004). The relative effectiveness of external, peer, and self-coaches. *Applied Psychology: An International Review, 53*(2), 260–278.

Taubner, S., & Kotte, S. (2022). Mentalization in coaching. In S. Greif, H. Möller, W. Scholl, J. Passmore, & F. Müller (Eds.), *International handbook of evidence based coaching: Theory, research and practice* (pp. 587–598). Springer.

Tavis, A., & Woodward, W. (2024). *The digital coaching revolution: How to support employee development with coaching Tech Kindle*.

Taylor, F. W. (1919). *The principles of scientific management*. Harper & Brothers.

Taylor, S. N., Passarelli, A. M., & Van Oosten, E. B. (2019). Leadership coach *effectiveness* as fostering self-determined, sustained change. *The Leadership Quarterly, 30*(6), 101313. https://doi.org/10.1016/j.leaqua.2019.101313

Terblanche, N. (2023). Artificial intelligence coaching. *Institute of Coaching Annual Conference – Coaching in Leadership & Healthcare Conference*. Boston.

Terblanche, N. (2024). *The current state of research on AI in coaching*. (Online Seminar, Belmont, MA, Institute of Coaching, 2.12.24) https://instituteofcoaching.org/conferences-events/current-state-research-ai-coaching

Terblanche, N., Molyn, J., de Haan, E., & Nilsson, V. O. (2022). Comparing artificial intelligence and human coaching goal attainment efficacy. *PLoS One, 17*(6), e0270255. https://doi.org/10.1371/journal.pone.0270255

Terblanche, N., Molyn, J., De Haan, E., & Nilsson, V. O. (2022b). Coaching at scale: Investigating the efficacy of artificial intelligence coaching. *International Journal of Evidence Based Coaching and Mentoring, 20*(2), 20–36.

Theebom, T., Beersma, B., Vianen, A. E. M., & v. (2014). Does coaching work? A meta-analysis on the effects of coaching on individual level outcomes in an organizational context. *The Journal of Positive Psychology, 9*(1), 1–18.

Thomsen, K. (2024). Die Entwicklung des Reflecting Functioning at Work Interviews (RFWI) zur Messung der Mentalisierung im Coaching. In F. Strikker, A. Bergknapp, I. Holtschmidt, C. Moscho, & S. Stenzel (Eds.), *Coaching und Change im Blickpunkt* (pp. 77–122). ibidem.

Tierney, S., Mamas, M., Skelton, D., Woods, S., Rutter, M. K., Gibson, M., et al. (2011). What can we learn from patients with heart failure about exercise adherence? A systematic review of qualitative papers. *Health Psychology, 30*(4), 401–410.

Todorova, I. (2022). Health coaching research. In S. Greif, H. Möller, W. Scholl, J. Passmore, & F. Müller (Eds.), *International handbook of evidence-based coaching* (pp. 429–447). Springer Nature.

Trist, E. L., & Bamford, K. (1951). Some social and psychological consequences of the longwall method of coalgetting. *Human Relations, 4*, 3–38.

Ulich, E., Groskurth, P., & Bruggemann, A. (1973). *Neue Formen der Arbeitsgestaltung – Möglichkeiten und Probleme eine Verbesserung der Qualität des Arbeitslebens*. Europäische Verlagsanstalt.
UNESCO. (2021). *Recommendation on the ethics of artificial intelligence*. United Nations Educational, Scientific and Cultural Organization.
Urbina, S. (2014). *Essentials of psychological testing*. Wiley, Kindle Edition.
Vaziri, H., Casper, W. J., Wayne, J. H., & Matthews, R. A. (2020). Changes to the work–family interface during the COVID-19 pandemic: Examining predictors and implications using latent transition analysis. *Journal of Applied Psychology, 105*(10), 1073–1087.
Verplanken, B. (Ed.). (2018). *The psychology of habit theory, mechanisms, change, and contexts*. Springer.
Vogel, H. (2020). Psychoedukative intervention. In M. A. Wirtz (Eds.), *Dorsch – Lexikon der Psychologie* (19th ed. pp. 1423).
Vollmer, A., & Vetter, A. (2022). Conflict transformation in coaching. In S. Greif, H. Möller, W. Scholl, J. Passmore, & F. Müller (Eds.), *International handbook of evidence based coaching: Theory, research and practice*. Cham, Switzerland.
von Schlippe, A. (2022). Family business in coaching: Specific dynamics. In S. Greif, H. Möller, W. Scholl, J. Passmore, & F. Müller (Eds.), *International handbook of evidence based coaching: Theory, research and practice* (pp. 325–336). Springer Nature.
von Schlippe, A., & Schweitzer, J. (1996). *Lehrbuch der systemischen Therapie und Beratung* (2nd ed.). Vandenhoek & Ruprecht.
von Schlippe, A., & Schweitzer, J. (2019). *Gewusst wie, gewusst warum – Die Logik systemischer Interventionen*. Vandenhoek & Ruprecht.
Wahren, H.-K. E. (1997). *Coaching*. Rationalisierungs-Kuratorium der Deutschen Wirtschaft.
Wang, Y.-Y., & Wang, Y.-S. (2022). Development and validation of an artificial intelligence anxiety scale: An initial application in predicting motivated learning behavior. *Interactive Learning Environments, 30*(4), 619–634. https://doi.org/10.1080/10494820.2019.1674887
Watson, D., Clark, L. A., & Tellegen, A. (1988). Development and validation of brief measures of positive and negative affect: The PANAS scales. *Journal of Personality and Social Psychology, 54*, 1063–1070.
Watzlawick, P., Beavin-Bavelas, J., & Jackson, D. (1967). Some tentative axioms of communication. In *Pragmatics of human communication – A study of interactional patterns, pathologies and paradoxes*. W. W. Norton.
Webers, G. (2008). *Die Untersuchung der Selbstwirksamkeitserwartungen, Selbststeuerungskompetenzen und Selbstreflexion im Kontext eines Coachings zum Thema Procrastination.* Diplomarbeit im Fachgebiet Arbeits- und Organisationspsychologie. University of Osnabrück.
Webers, T. (2020). *Systemisches coaching – Psychologische Grundlagen* (2nd ed.). Springer.
Wechsler, T., & Schütz, A. (2022). Self-concepts, self-discrepancies, and their significance in coaching. In S. Greif, H. Möller, W. Scholl, J. Passmore, & F. Müller (Eds.), *International handbook of evidence based coaching* (pp. 815–826). Springer Nature.
Wehrle, W. (2012). *Die 500 besten Coaching-Fragen: Das große Workbook für Einsteiger und Profis zur Entwicklung der eigenen Coaching-Fähigkeiten*. Manager Seminare, Edition Training aktuell.
Weihrauch, L., Kugler, S., Mausz, I., & Frey, D. (2022). Leadership coaching. In L. Weihrauch, S. Kugler, I. Mausz, & D. Frey (Eds.), *International handbook of evidence based coaching: Theory, research and practice* (pp. 521–530). Springer Nature.
Weizenbaum, J. (1966). ELIZA—a computer program for the study of natural language communication between man and machine. *Communications of the ACM, 9*(1), 36–45.
West, M. (2004). *Effective teamwork*. PBS Books.
West, M. (2012). *Effective teamwork: Practical lessons from organizartional research* (3rd ed.). Blackwell.

West, M., & Anderson, N. R. (1996). Innovation in top management teams [Print]. *Journal of Applied Psychology, 81*(6), 680–693.
White, M., & Epston, D. (1990). *Narrative means to therapeutic ends*. W.W. Norton.
Whitmore, J. (1992). *Coaching for performance: GROWing people, performance and purpose* (4th reprinted ed. 2010 ed.). Nicholas Brealey Publishing.
Whitmore, J. (1996). *Coaching für die Praxis: Eine klare, prägnante und praktische Anleitung für Manager, Trainer, Eltern und Gruppenleiter* (2nd ed.). Campus.
WHO. (2019). *ICD-11 International statistical classification of diseases and related health problems 11th revision*. World Health Organization.
Wildflower, L. (2013). *The hidden history of coaching (coaching in practice)*. Open University Press, Kindle Edition.
Wildt, J., & Wildt, B. (2009). *Handout: Grundlagen des Lehrens und Lernens*. Technischen Universität Dortmund.
Wilks, D. (2018). Twenty-first-century counseling theory development in relation to definitions of free will and determinism. *Journal of Counseling & Development, 96*(2).
Windlinger, L. (2021). Action regulation theory. In R. Appel-Meulenbroek & V. Danivska (Eds.), *A handbook of theories on designing alignment between people and the office environment* (pp. 54–67). Routledge.
Wong, A. P.-H. & Simon, J. (2020). Thinking about "ethics" in the ethics of AI. *IDEES*.
Wood, W. (2019). *Good habits, bad habits: The science of making positive changes that stick*. MacMillan (Kindle Edition).
XING, & Jonas, E. (2018). *Whitepaper: Coaching: Erfolgreiches Instrument der Personalentwicklung? – Wie Personaler darüber denken und wie sie Coaching konkret im Unternehmen einsetzen*. XING.
Yin, H. H., & Knowlton, B. J. (2006). The role of the basal ganglia in habit formation. *Nature Reviews Neuroscience, 7*(6), 464–476.
Zaharia, C., Reiner, M., & Schütz, P. (2015). Evidence-based neuro linguistic psychotherapy: A meta-analysis. *Psychiatria Danubina, 27*(4), 355–363.
Zapf, D., & Beitler, L. A. (2022). Bullying as a topic in coaching. In S. Greif, H. Möller, W. Scholl, J. Passmore, & F. Müller (Eds.), *International handbook of evidence based coaching: Theory, research and practice* (pp. 99–110). Springer Nature.
Zapf, D., & Semmer, N. K. (2004). Stress und Gesundheit in Organisationen. In H. Schuler (Ed.), *Organisationspsychologie – Grundlagen und Personal psychologie* (pp. 1007–1112). Hogrefe.
Zhao, S., Sampson, S., Xia, J., & Jajaram, M. B. (2015). Psychoeducation (brief) for people with serious mental illness. *Coachrane Database Systematic Review, 9*(4 CD010823).

The manufacturer's authorised representative in the EU is Springer Nature Customer Service Centre GmbH, Europaplatz 3, 69115 Heidelberg, Germany. If you have any concerns regarding our products, please contact ProductSafety@springernature.com

Printed and bound by CPI Group (UK) Ltd, Croydon, CR0 4YY
01/10/2026
02225971-0008